H. G. J. Moseley

H. G. J. Moseley

The Life and Letters of an English Physicist, 1887-1915

J. L. Heilbron

University of California Press
Berkeley·Los Angeles·London

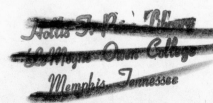

QC.16
B65
A44

74571

University of California Press
Berkeley and Los Angeles, California

University of California Press, Ltd.
London, England

Copyright © 1974, by
The Regents of the University of California

ISBN: 0-520-02375-7
Library of Congress Catalog Card Number: 72-93519

Printed in the United States of America
Designed by Jean Peters

Contents

You see actually the Rutherford work [the nuclear atom] was not taken seriously. We cannot understand today, but it was not taken seriously at all. There was no mention of it in any place. The great change came from Moseley.

—Niels Bohr, 1962

La loi de Moseley justifie la classification de Mendéleeff; elle justifie mêmes les coups de pouce que l'on avait été obligé de donner à cette classification.

—Maurice de Broglie, 1920

Preface

HENRY GWYN JEFFREYS MOSELEY, whom his family called Harry, was born at Weymouth, England, on November 23, 1887. He died two months before his twenty-eighth birthday, in the battle for Gallipoli. Like his friends and exact contemporaries Julian Huxley and Charles Galton Darwin, he came from a family long distinguished for its contributions to science. Unlike them, and luckily for him, he had made his reputation before the war, after a research career that lasted only forty months. That he could accomplish so much so quickly doubtless must ultimately be referred to native genius and energy. It also required unusual opportunity, luck, and perfect timing. It was luck that brought him to the research front at precisely the right moment, and with precisely the right preparation, to exploit the exceptionally fruitful discovery of von Laue in the cause of the atomic theories of Rutherford and Bohr. It was also luck that the research proved "so very easy," as he said, and gave "so rich a return for a minimum of work." As for opportunity, it almost appears that the chief joint objective of British scientists and educational reformers of the nineteenth century was to smooth the path of Harry Moseley.

Moseley's father and grandfather contributed to and profited from these reforms. In the biographical memoir that follows I have sketched—in so far as the very meagre documentation permits—the Moseleys' adaptation to the gradually increasing opportunities for scientific careers in nineteenth-century England. In 1901, when he entered Eton, Harry began to draw upon these opportunities; the possibilities for the cultivation of science there might surprise those familiar with Edwardian blasts at the curricula of the public schools. Moseley's self-conscious utilization of these possibilities, and of parallel ones at Oxford and the University of Manchester, is a chief theme of this book.

A second theme is the development of Moseley's research interests, which encompassed several branches of modern physics: radioactivity, the periodic classification of the elements, X-ray spectroscopy, the theory of atomic structure. His contributions to these fields were usually important and sometimes vital. They invite attention in their own right, as artifacts of Rutherford's school, as complements to the work of Bohr and Bragg, and as terms of comparison between English and continental physics.

The correspondence here published includes all known letters written to or by Moseley. Most are given in their entirety. Occasionally paragraphs dealing with nonscientific matters fully covered in other letters have been omitted and résumés provided; in no case has an item been dropped altogether. The letters seem to me to be of very great value. They document the interaction of a strong mind with the system established to educate it; they illuminate the development of physics during the years when classical theory began to yield to the quantum; they give glimpses of famous men; they chronicle one of the most important and dramatic researches in the history of modern physics. And, into the bargain, they are good reading, vigorous in thought and economical in expression, tributes to an educational system that bred its brains on Latin and English classics.

In preparing this book I have incurred three sorts of obligations which it is a pleasure here to acknowledge. The first is to former associates and acquaintances of Moseley's: Professors K. Fajans and A. S. Russell; the Reverend Prebendary A. L. Moir and Sir Thomas Merton; Mrs. Doris Wilkinson and Mrs. Henry Jervis; Mr. F. P. Walters, who has given me valuable information about Edwardian Eton; the late Sir Harold Hartley, who encouraged the project in its early stages; and, above all, Mr. A. Ludlow-Hewitt, who in the kindest and most generous manner has made available to me all pertinent correspondence and documents preserved by Moseley's mother and sister.

The second set of obligations is to those who have granted

permission to publish manuscript or copyright material: Mr. Ludlow-Hewitt; the Cambridge University Library; Professor Peter Fowler, F.R.S., Mr. E. P. Fowler, Dr. Ruth Edwards, and Dr. E. R. Taylor (permission to quote from the Rutherford Papers); Professor J. P. M. Tizard (the papers of Henry Tizard); Nuffield College Library (the Cherwell Papers); the Royal Institution (the Bragg Papers); the Royal Society of London (the Schuster and Larmor Papers); the Oxford Museum for the History of Science (the Moseley Papers and the Alembic Club Minute Books); Professor Aage Bohr (the Bohr Archives and the Hevesy Papers); the American Philosophical Society (the C. G. Darwin Papers).

Finally, I am obliged to friends and colleagues who have provided further leads or documents: Professors E. J. Bowen, Paul Forman and Sheldon Rothblatt; Drs. Ruth van Heyningen and Peter Heimann; Mr. R. H. L. Jervis; Mr. I. Kaye; and Dr. G. L'E. Turner, of the Oxford Museum for the History of Science, who has most generously obtained material for me when I was unable to be in England.

A Note on the Notes

THE NOTES give short titles of books and omit those of journal articles; Moseley's papers are cited by bold-face roman numerals, and his correspondence, published in this volume, by bold-face arabic numerals. Full titles to works mentioned in the notes will be found in the bibliography. Small superscripts thus (^{2}) indicate the edition cited. Year dates in the twentieth century usually omit the first two digits. The following abbreviations are also used:

AHES	*Archive for History of Exact Science*
AP	*Annalen der Physik*
AHQP	Archive for History of Quantum Physics (deposited in the libraries of the University of California, Berkeley; the American Philosophical Society, Philadelphia; and the Niels Bohr Institute, Copenhagen)
BA	British Association for the Advancement of Science
Badash	L. Badash, ed., *Rutherford and Boltwood: Letters on Radioactivity* (New Haven, 1969)
Birks	J. B. Birks, ed., *Rutherford at Manchester* (London, 1962)
BJHS	*British Journal for the History of Science*
CR	L'Académie des sciences, Paris, *Comptes rendus*
Diary	A series of pocket diaries, 1901, 1903–1915, 1918, kept by Amabel Moseley Sollas (LH)

DNB   *Dictionary of National Biography*

DSB   *Dictionary of Scientific Biography*

FAL   The papers of F. A. Lindemann (Lord Cherwell), Nuffield College, Oxford

HM   H. G. J. Moseley

HSPS   *Historical Studies in the Physical Sciences*

IWM   Imperial War Museum

J   *Journal*

JACS   *Journal of the American Chemical Society*

JRE   *Jahrbuch der Radioaktivität und Elektronik*

LH   Manuscripts in the possession of A. Ludlow-Hewitt

OB   Bodleian Library, Oxford

OHS   Museum of the History of Science, Oxford

ORS   Royal Society, *Obituary Notices of Fellows*, vols. 1–9 (1932–1954), continued by *Biographical Memoirs*, vol. 1+ (1955+).

PM   *Philosophical Magazine*

PRS   Royal Society, *Proceedings*

PT   Royal Society, *Philosophical Transactions*

PZs   *Physikalische Zeitschrift*

R   Rutherford papers, Cambridge University Library

RI   Royal Institution, London

RS   Royal Society, London

Sb (Munich)   Akademie der Wissenschaften, Munich. Mathematisch-Naturwissenschaftliche Klasse, *Sitzungsberichte*

Sb (Vienna)   Akademie der Wissenschaften, Vienna. Mathematisch-Naturwissenschaftliche Klasse, *Sitzungsberichte*

VdpG   Deutsche physikalische Gesellschaft, Berlin. *Verhandlungen*

Zs   *Zeitschrift*

I

Ancestry and Childhood

THE EARLIEST MOSELEY to flirt with science was Harry's great-grand-father William (c. 1760–c. 1850), the son of the founder of the family, a "very clever and strong minded" postilion who ended as a proprietor of hackney coaches. William was articled to an engraver but (according to the patchy family records) a stroke of lightning addled his brains and he ran off, brandishing an umbrella, to join the nearest college of Dissenters. He emerged a Calvinist and set about translating the Scriptures into Chinese. He came to science through Dr. Thomas Beddoes, the friend of Erasmus Darwin and the promoter of "pneumatic medicine," who invited him to Bristol to preach and to enjoy the benefits of laughing gas. William became an enthusiastic unlicensed physician. He generously shared his knowledge, such as it was, with his parishioners at Stoke-on-Trent, to whom, as the chronicles report, "he continually gave gratuitous medical treatment using iron and cold water." We find him next in Portsmouth and then in London, where he bought a school that catered to foreign boys and a medical establishment that specialized in lunacy. Here he overreached himself. The relatives of one crazy patient, unacquainted with William's history, brought suit against him for practicing without qualification. He regarded his sentence as a professional opportunity; for in prison, as he rightly observed, he would have "noblemen to practice on." [1]

---

[1] "Copy of Family History collected from unknown sources by Prof. H. N. Moseley," in

William married a nonconformist lady, one Margaret Robins, the daughter of a tailor and, on her mother's side, a distant relation of General Stonewall Jackson. She gave William nine children, of whom the second, Henry, born in 1801, was Harry's grandfather. Henry began his career as a teen-age manager of his father's school and madhouse. As preparation he had received a little learning at a school in Portsmouth which prepared people for "shipping matters" and inspired him with the ambition to be a shipwright. He attained this objective and indeed somewhat more—he became Vice-President of the Institution of Naval Architects—by a most indirect approach. His father William, whose shrewdness had by no means been impaired by his bout with lightning, perceived that he could enhance the reputation of his establishment among the foreigners it served by sending Henry to France to learn the classical French mathematics then not taught in English schools and only just entering the curriculum at Cambridge. Henry got a tight grip on the methods of Laplace and a just evaluation of his own powers; and on his return he announced to his father that he wanted to go to Cambridge. That good man, unwilling simultaneously to lose a son, a mathematical master and a Calvinist (for only Anglicans could then obtain a university degree), refused. Henry insisted, earned what he needed by tutoring, and, towards 1820, matriculated at St. John's.[2]

The university was then just emerging from a century of sloth and indulgence. Many of the professors still did not lecture and most of the students never thought to study; the institution as a whole specialized in filling the pulpits and the congregations of the established church and in granting "pass degrees," for which the candidate prepared, often taking his tutor as his guide, by drinking and idling. But there existed one course of study seriously pursued and rigorously examined, namely forty-two months of mathematics culminating in a week-long examination known as the tripos, conducted in a large unheated room in January. The wranglers, or those who passed this ordeal with first-class honors,

HM's hand (LH); cf. R. E. Schofield, *The Lunar Society of Birmingham* (1963), pp. 372–377.

[2] The family history dates Henry's sojourn in Abbeville in 1819 or 1820. Since he graduated BA in 1826, he probably entered in 1821, reckoning a year or so for recovery from an almost fatal attack of typhus. The *DNB* (XIII, 1072–1073), however, makes him matriculate in 1819, which implies a more serious interruption of his studies.

were listed in order of merit, and constituted the only recognized academic over-achievers in the university.

When Henry matriculated, reforming forces were urging the creation of other honors degrees and the inclusion of analytical techniques in the subject matter of the tripos. They had mixed success. On the one hand, new honors degrees came slowly. Classical languages won the privilege in 1822, but it was the only subject to do so before 1850; and to earn the right to examination its candidates had first to secure honors in mathematics. On the other hand, analysis, including applications to mechanics, hydrostatics, hydrodynamics, and optics, quickly entered the tripos. At the same time progressive professors of science, willing to lecture and to proselytize, began to have some influence. In 1819, for example, some thirty-three men, including the Lucasian Professor of Mathematics, Robert Woodhouse (said to be the first teacher of calculus in England), and William Whewell, wrangler and polymath, established the Cambridge Philosophical Society. Its second president, another old wrangler, James Wood, was the master of Henry's College, St. John's.[3]

Henry read for the tripos with his friend James Challis, who emerged first wrangler in 1825 and became a Fellow of Trinity and Plumian Professor of Astronomy. Henry came out seventh in 1826. It gave him little hope for a fellowship or professorship; only the church, to which he was in any case inclined, seemed to offer an adequate independence. He became priest in 1828 and received a curacy near Taunton in Somerset.

He was rescued from rustication partly by his own efforts and partly by the continuing operation of educational reforms. On his own he issued a *Treatise on Hydrostatics and Hydrodynamics for the Use of Students in the University* (1830), an admirable and original text which, together with Whewell's *Treatise on Dynamics* (1823), gave the intending wrangler the elements of applied analysis.[4] Then the reforms

---

[3] A. R. Hall, *The Cambridge Philosophical Society* (1969), pp. 1–9; D. A. Winstanley, *Early Victorian Cambridge* (1940), pp. 65–70, 83–85, 159–160, 168; J. W. L. Glaisher, *Proceedings of the London Mathematical Society* 18 (1886), 11–22; W. W. Rouse Ball, *Mathematics at Cambridge* (1889), pp. 187–219; T. Baker, *The College of St. John* (1869), II, 1095.

[4] Moseley, *Treatise*, preface; Challis, *BA Reports* (1833), 134.

intervened. The founding, in 1826, of University College, London, modern in curriculum, liberal in politics and indifferent in religion, had inspired the birth of a tory competitor, King's, "a College in which instruction in the doctrines and duties of Christianity, as taught by the Church of England, should be forever combined with other branches of usefull information." Moseley's combination of hydrodynamics and Christianity exactly fitted the objectives of the new college, which opened in 1831 with him doubling, or perhaps tripling, as chaplain and professor of natural philosophy and astronomy.[5] He remained for twelve years, and more than fulfilled the expectations of the trustees: he wrote several texts on applied mechanics, one of which, *The Mechanical Principles of Engineering and Architecture* (1843), became an international standard; and he improved religion with articles on "Astro-Theology" and with arguments from design in the style of the *Bridgewater Treatises*.[6]

In 1844 Moseley resigned his professorship to become one of Her Majesty's Inspectors of Schools, an agent of a Committee of Privy Council charged with administering funds newly granted by parliament for the improvement of primary education. The thoroughness of his reports, which at once established him as the most critical and constructive of all the inspectors, and the smallness of his staff—namely himself—can still teach us something. So too can his insistence that children must learn not only to read, but to like to read. Here, according to him, science must precede religion; rather than teach reading from Scripture, as was the universal practice, the Reverend Moseley proposed using elementary presentations of "laws of nature" applicable to the future callings of the children. Progress both intellectual and moral will result, he said, for whoever has mastered a law of nature "holds within his hands one link of a chain that leads up to God." [7] Moseley's value did not go unrewarded. In 1853, "for the great services [he had] rendered to

---

[5] *The Historical Register of the University of London* (1926), p. vi; F. J. C. Hearnshaw, *History of King's College* (1929), pp. 13–69, 91, 110–112.

[6] E.g., *Illustrations of Mechanics* (1859[6]), pp. v–vii, xv.

[7] See especially Moseley's report, based on an inspection of 247 schools, "Elementary Schools of the Midland District," in *Minutes of the Committee of Council on Education, 1845* (1846), I, 224–323. Cf. Frank Smith, *English Elementary Education 1760–1902* (1931), pp. 200, 211–212; A. S. Bishop, *Rise of a Central Authority for English Education* (1970), pp. 33–36, 79–87.

the cause of education," he received a canonry in the Bristol cathedral and a nice country living in Gloucestershire. He continued active in the cause, attending particularly to the high withdrawal rate from primary schools and the problem of introducing science into secondary education.[8]

Moseley's great energy was by no means exhausted by his public service. In 1850, while still an inspector, he presented to the Royal Society, which had elected him a fellow in 1839, a memoir which was to fulfill the ambition of his childhood. It dealt with the stability of ships and developed formulae, easily applied in practice, which (according to a Chief Constructor of the Royal Navy) soon became "established rules and principles" for the naval architects of Europe. Nor did Moseley's translation to Bristol end his contributions to science. Shortly after assuming his duties there he noticed a peculiar slippage of the lead plates of the roof of the cathedral. The sun's diurnal motion, or rather the consequent heating and cooling of the roof, turned out to be the culprit. The character of Moseley's mind will appear from his immediate generalization of his explanation of the slippage of the plates to an ingenious, if erroneous, theory of the motion of Alpine glaciers.[9]

"The sons of clergymen rarely take a lead in science," concluded Francis Galton, the eminent Victorian geneticist, after an exhaustive study of the breed.[10] Canon Moseley's son, Henry Nottidge Moseley (1844–1891), began as no exception to the rule. He grew up in rural Gloucestershire with a fondness for rabbit-shooting and *Robinson Crusoe*, a profound skepticism about the truth of anything in print, and no interest in mathematics or ancient languages, still the only paths to academic glory. On graduating from Harrow in 1864, force-fed on classics and cricket and with no reputation at either, he proceeded to Exeter College, Oxford, where, at his father's insistence, he was to read for

---

[8] Lord Aberdeen to Moseley, 23 May 1853; Lyon Playfair to Moseley, 10 Oct 1867; and correspondence re a conference organized by Moseley on "Early Age at which Children Are Taken from School," held in London in 1857 (LH).

[9] H. Moseley, *PRS* 5 (1850), 954–957, and *PT* 140 (1850), 609–643; *Transactions of the Institution of Naval Architects* 13 (1872), 328–330; H. Moseley, *PRS* 7 (1854/5), 333–342, and many papers in *PM*, 1869–1872. Cf. *More Letters of Charles Darwin*, ed. F. Darwin (1903), II, 163, and referee reports by Hopkins and Forbes, R.R.2. 162–163 (RS).

[10] Galton, *English Men of Science* (1874), p. 24.

honors in classics or in mathematics. He rejected both, and returned to hunting rats and collecting beetles.[11] Fortunately for him, the tentative reforming forces of his father's day, stiffened by a parliamentary commission set up in 1850 to bring the ancient universities into the nineteenth century, had won a series of victories which offered him salvation.

First, they forced Oxford to establish an Honours School in Natural Science, whose candidates, however, had first to satisfy the examiners in classics. Next, in 1863, the year before Moseley came up, they managed to excuse science classmen from the final examination in classics and to make honors in a single science school a sufficient achievement for a bachelor's degree. Third, they succeeded in diverting substantial sums to the support of science. In 1854, for example, Convocation reluctantly released profits of the University Press to build a museum, part depository and part laboratory; and in 1860 a new professorship attached to the museum, the Linacre Chair of Human and Comparative Anatomy, was established on the income derived from four superfluous fellowships extracted from Merton College. In 1866 H. N. Moseley began to read for honors under the Linacre professor. Canon Moseley agreed to the switch, but with misgivings, doubtless because he correctly anticipated that the traditional dons, who controlled the fellowships, would regard even a top science degree as "a dirty little first in Nat Phys or whatever it is." [12]

The first Linacre Professor, George Rolleston (1825–1881), another exception to Galton's clerical rule, had always liked to cut up animals; but as he came up to Oxford before the reforms, he had had to base his career on classics. He obtained a first in 1850 and a newly established fellowship, which obliged him to study medicine and thereby determined his calling. After practical training in London and service in the Crimea, he returned to Oxford as physician to the Radcliffe Infirmary, whence he slipped into the Linacre Chair. As one might have expected, he had no gift for research and inspired no school; but he proved an

---

[11] G. C. Bourne in H. N. Moseley, *Notes by a Naturalist* (1892[2]), pp. v–xvi; cf. H. T. Wood, *Cornhill Magazine* 50 (1921), 394–412.

[12] C. F. Mallet, *Modern Oxford* (1927), pp. 309–316, 329, 360–366; W. R. Ward, *Victorian Oxford* (1965), pp. 218–223; F. S. Taylor, *Annals of Science* 8 (1952), 88–104. See the discussion on science at Oxford in *Nature* 54 (1896), passim.

excellent teacher, despite a tendency to transform a lecture on, say, ancient shells into a criticism of the literary merits of Diodorus Siculus. Under Rolleston, Moseley's intellect quickly opened, spurred by the totally unexpected discovery that the specimens he dissected "were like the pictures after all"; and probably also by the challenge of defending the theories of Darwin, whom he greatly admired, against the objections of his teacher. In 1868 he obtained his "dirty little first"; and in the following year, in company with his close friend and fellow student E. Ray Lankester, he worked in Vienna as a Radcliffe Traveling Fellow. Still, despite his taste and talent for research, no permanent academic opportunity presented itself; and in the fall of 1870 he entered the medical school of the University of London.[13]

Once again new opportunities generated by government encouragement of science changed his course. First, in the fall of 1871, he went to Ceylon to work a spectroscope for the Government Eclipse Expedition headed by Norman Lockyer; he brought back a sackful of worms (planaria), which he sliced up at Oxford to the applause of Rolleston, who communicated the results to the Royal Society of London. Then, the following year, with the help of connections made in the Ceylonese excursion, Moseley joined the scientific staff of H.M.S. *Challenger*. The main purpose of her voyage was to study ocean bottoms which had become particularly interesting to the government after the successful laying of the Atlantic cable in 1866. Before then the English left scientific dredging to private citizens like Moseley's future father-in-law, John Gwyn Jeffreys (1809–1885), F.R.S., a solicitor devoted to molluscs. In the early sixties Gwyn Jeffreys dredged English waters from a private yacht; in 1869 he directed the scientific operations of H.M.S. *Porcupine*, a gunboat temporarily adapted for dredging; and only accident prevented him from sailing on the well-equipped *Challenger*, along with, or perhaps in place of, his future son-in-law.[14]

---

[13] E. B. Tylor in G. Rolleston, *Scientific Papers* (1884), I, x–lx; H. M. and K. D. Vernon, *History of the Oxford Museum* (1909), pp. 55, 63; A. V. Harcourt, *Cornhill Magazine* 28 (1910), 350–363; Lankester, *Nature* 45 (1891), 79–80.

[14] C. W. Thomson, *Voyage of the 'Challenger'* (1877), I, 2–11; *PRS* 38 (1885), xiv–xvii; J. N. Lockyer, *Contributions to Solar Physics* (1874), pp. 350, 379; A. J. Meadows, *Norman Lockyer* (1972), pp. 68–70; P. Pelseneer, *Bulletin scientifique du département du Nord et des pays voisins* 16 (1884/5), 258–262.

During the three-year voyage of the *Challenger* Moseley built his reputation with careful reports of tiny creatures unable to elude his extraordinarily penetrating eye. "You had only to put down Moseley on a hill side with a piece of string and an old nail [Rolleston used to say] and in an hour or two he would have discovered some natural object of surpassing interest." A typical example of his powers was noticing that the jointed shell of the common mollusc chiton, which everyone, including Gwyn Jeffreys, had carefully observed, was covered with eyes, which nobody had ever seen. On his return Moseley wrote a semi-popular account of his experiences, *Notes of a Naturalist on the 'Challenger'* (1879), which earned him the warmest praise from the dean of English naturalists. "It has excited in me greater interest than any other scientific book which I have read for a long time," Charles Darwin wrote Moseley shortly after receiving his copy. "Your volume is a mass of interesting facts and discoveries, with hardly a superfluous word." The *Challenger*'s naturalist became a fellow of his old college in 1876, and of the Royal Society in 1879; and two years later, on the death of Rolleston and with the active support of Darwin and Huxley, he succeeded to the Linacre professorship.[15] In the same year he married Gwyn Jeffreys' clever daughter Amabel, who had learned enough zoology from her father to be able to assist her husband.

The new professor settled his young wife, his Japanese and Melanesian curios, and his bottles of flatworms into a comfortable house in St. Giles' Circus, a short walk from the museum. Amabel bore him three children, of whom Harry was the youngest; the eldest, Betty, born c. 1883, died at sixteen; the second, Margery, born in 1884, became her brother's closest friend and confidante. The family started in promise and prosperity. The professor proved brilliant, "unsurpassed and unsurpassable," according to a former student, a captivating talker—in this quite unlike Harry—who "would often keep the attention of his

---

[15] E. B. Poulton, *John Viriamu Jones* (1911), pp. 184–187, 219–220, 234–235; Darwin to Moseley, 4 Feb 1879, in F. Darwin, ed., *Life and Letters of Charles Darwin* (1896²), I, 413–414; Huxley to Moseley, 25 Sept [1881] (LH); Darwin to Moseley, 25 Sept 1881 (LH): "I earnestly hope that you may be elected Linacre Professor at Oxford, for from my knowledge of your several works and from personal acquaintance with you, I am convinced that no other zoologist in Great Britain, who is competent to be a candidate, is so well fitted for the place & so likely to advance natural science in Oxford."

youthful hearers for a full hour beyond the appointed lecture time." [16] Unlike Rolleston, he knew how to do and how to guide research, and, with the help of college fellowships made available to his assistants, he soon assembled the nucleus of a leading school of physiology. He also did his part to improve facilities and training for science: with the powerful support of the Master of Balliol, Benjamin Jowett, who had already encouraged the building of the college laboratory in which Harry was to work, Moseley sought funds for a needed expansion of the museum; with Lankester and others he worked to establish a station for marine biology at Plymouth; and, in his father's spirit of public service, he frequently gave evening lectures in the larger provincial towns. But by no means did Moseley confine his activities to science or his acquaintances to scientists. The classicist Jowett and the archeologist Arthur Evans were among his friends; and travel to odd places, like Fez, Tangier, and Arizona, where he and Amabel journeyed expressly to visit the Pueblo Indians, was his favorite pastime.[17]

As these travels suggest, the family's activities were not limited by the income of the Linacre chair, which brought about £750. Canon Moseley had left his son a considerable estate, on the order of £15,000, and Amabel had brought a marriage settlement which, with a supplement from John Jeffreys' estate, reached £10,000. Invested with the utmost security in railroad shares and government funds, their capital gave an annuity of at least £750.[18] The life of a late Victorian or Edwardian family with £1,500 p.a. was extremely comfortable. A full-time maid earned about £20 p.a., an experienced cook and housekeeper about £50; a ton of coal, providing heat for a month, cost one pound; and food for an adult some 10 shillings a week. The Moseleys always had at least two in help.[19] The children were raised in upper-middle class luxury, both material and intellectual, attended by servants, exposed to professors, and surrounded by books, natural rarities, and foreign objets d'art.

---

[16] *Geological Magazine* 28 (1891), 575–576; Poulton, *Jones*, 234.

[17] Lankester, *Nature* 45 (1891), 79–80; letters from Jowett and Evans (LH); H. W. C. Davis, *History of Balliol College* (1963²), pp. 210–211.

[18] Wills of Henry Moseley (†20 Jan 1872), John Gwyn Jeffreys († 24 Jan 1885) and Henry Nottidge Moseley (†10 Nov 1891), in Somerset House, London; *Parliamentary Papers* (1876: lix), p. 343.

[19] M. Laski in S. Nowell-Smith, ed., *Edwardian England* (1964), pp. 145, 170–171; Diary, 1901–1915 (LH).

In 1887, at the zenith of his career, Professor Moseley was incapacitated by a neuromuscular disease. He, who had never known fatigue before, who preferred camping to city living, became a permanent invalid; he died in 1891, at the age of forty-seven, two weeks before Harry's fourth birthday. Amabel removed to Chilworth, near Guildford, in Surrey, where she devoted herself to the education of her children. Teachers were engaged in music, mathematics and languages. For recreation the children collected stamps, gardened, and put on plays in German. Their preoccupation with academic work appears in a few letters from Betty to Margery, who had gone away to school at High Wycombe. "Tell me a lot about your lessons in your next letter," she wrote. "Are you allowed to do any algebra?" "I do exceedingly hope that you have moved into lower fifth this week." "I want very much to know what lessons you are doing now, have you moved a peg or two in Latin?" "Yesterday Miss Fisher came to give us algebra . . . we shall get in front of you, as I suppose you are beginning again."

Harry, as the baby and the only male in this society, naturally felt himself apart. "Boy at present is carrying on a conversation with his bricks," Betty reported, adding the sovereign remedy, "he ought to have some dolls." He felt particularly alone without Margery. "Poor Boy feels rather dull without you [Betty wrote] as he hasn't much to do, yesterday he shed many tears in the first part of the walk & I think it was partly [due] to his feeling dull without you." [20] What Harry most missed were natural-historical excursions. He and Margery came to know every bird's nest in the neighborhood, learned to identify species by habitat, profile, song and egg, and grew expert in the delicate art of "blowing" (to use the *terminus technicus*) their finds. Margery kept a record of their sightings, and Harry acquired an imposing collection of eggs, partly by exchange, and later built himself a storage cabinet in the manner recommended by the best authority. [21]

Betty died in 1899 or 1900, apparently of consumption. Amabel returned to Oxford, where she resumed her old social life. For a time her amusements—chess, travel, concerts, lectures—included the Ashmolean Natural History Society of Oxfordshire, which gave her surviving

---

[20] Letters from Betty to Margery, 1895–c.1898 (LH).
[21] Lankester, *PM* 31 (1916), 173–174; F. O. Morris, *Nests and Eggs of British Birds* (1896⁴), I, viii–xi; 7.

children access to books, specimens, and guided field trips. Margery and Harry retained their interest in natural history throughout their lives. Margery, with the encouragement of Lankester, eventually produced a paper for the Royal Microscopical Society. Harry became an enthusiastic gardener in the family's cottage in the New Forest, and his last letters from the front are filled with observations of local fauna, of "frogs that sing all night, mantises that very seldom pray and grasshoppers innumerable." [22]

With Betty's death and the passage of time the patronized "Boy" gradually assumed the role left vacant by the death of his father, whom he strongly resembled both physically and intellectually. (In figures 18 and 23 one cannot miss the similarity of features, frame and hands, nor the common smallness of head, which, for what it's worth, Galton considered characteristic of successful Victorian scientists.) With the male role came a precocious sense of authority and responsibility which occasionally showed, as an unattractive obverse, an affectation of omniscience, a tendency to domineer, and an expectation of having his own way. But these traits rarely obtruded. School fellows remember him as "good-tempered but shy," a "likeable but very quiet boy, always pleasant, often smiling," "kind, modest, truthful and courageous," "unassuming, untidy, inhibited, golden-good, very likeable." [23]

Amabel entertained ambitious although unimaginative plans for the education of her clever son. The far goal was a good scholarship to Balliol, which at the turn of the century still enjoyed the ascendency it had acquired under Jowett, "a tranquil consciousness of effortless superiority." Harry had no financial need for a scholarship; winning one was the expected consequence of academic success in the public schools, which in turn reckoned their status by the number of their scholars. As for public school, Harry must go to Eton, again on a scholarship, although Amabel hedged her bet and provisionally enrolled him at Harrow. Eton was close; it too, under Edmond Warre, was at the height of its late Victorian prosperity; and, most important of all, its King's Scholars had an attractive reputation for what other boys called

---

[22] Ashmolean Society Papers (OB); F. A. Bellamy, *The Ashmolean Natural History Society* (1908), 478; **143**.

[23] Galton, *English Men of Science*, p. 98; private communication from J. Huxley; R. Knox, *God and the Atom* (1945), p. 136.

"sapping," i.e., for attending to their studies.[24] To ensure a fighting chance for a King's scholarship one required professional direction.[25] An excellent training ground, Summer Fields School, lay just north of Oxford, in beautiful meadows abutting the unpolluted Cherwell. Harry entered in 1896, as soon as he was eligible.

The headmaster, C. E. Williams (1852–1941), took the training of his gladiators seriously. The scholarship candidates had to study after dinner, while others read magazines. In the summer term a dress rehearsal took place, using Old Etonian papers; chocolates and sovereigns went to the top performers. When the great day came, Williams took his entries, some ten in number, to the White Hart Tavern in Windsor, where they approached the examination "as a team or crew, trained to the hour and full of the joy of battle." His results were remarkable: during the nineties he averaged five or six scholarships a year, slightly more than one-third the number available.[26] His success did not depend on mere cramming. His less able rivals, like Shane Leslie's tutor at Ludgrove, might make their pupils learn the New Testament by heart so that on meeting the Gospel in Greek they needed only to recognize a key phrase, take bearings, and spout the memorized translation. Williams attended to fundamentals (of ancient languages of course), invented catchy mnemonics, and trusted to his peculiar genius for anticipating examination questions. "Let's see, what have you got this morning," he asked his gladiators at breakfast at the White Hart during the Eton trials of 1900. "History and geography. Of course there's been all this talk of federating Australia. I suppose you all know the provinces of Australia and their capitals, but we'll just pass it around once." "So we passed it once round and it was the first question on the sheet that faced us in Upper School." [27]

Harry found several boys as clever as himself among his 125 school

---

[24] G. R. L. Fletcher, *Edmond Warre* (1922); Shane Leslie, *The Oppidan* (1922), pp. 48–49.

[25] Winifred Peck, *A Little Learning* (1952), pp. 99–100. There were of course noteworthy exceptions who won King's scholarships without private school training; see R. Knox, *Patrick Shaw-Stewart* (1920), p. 10.

[26] *Summer Fields Register* (1929), pp. 129–130; R. Usbourne, ed., *A Century of Summer Fields* (1964), pp. 19, 53–55.

[27] Shane Leslie, *Long Shadows* (1966), p. 63; R. Knox, *London Times*, 15 Mar 41, quoted in E. Waugh, *Ronald Knox* (1959), p. 49; Usbourne, ed., *Summer Fields*, p. 16.

fellows. Most conspicuous was Ronnie Knox, a recognized prodigy, who read Virgil at six and wrote Latin verses for fun. He was to become captain, or head academic boy, at Eton, a Balliol scholar, an apostate and a monsignor. There were Julian Grenfell, "wholly devoid of pettiness and humbug, cynicism and dishonesty," and his brother Billy, an excellent scholar, both killed in the first world war; Edward Horner, clever and artistic, who likewise died in battle; Alan Parsons, a future drama critic; and "a loutish little boy called Hugh Dalton," who became a baron and Chancellor of the Exchequer.[28] They were from similar social strata and quite representative of the population of the school: Knox's father was a bishop, the Grenfells' a peer, Horner's a feudal lord, Parsons' a rector with a good living, and Dalton's Chaplain to Windsor Palace, a position which had once been offered to Canon Moseley.

Harry was quite able to hold his own in this formidable competition. He won his form's classics prize in 1898 and again in 1899; he played respectable football and passable cricket; and he was a great power in the popular sport of bird-nesting. He made a fine collection of eggs, partly by trading duplicates from the great magazine he and Margery had assembled, and partly by depredations in the company of fellow aficionados like Parsons, with whom he shared the bruises of the hunt and the cool courage needed to "stand on a pointed stake with one leg nowhere." [29] Bird-nesting probably was Harry's strongest bond with his schoolmates.

In June of 1901 Harry took his place in the White Hart crew. Their performance was spectacular. Over one-half of the King's Scholars elected that year were from Summer Fields, including Parsons (who placed third in the election), Harry (fifth), G. L. Henderson (Harry's particular friend, an adventuresome youth later killed in an airplane accident), Horner, and Dalton. Six of the election, "including all who were natural leaders in work or play," were to die in the great war.[30]

---

[28] Waugh, *Knox*, pp. 45, 48–49; Lord Ribblesdale, *Charles Lister* (1917), p. 187; V. Tree, *Alan Parsons' Book* (1937), pp. vii–viii; E. A. P. Grenfell, baroness Desborough, *Pages from a Family Journal* (1916), pp. 41–43; F. J. Horner, *Time Remembered* (1933), pp. 213, 223.

[29] 1, 2, 4; private communication from P. Savage, present headmaster of Summer Fields.

[30] *Summer Fields Register*, pp. 129–130; Diary, 15 July 01; private communication from F. P. Walters; *London Times*, 22 July 30, pp. 14a, 16b. According to later notes by Margery (LH), Williams expected Harry to win the first scholarship to Eton in mathematics, but Harry was ill during the mathematics examination, and "took the fifth scholarship on his classics instead."

II

Eton

THE SEVENTY KING'S SCHOLARS or "Collegers," so-called because they dwelt within the school grounds, constituted only a small fraction of Etonians. The balance of the population of about 1,000 were paying students who lived in supervised houses in the town of Eton, and were consequently known as Oppidans (*oppidum*, town). Although both sets came from the governing and professional classes, and sat together in school, the Collegers tended to have little to do with the Oppidans, from whom the great Etonian bloods and future University Blues were primarily recruited. Harry formed all his few future friendships with fellow saps: with Julian Huxley, one year his senior, a favorite companion in bird-nesting explorations; with Henderson, whom he had known at Summer Fields; and with F. P. Walters, the son of the Principal of King Williams College (Isle of Man) and a future deputy Secretary General of the League of Nations.[1]

The Colleger began life in "Long Chamber," in one of fifteen curtained cubicles in which he slept and studied. Adjoining the chamber were seven rooms of relative luxury, equipped with fireplaces and inhabited by members of Sixth Form, which consisted of the top ten Collegers and the top ten academic Oppidans. The Sixth Former enjoyed great privileges: the rights to peculiar forms of dress, to the administration of justice, and to a fag to run his errands, light his fire and

---

[1] C. H. [Malden], *Recollections of an Eton Colleger* (1905), pp. 2–6, 37–41.

get his breakfast. Collegers were liable to this service for the duration of their time in Long Chamber. Harry accepted it good-humoredly, as appears from his first letter home from Eton. "They have the absurd fag plan here I find. The boy calls 'Here' and the last arrival is made useful. I am very near the 6th form rooms and have very little way to run, so I am lucky . . . . I am not a bit shy yet, because no old boy has yet deigned to look at me, except Summerfield boys. My bed is very uncomfortable and my pillow very low, but I shall soon get over that. The chief objection to the Long Chamber is that one can hear snores from one end of it to the other." [2] After his first year Harry received a room of his own, some 8 by 12 feet, papered in "hideous faded pink" and containing a folding bed, table, bureau, Windsor chair and, for a heater, a ledge beneath which ran a pair of hot water pipes. Here, or in similar quarters, he remained; for he left Eton a year earlier than most of his election, and consequently, although his general academic excellence insured him a place in sixth form, he never attained the seniority to take it.[3]

Harry's Eton had been largely fashioned by its huge headmaster, Edmond Warre, a splendid oarsman and a great expert on the naval operations of ancient Greece, who conceived it his duty to produce statesmen, bishops, generals, and solid imperial citizens for Victoria and Edward. His boys emerged with a "sense of unassailable primacy," "with training in leadership, power of decision, responsibility in running the affairs of a small but vital community," and, in a word, "with all the gifts requisite for dealing with their fellows." [4] They also tended to be intolerant, conventional, conservative, narrow-minded, healthy and un-educated. "Enthusiasm is reserved for games," one of Harry's unathletic classmates wrote. "To be too clever or intellectual is resented as

---

[2] *Ibid.*, pp. 26–28; **6**.

[3] Malden, *Recollections*, pp. 7–9. Harry ranked twenty-third, i.e., thirteenth Colleger, at the beginning of his last year, when the order is fixed; *A List of Eton College Taken at Election 1905* (1905), p. 8. Had he remained at Eton for another year he would probably have reached second place in the school, for his friend Walters, who was just behind him in 1905, ended there in 1906/7.

[4] These quotations come from, respectively, Shane Leslie, *End of a Chapter* (1916), p. 41; Hugh Dalton, *Call Back Yesterday* (1953), p. 35; and an anonymous writer in *Quarterly Review* 208 (1908), 409. See C. Hollis, *Eton* (1960), pp. 289–290; G. Drage, *Eton and the Empire* (1890); E. C. Mack, *Public Schools and British Opinion* (1941), pp. 246–250.

un-English." [5] To profit fully from the opportunity for intellectual improvement Eton offered one required independence as well as ability.

The common Etonian character was developed by carefully mixed doses of games, religion, patriotism, and ancient languages. The ritualization of athletics was largely Warre's doing. Until the middle of the nineteenth century games were casual affairs, only tolerated by the authorities, and boys making foreign expeditions to play cricket for the school thought themselves lucky if they escaped a flogging. Under Warre the best athletes, granted coveted "colours," were officially recognized as the leading boys. The Captains of the Boats and of the Eleven (the top oarsman and cricketer), invariably Oppidans, occupied an awesome height even Warre could not climb. Next to the captains in the line of heroes stood the two dozen members of "Pop," once a debating society which met above a cookshop (*popina*), but now the social and athletic elite "in which all privilege and glory culminates." To secure the right to a stick-up collar, patent boots, and a private fag, not to mention the power to flog the unconventional or the lawless, an ambitious boy would plot for years. "There is certainly a vital anxiety surrounding the entrance to Pop, an anxiety to which the proudest cannot be indifferent, an entrance which the most assured cannot take for granted." So Patrick Shaw-Stewart, a Colleger and contemporary of Harry's who, having no chance of election for athletics, conceived he might enter *ex officio* as Captain of the School. "I girt myself accordingly to a terrific struggle against endless obscurity." He committed most of the Greek scripture to memory and beat Ronnie Knox on a critical examination.[6]

Although Harry lacked the zeal and perhaps also the ability for athletic distinction, and consequently did not ascend to Pop, he participated willingly in all Etonian games except cricket. He played the Field Game (Eton football) indifferently, owing to his slowness which, however, admirably suited him to the Wall Game, a unique form of group mud-wrestling rewarding "weight rather than pace, endurance, [and] low cunning." Few ever fully grasped its rules. Goals occurred infrequently and fed arguments for generations; it is said that in 1900

---

[5] Leslie, *End*, p. 32.
[6] Hollis, *Eton*, p. 294; Mack, *Public Schools*, pp. 123–130, 210–211; Waugh, *Knox*, p. 59; Knox, *Shaw-Stewart*, pp. 15–17, 21. See Leslie, *Film of Memory* (1938), p. 207.

devotees still energetically disputed a goal of 1858.[7] Harry almost won a color at this sodden sport. He also rowed, encouraged by his tutor, who deplored the prevailing athleticism, and especially the cult of cricket, as "selfish" and "overspecialized." [8] He made the ante-finals in several races in the summer of 1905 and confidently looked forward to receiving his color during the distribution of spoils the following March. Much favoritism attended the business, however, particularly among the undistinguished; Harry, who was at first ignored by the Captain of the Boats, protested vigorously to the aquatic authorities the "wicked shame" of being passed over for two "worse oars." After several anxious weeks the captain "had woken up to a sense of his duties." Harry got his ribbon, the right to wear pink silk socks on the fourth of June, a berth among the inexpert eight on the sluggish *Alexandra*, and, most important, a place on the second College Four ("Coll:B") for the intramural bumping races in May.[9]

The competition proved as exciting as bird-nesting.[10] Harry had by no means discontinued his depredations on becoming a wet-bob; on the contrary, the river gave him a new route to the birds, and he thought nothing of rowing all day to visit the hole of a woodpecker. The Eton bloods regarded these expeditions with "the scorn reserved by English boys for kindergarten";[11] Harry's successful combination of such puerility with manly sport like rowing and the Wall Game is a good index of his inoffensive independence.

The second of Warre's educational medicines was religion. On Sundays prayers might consume six hours. On weekdays the boys spent a half hour in chapel enjoying the music, despising the preaching and escaping the exquisitely tailored penalty for shirking, namely, 500 lines of *Paradise Lost*.[12] This load of divinity was designed to inculcate fortitude, not piety, and decency rather than theology. Chapel appealed not to logic, fear, or mysticism, but to romanticism, generosity and patriotism;

---

[7] **14, 16**; Dalton, *Yesterday*, p. 26; Leslie, *Oppidan*, pp. 179–180; L. E. Jones, *Victorian Boyhood* (1955), p. 234.

[8] C. A. Alington, *Schoolmaster's Apology* (1914), pp. 29–30.

[9] **24, 26, 28, 29**; Malden, *Recollections*, pp. 187–196, 211; L. S. B. Byrne, *Eton Boating Book* (1933³), pp. 384, 393–396.

[10] Diary, 7 May 05; **32**.

[11] Leslie, *Oppidan*, p. 276.

[12] **7, 20**; Leslie, *Oppidan*.

it hallowed school friendships, consecrated school triumphs, and imposed a feeling of community. According to Knox, who was no friend of
the system, it worked "only too well." The housemasters reinforced it by
saying evening prayers and helping their younger boys prepare for
confirmation at the hands of the Bishop of Oxford.[13]

Harry's tutor and the master in college was the Reverend C. A.
Alington, a handsome and popular man of thirty, who became head in
1916 and ended his career as Dean of Durham and a writer of detective
stories. He was a good scholar, quick but not profound, and a tireless
apologist, unafraid of higher criticism or youthful skepticism, and
convinced of the overriding importance of communion, chapel, and
regular prayer; "it is these religious habits, indefinitely strengthened, as
they may be, by the companionship of like-minded friends, which are a
boy's greatest security when he goes out into the world." Alington had
been called to Eton in 1899 specifically to ensure that religion would
hold its own against athletics in the life of the school.[14] He won the
affection and respect of his charges by anchoring his explanations on
simple and basic propositions ("all through my life I have suffered from
those who would not begin at the beginning") and by using colorful,
even crude, parables to enforce a sense of duty to God, Eton and
England. His recipe for interesting boys in English poetry will illustrate
his methods. He invites them to his room, encourages them to range
among his books, "not unaided by tea"; and he advises them to begin
with strong meter, to "plunge into that great inheritance of admirable
nonsense which our age has provided for us." Start with W. S. Gilbert,
"the Aristophanes of the nineteenth century," and work through Kipling
to Clough and Whitman.[15] One suspects Alington would not even object
to Swinburne, then the favorite of the intellectual boys and a red flag to
Warre, who had proscribed the poet for what he judged to be
"unorthodox" sentiments. Boys found Alington "a witty man, an
immense relief from most masters." Tea or breakfast with him and his

---

[13] Leslie, *End*, p. 38, and *Shadows*, p. 66; Knox, *Spiritual Aeneid*, pp. 20–21.

[14] Alington, *Apology*, p. 128; *London Times*, 17 May 55, p. 13c; Alington, *A Dean's
Apology* (1952), p. 59. Alington issued his mysteries under the name S. C. Westerham;
Wilson Library Bulletin 30 (1955), 18.

[15] Alington, *Apology*, pp. 2, 64–79, 98–101, 120, 159, 189–202, and *Things Ancient and
Modern* (1936), pp. 108–109; Knox, *Spiritual Aeneid*, p. 28.

wife—she was a Lyttelton, related to dozens of prominent Edwardians—
was esteemed "a real treat." [16]

Harry attached a high value to his Etonian religion. In a later letter
to Margery, urging her to bring up her baby boy "as a Christian," he
wrote: "Personally I do not see how as a schoolboy I could have got on
without a definite religion, as Philosophic Ethics seemed even less
intelligible to me then, than they do now, and fear of discovery was
seldom a sufficiently strong motive for good behavior." [17] Those who
knew him best remarked the "purity of his life and conversation." While
the majority of public school boys swore like troopers, Harry "never said
a word [a friend wrote Amabel after his death] which could not have
been said in your presence." His Eton mess-mate, Frank Walters, recalls
that "any kind of 'dirtiness' in talk or act was utterly foreign to him;
nothing in him of the prig or the gossip." [18] Doubtless his goodness,
directness and unaffectedness had their roots deep in his character; but
they were strengthened by the Etonian ideals Alington instilled, notions
of duty, obligation and propriety, that simplified his life and hastened his
death.

The third ingredient of Warre's Eton was the study of ancient
languages, "the only sound basis of education," "the best instrument yet
devised for making a decent citizen out of the average English boy." [19]
Mathematics was also established and a few lesser subjects tolerated.
The boys began with Greek, Latin, mathematics, a little natural history,
and French, taught by classical masters who pronounced it like English.
They proceeded to a double choice, between Greek and modern history
and between German and science, and ended, at the age of sixteen or
sixteen and a half, by selecting a specialty from among modern
languages, classics, history, mathematics or science.[20] The curriculum did

---

[16] Julian Huxley, *Memories* (1970), p. 53; **21**; Leslie, *Oppidan*, pp. 188, 207. See Knox,
Shaw-Stewart, p. 36.

[17] **52**; see Jones, *Boyhood*, pp. 203, 210.

[18] H. Jervis to Amabel, 14 May 24; private communication from F. P. Walters.

[19] Alington, *Apology*, p. 14.

[20] Hollis, *Eton*, pp. 272–280, 285–290, 311; B. J. W. Hill, *Eton Medley* (1948), pp. 76–78,
129; Fletcher, *Edmond Warre*, p. 161; Jones, *Boyhood*, pp. 174, 190–191. Science
instruction had come in the wake of curricular and administrative reforms forced on Eton
by a Royal Commission appointed in 1861; Warre's greatness lay partly in his gracious
acquiescence to the inevitable. See E. D. Laborde, *Harrow School* (1948), pp. 59, 148.

not serve the great majority, who learned little and that useless; but the Collegers and occasional Oppidans who persevered, particularly in the classics, had well-nigh limitless opportunities to learn from accomplished and even inspired masters. In fashioning correct verses in dead languages they learned control of thought and expression, and began to see the classical texts as something more than grammatical puzzles.

They also thereby took what was still the most promising route to a university scholarship. Of the 126 scholarships which fell open at Oxford in 1906, the year Harry went up, 75 were reserved for classicists and only 14 for scientists. The serious imbalance, which persisted until the World War called attention to the recruitment of scientific manpower, could not help but stunt the growth of modern curricula in secondary schools specializing in the capture of university scholarships.[21] This practical consideration and counsel against scientific specialization came easily to older masters who, like Ronnie Knox's father, had been taught to regard scientists as "enemies of religion," allies of the Dissenters and Papists who had entered the universities along with science schools, laboratories, and professors of experimental physics. There is no doubt that the hostility of classical masters, as well as the pattern of university scholarships, depressed the number and caliber of science specialists at Eton, as it did in other public schools. For example, Harry's chemical friend Henry Tizard (whose father, the *Challenger's* hydrographer, had been a friend of Henry Nottidge Moseley) was the only scientist at Westminster. His peculiar interest brought the enmity of his master, who delighted in telling him that he had no chance for a close scholarship to the university: "We do not give such things to scientists." [22]

---

[21] A. Irving, *Nature* 66 (1902), 459; Lord Curzon, *University Reform* (1909), p. 77; *Natural Science in Education* (1918), p. 26. In 1905 there were four science masters at Eton in a staff of sixty-two; *List of Eton College*, p. 4. The hardback opposition appears from this blast from an old and distinguished Oxonian: "The attempt to foist these special physical researches on Oxford, which still [1910] remains an aristocratic gymnasium and essentially a theological seminary—where not one student in a hundred intends to pursue a scientific profession, where there is little scope for post-graduate study, in a world totally devoted to the 'humanities,' to Church, to 'good society,' and sport—this is a sheer waste of labour and money. . . . All this is only to distract and enfeeble the task of serious education for the average youth, who only needs at twenty-one to have his mind vivified, clarified, and organized." Frederic Harrison, *Memoirs* (1911), I, 134.

[22] Peck, *Little Learning*, p. 32; Campbell, *Nationalization of the Old English Universi-*

Harry proceeded easily through the set curriculum. He developed a good nose for "pot hunting," as non-saps called attempts at academic awards. He garnered prizes for Latin prose, which keen classicists like Knox disdained to write; for English poetry, with an agronometric adaptation of the story of Europa, carried off through "fields of corn and mangelworzel" by an "Aldernay First Prize" bull; and for natural history, where his precocious knowledge could be brought to bear. But he did not compete merely to win. He refused to play on his home court in a tourney which offered prizes for an "original essay on birds of Eton & neighborhood"; and later, having won one prize in chemistry and being certain of winning another, he declined to enter, "as it would be rather grabbing of me to take it, while if I am not in there will be quite a good competition for it." [23] *Nullum periculum nullum gaudium.* Algebra also came easily, at a level that may be judged from a question Harry solved "after much labour," namely, are the numbers "16, 1156, 111556, 11115556, etc., all squares?" He enjoyed doing problems "just hard enough to be interesting, just not too hard to prevent me from doing them all." The head mathematics master, J. M. Dyer, rated him par with the leading specialist, Hugh Marsden (who later taught mathematics at Eton), and far stronger than Dalton, "a fact [our peacock tells his mother] which I have never doubted for a moment." [24]

When it came time to exercise his academic freedom, Harry took Greek over modern history, doubtless with an eye to the Oxford Responsions, and science over German. He began with physics, imparted by Hugh de Havilland. Finding the instruction "too elementary" and his classmates "rather dense," Harry arranged to read on his own and to do practical work with William Douglas Eggar (1865–1945), the senior physics master.[25] Eggar, a scholar of Trinity College, Cambridge, thirteenth wrangler with second-class honors in natural science, had a lively sense of humor which he rigorously resisted. When it overcame him he wrote light topical verse for the *Pall Mall Gazette*; when he had

ties (1901); W. R. Ward, *Victorian Oxford* (1965), pp. 277–278, 289–290; E. Lyttelton, *Memories and Hopes* (1925), pp. 171–173; Tizard, Autobiography, p. 28 (IWM).

[23] **9, 10, 31.**
[24] **11**, where a proof is given; **22.**
[25] **13**; Jones, *Boyhood*, pp. 195–197.

the upper hand he compiled or revised his several pedantic textbooks. He was one of those unfortunate pedagogues who never catch the spirit of their subject. He could examine—after retiring from Eton in 1920 he did so regularly for Oxford, Cambridge, and the University of London— but he could not teach. Huxley recalls that Eggar's experiments "always seemed to go wrong." [26] Therefore, perhaps, he insisted that his students perform theirs precisely as the manuals directed and, in case of difficulty or obscurity, to consult a standard text. It was precisely the worst method for an original spirit like Harry's. "I have no respect for the man, because he either can not or will not explain anything and refers you to books," Harry complained to his mother. "The consequence is I don't do my work his way, but annoy him by introducing unnecessary complications, simply to prove that they don't matter, instead of taking everything for granted." The inevitable break occurred when Harry insisted on drawing a diagram of the apparatus he had used, rather than of the one pictured in the manual. "I told him even if I could conceivably remember it, I had not personally found [it] to work, as mine had. That enfuriated him, but I think my principle is right, as the differences were far from vital." [27]

Alington took alarm at his pupil's habit of dropping or circumvent- ing his colleagues, and hinted to Amabel that (as Harry put it) "I get my own way more often at Eton than is good for me." Her letter of admonishment, which coupled Alington's complaint with charges of "tyranny" (apparently in regard to holiday activities), touched Harry at his chief fault, and elicited the only passages in the surviving correspond- ence that betray any smallness of spirit. After an innocuous beginning, recording an unusually brilliant display of the Aurora Borealis, he breaks out petulantly: "You are the naughtiest, baddest, wickedest Mum ever seen." This ostensibly for playing bridge despite a bad headache, but in fact for her stinging references to his domineering. "My Mum is to have it all her own way next holidays, & she shan't reproach me for being a tyrant.—I never say anything half so nasty to you, and you see it still rankles." [28] This filial concession had no parallel in Harry's dealing with inept masters. In his penultimate term he approached Alington's

---

[26] *London Times*, 30 Apr 45, p. 6f; Huxley, *Memories*, p. 50.
[27] **16**.
[28] *Ibid.*

brother-in-law, Edward Lyttelton, who had succeeded Warre in 1905, to ask to be relieved of Paul Scoones, coauthor of the *Eton Algebra*, who had taken his degree at Oxford in 1896 with highest honors in physical science. "I represented that I could not work at mathematics in a room in which Scoones was teaching. I now therefore work in my own room. . . ." [29]

There were two science masters Harry could not bully. M. D. "Piggy" Hill, the Mr. Gill of Leslie's *Oppidan*, had obtained a first under Lankester at Oxford and then taught zoology at Owen's College, Manchester, before opening a Darwinian outpost at Eton. His lectures, "as good as a Jules Verne novel," supplied "the most exhilarating information about extinct animals and prehistoric man." For Julian Huxley, whose career he determined, he was "a genius of a teacher." [30] But not for Harry. A fussy man, Hill cared more for taxonomy than for physiology, a preference Harry could not appreciate. We perhaps see a trace of Hill in Harry's battlefield will which, while leaving his estate to the Royal Society for the "furtherance of experimental research," explicitly refuses support to "any branch of science which aims merely at describing, cataloguing or systematizing." Two other forces kept Harry from specializing under Hill: a strong physical intuition that early expressed itself in astonishment that helium, despite its lower boiling point, is heavier than hydrogen; and Hill's arch-rival, the Reverend Thomas Cunningham Porter (1860–1933).[31]

Porter had preached only once, some say on the gases let loose at the creation, others on the possible utility of asbestos in the fires of Hell. He taught lower boys chemistry "rather like the accomplishment of drawing-room comedy." He was reputed to have raised a cat from the dead with a galvanic battery. "This jar," he would say to new boys, "contains what is the most deadly explosive known to man. One drop would shatter this laboratory. A table-spoonful would damage lower chapel. If this jar was dropped I could not answer for the safety of

---

[29] 21. According to Leslie, *Film of Memory*, p. 191, all the mathematical masters were "weary mind-grinders."

[30] Huxley, *Memories*, p. 50; Leslie, *Oppidan*, p. 62; Hill, *Eton and Elsewhere* (1928), pp. 64–65, 79–81. See Hill in *Higher Education of Boys in England*, ed. C. Norwood and A. H. Hope (1909), pp. 395–400; and Hill and W. M. Webb, *Eton Nature Study* (1903/4).

[31] 134; 11; Hill, *Eton and Elsewhere*, p. 164.

Windsor Bridge. Now pass it round." The boys, awed by what probably
was water, then docilely learned the laws of Boyle and Gay-Lussac, which
their unorthodox master required them to repeat by heart, timed by a
stopwatch. Those who took notes faithfully were rewarded by special
"Good Boy Lecturers," illustrated by lantern slides Porter had made
from his own photographs, accompanied by music played through
speakers of his own design, and sometimes ending with ghost stories,
which he told brilliantly.[32] ("So sure his touch, that fame affirms / A boy
exists who caught a / Disease from only hearing germs / Described by Dr
Porter." [33]) Naturally he was despised by masters and loved by students.
The future writer, Shane Leslie, spent an entire term (or "half") with
Porter, happily trying to destroy a sixpence, and learning more, he says,
about the "actual workings of God" than he had from chapel services.
For a moment even the classical super-sap Ronnie Knox, "the cleverest
Etonian in human memory," thought to throw it all away and specialize
in chemistry.[34]

Porter was by no means a mere showman. He had a gift for practical
work, which perhaps explains his indifferent degree at Oxford, whose
bookish curriculum was also to trip up Harry. Porter had a private room
in the school laboratory where he developed his photographs, revived
dead cats, and repeated and extended experiments he read about in the
journals. He was one of the first men in England to work with Röntgen
rays and perhaps the earliest to recognize their inhomogeneity. His
ongoing research centered on problems of physiological optics, like
persistence of vision, to which he contributed an important phenomeno-
logical relation known as "Porter's law." [35] He accordingly had a fund of

[32] Leslie, *Oppidan*, pp. 62–63, 122; *J Chemical Society* (1933:2), 1650–1652; Jones,
Boyhood, pp. 208, 211; Knox, *Aeneid*, p. 30; Waugh, *Knox*, p. 73. See Porter's *Impressions
of America* (1899), illustrated by stereoscopic pictures and equipped with instructions for
inducing the necessary double vision without the use of spectacles. It is filled with original
observations of ocean currents, waterfalls, weather, landscapes, and the opium dens of San
Francisco.
[33] C. A. Alington, *Eton Faces Old and Young* (1933), p. 65.
[34] Leslie, *Film of Memory*, pp. 181–184.
[35] Porter, *Nature* 54 (1896), 110–111, 149–150; *PRS* 63:A (1898), 347–356, and *PRS* 70:A
(1902), 313–329, the last two communicated by Lord Rayleigh (cf., Rayleigh, *Life of . . .
Rayleigh* [1968²], pp. 196, 199). Porter's law states that the speed with which a
black-and-white sectored disk must be spun in order that flicker may just vanish is
proportional to the logarithm of the illumination of the disk.

challenging laboratory exercises to set his specialists, whom he trained with an eccentric combination of rigidity and freedom. He required absolute docility in small matters like the boring of a cork, which he forced students to do in the one true way; but he urged them to develop their own methods for complex problems, like the analysis of rare minerals, that lay quite beyond their competence. Textbooks loomed as small in his operations as they did large in Eggar's. "It never crossed Porter's mind for a moment," a former specialist recalls, "that some day one would have to pass an examination." [36]

Porter's magic easily captured Harry, who at the height of his infatuation planned to spend thirteen hours a week on chemistry. He was soon a showman. At the annual exhibition of the Eton Scientific Society he shared the program with H. A. Miers, F.R.S., Professor of Mineralogy at Oxford, who produced images of growing crystals by means of polarized light. "They were lovely, changing colour as they grew, and such colours." Harry then exhibited a foul explosive gas called phosphine (PH_3). "It worked beautifully. Each bubble as it bubbles up through water explodes on reaching the air with a little flash of light, making a little vortex ring of P_2O_5. The smell is of course appalling." [37] Porter also introduced Harry to quantitative analysis. He began by showing that certain crystals of oxalic acid were 99.6 percent pure, "a great triumph," he assured Margery, "as the result was probably very nearly exact, .4% impurity being just what one would expect [?], and the possibilities of accumulated error being great. Now I am to find the molecular weight of something by the lowering of the freezing, and raising of the boiling point, a very long and difficult business." [38]

It was as a science specialist that Harry tried for a Balliol scholarship. One of the examiners was Harold Hartley, who had just become a Balliol don and stood at the threshold of a distinguished career in physical chemistry. Sixty years later Sir Harold still remembered

---

[36] *J Chemical Society* (1933:2), 1650–1652; private communication from Sir Thomas Merton.

[37] **13, 19.** Harry also contributed a paper on deep-sea fishes to the Eton Scientific Society and showed it some elementary experiments on X rays (*Nature* 104 [1920], 444).

[38] **23.** For guidance in these matters Harry used W. A. Shenstone, *Elements of Inorganic Chemistry* (1900); A. F. Walden and B. Lambert, *Detection of the More Common Acid Radicals in Simple Salts* (1904); and the university-level texts of R. T. Glazebrook, *Heat* (1894), and *Light* (1902).

Harry's papers, the "answers very short, dead to the point," the writing clumsy, as if done with "a splinter of wood dipped in ink." Hartley wished Harry to have the science scholarship then available. It went, however, to Huxley, who had taken the examination the year before, done brilliantly and been refused, on the ground of immaturity; he returned to Eton, aged himself with bird-nesting and Greek iambics, reapplied and succeeded because, according to Hartley, the examiners felt pledged to him. So much for open competition.[39] Harry could not go to Balliol as a commoner, as that would clearly announce failure: "any scholarship," he wrote Hartley, "was better than none." Hartley replied with an offer of a second class scholarship, or "exhibition," which Harry considered briefly. He decided instead to settle for something other than Balliol. He succeeded at Trinity, much to the relief of himself and his backers. "I was of course delighted with the news, and very content to go to Trinity. My Tutor is very pleased, as it is his old college, and he naturally thinks well of it. . . . Porter seems to be very pleased, though rather disappointed at my not getting the Balliol as he evidently thinks me better than Huxley, in fact his butter is laid on with an obvious trowel." The outcome also disappointed Harry a little. "Butter is in season at times," he conceded to Margery.[40]

Most boys, like Ronnie Knox, felt leaving Eton "definitely as a tragedy."

> Masters and friends are not the care
> That racks my anguished mind;
> One numbing thought alone is there—
> I leave myself behind.[41]

Harry, who was notably unsentimental, took away poise and purpose without nostalgia. In October 1906 he took up residence at Trinity without a backward glance.

---

[39] Cf. Lord Curzon, *University Reform*, pp. 89–93, and A. Tillyard, *History of University Reform* (1913), pp. 244–250.

[40] 14, 18, 19.

[41] Knox, *Aeneid*, p. 53; Waugh, *Knox*, p. 79; private communication from F. P. Walters.

III

Oxford

HARRY RECEIVED a pair of rooms at the top of the northwest staircase in Trinity's third court. From his sitting room two windows overlooked the college laboratory, which in fifty years had made its way from the cellars of Balliol into an answering cavern in Trinity. The bedroom window, now cemented over to symmetrize the facade, gave onto the court and the gardens beyond. The internal arrangements reflected what Harry called his "economical tastes": a case filled with science books, including well-bound prizes from Eton; a mantelpiece surmounted by a valuable apothecary jar; a large Chinese tile decorated with a friendly dragon; and a few objects of solid silver, including a cigarette box, an inkstand, a lamp copied from a relic of Pompeii, and a cream pitcher in the form of a cow.[1] A few pots of the flowers of the season, the paraphernalia of a river man, and the usual college furniture completed his establishment.

Trinity sheltered about one hundred forty undergraduates, whose social mix will appear from the ancestry of the thirty-eight men of Harry's year: twenty-one sons of professional men (physicians, solicitors, teachers, ministers, army officers), fourteen of business men (merchants, bankers), and three of "gentlemen." More than half were graduates of one or another of the great public schools, and eight had come from

---

[1] H. Hartley, *Chemistry in Britain* 1 (1965), 522; E. J. Bowen, *Notes and Records RS* 25 (1970), 229; H. Jervis to Amabel, 18 Feb 20 (LH). Harry's old room is now 14/12.

Eton.[2] Harry found himself back in Warre's world in many respects. For one, like most Oxford undergraduates, and despite the recent multiplication of political clubs in the university, Trinity men were addicted to sports and given to extravagant admiration of the many Blues in their ranks. For another, as recommended by the student paper, *The Varsity*, they interested themselves in religion, and supported a thriving College Church Society "at which," as one participant recalls, "exotic papers were read and approved by the athletes." [3] Above all, the Trinity man, like the Etonian and most undergraduates, took care to avoid "bad form," "snobbishness," and excessive commitment of any kind; in a word, he strove to conform. "Nothing astonished me more than the uniformity of ideas and behavior among my fellow undergraduates." Thus the distinguished historian, E. L. Woodward, who came up in 1908, writing about ordinary old school boys, "numb to all intellectual interests," "bothered by public opinion [and] frightened by originality," "horribly afraid to say, do, or think anything unless they see everybody else setting them the example." [4] Finally Moseley found familiar the dominance of the classics, which drew most of the ablest men far from any contact with science or scientists. The resources devoted by the colleges to the pursuit of *Literae humaniores* may be illustrated by their redundant offering, in the summer term of 1907, of six *courses* of lectures on Aristotle's *Ethics*, of seven on the histories of Herodotus, and of six on the first few books of Plato's *Republic*.[5]

Most of the time Harry spent with Trinity men was on the river. During the season he trained most faithfully, kept his weight below 150,

---

[2] Admission Book (Trinity College); *Oxford University College Reports. Trinity* (1906–10). Two Rhodes Scholars, whose fathers were an oculist and an auctioneer, have been disregarded. Cf. C. A. Anderson and M. Schnaper, *Social Backgrounds of Oxford and Cambridge Students* (1952), p. 6, and S. Rothblatt, *Revolution of the Dons* (1968), p. 87.

[3] P. A. Wright-Henderson, *Blackwood's Magazine* 185 (1909), 336–338; private communication from A. L. Moir; *The Varsity* (1906/7), 9–10. Cf. the commendation of Trinity's "muscular Christianity" by "A Recent Under-Graduate, not of Balliol," *National Review* 48 (1906), 287.

[4] The quotations come from, respectively, Wright-Henderson, *Blackwood's Magazine* 185 (1909), 338; E. L. Woodward, *Short Journey* (1942), p. 29; P. Gardner, *Oxford at the Crossroads* (1903), p. 10; Woodward, *loc. cit.*; G. B. Shaw, *Sham Education* (1931), p. 335. Cf. Mack, *Public Schools and British Opinion* (1941), pp. 272–273.

[5] *The Varsity* (1906/7), p. 286; see D. O. Hunter-Blair, *Catholic University Bulletin* 14 (1908), 630.

and retired before 10 p.m.; he was rewarded with a seat in Trinity's second eight, which did well, and in Trinity's first torpid, which did not. He was shipped to the second torpid, which promptly sustained six spectacular losses. It was all the same to Moseley, who rowed for exercise, not for glory, and who might be found directly after a race enjoying some real sport in the Balliol-Trinity laboratory.[6]

Harry also participated occasionally in the Trinity Debating Society, where his quiet insistence, clear formulations, and great fund of knowledge won him a local reputation for omniscience. He enjoyed arguing, not "to inspire conviction or persuade to action," as Walters recalls, but as an "intellectual expression," a kind of mental exercise parallel to rowing.[7] His political and social views cannot be recommended for enlightenment or originality. Like many men who achieve great success from their own evident exertions, from hard pulling or hard studying in his case, Harry believed that the individual bore the primary responsibility for his own condition. "He took a laissez faire view of things, and believed that improvement would only come by individual initiative and enterprise." He had a very low opinion of, and almost no acquaintance with the "working classes." Doubtless he would have agreed with some colleagues of Galton, who had concluded from a count of academically distinguished father-son pairs (like Harry's father and grandfather) that they, the pairs, owed their success to superior racial stock. Naturally he opposed socialism, then indeed more a debating topic than a political force; he voted (or would have voted) exclusively for Conservative candidates; and he esteemed the House of Lords, whose caponizing by the Parliament Act he most vigorously disapproved.[8] These views were typical of Etonians of Harry's era. A notable exception was Hugh Dalton, who entered Parliament in 1924 as a Labour member. He then found himself facing "rows of Old Boys," a reunion which would have been happier had they not all occupied Tory benches.[9]

---

[6] *Oxford Magazine* 26 (1907/8), 326, 342–343; *ibid.* 27 (1908/9), 314, 331–332; *The Varsity* (1909/10), p. 286; private communication from Sir Harold Hartley.

[7] Private communications from F. P. Walters and A. L. Moir.

[8] H. Jervis to Amabel, 14 Apr 24 (LH); cf. **14, 21, 23**. E. Schuster and E. M. Elderton, *Eugenics Laboratory Memoirs* 1 (1907), find that over one-third of the fathers of men taking firsts or seconds at Oxford had themselves won similar honors, the sample being father-son pairs both of whom graduated from Oxford during the nineteenth century.

[9] Dalton, *Yesterday*, p. 33; Ribblesdale, *Lister*, pp. 11–14. *The Varsity* (1907/8), p. 118, opposes Lister's socialism.

The conservatism of Harry's generation expressed itself, among other ways, in a deep sense of duty towards king and country. Patriotism, instilled in the public schools and kept warm by memories of Mafeking, immediately responded to a government grown alarmed at the preparations of the kaiser and its own serious lack of reserve officers. Lord Haldane, Minister of War, rattled his saber at Oxford in May of 1908, announced the end of the old University Volunteers, and pled for recruits for a new Officers Training Corps. Men rushed to join. "It is not long since Oxford sent of her best at the Country's call, and now the Country is calling on her again," *The Varsity* reported, pointing out the "duty of every undergraduate to do *something* towards helping the military efficiency of the nation." Moseley joined the force, not as a militarist, he told Margery, but because he could "find no sound argument with which to confute the advocate of universal service." He took the training with his usual good humor. "We march around the fields—two men to a skipping rope make a section—imagining ourselves a large army. . . . Then we skirmish, open into extended order, and fire rapidly wooden cartridges at the trees." [10]

In none of these activities—pulling, wrangling or drilling—did Harry make any close friends. Nor did he exert himself to retain or improve his connections with Walters, Henderson or Huxley. The social void was filled primarily by Amabel and, before her marriage in 1909, by Margery; and by a new acquaintance, the only crony Harry ever had, a student of chemistry named Henry Jervis, who never learned the cause of his preferment. "I never did understand, and it still puzzles me," Jervis wrote Amabel just after the war, "why, out of all the people he knew, distinguished in learning, or position, or means, he chose me for his most intimate friend." For Jervis was an outsider. He had never been to public school; he was relatively old, a schoolmaster (and the son of a schoolmaster) already started on his career; and he had neither the money nor the leisure to participate in college life. He labored like an Horatio Alger hero in the Balliol-Trinity laboratory, "hating," as he put it, the debonair young demonstrators and "realizing very keenly the difference between myself and other people, many of them with

---

[10] *The Varsity* (1908/9), 410, and (1909/10), 4; *Oxford Magazine* (1907/8), 288–289. Reports of military maneuvers and summer camps became standard features in these journals. Cf. **37**, and Knox, *Shaw-Stewart*, p. 51.

substantial incomes or allowances, and the whole of their time at their own disposal." Harry, "almost a legendary being to me," befriended the unhappy schoolmaster for several reasons. First, a community of temperament: Jervis had a like reserve, a similar uprightness, and an even greater earnestness. Second, a common interest in physical science and, above all, in photography, about which Jervis was most knowledgeable.[11] And third, a certain noblesse oblige, a concern on Harry's part to improve the opportunities of an able, deserving and neglected fellow student. One summer he took Jervis on an Alpine walking trip, a common recreation of Oxford undergraduates, and one which Harry himself had first enjoyed during vacations from Eton. They made a "very sober and earnest pair," looking for flowers, admiring the view, and "arguing incessantly about politics." They returned to some good-natured jibes from a fellow worker in the laboratory for "discussing land nationalisation at the top of the Matterhorn." [12]

The intending specialist in physics faced three examinations. First came "Responsions," an entrance test requiring knowledge of arithmetic, elementary algebra or geometry, Latin, and Greek enough to render a prepared book into English. This last shibboleth was then the focus of debate between the moderns, who held it to be irrelevant and wasteful, and the ancients, who conceived that, "for the general good of the country, . . . a fair number of people should know a fair amount of Greek." Moreover, they said, dropping Greek from Responsions would lower the standard of English, depress culture, menace natural theology, and, worst of all, encourage that un-Oxfordian bugaboo, science. Scientists clever enough can learn Greek, and the rest go elsewhere; modern languages are no fit substitute for the tongue of Athens, which alone confers "general knowledge, culture, taste and humanity." The reformers lost the battle just before Harry came up. In any case he was fully prepared for Responsions at Eton; indeed, like many of his fellows, he had received a certificate of competence while still at school which excused him from the examination.[13]

[11] Letters of Jervis to Amabel, 18 Feb 20, 14 Feb and 14 Apr 24 (LH).

[12] Jervis to Amabel, 18 Feb 20 (LH); Diary, Aug 03, Aug 04, Aug 06; **36**. See Leslie, *End*, p. 32, and *Shadows*, pp. 68–69; and C. Bailey, *Francis Fortescue Urquhart* (1936), pp. 163–165.

[13] *Examination Statutes* (1906), p. 20. The argument for retaining Greek in Responsions

The next test, the "First Public Examination" or "Moderations," normally taken at the end of the freshman year, consisted of two parts, an examination in Holy Scripture and, for those reading for honors, an examination in either mathematics or ancient languages. Harry naturally took the first option, which, according to the statutes, was to cover most of the first four books of Euclid and algebra exclusive of the theory of quadratic equations. Anyone foolish enough to believe the statutes would have suffered as he deserved. The questions set Harry supposed acquaintance with infinite series, with the theory of numbers, and with some forms of cubic and quartic, to say nothing of quadratic, equations; and they required a firm grip on plane geometry and trigonometry. They tested not only knowledge and facility, but also mathematical sense: several could be done almost by inspection if one saw the straight path. The examination served well, therefore, in separating alphas from betas and in giving men like Harry, who obtained first class honors, just cause for celebration. But in toto the examination does not deserve high marks. Excepting one question about determinants, nothing on it could not have been set in the reign of George III; faithful, this time, to the advertisement in the *Statutes*, the examiners did not expect the least familiarity with the differential or integral calculus, which the specialists in physics and chemistry, who would not again be examined in mathematics, would soon need to know.[14]

The last test, the "Second Public Examination" or "Final Honours School," normally took place at the end of the fourth year of study. It occupied four days. On the first three the intending physicist wrote six papers, two elementary, one general and three special (heat, light and electricity); on the last day he showed his laboratory prowess by measuring properties, like focal lengths or capacitances, of objects given him. The written portion required a good general knowledge of physics and of the physical chemistry of solutions without—as one might expect from the level of the moderations—elaborate mathematics. None of the

---

has been assembled from several pamphlets dating from about 1904 (G. A. Oxon.b.141, ff. 183–185 [OB]); a counter-manifesto, signed by many scientists including Harry's tutor Nagel, appears *ibid.*, ff. 191, 199.

[14] *Statutes*, pp. 25, 32, where Euclid I, 7, 16–17; II, 8; III, 2, 4–10, 13, 23–24, 26–29; and IV beyond IV, 9, are excluded; "First Public Examination, Trinity Term, 1907," Radcliffe Science Library, Oxford.

papers set between 1906 and 1910, for example, asks about the methods of Lagrange or Hamilton in mechanics, or about those of Gauss, Green or Stokes in electricity; no question about the dynamics of rigid bodies, of tops or gyroscopes, anywhere appears, and the candidate who had never heard of phase space, spectral series or relativity would not be at the least disadvantage. The special papers on heat and light, however, required a firm grasp of advanced topics, like thermodynamic surfaces, birefringent systems, and the design of interferometers. Two other features of the examination deserve notice: it expected circumstantial knowledge of the methods normally employed to measure common theoretical quantities; and it supposed some acquaintance with the history and philosophy of science, with the achievements of a Galileo or a Cavendish, and with the true meaning of a "law of Nature."

As partial preparation for the final schools, the *Examination Statutes* recommended that the candidate familiarize himself with the fourth edition of Jamin and Bouty's *Cours de physique*. And indeed, anyone who confined himself to mastering the theory, practice and conventional history jammed into the 4,000 pages of this admirable text would be able to answer 90 percent of the questions he would face. Unfortunately, he would also be 100 percent ignorant of modern physics. The book recommended at Oxford in 1910 was initially issued between 1858 and 1866, as the standard text for the Ecole polytechnique; its fourth edition, completed in 1890, does not yet include the electromagnetic theory of light (1873), and perforce omits the electron, X rays, radioactivity, relativity and the quantum.[15]

The aspirant had several sources of guidance besides Jamin and the file of old examination papers. For one, he had a college tutor who, if he were lucky, would know something about physics. For another, he might attend his college's lectures on physical science, if any, or those of another College, like Balliol-Trinity, which were open to all members of the University. He might also have access to a college laboratory. And, of course, he would learn what he could from the professors of physics and their staffs.

---

[15] *Statutes* (1906), p. 66; *ibid.* (1910/11), p. 75; "Honour School of Natural Science. Final Examination, Physics," 1906–1910, Radcliffe Science Library, Oxford; J. Jamin, *Cours de physique*, ed. E. Bouty (1886–90). The *Cours* was modernized by three supplements issued between 1890 and 1905 but these, judging from the examination questions, were not included in the recommended reading.

In 1906 Oxford had two professors of experimental physics. The senior, Ralph Bellamy Clifton (1836–1921), had graduated sixth wrangler in what Harry called "quite prehistoric times." Two papers on optics and strong testimonials from Stokes, William Thomson and Whewell, among others, brought him to Manchester in 1860 as the first professor of physics at Owens College; five years later, having distinguished himself as a lecturer, he obtained the brand new chair of Experimental Philosophy at Oxford, another product of the agitation that simultaneously brought the Linacre professorship and the University Museum. It was said that the electors chose him above the great Helmholtz, who wished to come.[16]

Clifton's first task was to build a laboratory on the proceeds of the sale of a book. It happened that an heir of the first Earl of Clarendon (1609–1674) had left his ancestor's papers, including the manuscript of *The History of the Great Rebellion*, to the University on the understanding that some of the profits from their sale or publication would be used to build a riding academy. That was in the middle of the eighteenth century. The trustees procrastinated, the money grew, equestrianism declined, and the will was broken; Clifton found himself with £10,000, which he expended with the utmost care, planning every feature of the new laboratory and bringing the instruments into such perfection that he could not entrust them to a student of physics. Having created his monument Clifton retired without resigning; and by faithful abstinence from both teaching and research preserved himself and his professorship for over half a century. ("Show me a researcher," a Provost of Oriel once told Tizard, "and I'll show you a fool.") Only one investigation of any consequence was ever conducted in Clifton's laboratory, and that by a visiting professor, C. V. Boys, who had never been his student. This unique investigation, for which the quiet caverns of the Clarendon were perfectly suited, measured the gravitational constant, which doubtless explains why the Final Honours Examination perennially demanded "an account of the determination of the constant of gravity." [17]

---

[16] F. A. Lindemann to his father, 19 Nov 13 (FAL, box 97). In fact since it appeared most unlikely that Helmholtz would accept, he was never formally asked. Helmholtz to his wife, 11 April 1866, in A. von Helmholtz, *Ein Lebensbild in Briefen* (1929), I, 131.

[17] R. T. G[lazebrook], *PRS* 99:A (1921), pp. vi–ix; C. V. Boys, *PT* 186:1 (1895), 12; Tizard, Autobiography, p. 38 (IWM). Clifton never troubled to wire for electricity and,

Clifton's much younger colleague, J. S. E. Townsend (1868–1957), was a man of an entirely different stamp. He had received a B.A. and several prizes for physics and mathematics at Trinity College, Dublin, under the guidance of G. F. Fitzgerald. In 1895, disappointed in his expectation of winning the coveted Trinity Fellowship, Townsend entered the Cavendish Laboratory at Cambridge as a "research student," a capacity then just introduced against the well-taken opposition of the traditional dons. These students were not only scientists, they were aliens, i.e., graduates of other universities, who could earn that coveted distinction, a Cambridge B.A., after two years given up to some wretched research. Townsend and his fellow research student Ernest Rutherford, who had been educated in New Zealand, soon found themselves as much disliked by the younger members of the laboratory as by the old guard. They were too good. They garnered prizes and scholarships that the natives had expected to win; Rutherford received the signal honor of collaborating with the professor, J. J. Thomson; Townsend became a demonstrator (assistant lecturer) over the heads of the younger men. And worst, perhaps, the research students secured professorships "bang-off," as Rutherford said, in a world where few desirable academic positions existed. In 1898 Rutherford received a research professorship at McGill University in Montreal; two years later Townsend was appointed to a new chair at Oxford, the Wykeham Professorship of Experimental Physics, established on the income of fellowships from New College.[18]

Clifton was of course delighted to share his burdensome teaching load with his new colleague; and Townsend willingly accepted responsibility for electricity and magnetism which (according to a letter from the vice-chancellor) had previously been "practically omitted from the subjects taught or studied" at Oxford. The old professor proved less eager to share his unused laboratory; and Townsend, unable to "find accommodation at the Clarendon" (as J. J. Thomson delicately observed), obtained the use of a few rooms in the observatory and the museum. In 1903 the university erected a "spacious" structure, according to Clifton, for Townsend's introductory courses, namely a large tin hut

---

toward the end of his reign, closed the laboratory three days a week; Lindemann, "Notes on a History of Physics at Oxford," p. 2 (FAL, box 13:I).

[18] A. von Engel, ORS 3 (1957), 257–260; A. S. Eve, *Rutherford* (1939), pp. 14–52; J. J. Thomson, *Recollections* (1937), p. 137.

known grandly as the Electrical Laboratory. Not until 1910 did the Wykeham Professor secure suitable quarters, a true Electrical Laboratory erected with funds provided by the Drapers' Company of London, which had for many years interested itself in the support of education. Despite the inconvenience of his scattered domain, Townsend continued to work fruitfully at the problem that had chiefly engaged him at the Cavendish: the behavior of gaseous ions and discharges. His fundamental studies of the multiplication of charges, for example, led among other things to the invention of the Geiger counter; and his theory of the mechanism of ionization guided the early researches of Franck and Hertz, which culminated in the experiments which won them the Nobel prize. Townsend brought an important part of contemporary experimental physics to Oxford, and even to the Final Honours Examination, which thenceforth regularly bristled with gaseous ions.[19]

Harry's nominal tutor was D. H. Nagel (1862–1920), a Senior Fellow of Trinity and the guiding spirit of the Balliol-Trinity Laboratory. Nagel had come to Oxford in 1882, after a solid classical grounding at the University of Aberdeen; he entered on the same science fellowship Harry was to hold and graduated in 1886 with first class honors in chemistry. He quickly found that his strength lay not in research but in public relations; his good sense, not to mention his strong classical background, made him an effective campaigner against the academic prejudice still "keenly felt" by Oxford scientists at the turn of the century. Although Nagel remained current in physical chemistry and gave a popular course, which Harry doubtless attended, he was no fit cicerone for the intending physicist.[20] Trinity accordingly provided Harry with an additional guide,

---

[19] *Nature* 53 (1897), 425–427; Engel, *ORS* 3 (1957), 260–264; Thomson to Rutherford, 15 Feb 01, in Eve, *Rutherford*, p. 76. The relative vigor of the two Oxford professors may be grasped from i.a. the number of their demonstrators: between 1903 and 1910 Clifton's declined from four to two, Townsend's rose from one to five. In the same period Clifton had no more than £150 p.a. for apparatus for research and teaching, while Townsend, who had to equip a new laboratory, had c. £500 for the years 1901–1903 before sinking to a level more typical of Oxford (e.g., £130 in 1910). For comparison, Rutherford's equipment budget at Manchester averaged £420 in the years around 1910, and Thomson's at Cambridge probably exceeded £500. P. Forman, J. L. Heilbron and S. Weart, *HSPS* 4 (1973), Tables A.4 and C.2–3; *Oxford University Gazette*; *Annual Abstract of Accounts* of Oxford University.

[20] H. B. Dixon, *Nature* 106 (1920), 186; *J Chemical Society* 119:1 (1921), 551–553; E. J.

a Balliol scholar named Idwal Griffith (1881–1941), who had obtained a first class degree in physics and a fellowship at St. Johns in 1903. Griffith later did some valuable work in aeronautics and materially assisted Clifton's successor in reviving Oxford physics.[21] But when he assumed responsibility for Harry, he was flirting with the photo-effect, with most indifferent success, for his chief result was a failure to confirm the proportionality between photo-current and intensity of illumination. He then drifted leisurely towards photometry, and the optical-indolent school of Clifton, whose demonstrator he became in 1910; one doubts that he had much influence on Harry who, as Rutherford gently put it, pursued his studies "with a preference for his own methods." [22]

One of Harry's preferences was to set himself exercises to work off in the library or at the Balliol-Trinity Laboratory. If the results deserved it, he might present them to one of the science clubs—the Alembic and the Junior Scientific—of which he was an active member. The Alembic, founded in 1901, met once a week during term in the rooms of each of its twenty-one members in turn. Its surviving minutes show Harry as legislator and occasional humorist, as when, only half-facetiously per-haps, he opposed a trivial change of rules on the ground that it would add greatly to the difficulties of a future historian of the club. Following the defeat of his motion, the club proceeded to its main business for that evening, the "Stereochemistry of Pentavalent Nitrogen," which will convey some notion of its scientific level. Unfortunately, a gap in the minutes prevents our learning what high-minded subjects Harry chose to discuss. Some stylistic details have, however, survived. For his maiden performance he arrived "laden with large volumes of the Phil Trans" followed immediately by Jervis "carrying the remainder of his works of reference." He announced that he had lost his notes, but could easily reconstitute them; the audience shuddered; and Harry, having had his joke, "gave a masterly paper without the assistance of any notes at all." [23]

Bowen, *Notes and Records RS* 25 (1970), 229. Cf. Nagel and W. A. Spooner, *Exemption from Greek in Responsions* (1904).

[21] *Nature* 148 (1941), 589; H. E. Wimperis, in *Physics in Industry* V (1927), 12; R. W. Clark, *Tizard* (1965), pp. 30, 36; Diary, 1914, records Griffith as Harry's tutor.

[22] Griffith, *PM* 14 (1907), 297–306; G. M. B. Dobson, I. O. Griffith ["Fellow of Brasenose"], and D. N. Harrison, *Photographic Photometry* (1926); *Oxford University Calendar* (1910); E. Rutherford, *DNB* (1912–21), 388–390.

[23] Alembic Club Minutes, 18 Jan and 18 Oct 09, and 2 May 10 (MS Museum 140

The Junior Scientific was a more serious organization. Founded by Nagel, among others, as a club for all scientific men in the university, it drew its membership from both graduates and undergraduates, and even from the faculty, and met in the university museum. Besides its weekly seances in term and a gluttonous annual dinner, it occasionally sponsored an elaborate "conversazione" in the museum, with lectures, exhibitions by specially imported showmen like Porter, demonstrations of wonders like radium, and a continual serenade by the band of the Grenadier Guards. Harry was elected to the club in November 1906, two weeks after Huxley; in 1907 he served on its steering committee; and in 1910 he became its president, an unusual honor for an undergraduate. He had demonstrated his ability in at least three papers: one on "Electrotonic Theories" gotten up no doubt with an eye to the quasi-historical parts of the Honours Examination; another on C. T. R. Wilson's new expansion device, a proto-cloudchamber, of which Harry built a demonstration model in the Balliol-Trinity Laboratory; and one on "Electronic Theories and the Spectrum," certainly a suggestive topic for the future discoverer of Moseley's law.[24]

More suggestive still was a paper entitled "The Evolution of the Elements," which Jervis read to the club in the spring of 1908. It is an excellent review of recent work, and especially of an attempt to explain, on the basis of the electromagnetic theory of mass, why the relative atomic weights of the elements deviate from integers. One assumes that atoms are made of four different sorts of elementary particles, of which two are hydrogen and helium, and that heavier atoms arise through the combination of lighter ones; if mass is lost, as energy, during combination, the problematic deviations might well arise. This evolutionary view, according to Jervis, agrees well with the "provisional two-dimensional conception of the atom" introduced by J. J. Thomson, in which electrons distributed in concentric rings circulate within a spherical space that behaves as if it contains a diffuse positive charge. The whole business, Jervis concludes, is most promising, and permits the hope that the discrepancies between Rydberg's formula, $A = 2N + k$, and the

[OHS]); Jervis to Amabel, 18 Feb 20 (LH). Harry's legislation pertained to election of members. The first volume of minutes, 1901–1908, disappeared about 1910.
[24] Oxford University Junior Scientific Club, Miscellaneous Papers (OB); *Transactions of the OUJSC* (1905+), 129, 383; Hartley to Garrod, 23 June 25 (R).

facts, may soon be resolved. Here A represents the atomic weight of an element, N its *ordinal* number in the periodic table, and k either zero or one depending on the valence of the element. Plainly Rydberg's N has much in common with atomic number, the concept that was to guide Harry's classic study of the X-ray spectra. Doubtless Jervis discussed his paper with his only friend, who (one may recall) had already expressed interest in the peculiarities of atomic weights while still at Eton.[25]

These pleasant topics, evolving elements, spectral emission, the cloudchamber, etc., unfortunately had nothing to do with the set subjects of the Honours School. In the winter of 1909 Harry settled down to Jamin and his ilk. "Here in Oxford," he sighed to Margery, a "heavy eyed student pores unremittingly over dry 'School' books, merely ceasing to snatch an infrequent and unattractive meal, or to dream for a few hours that Schools are over, and he has squared the circle." "My poor eyes are worn out three days in each week measuring diffraction bands, Newton's rings, etc., which are only just faintly visible in a darkened room." [26] In the spring he intensified his efforts. He stopped rowing. He gave up outside projects. In early June his agitation broke through his customary reserve. The weather turned unusually hot. A squawking owl, an appropriate omen, kept him awake on the night of the 16th. The next day, a Thursday, the Final Honours Examination began with two papers on elementary physics. The questions, twenty in all, asked as usual for methods of measurement, or for simple applications of elementary formulae, or for brief essays on complex physical phenomena. The first two categories rewarded industry, the last, understanding; all required speed and instant recall. The "overpowering" heat, the pressure of time, and sleeplessness took their toll. Harry fought "inefficiently" and without "great success." [27]

Friday was general physics "and, most appropriately, heat." The general paper was an encouraging relief; it asked fewer questions, offered a choice, and included several old chestnuts. Then came heat, a subject Harry had studied with particular attention. The questions, as he said,

[25] Jervis, *Transactions of the OUJSC* (1905 +), 241–249; *supra*, p. 23. Jervis' principal sources were D. F. Comstock, *PM* 15 (1908), 1–21, and A. C. and A. E. Jessup, *ibid.*, pp. 21–55.

[26] **37**.

[27] **40**.

were "extremely fair and well arranged"; for a moment the coveted "first" looked possible, even likely. But the weather and hay fever struck, and he did "disgracefully." "It was a chance that could not be guarded against." Neither he nor the weather improved for light and electricity on Saturday. And so Harry left Oxford with a second class degree, a "failure" as he saw it and a source of "continuing surprise" to his future colleague, C. G. Darwin, who rated him "without exception or exaggeration the most brilliant man" he had ever met.[28] No one in fact obtained a first in physics in Harry's year; and only one Trinity man, a second in 1887, had ever before taken honors in the subject.[29]

For solace and recreation Harry betook himself to the chief love of his life. This was not a girl: Harry knew few, and like most undergraduates did not cultivate their acquaintance; he would have survived the visit of Zuleika Dobson without a flutter.[30] The love in question was a cottage called Pick's Hill, near Romsey in Hampshire. Amabel had bought the property, then unimproved, in the spring of 1908. Harry, then twenty, had drawn up plans for a large cottage, which was completed a year later at a total cost, including the land, of £618/7/6, less than one year's salary for a good professorship. Harry laid out the extensive garden, directed the gardeners (who came for one pound a week), and selected the plants, which soon represented several hundred species, duly recorded by their Latin names in a book kept for the purpose. He grew very attached to the place, to which he would retreat at every vacation and even over weekends, despite the length and inconvenience of a journey whose last stage was accomplished by foot or by donkey cart.[31]

In 1904 or 1905 Amabel moved to 48 Woodstock Road, just opposite the entrance to the university observatory. It was a large house—it currently accommodates twelve girls, a tutor and a caretaker of

---

[28] 41. Darwin as quoted by Lankester, *PM* 31 (1916), 173–174; Darwin in Birks, pp. 17–26.

[29] The *Oxford University Calendar* gives the subjects of science honors degrees from 1876. Harry's chances might have been better had he won the Balliol scholarship; Balliol had seven honors winners in physics, two of them firsts, between 1901 and 1914, and had a better overall record than Trinity in producing honors graduates in science. Cf. R. T. Gunther, *The Daubeny Laboratory Register* (1904–1924), p. 160.

[30] Margery's notes (LH); Dalton, *Yesterday*, p. 37.

[31] Diary; LH papers; 40.

Lady Margaret College—and well suited to dinner parties. Amabel's guests included many heads of colleges; most of the leading men of science, and especially Townsend, Love, Poulton, Sir Arthur Evans, and W. J. Sollas, the Professor of Geology, whom she was to marry in 1914; and of course Lankester, who frequently came up from London, where he had moved in 1898. Moseley often attended these parties, especially in his last year, when he moved out of college (as was customary) and into his mother's house.[32] He doubtless profited greatly from Amabel's vigorous social life: her accomplished guests not only added to his fund of general information; they also confirmed his impression that he belonged among them.

The problem was how to get there. Moseley faced what his father and grandfather, at similar points in their careers, would have considered an *embarras de richesses:* for where Canon Moseley, on graduation, had no realistic alternative to the church, and where Professor Moseley had, at first, no promising avenue but medicine, Harry had only to choose between available strategies for reaching an already open goal. In the last week of May 1910, in intervals between studying and worrying over schools, he considered two chief alternatives. First, he might go directly into research, accomplish something quickly, and emerge a fellow in some Oxford College and perhaps also a demonstrator in Townsend's laboratory. This course of action was urged by Townsend's senior demonstrator, the Reverend Paul J. Kirkby, who, having spent several quiet years exploding mixtures of hydrogen and oxygen, was about to take a country living in Norfolk. Second, he might try for a demonstratorship at Manchester, which had recently been advertised in *Nature*. Griffith advised strongly in favor of this course, which Nagel and Clifton, who still had connections in Manchester, supported; it would bring Harry under Rutherford, expand his horizon beyond Oxford, and give him teaching experience necessary for a persuasive candidacy for a professorship.[33]

Harry viewed this conflicting advice with his usual clear-eyed realism. Kirkby need not be taken too seriously, he observed, because "he is by nature rather lazy himself, and therefore his ideal is on a less strenuous plane than my own—he would probably think an Oxford fellowship would be the full stretch of my ambition." Again, "as an Oxford man [Kirkby] looks down on all things outside, whereas it is a fact that recommendations from Oxford are apt to carry less weight than from places where Science is treated as a more serious profession, and a year or two teaching in a very large well organized Laboratory at Manchester count for more than several years of the easy-going, and less responsible demonstrating at Oxford." Against the Manchester job was the "exceptionally low wage," £125, and, more important, the possibility that teaching would leave little time for the research necessary to support an eventual candidacy for "research posts such as I will want." This consideration raised a third possibility, namely to go to Rutherford as a research student and "then [to] try for a demonstratorship, if I find they have not immensely much to do, and if there appears to be a vacancy." [34]

At no point in these deliberations did Harry consider the Cavendish Laboratory, which still produced most English professors of physics, not to mention Nobel laureates, and boasted twice as many demonstrators as Manchester.[35] Harry's prejudice perhaps owed something to Townsend's increasing hostility to Thomson, whom he wrongly accused of building a reputation on the ideas of other men, and most notably his own. Again, Thomson did not guide his research students with the care exercised by Rutherford, and which Harry felt he needed after the casualness of Oxford. On the positive side, Rutherford was clearly the new power in English physics, "an excellent stepping stone," as Harry put it, whatever happened; and (not least) the discoverer of the spontaneous disintegration of the natural elements might be expected to set his junior associates interesting and even important work.[36] Harry knew Rutherford's work well, and had heard him lecture at Oxford. He concluded for Manchester, and in the middle of May visited Rutherford to inquire into the duties of the demonstratorship. Two weeks later, having weighed all advice and discounted Kirkby's, Harry began to assemble testimonials.

[34] 39.

[35] Ten against four. See J. J. Thomson in *History of the Cavendish Laboratory* (1910), p. 101, and *Recollections*, pp. 435–438.

[36] *Ibid.*; Townsend to Rutherford, 24 Feb 15 (R); Lord Rayleigh, *Sir J. J. Thomson* (1942), pp. 115–119.

"What a coup it would be [he told his mother] to get the post on the strength of the good testimonials I believe I would get before July 1st and then get a 2nd." And so it was. "Thank you very much for your letter informing me of my appointment," Harry wrote Rutherford on July 17. "It will be a great pleasure for me to work in your laboratory, and after my failure in 'schools' I consider myself very lucky to have got the opening which I coveted." [37]

Harry spent most of the summer tending his garden and reading radioactivity. In September he moved to Manchester, took the preliminary course of experiments on radioactivity offered to local and visiting neophytes, and prepared for "teaching idiots elements." [38]

---

[37] **39, 42**. Rutherford delivered his Boyle lecture, "The Transformation of Radioactive Matter," at Oxford on 5 June 08. The visit to Manchester appears from Diary, 13 May 10; it is perhaps the occasion Rutherford later recalled (*Nature* 116 [1925], 316–317), when Harry came to inquire about the feasibility of beginning radioactive research at Oxford. If so, Harry must have intended to do the work during the summer and not (as Rutherford says) during his last year. In any case Rutherford dissuaded him from it.

[38] Diary, 1910; **42, 43**.

IV

Apprentice

THE MAGNATES OF MANCHESTER, who perceived the connection between industrial advance and scientific training, regarded science far more favorably than did the Oxford Convocation. Before the end of the eighteenth century they had established a Literary and Philosophical Society, given over largely to physics and fortunate in the membership of John Dalton, the inventor of the first useful theory of the chemical atom. The society was still vigorous in Harry's time; its "grey-haired fogeys," as he told Margery, maintained a "lively interest" in modern science quite foreign to his Oxonian experience.[1] It was the same sort of interest which had supported the growth of the laboratory in which he planned to work, and which in fifty years had transformed the little college established by an earlier magnate, John Owens, into the Victoria University of Manchester.[2]

Owens College had strongly emphasized physics, and after the lucky loss of its first professor, Clifton, in 1867, it began to develop a school of great distinction. Future Cambridge physicists, like J. J. Thomson and C. T. R. Wilson, studied there alongside men like Edward Hopkinson, who became an important electrical engineer and a faithful supporter of his alma mater. The chief expansion of the physics department occurred under Clifton's successor one removed, Arthur Schuster (1851–1934),

---

[1] 64.

[2] E. Fiddes, *Owens College* (1937), *passim*; H. B. Charlton, *Portrait of a University* (1951), pp. 13, 28–30.

who differed from the usual English academic by the breadth of his culture and the depth of his pocketbook. He was a German Jew, the son of a Frankfurt cotton merchant who moved to Manchester in 1869, when Prussia annexed his city, in order to spare his sons the obligation of military training. Schuster was intended for the family business, but an evening course in chemistry at Owens College captured him for science. His infatuation took him back to Germany, to study under Helmholtz and Kirchhoff. He stayed just long enough to acquire a Heidelberg doctorate (for which, following the local custom, he submitted a fine instead of a thesis), and moved on to Cambridge, where he worked for several years at his father's expense. In 1881 he returned to Owens as its first Professor of Applied Mathematics, and in 1886 he succeeded to the chair of physics. His personal acquaintance with continental physicists, his knowledge of the literature, and his own wide interests, which ran from spectroscopy to meteorology, made him an ideal department head. So did his effective advocacy of science within the highest circles of the university and his private fortune and family connections, which gave him easy access to potential departmental benefactors.[3]

In the 1890s the friends of the physics department raised enough money to build a new, four-story laboratory, which opened in 1900 furnished with the latest instruments of instruction and research. When Harry entered scientifically backward Oxford, Schuster presided over a thriving establishment which instructed some 250 undergraduates— almost one in every six students in the university—and employed four demonstrators, a mechanic, and the professor's own research assistant. This last post, in the academic year 1906/7, belonged to Hans Geiger (1882–1945), a student of one of Schuster's German acquaintances, who had just obtained his dectorate with a thesis on the study of gas discharges at high currents. Among the demonstrators was W. D. Makower (1879–1945), a former student at the Cavendish and Manchester's authority on radioactivity, with whom Harry was to collaborate. The activity of the laboratory and the continuing generosity of the university toward physics induced an excellent instrument maker, C. W. Cook, and a masterful German glassblower, Otto Baumbach ("who can

---

[3] *Nature* 76 (1907), 640–642; G. C. Simpson, ORS 1 (1932/35), 309–323; Schuster, *Biographical Fragments* (1932), pp. 3–65; Charlton, *Portrait*, pp. 78–96.

do anything that is possible and what is more can do it well"), to set up shop across the street from the physics department. They were to build much of Harry's apparatus.[4]

With his laboratory established, Schuster determined to retire, provided he could secure a suitable successor. He chose a man altogether different from himself, namely Rutherford, the son of a New Zealand flax farmer, who possessed neither languages, nor culture, nor wealth, nor mathematics, and who regarded with indifference most of the many branches of physics which Schuster had encouraged. But Rutherford, then thirty-five, vigorous and outspoken, already an international authority, had shown that he could build the sort of coherent and prolific research school that Thomson guided at the Cavendish, and that Schuster wished to see established at Manchester. He angled anxiously, for his fish had already refused hooks baited by Columbia, Yale, and the University of London. His well-supported and well-equipped department, however, and Rutherford's desire to return to England, brought a positive reply. "I am so strongly attached to the place [Schuster wrote his successor-designate in October 1906] that I could not bear to leave my position except to someone who will keep up its reputation and increase it. There is no one to whom I would leave it with greater freedom from anxiety than yourself." To relieve his lingering uneasiness and to keep some mathematics in the laboratory, Schuster established a temporary Readership in Mathematical Physics, at the munificent salary of £350 per annum. Were it not for his forethought, Harry's collaborator, Charles Galton Darwin, would doubtless never have gone to Manchester.[5]

When Harry arrived in Manchester in September 1910 Rutherford had been professor there for three years. The number of research students had increased somewhat while the range of research topics, and the curriculum itself, had conspicuously narrowed; honors candidates

[4] *Nature* 58 (1898), 621–622; *The Physical Laboratories of the University of Manchester* (1906), pp. 1–38, 135–142; Fiddes, *Chapters*, pp. 210–211; Schuster to Rutherford, 7 Oct 06, in Birks, pp. 48–52; Rutherford to Boltwood, 15 Feb 08, in Badash, p. 180; M. von Laue, *Jahrbuch der deutschen Akademie der Wissenschaften zu Berlin* (1946–49), pp. 150–158; H. Geiger, *AP* 22 (1907), 973–1007. Cf. Badash, pp. 238n, 306, 313, and 87.
[5] Birks, pp. 47, 52; Schuster to Rutherford, 15 Jan 07 (R).

took their general examinations at the end of their second year and then, after a brief initiation by Geiger, launched into full-time research, usually on a little radioactive subject picked by Rutherford. "This scheme of instruction," writes a veteran, H. R. Robinson (1889–1955), a one-time collaborator of Harry's, "had the grave disadvantage of leaving wide gaps in our knowledge of some important sections of classical physics—and this is putting it euphemistically, for the word gap normally connotes at least something more or less solid in which a gap can exist." Harry lectured second-year honors students on electricity; but his main job, for nine or ten hours a week, was to teach intending engineers whatever physics they required.

He disliked the students, not only because they were "mostly stupid," but also because they offended his usually inoperative patrician sensibilities. "On Saturday," he wrote home shortly after term began, "I was disgusted to find a large proportion of coloured students with the thickest heads among those doing lab: work. These seemed to include Hindoos, Burmese, Jap, Egyptian and other vile forms of Indian. Their scented dirtiness is not pleasant at close quarters." He eventually found a few students with "the saving grace of intelligence," but he never considered his teaching anything more than a "chore that must be got through"; "he did the minimum work to hold the job, rarely arriving before demonstration time started, leaving the moment time was up." [6] The energy spared from teaching went into research.

Rutherford, who did not expect his new demonstrators to have spare energy, had told Harry to wait until Christmas before starting experimental work. Harry had not the slightest intention of complying: "I will kick when I have found out exactly how much is expected of me," he promised his mother, and did so, with his usual success. By the beginning of November he was assembling apparatus for a project which (as was only just) he did not find very interesting, "only repeating someone else's work" on the number of β particles shot out during the

---

[6] Robinson in Birks, pp. 68, 78; **44, 45**: A. S. Russell, private communication. With respect to Harry's sensibilities Griffith's reaction to *his* first exposure to Manchester may be of interest: "It is a ghastly place and I feel sorry for anyone who is condemned to profess and teach in its murky atmosphere. The place swarms with obese and horrid looking Jews"; Griffith to Lindemann, 18 Dec 19 (FAL, box 13:I).

transformation of radium.[7] The problem, as Harry recognized, had some theoretical importance.

According to the disintegration theory, a radium atom transforms itself into successive atavars by releasing charged particles in accordance with the scheme shown in figure 1.

$$Ra(1620y) \xrightarrow{\alpha} RaEm(3.82d) \xrightarrow{\alpha} RaA(3.05m) \begin{cases} 99.98\% \xrightarrow{\alpha} RaB(26.8m) \xrightarrow{\beta} \\ 0.02\% \xrightarrow{\beta} Astatine(2s) \xrightarrow{\alpha} \end{cases}$$

$$RaC(19.7m) \begin{cases} 99.96\% \xrightarrow{\beta} RaC'(0.00014s) \xrightarrow{\alpha} \\ 0.04\% \xrightarrow{\alpha} RaC''(1.32m) \xrightarrow{\beta} \end{cases} RaD(19.4y) \xrightarrow{\beta} \dots$$

1. The first few generations of the radium family. RaEm signifies the "emanation"; half lives are given in parentheses, where s, m, d, y stand for seconds, minutes, days and years.

A sample of radium gradually transforms itself by α emission into radium emanation (^{222}Rn) which, being a gas, generally diffuses from the place of its production, decaying as it goes into the short-lived RaA (^{218}Po). Note the duplicity of RaA and its granddaughter RaC (^{214}Bi), which decay by releasing both α and β particles. The entire short-lived family from RaA up to the comparatively patriarchal RaD (^{210}Pb) is known as the "active deposit."

Now a central assumption of the theory is that each disintegrating atom releases but a single particle. Therefore, as one sees immediately from figure 1, in "radioactive equilibrium," when the number of atoms exploding in unit time is the same for each generation, the rate of production of α particles by radium alone (n_α, say) should be half the rate of production of β particles in the active deposit (n_β). One can test this inference by driving off the emanation; n_α can then be determined directly, and n_β calculated from the β emission of the active deposit thrown in a few hours by the separated emanation. (One can ignore the radiation from the relatively long-lived RaD that builds up during the course of the experiment.)

Rutherford had tried to confirm the relation $n_\beta = 2n_\alpha$ as early as 1905, when neither RaC', nor the radiation from RaB, nor the unpopular decay routes of RaA and RaC were known. He used as β source the active deposit on a lead cylinder which had been exposed for several hours to the emanation; a covering of aluminum foil stopped the α's from RaA and RaC' (^{214}Po). He expected, and found in a rough

[7] 43, 44, 45, 47.

experiment, that $n_\alpha = n_\beta$, a spurious result secured by neglecting particles reflected from the cylinder, by overlooking the soft β rays of RaB, and by using erroneous values for the charge e of the particles ($e_\alpha = e_\beta = 3.4 \cdot 10^{-10}$ esu).[8] Sometime after the discovery of the β activity of RaB, Rutherford asked Makower to repeat the determination of n_β. Makower took as β source a thin glass tube filled with fresh emanation; he therefore avoided the abundant reflection from Rutherford's cylinder, at the price, however, of having to correct for the absorption of the β's in the walls of the glass, which were thick enough to stop all the α's. Using Rutherford's latest values for e ($e_\beta = 4.65 \cdot 10^{-10}$ esu) and for n_α, Makower reckoned that $n_\beta = 3n_\alpha$, that is, about 1.5 β's appeared to arise in the disintegration of an atom of RaB or RaC. But half an electron *non datur*. Makower concluded that, in such disintegrations, the atom lost a single β, "or possibly two."[9]

Harry's job was to remove the uncertainty left by Makower. Like most of Rutherford's research men, who habitually completed two or three little projects a year, Harry expected an easy conquest: a few weeks building the apparatus, a few hours making it airtight, a few days taking readings. On the last day of November, after some unanticipated sulkiness, the experiments began to act "like lambs"; "most of the difficulties are behind me," Harry wrote Margery a week later, at the end of term, as he settled down to finish the business off. But the β's would not behave. "I hoped today [about ten days before Christmas] to have got many of the results I wanted, but alas things went wrong as always when not wanted to, and today and tomorrow are wasted at the least, in remaking much of the apparatus." Again he was too sanguine: the laboratory assistant was busy repairing Rutherford's new automobile, and he had to make everything himself, including the brass fittings.

---

[8] Rutherford, *PM* 10 (1905), 193–208 (*Collected Papers* I, 816–829). Rutherford never doubted, as did an occasional colleague, that each transition involved but a single particle (cf. Badash, p. 99).

[9] Makower, *PM* 17 (1909), 171–180, who presents his results in terms of the presumed α rays from RaC. The β rays of RaB were found by H. W. Schmidt, *PZs* 6 (1905), 897–903, and confirmed by Rutherford's group in the spring of 1906 (Rutherford to Boltwood, 9 May 06, in Badash, p. 136). Rutherford and Geiger (*PRS* 81:A [1908], 141–161 and 162–173, = *Papers* II, 89–120) obtained the new values of the critical constants by counting the number, and measuring the charge, of the α particles emitted by a known quantity of radium.

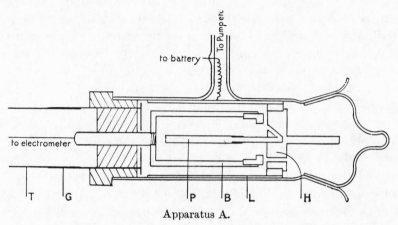

Apparatus A.

2. Moseley's apparatus for counting β particles. The source is contained in a thin glass tube within the silvered paper cylinder P, which is supported by the brass collar H and the brass tube L. B signifies the collecting cup, G a guard ring, and T a metal tube shielding the electrometer wire. From **III**.

Before the experiments could begin again the holidays arrived.[10]

The chief difficulty was the secondary radiation. Harry's source— emanation contained in a thin glass tube placed inside a silvered paper cylinder—gave off α and γ rays in addition to the β particles of interest. The α's, although stopped in the glass and paper, produced slow electrons, called δ rays, in their passage; the β's, as Harry was the first to observe, caused a similar radiation wherever they struck; and the penetrating γ's generated fast electrons throughout the apparatus and the measuring instruments. In addition, stray electrons arose from ionization of the residual gas, and some β particles, after reflection from the collecting cup, were lost either by reabsorption in the central cylinder or by escaping from the open end of the cup (fig. 2). Harry eventually succeeded in correcting for, or eliminating, the uncertainties introduced by these effects. He shielded the measuring instruments; he coated the inside of the brass cup with dry aluminum to reduce secondary emission; and, by electrifying the central silvered cylinder, he

---

[10] **46–49**. From the bibliography in Birks, pp. 334–361, one computes that the research men at Manchester published, alone or in collaboration, an average of 2.1 papers/year.

determined the amount (i_β, say) of the current received by the cup which derived from the primary β particles.[11] It remained to determine the relative contributions to i_β of RaB and RaC. Here Harry confronted the difficulty that the β's of RaB, being softer than those of RaC, were more effectively absorbed by the glass and the paper cylinder. He used the then recent discovery that pure RaB could be obtained by collecting recoiling, disintegrating atoms of RaA; the current from such a deposit, when corrected for the contribution of the calculable amount of RaC grown during the experiment, gives the relative contributions of RaB and RaC to i_β for the particular thickness t of absorbing materials employed. Of course Harry wanted to know the relative contributions and i_β itself in the unrealizable case $t = 0$. He had no recourse but to *increase* t, which he did by wrapping the silvered cylinder with sheets of India paper (supplied gratis by the Oxford University Press, still supporting science); from the resultant values of i_β and the relative contributions he extrapolated backwards to $t = 0$ to obtain a value for n_β.[12] The answer, after eighteen months of effort: $n_\beta = 2.2$, or each atom of RaB and of RaC, in disintegrating, releases precisely one and one-tenth particles. The deviation from unity arose partly, as Harry guessed, from uncertainty in the extrapolation, but mainly, as will appear, from the overlooked contribution of fast secondary electrons knocked out of the exploding atoms by their own γ rays.[13]

No one doubted the disintegration theory when Harry concluded his investigation in the spring of 1912. His results, however, were not without interest, for meanwhile continental physicists had found that most β emitters sent out groups of rays with distinct velocities; in particular, twenty or thirty different kinds of mono-energetic particles seemed to escape from RaB and RaC. According to Harry's findings, *one* disintegrating atom could not shoot off one particle of each kind. "It is

---

[11] With the central electrode negative, the cup receives a maximum current $i_1 = i_\beta + j$, where i_β is the primary β current and j that of secondary slow electrons; with the potential reversed, the current reaches a minimum $i_2 = i_\beta - k$, k measuring the slow electrons ejected from, or no longer able to reach, the cup. A special series of experiments (**III**, 250–254), gave $k = 1.5j$, whence $i_\beta = .6i_1 + i_2$.

[12] Makower had extrapolated in the same general way, but he had not separately determined the relative contributions.

[13] The extrapolation rested on assumptions about the absorption coefficients of β rays at small t, a matter then much in doubt; cf. J. L. Heilbron, *AHES* 4 (1968), 265–280.

therefore safe to conclude [according to Harry] either that different atoms of the same substance give rise to different radiations, the process of disintegrating being different in each case, or that the radiation that results from their disintegration is originally uniform but becomes modified by its passage through the atom." [14] Nature in fact uses both alternatives; Rutherford, basing himself on Harry's work, tried to make do with one.

The several types of β rays associated with a given transformation (Rutherford said) must be modifications of original, mono-energetic particles, which surrendered different amounts of energy to an unknown atomic agency. A natural recipient would be the electronic structure, presumably rings arranged about the nucleus in accordance with the model he had invented in 1910; and the ultimate beneficiary would be γ rays somehow produced during the rearrangement of rings disturbed by the production or the passage of the β particles. The energy of the β's should therefore differ by multiples of the energies of the γ's; if, for example, RaC produced only two kinds of γ's of energies E_1 and E_2, the energy of each of its β groups should be expressible as $E_0 - pE_1 - qE_2$, where E_0 is the initial uniform energy of projection and p and q are integers. Rutherford managed to fit the published data on the β spectrum of RaC to such expressions, and indeed using only two types of γ's, whose energies he chose to give the best agreement; no doubt he was delighted and perhaps also surprised at so elegant a confirmation of his bold theory, which expressly assimilated the γ's to characteristic X rays and assigned an extra-nuclear origin to all but the most energetic β's. Unfortunately it all rested on a "sad blunder," as he learned from Harry, who found on repeating the calculations that his master, like many neophytes in relativity, had taken $kmv^2/2$ rather than $mc^2(k-1)$ as the relativistic energy. (k is $[1 - v^2/c^2]^{-1/2}$.) "I fear all his calculations are wrong [Harry wrote his mother], but when I demonstrated it to him he philosophically acknowledged his error, and declared that even if the calculations did not fit the theory (which was made to suit them) he is sure the theory is right all the same." And in fact, when Rutherford recomputed the particle energies, he found the equations could again

---

[14] **III**, 230. The chief continental authorities were Baeyer, Hahn and Meitner (Berlin), *PZs* 12 (1911), 273–279, 1099–1101; and J. Danysz (Paris), *Le radium* 9 (1912), 1–5.

be satisfied, albeit with different values of the E's and the integers.[15]

The tarnished theory guided much of the work at Manchester during the last prewar years. Harry's β paper can be considered a contribution before the fact, as can the work he next turned to, a brief collaboration with Robinson, who then (the late spring of 1912) was serving his radioactive apprenticeship by measuring the heating effects of the various radiations of radium. Rutherford, with whom Robinson worked closely on this project, asked Harry to help in estimating the contribution of his old friends, the β's and γ's of the active deposit. Now, according to Rutherford's theory, the observed energy of the β and γ rays emitted by a disintegrating atom must be less than the kinetic energy of its fastest β particle, a proposition Harry and Robinson found to hold within 30 percent, a discrepancy hardly greater, as they say, than their experimental uncertainty. It was indeed a rough piece of work, and "not very interesting" for Harry, who delayed writing it up for almost two years.[16] By then, the spring of 1914, a great advance in the understanding of β decay had occurred. Rutherford and Robinson and a new recruit, W. F. Rawlinson, had found that the discrete β spectra arose from extra-nuclear electrons liberated from the disintegrating atom by its own γ rays; while James Chadwick, a former student of Rutherford's working in Berlin, discovered that the discrete spectrum was superposed on a continuous one, which in fact represented most of the energy of the β decay. Rutherford modified his theory to suit: the primary β particle in traversing its parent atom either loses its energy in old-fashioned, non-quantum collisions with the electronic structure, or it passes through special electronic regions, exciting characteristic γ rays of definite energy, some of which liberate by a quantum process the electrons which give rise to the line spectrum.[17] As Harry observes in his paper with Robinson, his earlier results show that such liberation does occur; or, more accurately, the new theory explained very nicely the puzzling extra

---

[15] Rutherford, *PM* 24 (Oct 1912), 453–462, = *Papers* II, 280–287; **62**; Rutherford, *PM* 24 (Dec 1912), 893–894, = *Papers* II, 292–293.

[16] **57, 59, 64**; Rutherford and Robinson, *PM* 25 (Feb 1913), 312–330, = *Papers* II, 312–327, esp. p. 324; **X**, 337.

[17] Rutherford, Robinson, and Rawlinson, *PM* 28 (Aug 1914), 281–286, = *Papers* II, 466–470; Chadwick, *VdpG* 16 (1914), 383–391; Rutherford, *PM* 28 (Aug 1914), 305–319, = *Papers* II, 473–485. Cf. **54**; Robinson in Birks, pp. 77–78; Rutherford, Chadwick and Ellis, *Radiations from Radioactive Substances* (1930), pp. 347–350, 391–392.

two-tenths of a β particle that he had found in the active deposit of radium.[18]

Collaborative experiments contributed greatly to forming the team spirit that distinguished Rutherford's research men. Through a complicated network of joint ventures most men participated directly or vicariously in the chief investigations of the laboratory; typically one began, as did Harry, with a personal project assigned by Rutherford, and while working on it collaborated with fellow laborers on small matters of mutual interest. Harry's first partner was a man of his year, Kasimir Fajans, a Heidelberg Ph.D. who had come to Manchester to transform himself from a straight- to a radio-chemist. His personal project was to repeat experiments from which Otto Hahn and Lise Meitner had deduced the existence of two new radioelements *between* RaC and RaD. Fajans found that the product called "RaC" was indeed complex, but not in the way supposed by Hahn and Meitner: it contained a β-emitter, now called RaC″, which plainly descended from RaC (i.e., from the daughter of RaB with $\tau = 19.7$ m) but which, equally plainly, could not be the α-emitting ancestor of RaD. Fajans came to the important conclusion that RaC can decay in two different ways, one resulting in RaC″ and an uncertain progeny, the other creating RaD. It was the first recognition of a branching product. "An able fellow, Fajans," Rutherford concluded. "The whole behavior is certainly very curious." [19]

One puzzle was the nature of the complex decay. In keeping with the Rutherfordian principle—one explosion, one particle—Fajans expected that, in *each* of its decay modes, RaC would emit the same sort of radiation, namely α particles. His experiments neither confirmed, nor caused him to reject, the hypothesis; and, as will appear, it guided, or rather misguided, part of his work with Harry. Subsequently Fajans recognized that a different kind of particle characterized each of the

---

[18] **X**, 336. In fact Harry's result, $n_\beta = 2.2$, is a little low; cf. Gurney, *PRS* 109:A (1925), 540–561. As for Rutherford's theory, internal conversion has survived, but not the extra-nuclear origin of the γ rays and the continuous β spectrum.

[19] Fajans, private communication; *Naturwissenschaften* 4 (1916), 381–382; *PZs* 12 (1911), 369–378 (received 27 Mar 11); Hahn and Meitner, *PZs* 10 (1909), 697; Rutherford to Hahn, 26 Apr 11, in Eve, p. 202.

suicidal routes of RaC, and that still another product, the short-lived RaC' (^{214}Po), intervened between RaC and RaD. In the summer of 1912, about a year after his return to Germany, he was able to publish a revised account of the options of RaC which differed from that of figure 1 only in not identifying the offspring of RaC".[20]

While Fajans was investigating "RaC," Geiger discovered that the active deposits of thorium and actinium each descended from a different, previously unknown and very short-lived α emitter. Fajans' results bore directly on Harry's research, and Geiger's suggested probable analogies to Fajans'; Harry and Fajans joined company to determine the half-lives of Geiger's ephemera and to devise a general scheme for probing the constitution of active deposits produced by α decay. Atoms so derived generally recoil with a *positive* charge; they may therefore be drawn through a negative grid and deposited, say, on a rapidly spinning disk. One can then determine the rate of the deposit's decay from measurements made by electroscopes placed around the disk. With the help of an old motor-driven wheel that Schuster had made for studying sparks and Harry had discovered in a storeroom, he and Fajans fixed the half-life of Geiger's most fleeting product at 0.0020 sec, about 2000 times smaller than the shortest half-life previously measured.[21] Furthermore, they used it to look for a suppositious short-lived α emitter in the active deposit of actinium, which, having been glimpsed in Paris by a Mlle Blanquies, had found a provisional place between AcC and AcC" in Mme Curie's latest disintegration table.[22] Only AcC" precipitated itself onto the whirling wheel at Manchester. Consequently Mlle Blanquies' product, if it existed, could not be the father of AcC", but rather a cousin, a collateral relative of the kind Fajans had discovered in the radium family. The collaborators began their search for this cousin *on the disk*, where, of course, it would be present in quantity only if it originated via α decay. Apparently they entertained Fajans' assumption that, in the case of a branch, both products derive from the same sort of disintegration. They found nothing. No doubt had Fajans' hurried

---

[20] Fajans, *PZs* 13 (1912), 699–705 (received 7 July 12).

[21] **I**, 633; the product, AcA (^{215}Po), has a half-life of 0.00183 sec.

[22] M. Curie, *Radioactivité* (1910), II, 429, 434. AcC" (^{207}Tl) was called AcD in Harry's time; cf. Rutherford and Geiger, *PM* 22 (1911), 621–629, = *Papers* II, 255–261, on p. 259.

departure for Germany not brought the experiments to a frenzied stop, he and Harry would have discovered the shy α-emitter, AcC′ (^{211}Po, τ = 0.52 sec).[23]

The work with Fajans concluded Harry's first year at Manchester. A retreat to Pick's Hill and a tramp through the Austrian Alps recruited his energies; and at the end of September 1911 he returned to the laboratory for a second go at the frustrating β rays, and for a new round of teaching and collaborating. His partner this time was Makower, who had also just finished with Fajans. The problem they chose, although of little interest in itself, exemplifies the crude analogies that often guided the routine work of the laboratory. Both RaB and RaC gave penetrating β rays, as Harry well knew; since, in addition, RaC emitted hard γ's, he and Makower conjectured that RaB would do so as well. They found no hard γ's, but a substantial amount of soft ones, whose absorption coefficient in aluminum they roughly measured. Since the γ's from RaC were always present, the properties of the new soft rays could only be obtained by curve-fitting, that is, by computing how various mixtures of γ radiations ought to be absorbed, and by comparing the results with experiment. "The work has been at times tedious more arithmetic than experiment," Harry complained. But it had the great merit of a short life, "only . . . ten days experimenting, followed by calculations in our spare moments for a fortnight." By keeping "Makower calculating . . . every night until he dropped asleep over his slide rule," Harry got their joint paper in the mail before Christmas, and brought his own rate of production closer to the Manchester average.[24]

Neither the collaborations, nor the fortnightly seminars of the physics department, nor the afternoon teas in the laboratory, brought Harry any closer to his fellow man. Nothing ruffled the reserve which grew increasingly in him, and which relaxed only in the company of his immediate family. Not that he was unpleasant or disdainful towards his colleagues. Quite the contrary. A. S. Russell, a shrewd Scot who worked in Manchester from 1911 to 1913, was "very surprised" to learn that Harry, who was neither "stuck-up" nor "vain," had been to Eton. "He

---

[23] Private communication from K. Fajans; **I**, 634. The branching of AcC was fully established by E. Marsden *et al.*, *Nature* 92 (1913), 29, and *PM* 28 (1914), 818–821.
[24] **II**; **53, 54, 56**.

was so reserved [Russell wrote] that I could neither like him nor not like him." In seminars Harry seldom spoke unless the discussion touched on one of his specialties; he then expressed himself with his usual admirable economy, and relapsed into silence. He indulged his old fondness for argument by challenging "all loose statements" passed in casual conversation. He argued quietly and in very few words, and if he failed to convince his opponent, he would quietly hold up a sixpence as a bet, and announce his readiness to appeal to the recognized authorities.[25]

Toward Rutherford, who had welcomed him to the laboratory in the friendliest way, Harry behaved with an independence entirely unknown in that paternalistic establishment. Although he admired Rutherford's work without qualification, he did not hesitate to contradict the master on any point he thought in error. There is no doubt that Harry's presence inhibited Rutherford's tea-time talk, a compound of banter, slang, wisecrack and burlesque that his restrained demonstrator thought more appropriate to a stage colonial than to a professor of physics. No more did Rutherford's exaggerated manly manner, which most of the research men, who called him "Papa," admired, amuse Harry. It was not entirely a joke when he warned Robinson that Rutherford would consider a certain part of their apparatus "very effeminate." [26]

For recreation and relaxation Harry took advantage of the many high-minded amusements Manchester offered. The city had an excellent orchestra, the Hallé, supported primarily by wealthy Anglo-Germans like Schuster, and a first-class repertory theatre, the Gaiety, which specialized in Shaw and Galsworthy, and enjoyed the services of (Dame) Sybil Thorndyke.[27] Harry attended plays and symphonies and even the cinema, where he saw, and much enjoyed, a lengthy version of *Les miserables*. "It was all done by first rate French actors and wonderfully well staged, with real scenery throughout, and quite exciting and easy to

---

[25] Private communication from A. S. Russell; Russell in Birks, p. 93.

[26] **43**; Russell, private communication, and in Birks, p. 89; Robinson in Birks, pp. 72, 76, 85; Marsden in Birks, p. 16; Andrade in Birks, pp. 28–31. The "effeminacy" was measuring current by a null method, namely Townsend's induction balance (*PM* 6 [1903], 603–605), which Harry habitually used (**I**, 631; **III**, 234; **X**, 329), and not by the deflection of an electrometer.

[27] W. H. Brindley, ed., *Soul of Manchester* (1929), pp. 176–192; R. Pogson, *The Gaiety Theatre* (1952), pp. 91–115, 135–141; Russell in Birks, p. 88.

follow without knowing the story." For less passive entertainment he
played bridge and tennis, went on long walks, and dined with old family
friends. Every now and then, with the slightest touch of noblesse oblige,
he would invite a few of the research men to his lodgings for dinner. No
one else did so except Rutherford and Schuster, and none of Harry's
guests, who had to live on their meager salaries, ever returned his
hospitality. As a host he was quietly efficient, and discoursed easily about
foreign travel, anthropology, zoology, Oxford professors, and the latest
performance of the Hallé or the latest play at the Gaiety. As Russell
remembers these dinners, Harry was not the least arrogant or conde-
scending, and never affected sophistication; nonetheless, his guests
perceived their place and left realizing that they were hayseeds, clever, no
doubt, but unfinished and provincial.[28]

"I have just finished my β ray paper." These glad tidings, sent
Margery on April 7, 1912, mark the end of Harry's apprenticeship.
Rutherford was "very complimentary" and sent the paper off to the
Royal Society for publication. He also offered Harry the John Harling
Fellowship, or anyway half of it, for the next academic year (1912/3).
The fellowship, established in 1900 in connection with the opening of
the new physics laboratory, paid the same stipend as a demonstrator
(£125) and imposed the congenial obligation of doing nothing but
research. Although nominally open and annually advertised, it was in
fact entirely at the disposal of Rutherford, who had already promised
part of it to a professor from Illinois.[29] Luckily Harry could afford the
unexpected honor and he happily resigned from the teaching profession.
    He observed the ending of his apprenticeship by taking a new
research line, though one well within the Rutherfordian ambit. As a
check on the results he had obtained by catching and counting β
particles, Harry had developed an apparatus for measuring the *positive*
charge generated in the source by their loss; now he proposed to use
much the same technique to attain unprecedentedly high potentials.[30]

---

[28] **46, 58, 69**; W. H. Bragg to Rutherford, 30 Mar 13 (R); Russell, private communication.

[29] **56, 57**; the joint award to Harry and T. S. Taylor was announced on 5 July 12. Cf.
Physical Laboratories, pp. 11, 129, and Badash, pp. 202, 210.

[30] **III**, 233–235. The technique was first tried, with indifferent success, by W. Wien (*PZs*
4 [1903], 624–626), whose work Harry knew through Makower (*PM* 17 [1909], 171).

Plainly a tube filled with radium emanation and hung up in a good vacuum will continue to increase its potential V until either its insulation fails or its activity ceases or V becomes large enough to arrest the fastest of its β particles. Hoping the last might occur first, Harry planned to determine the kinetic energy of emission, namely eV, free from the difficulties of the usual procedure, which depended upon the bending of the particle's trajectory in a magnetic field. In particular, he hoped to supply better evidence than yet existed for deciding between theories of the dependence of mass on velocity.[31] Unfortunately it takes about a million volts to stop fast β particles. Neither the "vacuum" nor the source's insulating support could withstand such stresses. After a few trials, which "ended in failure," Harry allowed that he would be satisfied with 300,000 volts; by the end of July 1912, after four months' work, he had reached half that, about 50 percent more than the highest potential then attainable by other means. Still, as he told Margery, he had "not yet had an experiment which consents to work properly." [32] He broke off for the summer optimistic about the future of his radium battery and full of plans for improving it.

---

[31] IV, 471. Harry points to the ambiguous results of Kaufmann and their evaluation by Planck (*PZs* 7 [1906], 758, 761); Harry's control of relativity (*supra*, p. 52), and his desire to test it experimentally, distinguish him from most English physicists of his time (S. Goldberg, *HSPS* 2 [1970], 120–121).

[32] **56, 58, 59**; cf. Rutherford to Boltwood, 15 Mar 12, in Badash, p. 265.

V

Journeyman

THE MOST EXCITING EVENT in physics in 1912 was the discovery, made in Munich in April, that X rays could be made to interfere in much the same way as light. Acting on a suggestion by Max von Laue, W. Friedrich and P. P. Knipping had obtained symmetrical images on photographic plates placed behind crystals irradiated by a soft, fat beam of X rays (fig. 3). In June the three collaborators submitted their results to the Bavarian Academy of Sciences. A month later Laue sent the same body a quantitative theory of the positions of the images, which assimilated X radiation to waves and claimed thereby to have decided at last the true nature of Röntgen's rays. Reprints of both papers had reached Manchester by the time Moseley returned from his summer at Pick's Hill.[1]

Laue's claims did not convince the most knowledgeable of his English readers. W. H. Bragg (1862–1942), Professor of Physics at the University of Leeds, refused to discount the weighty evidence he had been adducing for five years in support of the theory that X (and γ) rays consist of "neutral pairs" of charged particles. Bragg's theory had its own difficulties; but it could account persuasively for phenomena unintelligible on Laue's, for example, the transfer of the *entire* kinetic energy of a

---

[1] Friedrich, Knipping and Laue, *Sb* (Munich) 42 (1912), 303–322; Laue, *ibid.*, 363–373; P. Forman, *AHES* 6 (1969), 38–39. H. A. Lorentz notified Rutherford of the German discovery on 17 Sept 12 (R).

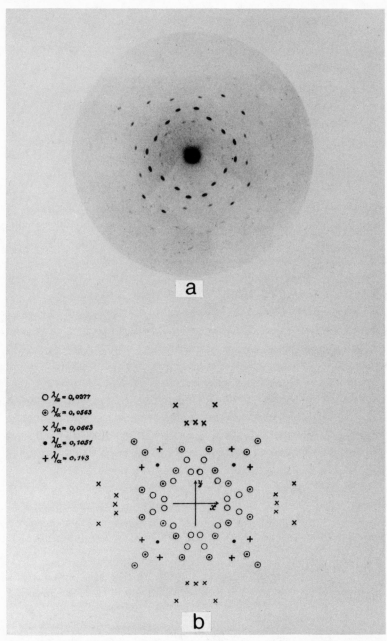

3. The Laue spots (a) a photograph made by Friedrich and Knipping (b) Laue's analysis, associating sets of spots with suppositious monochromatic rays. From Friedrich Knipping and Laue, *Sb* (Munich) 42 (1912).

cathode-ray particle via an X ray to a secondary electron. Were X rays waves, such a transfer could no more occur than (to use a favorite analogy of Bragg's) could a spreading water wave, produced by the fall of a rock, encounter an identical rock, surrender to it its entire energy, and project it to the height from which the original fell.[2]

But one did not have to follow Bragg to object to Laue. Bragg's arch enemy, C. G. Barkla (1877–1944), had based his career, which was to lead to the Nobel Prize, on finding analogies between X rays and waves. He had begun by confirming that the rays scattered like waves,[3] and continued by showing how to polarize them. Then, under Bragg's attack, he had made a splendid discovery, which, he said, "verified the [wave] theory in a more striking way than I ever anticipated." He had found that under bombardment from an X-ray tube an element can emit *homogeneous* X rays with penetrating powers (as measured by absorption in aluminum) *characteristic* of itself.[4]

Two features of this characteristic radiation supported the analogy to light. First, each element examined gave two rays of different penetrating power, which Barkla and his collaborators named K and L, in order to leave alphabetical space for future discoveries. These rays, and the expected novelties harder than K or softer than L, bear an obvious analogy to optical emission spectra. Second, Barkla found that to obtain a given characteristic ray he had to illuminate the appropriate element with radiation *harder* than that desired. Here the optical analogy is so strong that physicists often referred to Barkla's rays as "fluorescent" X radiation. Despite his great investment in the wave theory of the rays, however, and despite his eagerness to annihilate Bragg, Barkla doubted Laue's explanation of the tantalizing spots. "I have had a copy of Laue's paper for some little time," he wrote Rutherford on October 28, 1912, "and certainly am sceptical of any interference interpretation of the results. A number of features do not

[2] Bragg, *PM* 14 (1907), 429–449; *PM* 20 (1910), 385–416; *Nature* 90 (1912), 529–532, 557–560; Forman, *DSB* II, 397–400, and R. H. Steuwer, *BJHS* 5 (1971), 258–281.
[3] Barkla, *PM* 5 (1903), 685–698; J. J. Thomson, *Conduction of Electricity through Gases* (1903), p. 270; Rutherford to Bohr, 24 Feb 13 (AHQP); Forman, *DSB* I, 456–459, and Steuwer, *BJHS* 5 (1971), 260–267.
[4] Barkla, *PRS* 77:A (1906), 247–255; *PM* 11 (1906), 812–828; *Nature* 78 (1908), 7; Barkla and Sadler, *PM* 16 (1908), 550–584.

point in that way. . . . . This in no way affects my absolute confidence in the wave theory of X rays." [5]

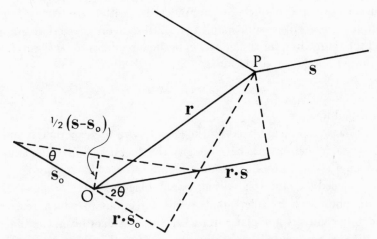

4. The scattering of X rays by the atoms (or molecules) of a crystal. Note that the phase at O is ahead of that at P by $2\pi \mathbf{r} \cdot \mathbf{s}_0/\lambda$; and that the phase of waves scattered from O in the direction $\mathbf{s}$ is behind that of parallel waves from P by $2\pi \mathbf{r} \cdot \mathbf{s}/\lambda$.

Laue's difficulty arose through his carrying over the standard analysis of the one-dimensional grating to a network of scattering centers distributed in space. His procedure will be clear from figure 4, where $\mathbf{s}_0$ and $\mathbf{s}$ are unit vectors along, respectively, the incident beam and radiation scattered at angle 2θ to it, and O is an atom in the crystal's center chosen as origin of coordinates. Assume for the moment that the radiation is homogeneous of wavelength λ. The amplitude $A(\theta)$ of the radiation scattered from O in direction $\mathbf{s}$ at distance R may be written $f(R) \cdot \exp[(2\pi i/\lambda)(R - ct)]$; that from a neighboring atom P at the directed distance $\mathbf{r}(r \ll R)$, $f(R) \cdot \exp[(2\pi i/\lambda)(R - ct) - i\Delta_r]$, where Δ_r is the difference in phase of the initial beam at P and at O. Evidently $\Delta_r = (2\pi/\lambda)(\mathbf{s} - \mathbf{s}_0) \cdot \mathbf{r}$. Now $\mathbf{r} = a(l\mathbf{i} + m\mathbf{j} + n\mathbf{k})$, where a is the distance between

[5] Barkla and Sadler, *PM* 17 (1909), 739–760; Barkla, *PM* 22 (1911), 396–412; Forman, *AHES* 6 (1969), 65. Continental physicists, like Maurice de Broglie, also had trouble understanding Laue; de Broglie to Lindemann, 20 Nov 12 (FAL, box 80).

nearest neighbors in the crystal, which we shall suppose cubical; l, m, n are integers; and **i**, **j**, **k** are unit vectors along axes parallel to the sides of the element from whose iteration the crystal may be constructed. So much for physics. If one now computes the scattered intensity $I(\theta) = \Sigma_r A_r^2(\theta)$, one recovers sums familiar from the theory of the line grating, and the result that, for the radiation in the direction **s** to be sensible, the following relations must hold:

$$(\mathbf{s} - \mathbf{s}_0)/\lambda \cdot (\mathbf{a}, \mathbf{b}, \mathbf{c}) = (h_1, h_2, h_3), \qquad (1)$$

the h's all integers.[6]

Now $\mathbf{s}_0$, **a**, **b**, **c** are fixed by the geometry of the experiment and of the crystal; equations (1) therefore give the directions **s** in which a ray of wavelength λ will produce maxima of order h_1, h_2, h_3. A photographic plate placed behind the crystal would blacken only in those spots corresponding to h-triplets that define directions in which scattered radiation can reach the plate. But what if the incident beam contained a continuous or "white" spectrum representing all values of λ within a certain range? Triplets could then be found to give directions as close as desired to any arbitrary **s** within a comparable range. It would seem that the plate should darken uniformly over a wide area, and no interference pattern whatsoever appear.

Laue and his associates were perfectly aware of this inference and also of the fact that their beam included pulses from electrons stopped by their anticathode as well as Barkla radiation characteristic of it. Since they assumed that the pulses were made up of (or could be analyzed into) radiation of wavelengths continuous over a certain range,[7] they looked to the characteristic rays of the anticathode, or perhaps to Barkla rays generated in the crystal itself, to impose an interference pattern on top of the general darkening caused by the pulses. They were accordingly very much surprised by the crispness of the patterns they obtained.[8]

Although the crispness probably perplexed him, Laue analyzed the

---

[6] Cf. R. W. James, *Diffraction of X Rays* (1948), pp. 2–5.

[7] The "wave theory" had generally regarded X rays as a stream of electromagnetic pulses created by the stoppage of cathode rays; its modern form in 1912 was Sommerfeld's theory of Bremsstrahlung (*PZs* 10 [1909], 969–976; and *PZs* 11 [1910], 99–101).

[8] Laue, Friedrich and Knipping, *Sb* (Munich) 42 (1912), 311, 314, 322; cf. Forman, *AHES* 6 (1969), 59–63.

photographs from his initial point of view, and sought values of λ for the suppositious monochromatic rays responsible for the spots. In the experiment of Friedrich and Knipping, the plate lay in the xy (**ij**) plane and $s_o = \mathbf{k}$; equations (1) reduce to

$$a/\lambda \cdot (\alpha, \beta, \gamma - 1) = (h_1, h_2, h_3), \qquad (2)$$

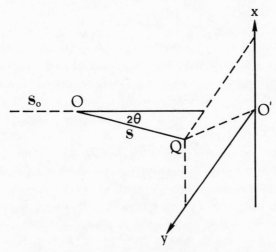

5. The geometry of the Friedrich-Knipping experiment. The center of coordinates of the scatterer is at O, and the photographic plate occupies the xy plane (cf. fig. 3b). OO′ is z and O′Q, q.

where $\alpha\beta\gamma$ are the direction cosines of **s**. The coordinates of a spot relative to the origin at O are then $z(\alpha/\gamma, \beta/\gamma, 1)$; and the radial distance q (fig. 5) of the spot at Q from O′, the center of symmetry of the diffraction pattern, is $z/\gamma \cdot (1 - \gamma^2)^{1/2}$. Curves of constant γ are therefore circles. Laue measured q for the circle passing through eight of the darkest spots on the photograph (fig. 3) and computed γ; the rest was guesswork. It emerged that the same ray could produce eight spots ($h_1 = \pm 3, \pm 5, h_2 = \pm 5, \pm 3$) on the circle $\gamma = 1$, and simultaneously satisfy equations (2); and that most of the rest of the pattern could be similarly saved by supposing four more monochromatic rays in the incident beam. "It may not be that complete truth has been reached," Laue concluded, referring particularly to his five funny values of λ. "But one thing is

certain: the theory is on the right path." One might nonetheless worry
why other sets of h's, not obviously less eligible than those Laue found,
were not represented; and why the penetrating power of the scattered
radiation, as measured by Friedrich and Knipping, differed from that of
the Barkla radiation they supposed it to be.[9]

These questions particularly bothered Bragg, for whom Laue's five
λ's were five too many. By the middle of October 1913, Bragg had found
a way to suggest that, as he later put it, "the positions of the spots give
no information concerning the wavelength of the incident radiation."
His son, W. L. Bragg, then about to return to Cambridge where he was
still an undergraduate, had observed that most of the spots lay in
directions given by "avenues" in the crystal, that is, by lines of length na
drawn between pairs of atoms; evidently this condition allows only those
directions s (in fig. 5) for which $x = (k_1/k_3)z$, $y = (k_2/k_3)z$, and $\Sigma k^2 = n^2$,
n and the k's all being integers. Bragg found indeed that he could get
most of the spots merely by finding three integers the sum of whose
squares is also a square.[10] In particular, the k-set ± 6, ± 10, 33 (which
Bragg does not mention) give the spots of the h-set ± 3, ± 5, 1. What
might the rule signify? "It is difficult to distinguish between various
explanations which present themselves," Bragg said, without presenting
any. We might suppose, however, that he pictured X-ray particles
careening down atomic avenues whose directions were given by the rule
of squares.[11]

Meanwhile the younger Bragg had returned to Cambridge, where
the pulse model had long been cultivated. There his late close study of
the spots, informed by the prevailing genius of the place and by
Schuster's classic analysis of optical diffraction, yielded a splendid
dividend. According to Schuster, white light consists of a "confused
pulse" (to borrow an old tag from Robert Hooke) of energy which is
divided into monochromatic constituents *by the action* of the diffracting

[9] Laue, *Sb* (Munich) 42 (1912), 363; Laue, Friedrich and Knipping, *ibid.*, 321–322.

[10] Bragg, *Nature* 90 (24 Oct 12), 219 (dated 18 Oct 12); *ibid.* (28 Nov 12), 360–361.

[11] Laue understood Bragg to entertain an hypothesis similar to Stark's (*PZs* 13 [1912],
973–977; Forman, *AHES* 6 [1969], 53–54), according to which "Lichtquanten" pass
through "shafts" between the molecules of the crystal lattice; this from Laue to Bragg, 10
Nov 12 (Bragg Papers, RI), in which Laue reaffirmed his belief that the spots derived from
"eine oder einige spectral-homogene Strahlungsarten," now, however, of "unbekannter
Herkunft."

mechanism; in the case of a grating of spacing e, for example, diffracted pulses proceeding at an angle φ to the direction of incidence follow one another at intervals of $e \sin \varphi$, and so appear to have a wavelength $\lambda = e \sin \varphi$.[12] In the case of a crystal, families of planes passed through the molecules would play the part of the grating's lines. Of course, just as in Laue's theory the initial pulse must contain a disturbance of appropriate period if the diffracted pulses are to be in phase in the direction s; the peculiar advantage of Schuster's point of view is to draw attention to the crystal *planes* as diffracting agents.

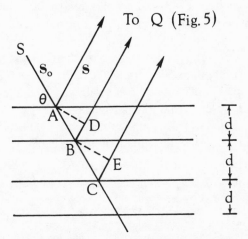

6. Bragg's theory of the Laue spots. The horizontal lines represent crystal planes, SA the direction of incidence (s_o), BC and DE the direction of reflection (s), and θ the glancing angle.

From this perspective Bragg saw the same crystal would generate Laue spots provided that the planes between which, in his father's theory, the X rays fly, in fact force upon them, by reflection, the necessary periodicity (fig. 6); a white pulse incident at "glancing angle" θ will give, after reflection, a series of pulses following at regular intervals

[12] A. Schuster, *Theory of Optics* (1909²), pp. 117–119. Priority in this conception of the character of diffraction appears to belong to G. Gouy, *J de physique* 5 (1886), 354–362; cf. his *Notice sur les travaux scientifiques* (1913), pp. 11–12.

of $\lambda = AB + BD = BC + CE = 2d\sin\theta$, d being the distance between reflecting planes. One sees immediately that, contrary to Laue's analysis, there is no need to ascribe the spots to a few monochromatic waves assumed present *ab initio;* the experimental arrangement fixes θ, and thereby selects the monochromatic ray that the crystal will construct. Of course one can imagine an infinity of sets of planes drawn through the crystal. But if one requires that only planes that pass through a relatively large number of atoms give rise to rays of detectable intensity, one understands immediately that, in a given relation to the incident beam, the crystal constructs but a few effective monochromatic rays.[13]

Young Bragg had now to express the effective direction s to a spot Q in terms of integers p characterizing the set of responsible crystal planes. We pass over his arithmetic,[14] and over the slight complication introduced by the fact, revealed to him by the Cambridge mineralogist W. J. Pope, that the ZnS crystal used by the Germans has a face-centered cubic and not, as Laue thought, a simple cubic structure. But we should observe that the k-triplets of the older Bragg, when expressed in terms of his son's integers p, identically satisfy the numerological rule $\Sigma k^2 =$ the square of an integer.[15]

---

[13] W. L. Bragg, *Proceedings of the Cambridge Philosophical Society* 17 (1912/14), 46. The argument restricting effective "reflection" to atom-rich planes is not sufficient, for it does not explain (1) the weakness of the "reflection" at higher orders n or (2) the ineffectualness of the scattering centers when considered as lying on atom-poor planes (the number of scatterers in unit volume is much the same for all *sets* of planes, the less populated planes lying closer together). An adequate account requires i.a. attention to the heat motion of the scatterers, which mars the regularity of the crystal, and to details of the electronic distribution. The successful quantitative theories use Laue's approach with appropriate factors in $f(R)$. The matter was not fully resolved (and therefore the crispness of the Laue diagrams not fully understood) until after the First World War. Cf., Laue's report to the second Solvay congress (1913) and the remarks of Sommerfeld and Lorentz in *La structure de la matière* (1921), pp. 99–102, 109–112; W. H. and W. L. Bragg, *X Rays and Crystal Structure* (1915), p. 199; and James, *Diffraction of X Rays*, chs. 2–5.

[14] W. L. Bragg, *X Rays*, pp. 47–49. Bragg considered (Research Notebook, RI) only to reject as "clumsy" the classification of the reflecting planes by their intercepts along the coordinate axes which he later employed (*PRS* 89:A [1913], 248–277).

[15] Bragg's rule can also be obtained from Laue's analysis. From equation (2),

$$(\alpha, \beta, \gamma) = L(-2h_1h_3, -2h_2h_3, h_1^2 + h_2^2 - h_3^2),$$

where

$$L = (\Sigma h^2)^{-1};$$

(k_1, k_2, k_3) may be taken as L^{-1} (α, β, γ), whence $\Sigma k^2 = (\Sigma h^2)^2$, a relation which Laue pointed out to Bragg in a letter of 10 Nov 12 (RI).

With the arithmetic in hand, Bragg could identify the set of planes responsible for the production of a given spot. The common spacing d between the planes of the set, which may be found by geometry, then give the constructed wavelengths λ via the condition $\lambda = 2d\sin\theta$.[16] In this way Bragg required eighteen values of λ where Laue had assumed only five. His inflation brought great simplification: one could now regard the spots not as an arbitrary pattern produced by suppositious homogeneous rays, but rather as a *complete collection* of interference maxima constructed from the inhomogeneous incident radiation by *all sets* of "atom-rich" planes from which, under the experimental conditions, reflected beams could reach the photographic plate. It also appeared from Bragg's theory that the Germans had proceeded in an unnecessarily cumbersome way: rather than pass rays through the crystal, one needed only to reflect them from its face, provided the surface contained a relatively large number of atoms. The cleavage planes of crystals present such surfaces. By the end of November 1912, W. L. Bragg was easily obtaining spots by reflection from standard slips of mica. On December 5, a week before this discovery became public, W. H. Bragg (who did not hold dogmatically to his corpuscularism) notified Rutherford of his son's success: "My boy has been getting beautiful X-ray reflections from mica sheets, just as simple as the reflection of light in a mirror. They can be got in five minutes' exposure. . . ." [17]

Meanwhile Harry had begun fishing these muddied waters. He had had to suspend work on the radium battery because a fitting for the liquid-air machine, whose product he needed in his vacuum system, had failed to arrive from its German manufacturer. Not knowing, as he said,

---

[16] This formula can easily be obtained from Laue's equations (1). Let α', β', γ' be the direction cosines of $\mathbf{s} - \mathbf{s}_0$ with respect to $\mathbf{a}$, $\mathbf{b}$, $\mathbf{c}$; then, since $|\mathbf{s}-\mathbf{s}_0| = 2\sin\theta$ (cf. fig. 4), we have instead of equation (2)

$$2\sin\theta \cdot a/\lambda \cdot (\alpha', \beta', \gamma') = (h_1, h_2, h_3). \tag{2'}$$

Evidently the vector (h_1, h_2, h_3) is parallel to $(\alpha', \beta', \gamma')$, which implies that $\mathbf{s} - \mathbf{s}_0$ is normal to the plane that intercepts the axes $\mathbf{a}$, $\mathbf{b}$, $\mathbf{c}$, at a/h_1, a/h_2, a/h_3. If this plane is rich in atoms, it (or rather its set) can construct spots; if d is the distance between successive members of the set, $d = a\alpha'/h_1 = a\beta'/h_2 = a\gamma'/h_3$, and equation (2') collapses to the "Bragg law," $2d\sin\theta = \lambda$, or more generally, $n\lambda$, where n is the order of the interference.

[17] Bragg to Rutherford, 5 Dec 12 (R); W. L. Bragg, *Nature* 90 (12 Dec 12), 410.

"how long they will keep me waiting," he looked about for other amusements and, by October 10, had lighted on Laue's spots. He decided to try to adapt the German technique to a familiar Manchestrian agent, namely γ rays. Preliminary photographs were spotless, doubtless because of the low intensity of the radiation. Nonetheless the project greatly appealed to Harry, partly, perhaps, in connection with Rutherford's theory of γ-ray production, which he was then studying carefully. When the liquid air flowed again he made one last try for super potentials and conceded defeat at 150,000 volts.[18] That was in the middle of October. He was then "already devising new methods for my next piece of work, which will be a thorough frontal attack on the γ ray, and will probably keep me good and quiet for the best part of a year." In fact it engaged him only momentarily. When he looked more closely at the German work he concluded that Laue and company "entirely failed to understand what it meant, and gave an explanation which was obviously wrong." Before proceeding with the γ's he felt that he should understand the experiment he proposed to adapt, and, anticipating mathematical difficulties, he invited C. G. Darwin to join him in the project.[19]

Darwin (1887–1962) carried a scientific pedigree higher even than Harry's: he was the grandson of Charles Darwin, the son of Sir George Darwin (a Cambridge professor and the Astronomer Royal), and the Fourth Wrangler of 1910. He had come to Manchester in that year to succeed Henry Bateman as Schuster's mathematical reader.[20] That, of course, had not prevented Rutherford from "encouraging" him to do experiments on radioactivity; and in 1911 the only wrangler at Manchester was busily helping Ernest Marsden, one of Harry's fellow demonstra-

---

[18] 6o, 61, 62. Harry read a little paper on his radium battery to the "fogeys" of the Literary and Philosophical Society, which had elected him a member, for a fee of two guineas, on 9 May 11, a month after Darwin had been similarly elevated; *Memoirs and Proceedings of the Manchester Literary and Philosophical Society* 57 (1912/13), viii–ix, xlii–li; 64.

[19] 62, 63; Darwin in Birks, p. 21. Harry had been interested in X rays already at Eton where (according to Eggar) he demonstrated their "simpler properties" to the College Scientific Society in 1905 (*Nature* 104 [1920], 444).

[20] His application may be of interest. It consisted of a note from the Astronomer Royal: "I find that my son Charles would very much appreciate the studentship." G. Darwin to Schuster, 22 June 10 (Schuster Papers, I.59, RS). See C. G. Darwin to Schuster, 27 June 10 (*ibid.*, I.54).

tors, in analyzing the complex product then called "ThC." They found, as expected, that ThC (^{212}Bi) branched in the manner Fajans had discovered in RaC, and they succeeded in determining the periods and relative occurrences of the two modes of decay. Darwin finished this investigation in April of 1912, and a month later he concluded a theoretical examination of α absorption which was to prompt Bohr, then also in Manchester, to develop the nuclear model. He consequently had no pressing project in hand, and perhaps had already begun to think about X-ray diffraction, when Harry proposed the collaboration to him.[21]

Their first order of business was to discover "the real meaning of the [German] experiments." The surviving records do not disclose their line of thought which, "after much hard work," succeeded quite independently of the Braggs. The foregoing account of the approaches of Laue and Bragg will suggest the sorts of difficulties they faced; and the ingenious analogy between the action of a diffraction grating and that of a set of reflecting planes, which Moseley concocted and Darwin later developed, may indicate that they, too, profited from Schuster's optical theories.[22] On November 1, 1912, Harry revealed their theory before the fortnightly Friday physics colloquium. W. H. Bragg was in attendance. "It was rather anxious work, as Bragg the chief authority on the subject (Physics Professor at Leeds) was present, and so I had to be cautious. However, it proved quite successful, and I managed completely to disguise my nervousness." There was little cause for alarm, for Bragg had by then fully adopted his son's yet unpublished theory; and in the ensuing discussion Harry discovered that that theory, of which he had heard rumors, differed little from the explanation he and Darwin had devised.[23] They thereupon decided to leave the matter entirely to the Braggs.

Having resolved their initial problem, Harry and Darwin decided to

---

[21] Marsden and Darwin, *PRS* 87:A (1912), 17–29; Darwin, *PM* 23 (1912), 901–920, and J. L. Heilbron and T. S. Kuhn, *HSPS* 1 (1969), 237–240; G. P. Thomson, *ORS* 9 (1963), 69–71.

[22] Darwin, *PM* 27 (1914), 317; **63**; *infra*, p. 223.

[23] **63**. Cf. *infra*, n. 36, and Rutherford to J. A. Gray, 6 Nov 12 (R): "Moseley gave an account of the [German] work, and shewed that all the spots could be explained by assuming a scattering of the X rays and the interference of the scattered rays. Bragg came over and he had come to practically the same view." According to later notes by Margery (LH), Harry and Darwin were two days behind the Braggs.

give themselves entirely to the study of X rays and to the attempt to find a theory that might reconcile the corpuscular properties emphasized by Bragg with the diffraction effects they now understood.[24] Their first obstacle was Rutherford. No one at Manchester had had any practical experience with X rays; he certainly had none, and without his paternal guidance Harry and Darwin might well run astray and tarnish the reputation of the laboratory. He had misgivings enough in the still unsettled matter of G. N. Antonoff, a student who had announced, with his blessing, the existence of a new radioelement (UY, ^{231}Th), which the radiochemists regrettably could not confirm.[25] Our hopeful Röntgenologists found their leader "distinctly discouraging." Of course it was not long before Rutherford, like everyone else, let Harry have his way. Doubtless he acquiesced the more willingly when W. H. Bragg generously invited Harry to Leeds to learn the tricks of experimental X-ray work.[26]

The first objective Harry and Darwin set themselves was to test whether the rays which produced the spots, and consequently which must be assumed to have an extended wave-front, also "possessed those properties which have led Prof. W. H. Bragg to suggest that X rays are corpuscular." It might well be that the incident beam contained a wavelike and a particulate constituent, which the crystal merely separated. The proposed test consisted of measuring the ionizing power of interfering rays produced in the manner of Friedrich and Knipping. In the middle of November Harry began to assemble the apparatus suggested by Bragg, who himself intended to pursue the same line. The installation was expensive. An essential component, the break used to interrupt the primary current in the induction coil used to drive the

---

[24] Bragg also called for "a theory which possesses the capacities of both the wave and particle models," e.g., in *Nature* 90 (28 Nov 12), 360–361; cf. Steuwer, *BJHS* 5 (1971), 272.

[25] Antonoff, *PM* 22 (1911), 419–432; Rutherford to Boltwood, 16 May 11, in Badash, p. 250; **86**. The matter was resolved in Antonoff's favor by Soddy, *PM* 27 (1914), 215–221. "I am very glad things turned out all right [Rutherford wrote Hervesy on 7 Jan 14 (Eve, p. 228)], for I should have been very sorry to feel that the laboratory had one piece of bad work to its discredit."

[26] Darwin in Birks, pp. 21–22; **66, 67**. Against this background Rutherford's request to the Royal Society in 1915 for funds to do X-ray research makes curious reading (Schuster Papers, II.221, RS): the grant, he says, is to insure for England the lead in the field given it by the work of Moseley, "started under my direction in my laboratory."

X-ray tube or "bulb," cost 10 gns, about 5 percent of the annual research budget, and about half the price of a good mercury-vapor vacuum pump, which the laboratory sorely needed. Then there were the bulb itself and the crystal sections, which had to be procured in Germany. Rutherford, who controlled the laboratory purse, consented to the expenditures after a little "squeezing" from Harry.[27]

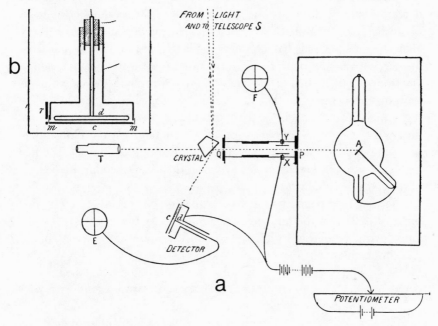

7. The definitive Moseley-Darwin apparatus (a) the general layout (b) the detector. From **VI**.

The German crystals proved unnecessary. As Harry was completing his apparatus he learned of Bragg's reflections from good English mica; and, always ready to rebuild to effect the slightest improvement, he immediately adopted the new technique. In his definitive version, an extremely sensitive device (fig. 7), an X-ray beam from a platinum anticathode (A), narrowly collimated by the slits P, Q, fell on the face of

[27] **VI**, 211; **66**; Robinson in Birks, pp. 74–75; [Max Kohl, A.G.], *Price List Fifty. Physical Apparatus* (c. 1912), pp. 399, 985. Cf. *supra*, p. 36, n. 19.

a crystal mounted on a spectrometer table, the line of impact coinciding with the axis of the instrument. The reflected beam entered the detector, carried by the arm of the spectrometer, through the lead slit r and the mica window m. Because of the narrow collimation, the small reflectivity, and the absorption of the beam in the air it traversed (40 cm from anticathode to crystal and half that again from crystal to detector), the rays entering m were very much less intense than those leaving A. The detector had therefore to be very sensitive.[28] It exploited the fact, discovered by J. J. Laub, that X rays striking a metal plate at very oblique angles produce a rich harvest of secondary electrons. These particles, knocked out of the plate c and accelerated toward the positive central electrode d, could then create many more self-reproducing electrons by ionizing the helium gas that filled the detector. The device embodied techniques introduced by several of Harry's mentors: Townsend had initiated the study of amplification by multiple ionization, Griffith had been the first to use it in practice, and Rutherford and Geiger had perfected it, inter alia, by using helium in their classic counting of the α particles from radium.[29]

It is a great testimony to Harry's skill and quickness that in their first order of business—the hunt for ions produced by the reflected rays—he and Darwin were able to keep pace with the more experienced Bragg. The hunt extended into the new year, spurred by C. T. R. Wilson's failure to find any evidence of ionization on photographs taken in his cloudchamber. On January 16, 1913, Harry and Darwin found what they sought, and rushed to settle "some of the interesting points which arise" before announcing their discovery. Their delay brought instant disappointment. The following day Bragg, who had also succeeded, sent his good news to *Nature*, and on the 18th he told Rutherford. "I found the ionization from the reflected radiation from mica quite easily. . . . The ray [therefore] travels from point to point like a corpuscle: the disposition of the lines of travel is governed by a wave theory. Seems pretty hard to explain; but that surely is how it stands at present."[30]

---

[28] **VI**, 211–214; Darwin in Birks, p. 22.

[29] **VI**, 214–215; J. J. Laub, *AP* 26 (1908), 712–726; Townsend, *PM* 3 (1902), 557–576, and *PM* 6 (1903), 598–618; Griffith, *PM* 14 (1907), 297–306; Rutherford and Geiger, *PRS* 81:A (1908), 141–161, and *PM* 24 (1912), 618–623 = *Papers* II, 89–108, 288–291.

[30] **68**; Bragg to Rutherford, 9 and 18 Jan 13 (R); Bragg to *Nature*, 7 Jan 13 (*Nature* 90 [23 Jan 13], 572).

Thus anticipated, Harry and Darwin had either to remain silent or to echo Bragg in the pages of *Nature*. They chose to echo, "fearing that if we kept silence until really ready for publication, all the others who have been writing to *Nature* on the subject would regard us as interlopers into their preserves." A letter duly appeared, "confirming and extending" Bragg's results and emphasizing that they showed the energy of X rays to possess the "contradictory properties of extension over a wave front and concentration in a point."[31]

Having staked their claim, Harry and Darwin settled down to a leisurely study of this "most mysterious property of energy which [Harry wrote Margery] the Germans have for some time been groping after, but which we see no immediate hope of comprehending." Since they had no particular hypothesis to test—"mechanics," Harry said, "have in this direction been for some time a broken reed"—they began by collecting data on the reflected energy or intensity $I(\theta)$. They took readings with great industry, frequently at intervals of 30' of arc, and at each determination were plagued by the unsteadiness of the bulb. (The plates XY in figure 7 monitored the output of the bulb by measuring the ionization produced by the primary beam in the air between them.) Their preliminary results showed that $I(\theta)$ decreased quickly and regularly from glancing incidence to $\theta \sim 35°$, when it became undetectable, except for small "singularities," which they supposed to arise from flaws in the structure of their crystal, and which they proposed to investigate when more important matters had been dispatched.[32] Before they could proceed further, the Braggs, who had begun to work together, again intervened: they found that the intensity of reflection was abnormally high at three well-defined angles, a fact which W. H. Bragg generously reported to Harry. On March 30, 1913, he sent Rutherford further particulars: each of the special rays had a different penetrating power, which remained constant independent of the nature of the reflecting crystal or of the state of the bulb; Bragg did not know (nor guess) whether the powers would alter if a metal other than platinum served as anticathode. As for the special angles, $\theta = 9.8$, 11.5, and 13.6 degrees, they appeared to be roughly in harmonic progression,

[31] **67, 68**; HM and Darwin to *Nature*, 21 Jan 13 (**V**).

[32] **69**; **VI**, 211–212. The vagaries of the bulb were diminished somewhat by lighting an electric lamp in the lead box containing it (**VI**, 218).

and so seemed to "hint that the 'frequencies' or 'energies of the quanta' are in A[rithmetic] P[rogression]"; and that, Bragg concluded hopefully, "hint[s] vaguely at some relation like yours with β and γ rays." [33] Four days later Bragg wrote to confirm his results, and on April 7 he presented the Royal Society with the work he and his son had done to date: a rough survey of the general reflected radiation and the angles, accurate to about 1 percent, for reflection of the three special rays from the surfaces of six different crystals.[34]

Alerted by Bragg, Harry and Darwin reexamined their singularities, taking readings at intervals of 1' of arc; the fine collimation of their instrument, which had caused them to miss the peaks on their first survey, now paid a handsome dividend by resolving the three Bragg mountains into five separate pinnacles. By May they were feverishly at work measuring absorption coefficients, disentangling the contributions of the different orders of reflection to $I(\theta)$, and trying to estimate such important details as the length of the wave trains in the singular rays. Harry would work at the experiments for fifteen hours at a stretch, into the "last stages of exhaustion"; he dined on cheese at three in the morning and breakfasted, invariably on fruit salad, the following noon.[35] The result of this terrific effort, published in the *Philosophical Magazine* for July 1913, is a masterpiece of accuracy, comprehensiveness, and economical expression. It plainly describes the experimental arrangement and its pitfalls; it gives precise curves of the reflected white radiation, i.e., of $I(\theta)$ less the singularities, and an elementary theory of the curves' shapes, which the Germans especially appreciated, and accepted as a demonstration of the existence of a continuous X-ray

---

[33] Bragg to Rutherford, 10 Mar 13 (R). Assume that the singular rays are produced by the impacting electrons in the manner Rutherford envisaged γ rays to come from β's: we would expect the energies of the singular rays to differ by a constant, i.e., should stand in A.P. Since, according to Planck, the energies are proportional to the reciprocals of the wavelengths, $1/\lambda$ or, what is almost the same for small angles, $1/\theta$, should also be in A.P. That the reciprocals of 9.8, 11.5 and 19.6 are in A.P. is of course merely a coincidence.

[34] Bragg, *PRS* 88:A (1913), 428–438. The paper includes rough figures for the absorption coefficients of the special rays in aluminum (which showed, i.a., that such rays could not give rise to Laue's spots), and hints at the connection between the A.P. of $1/\theta$ and Rutherford's ideas.

[35] **74**; Darwin in Birks, p. 22; Rutherford, *PRS* 93:A (1917), xxviii; interview with Hevesy, 25 May 62 (AHQP).

spectrum; and it supplies values for the singular angles to an accuracy about an order of magnitude better than the Braggs'.[36]

They also made explicit what the Braggs had only hinted, namely, that the singular rays were nothing other than Barkla radiation character- istic of their platinum anticathodes. One might well wonder at their caution, and indeed at neither party having *sought* the singular rays from the beginning of its experiments. In 1913 one even knew how hard the bulbs must be to produce rays characteristic of a platinum anticathode, for in 1911 a Cambridge physicist, Richard Whiddington, had found the very important empirical rule that the velocity which cathode rays must possess to produce X rays just hard enough to excite K radiations from an element of atomic weight A is about $A \cdot 10^8$ cm/sec. Calculation by this well-known rule would have placed the platinum K rays at about 100,000 volts, above the range of the Müller bulbs the Leeds and Manchester groups used; but they might still have expected the platinum L rays, which were known to correspond in hardness to the K rays of the iron family (10,000 volts).[37] Perhaps one should regard their failure to look for platinum L rays as the obverse of their rejection of Laue's theory, and with it the supposition of strong monochromatic beams in the original radiation. In any case their oversight provides an excellent index of the highly exploratory nature of the early experiments on X-ray diffraction, and of the tentative, disjointed state of the theory, which Laue himself had not yet fully mastered.[38]

The connection between Braggs' peaks and Barkla's radiation emerged when (if not before) Harry and Darwin found that the absorption coefficient of one of their singular rays, which they called "β,"

---

[36] *Fortschritte der Physik* 69:2 (1913), 194; Friedrich, *PZs* 14 (1913), 1079–1084; Laue, *JRE* 11 (1914), 317–319. The Braggs with their customary generosity pointed out the merits of their rivals, e.g., W. L. Bragg, *JRE* 11 (1914), 361–362, and W. H. Bragg to R. W. T. Harrison, 6 June 13 (RS): "Having got my results out, I gave them ['two keen young Manchester students'] very material help. They have repeated my experiments and pushed some of them to a higher degree of accuracy. . . ."

[37] Whiddington, *PRS* 85:A (1911), 323–332. Cf. N. Feather, *ORS* 17 (1971), 741–756.

[38] Laue, *AP* 41 (1913), 989–1002. Cf. Rutherford to Bohr, 11 Nov 12 (AHQP), *re* Harry's lecture of 1 Nov 13: "There seems to be no doubt that the positions of all the spots can be simply explained by supposing there is some kind of interference between the pulses. The position of the spots, however, is determined by the crystalline arrangement and has apparently nothing to do with the wave length."

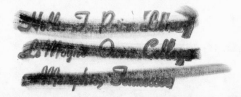

closely approximated that of the platinum L ray. From Bragg's equation, $n\lambda = 2d\sin\theta$, one can find λ_β in terms of d, or better, of k, the number of molecules in an element of side d; evidently, $d^3 = kM/N\sigma$, where M is the crystal's molecular weight, σ its density, and N Avogadro's number. Harry's figures made $\lambda_\beta = 1.397k^{1/3} \cdot 10^{-8}$ cm for the case of rocksalt; since for the most probable arrangements, $k^{1/3} \sim 1$, λ_β agreed nicely with earlier estimates based on various classical considerations. They did not stop with this agreement which, in their opinion, fixed X rays too tightly to classical theory; and so, doubtless with an eye to Bragg's theories, they sought a quantum-physical correspondence of *energy* as well. Their procedure was to equate $h\nu_\beta = hc/\lambda_\beta = 1.37 \cdot k^{-1/3} \cdot 10^{-8}$ erg with the energy Whiddington's law required for the excitation of rays as penetrating as β. Extrapolating Barkla's results on the relation between atomic weight and absorption coefficient, they deduced that if β were a K ray, it would belong to an element of $A = 75.5$, and consequently, according to Whiddington, represent an energy $W_\beta = (m/2)(75.5 \cdot 10^8)^2 = 2.6 \cdot 10^{-8}$ erg. They considered the agreement with $h\nu_\beta$ satisfactory. This time they anticipated Bragg, who reciprocated by being more thorough. He obtained the penetrating powers and frequencies of characteristic rays from anticathodes of tungsten and nickel. The values of $h\nu_\beta$ from Ni, W and Pt stood as 100:132:151; the values of W_β, computed from the "equivalent" K emitter, were as 100:130:150! [39]

In the spring of 1913 Rutherford offered Harry the undivided John Harling Fellowship for the academic year 1913/14 "as slight inducement" for remaining at Manchester. It was tempting: Harry could then continue his X-ray work without interruption and retain access to the services of Cook and the omnicompetent Baumbach. Moreover, he had no other position and no desire to become "an amateur." Nonetheless he refused, judging it "unwise at the present stage to be long in one place." He had learned from Rutherford, as he gratefully acknowledged, "how research work ought to be done"; further exposure promised little gain.[40] Indeed, their roles were soon reversed. After the summer vacation

[39] **VI**, 223–224; W. H. Bragg, *PRS* 89:A (1913), 246–248, received 21 June 13. Bragg's absolute values of $h\nu_\beta$ (made possible by his son's determination of k) also agreed reasonably well with W_β. W. L. Bragg, *PRS* 89:A (1913), 272–276, received 21 June 13.
[40] **71, 82, 91**.

Rutherford "caught the prevailing X-ray fever" and began bouncing γ rays off a beautiful crystal of potassium ferrocyanide that Harry lent him for the purpose. The professor thus took up the work his student had long abandoned; and, with the technique perfected by Harry and Darwin and the help of Andrade, he obtained frequencies for the γ rays that appeared to support his theory of β decay.[41]

Harry considered several alternatives for the fall. He might go abroad, say to Germany. But "after consulting several people [he told Amabel] I consider that a few months are as much as could profitably be spent there simply because there is no laboratory there which comes up to England in the experimental side of modern physics. They run away after strange theories and experiment gets neglected." [42] Certainly a curious view when one considers, say, the large X-ray installations in Munich, the precise spectrometers of Bonn and Tübingen, and the several laboratories of Berlin where, among others, Hahn and Meitner and Franck and Hertz were busily at work. Despite the presence of counter-examples like Geiger and Fajans, the insular Manchester group maintained the fiction that German physicists were incompetent, long-winded, and light-headed. Traces of this attitude appear in Rutherford's effort to bowdlerize Bohr and in Harry's review of Svedberg's *Die Existenz der Moleküle*, whose Swedish author he took to be a German and consequently a tedious and "horrid" fellow.[43]

To continue Harry's deliberations. "Also their national bigotry is rather a serious obstacle in the path of any foreigner." Here is another fiction, fed by the kaiser and the War Office; Andrade, for example, who succeeded Harry as John Harling Fellow, worked quite happily in Heidelberg in 1910/11 under the extravagant nationalist Philipp Lenard. But Harry, despite his friendly collaboration with Fajans, did not care to discriminate; even his great admirer Jervis recalled that he suspended his usual kindliness when it came to Germans and "the rowing men at

---

[41] **83**; Rutherford and Andrade, *Nature* 92 (30 Oct 13), 267, and *PM* 27 (1914), 854–868, = *Papers* II, 361, 432–444.

[42] **71**.

[43] Rutherford to Bohr, 25 Mar 13: "As you know it is the custom in England to put things very shortly and tersely in contrast to the German method, where it appears to be a virtue to be as long-winded as possible." L. Rosenfeld, ed., *On the Constitution of Atoms and Molecules* (1963), p. xlv; HM, *Nature* 92 (27 Nov 13), 367–368; **64, 79, 80**.

Trinity." As for the French, Harry solemnly told his mother, they are in point of bigotry "a hundred times worse [than the Germans], and their suspicion that their pet ideas will be stolen seems in some cases to be such that conditions become intolerable." [44]

Needless to say Harry did not study abroad. He decided instead to apply for a special fellowship advertised by Brasenose College, Oxford, even though Townsend was supporting another candidate and the college did not wish a physicist. "But," as he said, "it never does any harm to remind people of one's existence." The post went to the Demonstrator of Mineralogy at the Oxford Museum, T. V. Barker, whom the college chose from among thirty-five applicants. Harry decided to return to Manchester in the fall to complete a new project he had started before the summer recess, and then to remove to Oxford, to work in Townsend's laboratory as an independent, self-supporting investigator. "I will have a much better chance of a research fellowship," he reasoned, "if I am on the spot clamorous." [45]

---

[44] E. N. da C. Andrade, *Physics Education* 1 (1966), 69–78; Fajans, private communication; **71**; Jervis to Amabel, 18 Feb 20 (LH).

[45] **72, 73**; *London Times*, 16 June 13, p. 4c.

VI

Master

"WE FIND THAT an X ray bulb with a platinum target gives out a sharp line spectrum of five wavelengths," Harry wrote his mother on May 18, 1913. "Tomorrow we search for the spectra of other elements. There is here a whole new branch of spectroscopy." The same point occurred to W. H. Bragg and to the leading French authority on X rays, Maurice de Broglie. But whereas Bragg and de Broglie focused their attention on the rays themseves—on their number, penetrating powers, and fine structure —Harry regarded the new spectroscopy as a most welcome tool in atomic physics, a technique which, he said, "is sure to tell one much about the nature of an atom." [1]

At Manchester, in the spring of 1913, one could not avoid the theory of atomic structure. Hevesy and Russell were then publishing their respective contributions to what would shortly be the theory of isotopy. Niels Bohr, having imbibed the spirit of the laboratory during a five-month stay in 1912, had recently paid it another visit in order to defend a draft of his first paper on "the constitution of atoms"—the famous paper deriving the Balmer formula for the spectrum of hydrogen —from Rutherford's heavy editorial hand. And Geiger and Marsden had just completed their classic investigation of the large-angle scattering of α particles, which strongly supported the nuclear model of the atom that

---

[1] 74; Bragg, *PRS* 89:A (1913), 246–248; de Broglie, *CR* 157 (17 Nov 13), 924–926, and *CR* 158 (19 Jan 14), 177–180. These last papers describe the method of the rotating crystal (*infra*, p. 224).

Rutherford had proposed, on very sketchy evidence, two years before.[2]

To interpret the Geiger-Marsden experiments Rutherford assumed that the α particle and the nuclei of the scattering atoms interacted like *point charges*. Since α particles, as everyone knew, became helium atoms on capturing two electrons, it followed for Rutherfordians that the helium nucleus was none other than an α particle, and consequently carried two positive charges. Now the deflection of α's from heavy metals, when interpreted according to Rutherford's scattering theory, showed that C, the charge on the nucleus of a target atom, was about one-half its atomic weight A. But, as we have just seen, precisely the same relation, $A = 2C$, holds for helium $(A = 4)$. Bohr, Darwin, and Rutherford himself regarded the success of this relation, which was known on other grounds to be correct to order of magnitude, as a particularly striking confirmation of the nuclear model.[3] So did one A. van den Broek, a lawyer and amateur physicist in Amsterdam. The true significance of the Rutherfordian relation, he said, appears when one views it in the light of another approximation, $\overline{\Delta A} = 2$, where $\overline{\Delta A}$ is the average difference in atomic weight between neighboring elements in the periodic table. For from these two imprecise relations it follows that ΔC is approximately unity, a result van den Broek proposed to consider an exact law; and since, on Rutherford's scheme, $C_{He} = 2$, his Dutch interpreter could only conclude that $C_H = 1$ and that, in general, an element's nuclear charge equaled its serial number (let us call it Z) in the table of Mendeleev.[4]

"Broek's hypothesis," as Harry called the doctrine of atomic number, evidently differed from Mendeleev's fundamental principle, to which most chemists still gave allegiance, namely that the chemical properties of an element depend unambiguously on its atomic weight. According to Rutherford's model as understood by Broek and Bohr, the

[2] Geiger and Marsden, *PM* 25 (1913), 604–623; Hevesy, *PM* 25 (1913), 390–414; L. Rosenfeld, ed., *The Constitution of Atoms and Molecules* (1963), p. xlv.

[3] Heilbron, *AHES* 4 (1968), 285–299; Heilbron and Kuhn, *HSPS* 1 (1969), 245–255; Darwin, *PM* 23 (1912), 909.

[4] Van den Broek, *PZs* 14 (1 Jan 13), 32–41; see T. Hirosige, *Japanese Studies in the History of Science* 10 (1971), 143–162. It is curious that van den Broek did not have the idea of isotopy; like W. Ramsay, *Smithsonian Institution Reports* (1911), 190, he considered β emitters "pseudoelements," and assigned them the same place as their daughters.

outermost of the planetary electrons surrounding the nucleus determine the chemical character of an atom; and since the electronic structure is regulated by the nuclear charge, it follows from Broek's hypothesis that Z, and not A, controls the periodic table. Chemists had already discovered that at three places in the table—nickel-cobalt, argon-potassium, and iodine-tellurium—the chemical order inverts that of weight.[5] Since the electronic structure also determines spectral properties, one might expect that the characteristic radiations from atoms would also follow Z, and confirm the inversions apparently required on chemical grounds. Moreover, in the spring of 1913, one could readily find a very promising subject for such a test. Whiddington's rule, one will recall, had revealed a physical property other than weight, namely the hardness of K rays, that changed *regularly* and almost *monotonically* throughout the periodic table. Did the K-ray frequencies follow A, as Whiddington's rough results indicated, or Z, as Broek demanded and Barkla's old experiments on nickel and cobalt implied? On, or just after finishing his work with Darwin, Harry decided to measure these frequencies "for the express purpose [as he says] of testing Broek's hypothesis." [6]

The surviving documents do not disclose when Harry first projected this examination, which was very shortly to win him an international reputation. He did not begin to build the necessary apparatus until the beginning of August 1913; consequently, we may suppose, the hope expressed in his letter of May 18, viz., that the new X-ray spectroscopy "is sure to tell one much about the nature of an atom," did not refer to a test of Broek's hypothesis. Indeed, we may doubt that Harry had then studied Broek's lengthy paper.[7] He did not read German easily, and a glance at the first few pages, filled with egregious errors about radioactivity, would not have recommended the effort. He could of course have been directed to Broek by Darwin, who knew German well. Even so we may doubt that, in the last month of their collaboration, Harry and

---

[5] J. W. van Spronsen, *The Periodic System* (1969), pp. 237–242, gives examples of artifices devised by chemists to save Mendeleev's ordering principle.

[6] HM to *Nature*, 5 Jan 14 (**VIII**); Barkla and Sadler, *PM* 17 (1909), 740, and Barkla and Collier, *PM* 23 (1912), 997. Several physicists before van den Broek had taken the "position number" in the periodic table as fundamental and tried to express A as a function of Z; the most successful relation, $A = (Z+2)^{1.21}$, was found by a student of J. J. Thomson's, J. H. Vernon (*PM* 4 [1902], 103–115).

[7] **74, 77**.

Darwin started to test Broek's hypothesis; for Darwin, as Hevesy has recalled, was keenly interested in the test, and doubtless would have continued with it had he in fact begun it.[8] The great work appears to have been planned in July, after the collaboration had been amicably dissolved, and following the intervention of Niels Bohr.

Bohr visited Manchester towards the end of the first week in July 1913, in order to discuss the second and third installments of his paper on atomic constitution with Rutherford and to renew his acquaintance among the research men. There, for the first time, he had a long talk with Harry; Hevesy and Darwin were also present, and the conversation turned on the question whether the frequencies of the K rays, to which Bohr had given considerable attention, should follow A or Z.[9] Bohr then (according to his later recollections) expounded his views about the periodic table, no doubt as they appear in the second part of his pioneering paper, which made public for the first time the familiar qualitative picture of the nuclear atom, regulated by the quantization of the angular momentum and the principles of isotopy and atomic number. After the discussion, as Hevesy remembered it, Harry declared, "we will see what quantity determines the X-ray spectra" and started on his epochal researches.[10]

Only one of the problematic pairs of elements, Co ($Z = 27$) and Ni (28), gave K rays soft enough for investigation. Since, for the proposed test, their radiations had to be compared with those from neighboring elements, Harry decided to try to find the rays characteristic of the metals from Ca ($Z = 20$) through Zn (30), respectively the lightest and

---

[8] Van den Broek, *PZs* 14 (1913), 38; Hevesy, interview of 25 May 62, p. 8 (AHQP). Darwin continued to work on theoretical questions that arose from the collaboration, e.g., the effects of thermal motion (VI, 226); Darwin, *PM* 27 (1914), 315–333, 675–690.

[9] Bohr, interviews of 2 Nov 62, pp. 16–17, and 14 Nov 62, p. 5 (AHQP); Bohr to Rutherford, 31 Jan 13 (AHQP). Bohr was not in Manchester in June 1913 as he says in Birks, pp. 131–132; his whereabouts in July appear from his letters to Rutherford of 1 and 29 July 13 (AHQP). Harry was at Pick's Hill during Bohr's visit of c. 1–6 April 13; Bohr to Rutherford, 26 March and 8 April 13 (AHQP); Diary, 19 March and 1 April 13.

[10] Hevesy, *Naturwissenschaften* 11 (1923), 604–605; cf. **76**. It is of course possible that Harry first decided to test Broek and then asked Bohr's opinion; such a view is supported by Bohr's *published* account of the matter (in Birks, pp. 131–132), and, by implication, by Rutherford, *Nature* 116 (1925), 316–317; cf. Heilbron, *Isis* 57 (1966), 345–346.

the heaviest elements easily employed as K emitters. Commercial bulbs did not come equipped with anticathodes of these materials. Consequently Harry himself had to undertake the chore of constructing, exhausting and sealing X-ray tubes. He immediately perceived the advantage of building several different anticathodes into the same bulb: it saved time and expense, and freed him from continual dependence on the laboratory's "jealously guarded" vacuum pumps. He accordingly adopted the procedure G. W. C. Kaye had employed in 1909, in a well-known study of the penetrating powers of K rays. Kaye had put a pair of rails inside the tube, in a cross arm perpendicular to the branch containing the anode (fig. 8); the rail supported a little truck, and the

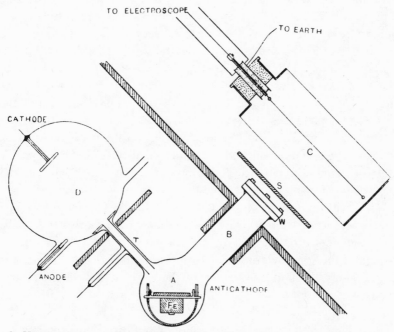

8. Kaye's apparatus for examining the penetrating powers of X rays. Cathode rays produced in the vessel D excite X rays in targets at A; rays traveling in the direction AB cross the aluminum window W and various absorbers S before entering the ionization chamber C. The targets sat on a truck which was drawn forward on a curved aluminum rail by an external magnet acting on pieces of soft iron (one of which is shown in the figure) fixed to the truck's axles. From Kaye, PT 209:A (1909).

truck carried the samples, which were towed into the line of fire of the cathode rays by a magnetic device. Harry at first used silk cords attached to weights floating on mercury instead of the magnetic guide; in his final version (fig. 9), he wound the cords on brass bobbins which could be turned without opening the vacuum.[11] Rays from the target under bombardment passed through a narrow platinum slit to fall on the face of the old crystal of potassium ferrocyanide; and, at first, the reflected beam was caught in an ionization chamber similar to the detector Harry had used in his work with Darwin.

The ionization method proved intolerably slow and, owing to the unsteadiness of the compound bulb, undependable. Harry switched to photography, at first with no better results: "horrid diffraction fringes then come round the lines of the spectrum and prevent their positions being measured very accurately." But he knew "roughly," as he told Margery, what caused the fringes, which Barkla had been studying for some months.[12] It appears that they derived from "white" radiation reflected from flawed patches on the crystal surface. To deal with them Harry had to rebuild his spectrometer, if he had not already done so, to take advantage of the curious "focussing effect" discovered independently by the Braggs and de Broglie: if the entrance slit A and the photographic plate near B (fig. 10) lie on a circle centered on the axis C of the spectrometer, and if, in a given position of the crystal, *characteristic* rays of wavelength λ are imaged at B, then, if the crystal is rotated through a small angle β, the rays of wavelength λ will again be reflected to the same point B. The facets producing the Barkla fringes, however, will rotate with the crystal; a set of fringes which overlapped the characteristic ray at B before the rotation will not do so afterwards. The geometry recommended by the Braggs not only allows one to distinguish the spurious fringes from the true interference maxima, but also to ignore the finite divergence of the incident X-ray beam. Harry accordingly cut down his earlier instrument to make AC = BC = 17 cm.[13]

By October 19, 1913, he had surmounted most of the experimental

---

[11] Kaye, *PT* 209:A (1909), 123–151; **77**; **IX**, 704. Whiddington, *PRS* 85:A (1911), 99–118, had also used Kaye's device.

[12] **77**; Barkla and G. H. Martyn, *PM* 25 (Feb 1913), 296–300, and *Proceedings of the Physical Society* 25 (1913), 206–213.

[13] **87**, esp. n. 7; **VII**, 1026.

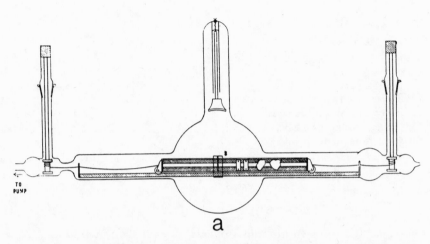

a

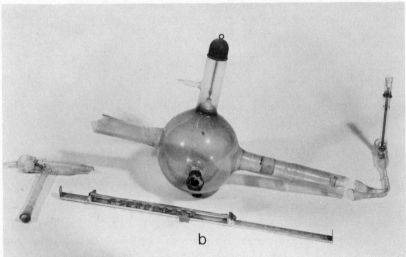

b

9. Moseley's definitive apparatus for obtaining hard X rays (a) schematic diagram, from **IX** (b) what remains of the apparatus, courtesy of OHS.

difficulties and expected the work to "go very well." The results surprised even himself. In ten days the project began to be "astonishingly successful." "I can now get in five minutes a strong sharp photograph of the X rays spectrum, which would mean days work by the ionization

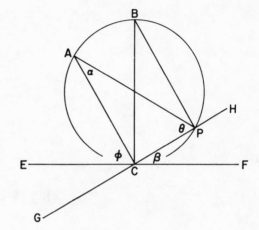

10. The geometry of the rotating crystal. When the crystal face swings from EF to GH the point from which rays of wavelength λ are sent toward B moves from C to P.

method." It had taken him only four days to get the rays from Ti, Cr, Mn, Fe, Co, Ni, and, for good measure, Cu and Ag. "The chief result [he wrote Amabel on November 2] is that all the elements give the same kind of spectrum, the result for any metal being quite easy to guess from the results for the others. This shews that the insides of all the atoms are very much alike, and from these results it will be possible to find out something of what the insides are made up of." In only a fortnight he got the spectra he wanted, the K rays from Ca through Zn; and, as expected, they followed Z rather than A. The whole business was indecently easy. "My work has turned out so extremely interesting and important that I will go on with it for a long time to come, and the only question is where to break off, publish, and start afresh in Oxford. I feel a very selfish fellow over it, as it is so very easy and so little trouble and gives so rich a return for a minimum of work that I should like to keep it all to myself. If I publish, a horde of hungry Germans will be down on it directly, and if I delay perhaps someone will get in ahead." [14] He decided to feed the Germans. On November 16 he informed Bohr of his progress. Two weeks later his preliminary measurements appeared in the *Philosophical Magazine*, illustrated by a diagram now celebrated as "Moseley's

---

[14] 78, 79, 80.

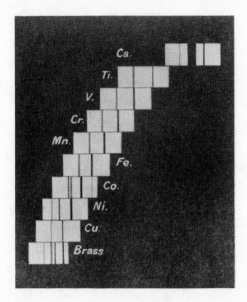

11. "Moseley's step ladder," arranged with frequency decreasing from left to right. The darker of the two lines in each spectrum is K_α, the other K_β; brass shows the spectra of both copper and zinc (not separately given). Plainly an element is missing between calcium and titanium; the truant, scandium ($Z = 21$), was well known, but Moseley had not yet examined a sample when he drew up the ladder. From **VII**.

step-ladder" (fig. 11), in which the regular progression of the K frequencies of the transition metals is brought strikingly before the mind.

The results, he told Bohr, were "exceedingly simple and largely what you would expect." Each element gave two main lines, an α and a β, the former being five times as intense and 10 percent softer than the latter. The frequency of the α component, $\nu_{K\alpha}$, obeyed to within 0.5 percent the formula

$$\nu_{K\alpha}/\nu_0 = (3/4)(Z-1)^2, \tag{3}$$

where ν_0 represents the Rydberg frequency familiar from optical spectra.[15] No doubt it was the dependence on Z^2 which Harry had in mind when he said his results coincided "largely" with his expectations. Very likely he had hit upon equation (3) by plotting the square root of $\nu_{K\alpha}$ against Z, a procedure which Whiddington's law, interpreted in the light of Planck's and van den Broek's hypotheses, would suggest.[16] But no

---

[15] 81; **VII**, 1028–1029.
[16] Equate $h\nu$ for the K ray to the kinetic energy $mv^2/2$ of the exciting cathode ray, and

one, not even Bohr, had anticipated the precision and simplicity of the formula; and we can easily imagine Harry's surprise and excitement at the discovery that the coefficient factored into exactly $(3/4)\nu_0$. For the rough relations from which he and Bohr inferred that ν_K would behave as Z^2 did not authorize exact predictions; and the nuclear model itself would suggest a more complicated dependence, since the electron involved in K emission must interact with other atomic electrons, and that interaction might well alter with Z.[17]

The tantalizing K_α formula, equation (3), was to perplex Harry for the rest of his life. Why did it contain $(Z - 1)$ and not Z? What did the factor 3/4 signify? The formula could be expressed much like Balmer's, by writing the 3/4 as $(1/1^2 - 1/2^2)$; and it could be interpreted, so Harry thought, as a strong support for Bohr's quantized atom. But his arguments, which we will examine later, were scarcely persuasive, and the first advance in the theory of X-ray spectra came from outside Bohr's circle. Fortunately confidence, not understanding, was needed to exploit the formula fully: for assuming, as Moseley did, that it held generally, it afforded an incomparable tool for identifying elements and for probing the periodic table in search of new ones. Only if the known elements had K_α frequencies increasing as $(Z-1)^2$, with no Z's missing, would chemists deserve high marks for discovery. Having used the chemical order, as planned initially, to test the Z dependence of the K frequencies, Harry had the splendid idea of inverting his procedure, making the X rays the final arbiter in a search for missing elements.[18]

The condition of the table in 1913 invited such a probe. Besides the well-known difficulties at cobalt, argon, and tellurium, there were three entire periods about which little agreement obtained. One of these, the elements beyond bismuth, need not concern us, for Moseley did not extend his measurements into the radioelements; the others were the

---

use Whiddington modified by van den Broek: $h\nu = m\nu^2/2 = 4Z^2 \cdot 10^{16}$, a calculation similar to that in **VI**, 223.

[17] Bohr considered his discussion of the frequencies of the K rays in *PM* 26 (1913), 498–502, as a "first approximation"; Bohr to Rutherford, 10 June 13 (AHQP). Hevesy, *Naturwissenschaften* 11 (1923), 604–605, emphasizes the "astounding simplicity" of Harry's results, "a simplicity which the then current state of atomic theory could not predict"; cf. Rutherford, *Nature* 116 (1925), 316–317.

[18] "It [the new X-ray spectroscopy] may even lead to the discovery of missing elements, as it will be possible to predict the position of their characteristic lines" (**VII**, 1030).

short first period, hydrogen and helium, and the sixth period, where the difficulty lay in the rare earths. The uncertainty in the light elements arose largely from hazardous assumptions about the behavior of atomic weights. Since the difference in A between hydrogen and helium is somewhat larger than the average difference, $\overline{\Delta A}$, between contiguous elements throughout the next four periods, it occurred to some bold spirits, like the future Nobel Laureate Alfred Werner, that one or more elements remained undiscovered before and/or between the two members of the first period (fig. 12).[19]

There was no lack of candidates for these positions. Mendeleev himself predicted a new fluorine-like element with $A = 3$, which would not only plug the gap between H and He, but also bring the number of the halogens up to that of the alkalis. He also admitted novelties at $A = 0.17$ and 0.4, which he supposed to be, respectively, the physicists' ether and the source of certain spectral lines in the solar corona. The Jessups, whose speculations about the evolution of the elements Harry had met at Oxford, added "proto-beryllium" ($A = 1.3$) and "proto-boron" ($A = 2$) to account for other lines unattributable to terrestrial substances. Three years later, in 1911/2, J. W. Nicholson succeeded in computing the frequencies of many such lines from three simple models consisting of a nucleus and a single ring of circulating electrons, and each representing, he said, an atom of an element lighter than hydrogen.[20] The claims of two of these elements, "nebulium" and "coronium," already most impressive because of the unprecedented agreement obtained by Nicholson, were further strengthened by the popular numerological system of Johannes Rydberg, which predicted precisely four elements beneath lithium.[21] These often plausible speculations

---

[19] Werner, *New Ideas in Organic Chemistry* (1911), pp. 6–9, computed $\overline{\Delta A}$'s for the second through fifth periods as 1.85, 2.4, 2.47, and 2.5, respectively; and extrapolated $\overline{\Delta A}$ for the first period as 1.5 which, happily, is also half the difference between A_H and A_{He}. He accordingly expected a new element at $A = 2.5$.

[20] D. Mendeleev, *Principles of Chemistry* (1905³), II, 509–529; A. C. and A. E. Jessup, *PM* 15 (1908), 21–55; J. W. Nicholson, *PM* 22 (1911), 864–889, and *Monthly Notices of the Royal Astronomical Society* 72 (1911/2), 49–64, 139–150, 176–177, 677–693, 727–739. Cf. van Spronsen, *Periodic System*, pp. 253, 326–327; R. McCormmach, *AHES* 2 (1966), 160–184; and the curious system of B. K. Emerson, *American Chemical J* 45 (1911), 162–164, 173: the electron, coronium, H, nebulium ($A = 2$), proto-fluorine (the missing halogen patriarch, $A = 3$), He.

[21] Rydberg, *Årsskrift Lund Universitet* 9:2 (1913), 1–41, suggested, on the basis of his own computation of $\overline{\Delta A}$, that the number of elements in the pth grand period is $4p^2$, where

WERNER'S ARRANGEMENT.

—																										He 4
H 1·008																										—
Li 7·03	Be 9·1																B 11	C 12	N 14·04	O 16·00	F 19	Ne 20
Na 23·05	Mg 24·36																Al 27·1	Si 28·4	P 31·0	S 32·06	Cl 35·45	A 39·9
K 39·15	Ca 40·1	Sc 44·1	Ti 48·1	V 51·2	Cr 52·1	Mn 55·0	Fe 55·9	Co 59·0	Ni 58·7	Cu 63·6	Zn 65·4	Ga 70	Ge 72	As 75·0	Se 79·1	Br 79·96	Kr 81·12
Rb 85·4	Sr 87·6	Y 89·0	Zr 90·7	Nb 94	Mo 96·0	—	Ru 101·7	Rh 108·0	Pd 106	Ag 107·98	Cd 112·4	In 114	Sn 118·5	Sb 120	Te 127·6	I 126·96	X 128
Cs 133	Ba 137·4	La 138	Ta 188	W 184·0	—	Os 191	Ir 198·0	Pt 194·8	Au 197·2	Hg 200·8	Tl 204·1	Pb 206·9	Bi 208·5	Te a ?	—	—
—	Ra 225	La.. ?	Th 232·5											Pb a ?	Bi a ?	Te a ?

Rare earths: La 138 | Ce 140 | Pr 140·5 | Nd 143·6 | — | Sa 150·3 | Eu 151·79 | Gd 156 | Tb 160 | Ho 163 | Er 166 | Tu 171 | Yb 173·0 | U 239·5 | Ac ?

12. Werner's periodic table, a typical pre-Moseley representation of the respectively speculative type. Of particular interest are the three spaces below hydrogen and helium, that between hydrogen and helium, and those in the rare earths. From Werner, *New Ideas in Chemistry* (1911).

regarding the population of the first period greatly obscured the idea of atomic number.

The difficulties in the rare earths had a more practical nature. As most of the more cautious chemists counted, beginning with one at hydrogen and leaving a space between molybdenum and ruthenium for a missing homologue of manganese ("eka-manganese," $Z = 43$), the rare earths commenced with lanthanum at number 57 and ended before tantalum; but as it was quite uncertain how many lanthanides existed, the serial number of tantalum could not be fixed. (These details may be followed with the help of the periodic charts of figure 17, which are correct except for including 72 among the earths.)

By heroic applications of the tedious methods of fractional crystallization the chemists of the last century had managed to separate twelve bona fide lanthanides from the highly complex minerals in which they occur. As it happened, only one of them, "ytterbia," split off by J. C. G. de Marignac in 1878, contained an undetected element; but that did not prevent enthusiasts from proposing a dozen more, and giving them names even more barbaric than those of the true earths.[22] With the splitting of ytterbia, which occurred in 1905/6 under circumstances we must briefly examine, chemists had reached the end of their powers, a fact which none could have known and few would have welcomed.[23]

Marignac's ytterbia was first divided by Carl Auer von Welsbach (1858–1929), who had had a similar success with "didymia" in 1885. About 1900, having invented the incandescent gas mantle and made himself a millionaire and a baron, Auer turned his attention to ytterbia, then the heaviest of the recognized lanthanides.[24] After thousands of

"grand period" denotes two consecutive ordinary periods. (Both the usual second and third periods correspond to $p = 2$, each having half the $4 \cdot 4 = 16$ elements; and likewise the fourth and fifth periods each have 18 of the $4 \cdot 9 = 36$ of the third grand period.) The first grand period, which should have four members, evidently wanted two elements. Cf. W. M. Hicks, *PM* 28 (1914), 139–142; *infra*, p. 114; and the similar system in Werner, *New Ideas*, pp. 6–9.

[22] See, e.g., C. Baskerville, *Science* 17 (1903), 77–81, and 19 (1904), 88–106; R. J. Meyer in R. Abegg, ed., *Handbuch der anorganischen Chemie* III:3 (1906), 139–142; G. Urbain in M. A. Haller, ed., *Les recents progrès de la chimie* III (1908), 37–66; and M. E. Weeks, *Discovery of the Elements* (1956⁶), pp. 695–727.

[23] Although there are 14 lanthanides in all (and 15 rare earths including lanthanum), one, promethium ($Z=61$), does not appear to exist naturally.

[24] J. d'Ans, *Berichte der deutschen chemischen Gesellschaft* 64:1A (1930), 59–92; A. Skrabal, *Neue österreichische Biographie* VII (1931), 46–56; C. R. Böhm, *Das*

fractionations carried out in the laboratory in his Austrian castle, Auer obtained crystals and a mother liquor of sufficiently different spectroscopic properties to enable him to notify the Viennese Academy of Sciences of the existence of a new earth. That was in 1905. He gave no details, however, until 1907, when he presented the Academy with measurements of the optical spectra and atomic weights of the two ytterbia components, which he proposed to call "aldebaranium" and "cassiopeium." [25] Meanwhile Georges Urbain (1872–1938), Professor of Chemistry at the École de Physique et Chimie Industrielles in Paris, had announced the partition of Marignac's earth. Urbain gave fewer lines than Auer was to provide and notably inferior weights, which showed that he had not carried the separation as far; but he was undoubtedly the first to publish data on the new elements, which he called "neo-ytterbium," after Marignac, and "lutecium," after the Latin name for Paris. In 1908 the International Committee on Atomic Weights, of which Urbain had just become a member, recognized his priority and adopted his names, to the intense and undying indignation of the Baron von Welsbach.[26]

The rivals redoubled their efforts. Auer picked on thulium whose spectra, he said, betrayed the presence of at least three new atomic species which, however, he was never able to isolate. Urbain was luckier. At the Sorbonne, where he became professor in 1908, he labored over his lutecium for three years, refining it through tens of thousands of crystallizations until, in 1911, he found a substance with entirely new magnetic and spectroscopic properties in the mother liquor of the most soluble fractions. He regarded this substance, which he called "celtium," as elemental. The International Committee declined to certify it, because Urbain had not determined its atomic weight. The committee

Gasglühlicht (1905), pp. 1–68. The cheap and plentiful wastes of the Welsbach lighting companies greatly stimulated the study of the chemistry of the lanthanides and the radioelements, for a principal ingredient of the Auer mantle, thorium, occurs naturally only in combination with rare and radioactive earths. Cf. Baskerville, *Science* 17 (1903), 77–81; Meyer in Abegg, *Handbuch* III:3, 138; and Badash, pp. 39, 81, 162, 209, 325–326.

[25] Auer, *Sb* (Vienna) 115:2b (1906), 737–747, and 116:2b (1907), 1425–1469. See F. Sedlacek, *Auer von Welsbach* (1934), pp. 66–68.

[26] Urbain, *CR* 145 (1907), 759–762; *Annales de chimie* 11 (1939), 5–9; *JACS* 30:1 (1908), 4; Auer, *Sb* (Vienna) 118:2b (1909), 507–512. See F. Exner and E. Hascheck, *Sb* (Vienna) 119:2a (1910), 771–778.

was quite correct—indeed its table of 1912 contained precisely the right number of éarths—for "celtium" was nothing other than lutecium of about the purity of Auer's cassiopeium.[27] Nonetheless celtium received a home in many contemporary periodic tables and, along with Auer's multiple thuliums, was regarded as the least problematic of the dozen or so supernumerary earths as yet unrecognized by the International Committee on Atomic Weights.

Among Harry's few surviving papers is a periodic table published by the Eton College Scientific Society and used by him in his earliest studies of chemistry. He has circled the rare earths, including their lighter homologue yttrium, and guessed that europium, which was not fully accepted until Urbain's work of 1904, should occupy one of the six spaces the society had left blank in the vain hope of fitting the lanthanides into the periodic system. He soon abandoned these precocious speculations and, like most physicists, knew little about the earths when the unexpected ease of X-ray spectroscopy returned his attention to them. He then carefully studied the literature, with the help of a Manchester friend who read German more easily than he did;[28] and he was doubtless amused to discover the extent of the chemists' confusion, which he proposed to dispel with a few blasts from his X-ray machine.

The great work was done in Oxford, where Harry moved at the end of November 1913, immediately after writing up his experiments on the K rays of the transition metals. He had no official position at Oxford. Townsend gave him space in the Electrical Laboratory and "every facility," but no financial support; and he required all his "patience and tact" to assemble enough apparatus to continue his researches. He captured a Gaede pump from the Balliol-Trinity Laboratory, and "after some difficulty" a spectrometer accurate to 1' of arc, perhaps from the Clarendon's excellent untouched collection of optical instruments. Other things had to be bought with the help of a grant Harry had

[27] F. W. C. Clarke et al., *JACS* 34 (1912), 1437–1440; cf. van Spronsen, *Periodic System*, pp. 260–273.

[28] Among Harry's papers at OHS are four sheets of notes in an unidentified hand on Meyer's introduction to rare-earth chemistry (in Abegg, *Handbuch* III:1, 129–142); and, in the same hand, on a letterhead from "15 Oak Road, Withington, Manchester," a list of the earths recognized in 1913.

received from the newly founded Solvay Institute. It all proved a great
drain on his small stock of patience, especially as his old X-ray tube
broke about Christmas time, when Townsend's overworked mechanic, "a
thorn in the flesh," could not be expected to mend or replace it. Other
lackadaisical "villains," like Messrs Cossor of London, from whom
Moseley had ordered many special bulbs, declined to rush about his
business.[29] "A natural and deserved run of ill-luck," as he put it, had
reduced him to half-speed just as he began to implement his most
ambitious research plans.

He envisaged a simultaneous, threefold investigation, which would
measure the hard K rays of the fifth period (Rb to I), the soft K's below
Al and the soft L's below Ag, and the moderately penetrating L's of the
rare earths. Each project had its own special difficulties. With the hard
K's the general "white" X radiation becomes important: to produce
them, the beam must strike the crystal at small angles ϕ, where the
general reflection is large; Barkla fringes then become prominent and
sometimes mask the high-frequency lines.[30] The soft K and L rays
required more elaborate arrangements. Too effete to penetrate the air or
the wrappings of the photographic plate, they recorded themselves only
in vacuo; so Moseley commissioned a spectrometer from Cook, the
instrument maker at Manchester, which admitted the X-ray beam
directly into an evacuated space containing the crystal and the plate (fig.
13). The rare earths offered a challenge of a different kind. Only a few
could be bought commercially, and they often were "fearful mixtures,"
with impurities amounting to over 50 percent. For the rare rare earths,
some of which existed only in the preparations of their discoverers, Harry
had to appeal to Crookes and Urbain, and to his friends Fajans and
Hevesy, whom he mobilized to search the Germanies.[31]

By the middle of January 1914, Moseley had acquired commercially
pure samples of eight rare earths, and was just beginning to break into
stride again. By the end of the month he had measured the strongest L

[29] 84, 85, 87; Hartley to N. G. Thomas, 23 June 15 (R). The Comité scientifique de
l'Institut International de Physique Solvay (of which Rutherford was a member) granted
HM 1,000 Belgian francs on 7 Nov 13 (Solvay Archives, Brussels, courtesy of J. Pelseneer);
Laue and Bragg received similar grants (1000 and 1500 francs, respectively).
[30] 87, 88; C. G. Barkla and G. H. Martyn, *Nature* 90 (1913), 647.
[31] 86, 87, 88, 90, IX.

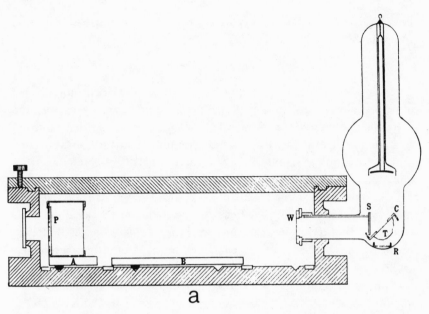

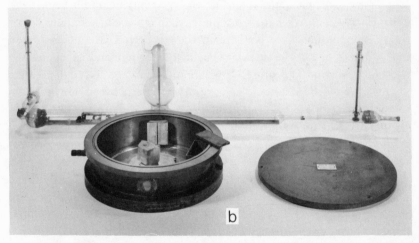

13. Moseley's definitive apparatus ror obtaining sott X rays (a) schematic diagram, where R designates the rails, C the carriage bearing the samples, S a collimating slit, W a window of gold-beaters' skin separating the generating tube from the spectrometer, B the spectrometer table, and A the table supporting the photographic plate P, from IX (b) what remains of the apparatus, courtesy of OHS.

line, L_α, in seven metals from ruthenium (44) to antimony (51), which he found to fit the expression

$$\nu_{L\alpha}/\nu_0 = (1/2^2 - 1/3^2)(Z - s_n)^2, \qquad (4)$$

and that was "a great piece of luck," as he told Darwin, for he had already published the formula, "on the slenderest of evidence," in the December *Philosophical Magazine*.[32] During February he marched forward on all fronts with his wonted rapidity, and early in March he sent Rutherford the results of a spotty survey of elements stretching from aluminum (13) to gold (79).

This report exudes a confidence remarkable even for Harry. He had measured K_α for eighteen elements from aluminum to palladium (46), including the ten from calcium (20) to zinc (30) he had already investigated. Of the eight new elements, four—yttrium (39), zirconium (40), molybdenum (42) and palladium (46)—were beyond zinc. Through some error in computation, he made these last four respectively 40, 41, 43, and 47, in order to preserve the factor $(Z-1)^2$ in the K_α formula. Since only eight elements were known between zinc and yttrium, and since Harry supposed that strontium, which he had not yet tried, would be 38, he announced to Rutherford the existence of an undiscovered element at $Z = 39$. He himself thought it "very probable" that this shy substance was nothing other than Urbain's celtium. Now all periodic charts left a place for a homologue of manganese between molybdenum and ruthenium (i.e., at $Z = 43$), but it was not the relocation of this hole that Harry had in mind; our fearless physicist, in opposition to three generations of chemists, wished to introduce *another* unknown element into the fifth period of Mendeleev's table. Forty-three became forty-four, and all the elements at least to the equivocal rare earths were pushed one place to the right. Among other inconveniences, bromine would then fall into the noble gases and krypton into the alkalis! One could scarcely find a better index of the strength of Harry's convictions and the independence of his mind.

With the help of the L_α lines Harry extended his curious attribution of atomic numbers up to gold (79), which he made 80. Having fixed molybdenum at 43 via K_α, he found that the L_α rays of fourteen elements

---

[32] **89; VII**, 1033. The "slenderest evidence" was L_α for Ta $(Z=73)$ and Pt $(Z=78)$.

from niobium to gold satisfied equation (4) with $s_n = 8.4$; the only space in the sixth period, ignoring the rare earths, was the second homologue of manganese located by the chemists at $Z = 75$, and by Moseley at 76. The poor quality of the commercial samples made the rare earths temporarily intractable. But with specimens recently received from Crookes, and with others coming from Urbain, Harry expected to be able to redeem his boast to Hevesy, and "to put every rare-earth element into its right pigeon-hole." [33]

After sending this report, Harry had misgivings. He repeated his calculations, and discovered an error which threw off all his numbers from yttrium on. Consequently his table did not differ from the chemists'; the missing element at 39 was a myth; and spaces did exist at 43 and 75. He sent these corrections to Rutherford immediately, and published the emended version in the April number of the *Philosophical Magazine*. The paper differs from the reports to Rutherford in giving scattered measurements of additional lines (K_β, L_β L_ϕ, and L_γ) and in treating the rare earths, of which Harry had by then investigated lanthanum to neodymium (57–60), samarium to gadolinium (62–64), dysprosium (66) and erbium (68). With those chemists who (largely on the basis of $\overline{\Delta A}$) recognized a gap between neodymium and samarium, he left 61 blank, and, following Auer, he admitted two thuliums. He consequently made rare earths of the sixteen elements from lanthanum up to tantalum, which he had fixed at 73 via L_α; the last four (69–72), which he had not fully measured, being thulium I, thulium II, ytterbium and lutecium (fig. 14). As for number 61, he hinted that it might be the elusive celtium, a conjecture he made explicitly in a letter to Hevesy, whom he assured as usual that "there can [now] . . . be no doubt" about the order of the lanthanides. In fact he had mixed up holmium and dysprosium, allowed two thuliums, made element 72 a rare earth and moved ytterbium and lutecium each up one unit, for five errors among the last six earths. By the last week in April, however, he had rectified his impetuous mistakes, and sent Hevesy the "correct order." The new scheme was indeed correct, with the exception of the irrepressible celtium, which Harry made element 72.[34]

---

[33] **88, 90.**

[34] **93, 94.** HM managed to correct the confusion between Ds and Ho before distributing reprints (J. R. Rydberg, *PM* 28 [1914], 144–149). It is amusing that in the published paper

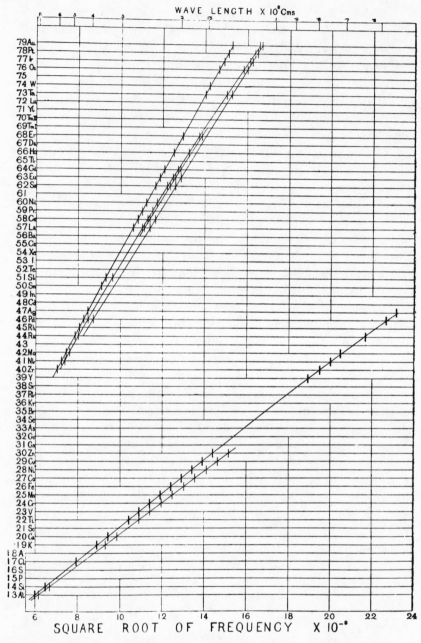

14. Moseley's last survey of the X-ray emission spectra. Reading from the bottom, the lines chart K_α, K_β, L_α, L_β, L_ϕ, L_γ, respectively, from **IX**.

The power of Harry's method appeared most convincingly in the rare earths, for he could know in minutes the contents of a sample which a chemist might take years to analyze. The practical possibilities did not escape Urbain, who in the middle of May 1914 decided to carry his specimens to Oxford; he was eager to try the last four earths, which he had fixed at thulium, ytterbium, lutecium and celtium, an arrangement that had the double advantage of establishing the elemental status of celtium and discrediting Auer's second thulium. Urbain and his wife arrived on June 2nd, and stayed two days. Although neither spoke English, and their host was restricted to what he called "dog French," no doubt learned on his Alpine expeditions, the visit proved most fruitful. The precious tubes containing the world's only celtium turned out to hold nothing more interesting than lutecium and neoytterbium, to Urbain's intense disappointment; which, however, eased somewhat when the celebrated thulium II likewise refused to put in an appearance. Elements 61 and 72 (as well as the long-expected homologues of manganese, 43 and 75) remained at large. The speed and reliability of Moseley's technique flabbergasted Urbain. He left eight samples for further analysis and returned to Paris, having untangled in a few days conundrums that had taken chemists six generations merely to propose.[35]

Moseley also learned something from Urbain. He had tried to engage his visitor in a discussion of the physical meaning of the K and L formulae, and found a barrier deeper than language. "I gathered from [Urbain] that the French point of view is essentially different from the English. Where we try to find models or analogies, they are quite content with laws." It is most interesting that Moseley had not met with Urbain's brand of continental positivism earlier. The fundamental difference between the French and English approaches had been widely discussed since the time of Maxwell, and the peculiar need of the British physicist for "the robust form and vivid colouring of a physical illustration," for something to lend "human interest" to the "tenuity and paleness of a symbolic expression," was recognized on both sides of the

---

Moseley calls elements 71 and 72 Yb and Lu (Urbain's names), while in his letter to Hevesy of 20 Mar 14 (**93**) he makes them aldebaranium and cassiopeium (Auer's names) so as not to hurt Hevesy's Hungarian feelings.

[35] **96, 97, 103**; Diary, 2–4 June 14; Urbain, *CR* 174 (1922), 1349–1351; Urbain to Rutherford, 26 Sept 15 (OHS). Cf. P. M. Heimann, *Annals of Science* 23 (1967), 249–260.

channel.[36] Perhaps the closeness and unself-consciousness of Rutherford's school had caused Moseley to overlook the existence of an alternative approach to physics.[37] He never doubted that part of his task was to link his formulas to an atomic model.

Bohr's second paper on the constitution of atoms and molecules, published in September 1913, touches twice on the problem of X rays and atomic structure. One consideration seeks to show that K rays originate in a disturbance of an electron in the *innermost* ring. Assuming that such an electron circulates about a nucleus of charge Z, and ignoring the effect of other electrons, the angular-momentum condition and the force balance give for v, the electron's orbital velocity,

$$v = (2\pi e^2/h)Z = 2.1 \cdot 10^8 Z \text{ cm/sec.}[38]$$

The total energy of an electron bound by an inverse-square force is the negative of its kinetic energy, which equals the energy required to remove it from the atom; a cathode-ray particle with velocity v could therefore just knock such an electron out of its orbit. But Whiddington's formula requires that the cathode-ray particle have a velocity $A \cdot 10^8$ cm/sec to excite the K radiation in an atom of weight A. Equating the two values for v, $Z = A/2$, the approximate Rutherfordian relation from which van den Broek proceeded. Bohr thought this result a convincing support for the assumption from which he derived it, namely that K radiation involves the innermost electron ring.

The second consideration concerned the population of the electron rings. Here Bohr, who had no principles sufficient to solve the problem, was much less successful and persuasive than anywhere else in his

---

[36] **96**; J. J. Thomson in *James Clerk Maxwell, A Commemoration Volume* (1931), p. 31; G. F. Fitzgerald, *Nature* 53 (1896), 441–442. See P. Duhem, *Aim and Structure of Physical Theory* (1954), pp. 55–104. Urbain did not deny the value of physical models or analogies—"Nous ne pensons que par des images et l'image atomique accroît notre pussance d'apprendre et de créer," (*Revue du mois* 7 [1909], 419)—but, like most of his countrymen, he did not care to elaborate them.

[37] Harry's missing this point is particularly interesting since the introduction to Svedberg's *Die Existenz der Moleküle* (1912), pp. v–vi, a book he reviewed, discusses an extreme form of the continental view, energetics.

[38] The quantum condition is $2\pi mrv = h$; the force balance gives $Ze^2/r^2 = mv^2/r$. By elimination, $v = (2\pi e^2/h)Z$. Note that this formula also suggests $\nu_K = \text{const}.Z^2$, if one equates the binding energy, $mv^2/2$, with $h\nu_K$.

fundamental papers of 1913. He could calculate the energies of electronic configurations, neglecting forces between rings and assuming the supposed universal condition on the angular momentum; but these calculations often gave for the lowest energy a ground-state configuration— such as a single three-electron ring for lithium—which seemed impossible for chemical reasons. Consequently Bohr had to sense his way through the first twenty-four elements of the periodic table, assigning ground-state configurations as much by instinct as by principle. Calcium, for example, he endowed with the structure 8,8,2,2, where the numbers from left to right designate the ring populations, counting from the nucleus outwards. For the theory of K radiation the innermost ring of eight electrons is of particular interest; Bohr thought it came in with neon (8,2) and persisted to the iron group, where it filled out to 18.

As soon as Moseley obtained the K_α formula and noticed its close resemblance to Balmer's law, he tried to relate his results to the special principles Bohr had used to explain the visible spectrum of hydrogen. In November 1913 he had excitedly informed Bohr that the X rays confirmed the quantum condition on the angular momentum. Assume, he wrote, that K radiation comes from an innermost ring of n electrons, and that n remains the same for all $Z > 20$. The equation of equilibrium for each such electron is

$$m\omega^2 r = (e^2/r^2)(Z - s_n), \tag{5}$$

where s_n represents the combined effect of the other $n - 1$ electrons on the one in question, ω being the angular velocity of the ring and r its radius. Since, by hypothesis, s_n does not change with Z, equation (5) implies that

$$(\omega^2 r^3)_{Z+1} - (\omega^2 r^3)_Z$$

is a constant. But from Moseley's measurements the same can be said of $(\sqrt{\nu})_{Z+1} - (\sqrt{\nu})_Z$. Therefore, he said, in a non sequitur he was to repeat in print, $\omega^2 r^3/\sqrt{\nu}$ must be a constant.[39] To obtain Bohr's principle from this last proposition Moseley had to show that $\nu \propto \omega$; for then $r^3 \omega^{3/2}$, and consequently the angular momentum $m(r^3\omega^{3/2})^{2/3}$, would be

---

[39] A non sequitur because it tacitly equates $Z - s_n$ with $Z - 1$. (If $\omega^2 r^3 = Z + a$, and $\sqrt{\nu} = Z + b$, $\omega^2 r^3/\sqrt{\nu}$ is independent of Z only if $a = b$.) Cf. **81**; **VII**, 1032; W. L. Bragg, *JRE* 11 (1914), 367.

constant. The demonstration committed him to a very curious view of K emission.

The emitted frequency ν will be proportional to the angular velocity ω if the K rays arise either from a *transition* of the innermost ring *as a whole*, or from the transverse vibrations of the ring in its ground state. For the latter case the proportionality follows directly from the ordinary mechanics, which Bohr thought applicable to oscillations perpendicular to the plane of the electron rings. For the transition of the ring as a whole Moseley probably intended the following argument. The ring's initial energy, on Bohr's principles, is $-nh\nu_0(Z - s_n)^2$, and its excited energy in a two-quantum level, $-nh\nu_0(Z - s_n)^2/4$; the assumption that the ring moves as a whole preserves the factor $Z - s_n$. Employing Planck's relation, $\nu = $ (difference in energy)$/h$, $\nu_K = (3/4)\nu_0(Z - s_n)^2$. But ω in the initial state is $4\pi\nu_0(Z - s_n)^2$, whence $\nu_K \propto \omega$, *quod erat demonstrandum*.

This argument has required two sleights of hand. The first, the non sequitur signaled earlier, tacitly made $s_n = 1$, and thereby caused Moseley explicitly to abandon Bohr's structures for elements beyond calcium. He took the innermost ring to contain just half the eight electrons Bohr had prescribed, for the only value of s_n close to unity, 0.96, occurs at $n = 4$. This conclusion, coupled with the assumption that the ring moved as a whole, required the second bit of legerdemain; for Planck's condition would lead one to expect *one* quantum $h(4\nu_K)$ from the transition of the four ring and not *four* quanta $h\nu_K$, as Moseley—who in this perhaps copied a discarded procedure of Bohr's—quietly assumed.[40] In his picture four K_α quanta each of frequency $(3/4)\nu_0(Z - 0.96)^2$ accompany the return to normal of a four-electron ring previously excited to the second Bohr stationary state. Among other difficulties this mechanism has the serious flaw, which Moseley himself emphasized, of requiring four times the excitation energy implied by Whiddington's relation.

Consequently Moseley half-heartedly proposed a second possibility

---

[40] HM also let this second sleight of hand pass into print (**VII**, 1033); it still succeeds (P. M. Heimann, *Centaurus* 12 [1968], 261–274), although Nicholson immediately caught it ([E. Rutherford *et al.*], *Discussion on the Structure of the Atom* [1914], p. 14). For Bohr's similar maneuver see Bohr, *PM* 26 (1913), 1–3, and Heilbron and Kuhn, *HSPS* 1 (1969), 270.

to Bohr, one which avoided the energy difficulty at the exorbitant price of altering van den Broek's hypothesis. Perhaps, he suggested, the innermost ring contains not four but only one electron, and two elements below calcium have the same atomic number! The electron would then feel a nuclear charge of $(Z-1)e$, and emit a frequency $(3/4)\nu_0(Z-1)^2$ in passing from the second to the ground state. Such a possibility would evidently undermine the entire periodic arrangement, and Moseley's probing of it, for there might then be any number of undiscovered elements associated with a given Z. Bohr replied that energy considerations ruled out the four-quantum mechanism, and passed over in silence his correspondent's lapse from orthodoxy. He was, however, unable to offer any "valuable suggestion," other than to propose that the energy radiated as K_α came from the rearrangement of the innermost ring following the expulsion of one of its members, viz.,

$$\nu_{K\alpha}/\nu_0 = n(Z-s_n)^2 - (n-1)(Z-s_{n-1})^2 \sim$$
$$[Z - \{ns_n - (n-1)s_{n-1}\}]^2.$$

But even if an n exists which makes the expression in curly brackets unity, the scheme cannot supply the essential factor $3/4$. Bohr saw no way to go. "For the present [he said] I have stopped speculating on atoms." [41]

Although Moseley could not quite interpret his results in terms of his friend's quantized atom, he did not doubt that they supported Bohr's theory, and he confidently said so in the *Philosophical Magazine* for December 1913. Bohr and Rutherford agreed;[42] people outside the Manchester group did not. Criticism came from physicists both friendly and averse to the Bohr theory, and among the latter the bellicose F. A. Lindemann led the van. Only a year older than Moseley, Lindemann already enjoyed an international reputation: in 1910 he had completed

---

[41] Bohr to Moseley, 21 Nov 13 (83). Although Bohr's suggestion led to a fruitless expression, it had the advantage (against Harry's) of remaining close to his new principles, which he was not prepared to relax to accommodate Moseley's formulae. Bohr here anticipated later work based upon the "true" mechanism of X-ray emission: the fall of an electron into a vacancy within the atom caused by the removal of a deep-lying electron by an external agent (*infra*, p. 129).

[42] Rutherford to Bohr, 11 Dec 13, and Bohr to Rutherford, 21 Dec 13 (AHQP); Bohr, *Nature* 92 (1914), 554; Rutherford, *Discussion*, pp. 4–5. The Braggs (*X Rays* [1915], p. 84) considered Harry's efforts to forge agreement with Bohr "interesting" and "remarkable."

experiments in collaboration with his mentor, W. Nernst, directed towards confirming Einstein's quantum theory of specific heats, and the following year he had joined his friend Maurice de Broglie as one of the secretaries of the first Solvay Congress. In 1912 Lindemann began to work on X rays in de Broglie's private laboratory in Paris. A practiced juggler with numbers, he took an immediate dislike to Bohr's theory, which he conceived to be nothing but numerology; and when Moseley asserted that X rays, on which Lindemann now fancied himself an expert, confirmed the obnoxious atom, "F.A." slashed out at him in the pages of *Nature*.[43]

Dimensional considerations alone, he wrote, could supply the general form of the K_α formula and, moreover, suggested how to handle K_β, which Moseley had unjustifiably neglected. For what can ν depend on but the amounts of positive and negative charge (Ze and $-ne$), the mass and separation of the electrons (m and r), and, "if we wish to introduce the quanta, upon Planck's element of action h"? These quantities may be combined in any number of ways to give the dimension of ν; and in the particular case where r is omitted,

$$\nu = \text{const.} n^2 Z^2 e^4 m / h^3,$$

or $\text{const.} \nu_0 n^2 Z^2$. If but a single electron vibrates, $n = 1$, and the K_α formula, or something very like it, appears; and if r is retained formulae emerge which might correspond to other lines, like the mysterious K_β. Moseley's experiments, according to Lindemann, only identified Z as the atomic number: they supported van den Broek, not Bohr. This pettifoggery appeared on New Year's Day, 1914. Two weeks later Bohr and Moseley each replied in separate letters to *Nature*. Bohr took his usual modest tack and limited himself to observing that he had computed the Balmer frequencies exactly, while dimensional analysis must necessarily leave numerical factors undetermined. Moseley gave a fuller and less satisfactory answer.

He argued from what he called the h hypothesis, which he might better have named the "h constraint," namely that the atom builder must introduce nothing but the quantities m, h and e into his

---

[43] Lindemann to *Nature*, 28 Dec 13 (*Nature* 92 [1 Jan 14], 500–501); Earl of Birkenhead, *The Professor and the Prime Minister* (1962), pp. 19–44; G. P. Thomson, ORS 4 (1958), 45–71.

calculations.[44] This premised, Lindemann's *r* falls out, together with all the alternatives it made possible, and dimensional analysis gives but one form for *ν*,

$$\nu = f \cdot e^4 m / h^3,$$

where *f* is a pure number derivable from *Z* and the geometry of the atomic model assumed. If $f = 2\pi^2$, one obtains ν_0, the Rydberg frequency; if $f = 2\pi^2 \cdot (3/4)(Z-1)^2$, the K_α formula results. "The simplicity of the expression *f* in these two cases [according to Moseley] is itself an argument in favour of the *h* hypothesis." Now of the three *h* atoms then competing,[45] he continued, only Bohr's explained why *f* is $2\pi^2$ in the optical case and "demanded" that the principal X-ray frequency be given by $f = 2\pi^2 \cdot (3/4)(Z-1)^2$! Since Bohr had published no K_α formula, and the view outlined in his letter of November 1913 suggested a quite different form for *f*, it was fortunate that Harry had discovered in the laboratory just what the theory "demanded." The factor $Z-1$ remained troublesome. Moseley repeated his earlier conjectures, again emphasized the energetic difficulty of the four ring, and conceded that neither scheme accommodated K_β. He ended rather less confident than he began. "Either Bohr's theory or my interpretation of it requires modification."

Moseley's defense failed to persuade. Lindemann's charge of number juggling remained colorable; for only by deriving the constant *f* could Moseley go beyond dimensional analysis, and it was precisely that derivation that he could not accomplish. Whatever one thought of Bohr's procedures—and many besides Lindemann thought them ad hoc—they were not corroborated by Harry's elucidation of the K_α formula. Lindemann did not content himself with this small victory, however, and he issued an outrageous reply, captious on the theoretical

[44] HM to *Nature*, 5 Jan 14 (**VIII**). The problem of fixing the size of atoms by universal constants goes back at least to J. Larmor's *Aether and Matter* (1900), pp. 189–193; it had concerned Bohr particularly in the summer of 1912, in his last weeks at Manchester (Heilbron and Kuhn, *HSPS* 1 [1969], 237–255).

[45] The other two being Thomson's, *PM* 26 (1913), 792–799, and Nicholson's, for which see Heilbron and Kuhn, *HSPS* 1 (1969), 258–263, and R. McCormmach, *AHES* 2 (1966), 160–184.

side and deceitful on the experimental. Moseley considered it dishonest, and declined to respond.[46]

It appears that more moved Lindemann than the thirst for knowledge. For one, Moseley's sudden intervention had cut across the bows of the duc de Broglie, who had confessed himself "annoyed" by it, and especially by Harry's grabbing the prominent lines alone, without stopping to "explore the total spectrum." No doubt Lindemann hoped that his attack might help even matters for his friend. And for himself. For Lindemann had begun to fish for Clifton's chair, and could not have failed to recognize a strong threat in Harry.[47]

A more friendly critic followed Lindemann into the lists. J. W. Nicholson, the designer of successful models of spurious atoms, thought Bohr's theory of one-electron systems "very attractive," but its extension to higher atoms wholly unjustified, either in Bohr's own view or in Moseley's interpretation.[48] Bohr's principles, according to Nicholson, made Saturnian atoms—coaxial electron rings—impossible, taking literally the requirements that in the ground state each electron possess angular momentum $h/2\pi$ and (except as regards radiation) obey the ordinary mechanics. Then, he claimed, the electrons either must move in different planes, or they must all lie on the same circle, whose radius might well change with time.[49] He did not prove this proposition in

[46] Lindemann to *Nature*, 25 Jan 14 (*Nature* 92 [5 Feb 14]), 631; **90**. The charge that Bohr had required an ad hoc hypothesis was not altogether ill-founded; cf. Heilbron and Kuhn, *HSPS* 1 (1969), 266.

[47] De Broglie to Lindemann, 18 Dec 13 (FAL, box 80): "J'ai été naturellement ennuyé de voir dans le Phil. Mag. le travail de Moseley, il est certain que nous faisons presque la même chose, bien qu'il semble ne pas explorer aussi bien l'ensemble du spectre." See Tizard to Lindemann, 9 Dec 13 (FAL, misc): "Moseley has been doing photos of X ray spectra of metals—I think probably on the same lines as de Broglie." Lindemann's designs on the Oxford succession appear from a New Year's card from de Broglie, 31 Dec 13 (FAL, box 80), wishing "en particulier que vous pourrez bientôt rendre à la chaise de physique d'Oxford la celebrité que le collaborateur de Townsend a laisseé un peu obscurcir depuis quarante années"; and from Lindemann to his father, 19 Nov 13 (FAL, box 97).

[48] Nicholson, *Nature* 92 (1914), 583–584; *PM* 27 (1914), 541–564; *PM* 28 (1914), 90–103; *Monthly Notices of the Royal Astronomical Society* 74 (1914), 425–442; Rutherford, *Discussion*, pp. 12–15.

[49] As would be the case if each electron described an appropriately phased elliptical orbit. Cf. G. A. Schott, *Electromagnetic Radiation* (1911); Bohr, *PM* 26 (1913), 21; and A. Sommerfeld, *Atombau und Spektrallinien* (1922³), p. 612.

general, but he neatly showed that it sufficed to destroy Bohr's lithium atom (2,1). Consequently lithium must be either a single ring or a three-dimensional structure, and in neither case could it consist of only three electrons. From Bohr's criteria that an atom of nuclear charge N and n electrons will only gain or lose an electron, respectively, when the energy of the configuration $(N, n \pm 1)$ is less than that of the arrangement (N, n), it follows readily that a neutral, single, three-electron ring is inert. Not until $N = 6$, carbon on van den Broek's hypothesis, does an atom appear with properties approaching lithium's. If, on the other hand, a spatial model is preferred, the simplest satisfactory arrangement Nicholson found involved four electrons. It seemed best to him to admit the existence of one or more unknown inert elements between helium and hydrogen.

Moreover, the K_α spectrum, as elucidated by Nicholson, implied more elements than van den Broek allowed. Assuming Moseley's mechanism and associating K_α with the "vibration" of the atom as a whole,[50] the nuclear charge N of, say, calcium, must satisfy the condition $N - s_N = 19$. But since s_N increases with N and exceeds three for $N >$ 10, N for calcium must be larger than 20: and therefore the serial number of the periodic table neither equals, nor even approximates, the nuclear charge. According to Nicholson, who in this respect gave less than Lindemann, Moseley's results neither supported Bohr's theory of the higher elements, nor confirmed van den Broek's hypothesis; they showed merely that the "frequencies of the principal X rays of the elements are proportional to the squares of natural numbers." This conclusion, which today might appear reckless, was neither ill-considered nor isolated.[51] In his last professional appearance, as we shall see, Moseley quite failed to persuade the physicists and chemists of the British Association for the

---

[50] Nicholson recognized the difficulty in the number of quanta emitted, and that Harry had misapplied the Bohr theory in this connection. It is noteworthy that even when using Bohr's radiation theory both Moseley and Nicholson misleadingly speak of "vibrating" rings.

[51] Bohr could not find fault with Nicholson's arguments, which had been closely examined by a former student of Hilbert's, L. Föppel (*PZs* 15 [1914], 707–712). Bohr's response (*PM* 30 [1915], 394–415) was not to allow them much force: rather than relinquish the general features of his ring atom, he was prepared to relax still further the dominion of mechanics in microphysics.

Advancement of Science that his results confirmed the doctrine of atomic number.

Whether or not one agreed with Moseley's interpretation of his experiments, one could not doubt their theoretical and practical importance. Urbain returned to France declaring that the "loi de Moseley" had put an end to the "joli roman" of Mendeleev. Closer to home the Royal Society invited Harry to participate in a discussion on the structure of the atom, "a great meeting," as he told Hevesy, at which the Rutherfordians celebrated the "funeral" of the old model of J. J. Thomson.[52] The Royal Institution inquired whether he would care to give one of their prestigious Friday Evening Discourses. His work aroused interest even at Oxford, where (as he wrote Rutherford shortly after his arrival) "there is no one interested in atom building." He expounded the theory of the nuclear model to the Alembic Club, which listened with very great interest before its president recalled it to sanity by criticizing "the optimistic character of the paper from the point of view of the ordinary chemist." [53]

As Harry's reputation rose so, naturally, did his hope of securing a good professorship. The position he most desired became open in the spring of 1914 when Clifton announced his imminent retirement. Clifton and Townsend had each his own candidate, both tepid Oxford men uninformed by the spirit or experience of modern research laboratories. Their division gave Harry a chance, as did the presence of Schuster among the electors, and he decided to try for the post. Meanwhile the University of Birmingham opened competition for its Chair of Physics, vacated in April by the death of J. H. Poynting. Harry decided to try for Birmingham as well, and consulted Rutherford about the number and nature of the testimonials he would need, and about the advisability of impressing the "uneducated elector" with the "opinion of foreigners." [54] In the event, Harry, who was "not acquainted with distinguished Germans" and could not ask Urbain without appearing to

---

[52] Urbain to HM, 29 June 14 (**102**); **93**; Rutherford to Boltwood, 17 March 14, in Badash, p. 292: "I am speculating whether JJT will turn up [at the funeral], because he knows that I think his model is only fitted for a museum of scientific curiosities." See Rutherford to Bohr, 16 March 14 (AHQP); **90**; and Rutherford, *Discussion*, pp. 5–9.

[53] RI to HM, 7 Nov 14 (**116**); **85**; Alembic Club Minutes, 18 May 14 (OHS); cf. *infra*, p. 114.

[54] **90, 96, 101.**

"request a testimonial as a return for hospitality received," had to content himself with enthusiastic endorsements from Rutherford and Bragg, and a routine recommendation from Townsend. But it scarcely mattered. Before either Birmingham or Oxford could choose its professor, the war broke out. Each university postponed its election until (as Sir Oliver Lodge, the Principal of Birmingham, wrote Harry) "conditions are more normal." [55] At the war's end Poynting's chair went to S. W. J. Smith, F.R.S., and—what would have irritated Harry immensely—Clifton's went to Lindemann.

---

[55] 96, 107, 108; Oliver Lodge to HM, 4 Nov 14 (115). Cf. testimonials of Bragg, Rutherford and Townsend, all dated 9 June 14 (98, 99, 100); and E. W. Vincent and O. Hinton, *The University of Birmingham* (1947), p. 228.

VII

Australia and Gallipoli

IN 1912, ENCOURAGED by a travel grant of £15,000, the British Association for the Advancement of Science agreed to hold its meeting for 1914 in Australia. After several changes of mind Harry decided that he was far enough ahead of that "horde of hungry Germans," his competitors, to spare the time to attend, and on June 12, 1914, he and Amabel, who went to see the scenery and some Australian cousins, sailed from Liverpool.[1] They spent a fortnight in the Canadian Rockies, at Lake Louise and Yoho, admiring the mountains, the waterfalls, and above all the flowers. Harry found something else to admire as well, a girl named Louise, a novel interest that Amabel warmly encouraged.[2] Apparently Harry had felt strange stirrings for some time. Two months earlier, as best man at the wedding of his friend Jervis, he had gone so far as almost to flirt with the bride's younger sister; his unusual attentions flabbergasted the groom, who had never before seen him voluntarily talk to a girl, and so impressed their object that she remembered every detail of the conversation over fifty years later.[3] Nothing came of either romantic interest.

The voyage from Vancouver, whence the Moseleys sailed on July 8,

---

[1] BA Report (1914), 680–681; **79, 89, 94.** Harry had bought himself a life membership in the association in 1913 (Report [1914], xvii).

[2] Margery's notes, dated 28 June 34 (LH), on a conversation with Amabel's most intimate friend; Amabel to Margery, 4 and 11 July 14 (LH); **104.**

[3] Private communication from the lady concerned; Jervis to Amabel, 18 Feb 20 (LH).

was pleasurable and instructive. Harry turned his thoughts from Louise to the rare earths, about which he planned to speak in Australia. He worked up his last results, analyses of the eight promising preparations Urbain had left at Oxford, which made possible determinations not only of the natures but also of the proportions of their constituents. They offered no chemical and only minor physical novelties, satellites of L_α and L_β that Harry had missed on earlier photographs.[4] Many people on board ship, which was crammed with what he called "B. Asses," were interested in his results. Harry particularly enjoyed talking with "old Professor Goldstein of Berlin," a pioneer in the study of gas discharges and a man of wide general culture, with whom he and Amabel explored Honolulu. Other notable adventures included a few nights in a native hut in the interior of Fiji and a fierce shipwide tussle, a "General Knowledge Examination," which Harry and Amabel easily won.[5] They arrived at Sydney on August 6, two days after England had declared war on the Central Powers.

The Australians had planned an intricate meeting, to commence at Adelaide on August 8 and to migrate successively to Melbourne, Sydney, and Brisbane. The opening in Adelaide, being merely social, held nothing for Harry, who rushed off into the bush with twenty-five kindred souls in search of the duck-billed platypus and the silver mines of Broken Hill, a town on the Western border of New South Wales. There, it is said, he put to shame the chemists and geologists of the group by seeing sooner than they the physical basis of local smelting practices. But the war cast gloom on such amusements, and Harry, who had planned to stay in Australia through October, decided instead to return home immediately after fulfilling his obligations to the Association. These consisted of reading a paper at Sydney on "High Frequency Spectra" and in participating at Melbourne in an unusually well-attended session on the structure of the atom.[6]

Rutherford opened the discussion by emphasizing the important corroboration of the nuclear model supplied by α scattering and van den Broek's hypothesis, securely anchored by Moseley's formulae. An old-line chemist, H. E. Armstrong, F.R.S., replied that he and his brethren could

---

[4] 103.
[5] Amabel to Margery, 11 July 14 (LH); Diary, 15–30 July 14.
[6] BA *Report* (1914), 305, 714–715; 101, 108.

not undertake to discuss the new views of the atom "with advantage," as "the arguments used are so novel and daring, the connections so original"; and yet, he said, it was clear enough that the physicists, who have "held aloof from chemists," had again gone astray, employing powerful methods with "little chemical significance," and contributing nothing to the understanding of the central problem of chemistry, valency. As to the doctrine of atomic numbers, it probably referred to atomic species of a certain "preferred type," ones able to compete particularly well, one imagines, in the struggle for survival; Moseley's work perhaps showed that almost all such atoms had been identified, but by no means proved that the age of the discovery of the elements had come to an end. It was people like Armstrong and Arthur Smithells, Professor of Chemistry at Leeds, who had earlier complained to the British Association about the invasion of his field by mathematicians, radioactivists and speculative philosophers, that made "dam'd fool" and "chemist" synonyms to Rutherford.[7]

After Armstrong had swung his rusty weapons a more formidable gladiator arose, the mathematical physicist H. M. Hicks, who claimed that the Rutherford-Bohr model gave no better purchase for understanding series spectra than did the old plenary atom of J. J. Thomson. Moreover, he said, the K_α law did not confirm van den Broek's atomic numbers, but Rydberg's ordinals R, greater by two than Moseley's Z's. Rydberg (to whom Harry sent an abstract of his second paper on X-ray spectra) had emphasized that he had predicted precisely thirty-two elements in the sixth period, including fifteen between barium and tantalum, and Moseley had found no more; and he had further argued that, in terms of his R's, the K and L formulae displayed striking (and therefore significant) numerological patterns, K_α depending on $(R-3)^2$, L_α on $(R-3.3)^2$, K_β on $(R-3.5)^2$, and L_β on $(R-3.3.5)^2$.[8] Hicks repeated these considerations which, he said, pointed strongly to the existence of

---

[7] *BA Report* (1914), 293–301; Smithells, *BA Report* (1907), 477, and *Nature* 76 (1907), 356–357. See O. Lodge, *Nature* 76 (1907), 414–415, and J. J. Thomson, *The Atomic Theory* (1914), pp. 14–15.

[8] *BA Report* (1914), 293–301; cf. Hicks, *PM* 28 (1914), 139–142; Rydberg, *ibid.*, 144–149; and van den Broek, *ibid.*, 630–632. To secure agreement with L_α Rydberg had to sacrifice the factor $5/36 = 1/2^2 - 1/3^2$ and with it the apparent connection with the Bohr-Balmer formula.

two elements between hydrogen and helium, elements he proposed to identify with Nicholson's "coronium" and "nebulium."

Nicholson replied affirming his regard for Bohr's handling of the one-electron case, and his conviction that the rest of the theory would not stand. Moseley contented himself with a neutral presentation of his work, mentioning neither Rutherford's atom nor the theories of Bohr. Regrettably he did not develop the ideas he had had some months earlier, when he wrote Darwin announcing confirmation of the L_α formula, equation (4). "An important point [he then said] is that the L s_n is much larger than the K for the same element. Evidently L comes from the second ring of somewhere about 18 electrons . . . and I believe this is the key to the atom['s] structure." He planned to look for an M series, $(1/3^2 - 1/4^2) \cdot \nu_0 (Z-s)^2$, and invited Darwin to work out the properties of an atom in which successive rings possess increasing amounts of angular momenta $h/2\pi$. In such a case Moseley recognized the inner rings would be less populous than Bohr required.[9] These last suggestions —the n-quantum character of the nth ring and the restricted population of the innermost one—anticipated the first successful explanation of X-ray production on Bohr's principles.

The quick mobilization of the Australians and their strong feeling for the mother country intensified Moseley's own sense of duty, and the unquestioning patriotism instilled by the public schools.[10] He left the commonwealth—whose sons he would meet soon enough again—on August 29, on the first ship he could get after delivering his paper at Sydney. Amabel remained in Australia to attend the last meetings in Brisbane. She then returned via Suez in the company of William Johnson Sollas (1847–1926), Professor of Geology at Oxford, whom she had known for many years. Sollas, a widower for three years, wished to remarry; Amabel accepted him, to the "uncommon surprise" of her son. Not that Harry disapproved of his step-father elect. He reassured Margery, who suspected Sollas of marrying for money, that the geologist

---

[9] 89. Harry probably guessed at the paucity of inner-ring electrons by considering the formula for the radius r_n of an n-quantum ring containing ρ electrons; for $r_n \sim n^2/(Z_{eff} - s_\rho)$, where the effective nuclear charge is approximately $Z - \Sigma p_i$, summing over inner rings; to keep the atom to within accepted sizes, Σp_i must be appreciably smaller than Z.

[10] P. F. E. Schuler, *Australia in Arms* (1916), pp. 15–23.

was "thoroughly a gentleman"; for the rest, he had "the merits of being an exceptionally enthusiastic and interesting talker, and the drawback of great deafness in one ear." Harry disapproved of the union because it involved a "gamble" which would never have occurred to him, risking a "modicum of happiness . . . on the excellent [but uncertain] chance of getting more " "I go through life perfectly contented so long as I am happy and do not bother to think whether I could not be happier." Despite his spring stirrings, Harry did not yet understand the need for companionship. But he did not press his objections and the marriage took place on December 17, 1914.[11]

Moseley had then been on active military service for precisely three months. He had begun to train on his return voyage, "reading up a smattering from War Office manuals, and practicing flag wagging, Morse and semaphore while crossing the Pacific." He and Tizard, with whom he had shared a cabin from Sydney, took the first train east from San Francisco. They ran to the dock in New York and jumped aboard the *Lusitania*, which sailed for England the evening of the day they arrived.

Harry had decided to commission himself in the Royal Engineers. The Engineers preferred engineers, and declined. That of course did not discourage Harry at all. "[I am] trying to pull private strings," he wrote Margery on October 10, "but unfortunately find them working rather rustily at present, since nobody seems to know which is the right string to pull. I wrote to Ray Lankester and told him to busy himself, but he replies that he does not know how to, and must first be told whom to attack." Harry himself, armed with an impotent letter of introduction, descended on the commanding officer of the Royal Engineers at their headquarters in Aldershot, but that worthy "flatly refused to be chivied." Thereupon he and Tizard, who had also made little progress, went up together to "bully" (as Harry put it) the War Office. "I spent the whole morning waiting in a passage [the bully wrote his mother] and was told about lunch time that the intended victim was too busy to see me." He returned to the attack in the afternoon and emerged victorious, a "very lucky" lieutenant in the Royal Engineers. Tizard was made an Artillery officer. Four days later, on October 17, Harry arrived at Aldershot.[12]

---

[11] 111, 117; Diary, Oct and Dec 14; *ORS* 2 (1936/39), 265–281. Cf. 119.

[12] 105, 106, 109, 110, 111; Tizard, Autobiography, p. 51 (IWM); Clark, *Tizard*, p. 23.

After a month's "strenuous and interesting" training, in which he learned to signal by semaphore and ride without stirrups, Harry was transferred to an "incredibly gloomy" camp at Bulford on the Salisbury Plain. There he lived in the mud with "splendid fellows, very keen and well-educated," who were learning to set up military communications systems.[13] He did not find the work altogether "amusing," however, and for a few weeks after Christmas he labored as hard to leave the Engineers as he had to enter them. The cause of his infidelity was his first airplane flight, which he made on a day miraculously free from rain. He immediately decided to transfer to the Royal Flying Corps. He then encountered an object even he could not budge: the inefficiency and indifference of the military bureaucracy. It took ten days for his application to proceed through the Engineers, the War Office and the "flying hierarchy to the people really concerned, who have written back through the same channel to enquire my weight. No doubt [he complained to Amabel] more enquiries will follow through the same chain concerning my eyesight and my moral character etc. each at an interval of ten days. If only the channel could be short circuited . . . ." He yanked what strings he could, but nothing moved. The matter was eventually settled by a General Order which forbade further transfers to the R.F.C. from units of Kitchener's New Army.[14]

In the middle of February Harry's company was attached to the 13th Infantry Division at Woking. He himself became responsible for the communications of one of the division's brigades, the 38th, "quite an interesting little job," he wrote Rutherford, since "I and my 26 men will be quite on our own as soon as we get to the Front." That happy event he foresaw for the end of April, and naturally he expected it to occur in France.[15] He reckoned without the mad planners of Whitehall.

At the beginning of April, when the 38th was enjoying springtime maneuvers in the Surrey countryside, General Sir Ian Hamilton was assembling an army in the eastern Mediterranean for an invasion of the peninsula of Gallipoli, which closes the northern face of the Dardanelles and the Sea of Marmara. The more enthusiastic promoters of the adventure expected that seizure of the peninsula would crush the Turks,

---

[13] 113, 114, 117, 118.
[14] 119–122.
[15] 127.

secure Egypt, open a much needed supply route to Russia, and enlist the wavering Balkan states in the cause of the Allies. On April 25, 1915, Hamilton's troops secured two beachheads, one at Cape Helles on Gallipoli's southernmost tip, the other some fifteen miles up on the northern coast, at a place named "Anzac Cove" after its gallant conquerors, the Australian and New Zealand Army Corps. The Turks proved unexpectedly stubborn. Engagements fought during the next few weeks scarcely improved the Allied position, and the condition of the troops deteriorated with every day spent in the trenches, exposed to the enemy, the elements, epidemic dysentery and an invincible plague of flies. Fresh troops were needed to storm the complex system of fortified hills and ridges which commanded the peninsula's interior.[16]

On June 7 the government agreed to Hamilton's request for more units and ordered three divisions of the New Army, including the 13th, to the East. Harry, who had inferred from the delay in shipping his brigade that it was reserved for the Mediterranean, had his suspicions confirmed by orders to draw sunhats and tropical kits. He was ferocious in providing for his men. Had their sun helmets not arrived? Harry located a shipment, commanded an axe from the stationmaster, and ran off with a supply destined for another unit. "I fear their quartermaster will not bless me when the remains reach him, nor will he love the stationmaster, who has no authority for the theft beyond my signature of receipt." Had they been issued boots in poor condition? Harry convened a board of officers to condemn the offending footwear, and his men drew anew. He collected his signal gear with the same determination. While Amabel searched for "any old tools which may be useful," Harry bypassed his quartermaster and cleared out every scrap of wire at the field stores in Aldershot. Thus prepared, and armed with a .32 caliber revolver and an air cushion, he set sail from Avonmouth on June 15, 1915.[17]

It soon became excessively hot. Alexandria, which he reached by June 27, was "full of heat flies native troops and Australians"; it reminded him of his mortality, and there he composed his will, leaving his entire estate to the Royal Society of London.[18] After a week in Egypt

---

[16] C. F. Aspinall-Oglander, *Military Operations, Gallipoli* (1928/32), I, 48–50, 58, and II, 59–67; Bryan Cooper, *The Tenth (Irish) Division in Gallipoli* (1918), pp. 43–48.

[17] 128–131.

[18] 132–135.

the 38th was sent to Helles to gain some combat experience before attempting the central highlands. The first few days were spent along the coast, the heat unrelenting, the "centipedes eight inches long and very fat," the food monotonous. "The one real interest in life is the flies, no mosquitoes, but flies by day and flies by night, flies in the water, flies in the food." Towards the middle of the month they went into the trenches to relieve elements of the original invasion force. "We moved yesterday [13 July 15] to a place where the road is worse than the flies. Sand in boots clothes mouth eyes hair. Sand in the food and the water and the air." There were also bullets and dysentery. Harry undertook to protect his flock from both, from the first by inculcating "prudence by example," from the second by Spartan diets and great doses of chlorodyne supplied by Amabel for the purpose. He lost three men to dysentery and one to the Turks.[19]

After three weeks at Helles the 38th proceeded to the harbor of Murdos, on the island of Lemnos, a staging area about seventy miles from Anzac. There Harry spent a few pleasant days swimming in the Mediterranean and hiking in the parched and barren hills, which he found to be "thick with worked flints." With fresh eggs and fruit collected from a nearby village and amenities like Bovril and silk pyjamas commanded from Amabel, he made himself almost comfortable.[20] He had no inkling of the preposterous plan he and his comrades would be called upon to effect.

The primary thrust for the new offensive, according to the generals, was to come from Anzac, a rough semicircle about one mile in radius and already so crowded that its 20,000 troops scarcely had standing room. To insure surprise, the attacking force, an additional 20,000 men, was to be smuggled ashore on three successive moonless nights, and hidden by day in caves and trenches prepared by the Australians. At 10:45 on the evening of Thursday, August 6, 1915, seasoned troops were to knock the Turks from low hills dominating the only practicable inland routes. Two columns of the new arrivals would then scale the fortified, critical ridge system called Sari Bair, and occupy all its chief heights before sunrise. Meanwhile other elements of the new force would land some six miles

---

[19] **137–144.** Aspinall-Oglander, *Gallipoli* II, 75–76, 98, 148; Cooper, *The Tenth*, p. 59.
[20] **144.**

north of Anzac, at a place called Suvla Bay, and thence proceed inland to cover the north flank of the principal attacking columns.[21]

The plan failed to provide adequately for the inexperience of the troops and the extreme difficulty of the terrain. The routes to Sari Bair lay through steep, dry gullies, or Deres, a complicated network of boulder-strewn passages through otherwise impenetrable scrub-covered cliffs. Even in the daylight, unopposed, and competently guided the new troops would have been pressed to reach their objectives; in the dark, heavily burdened, following inexperienced leaders over hostile and unknown ground, they found it impossible.

The first phase of the operation, the dislodging of the local Turks, succeeded, though somewhat behind schedule. The assault troops then advanced. The left-hand column, which included half of Harry's brigade, had some trouble entering the Aghyl Dere (fig. 15), lost precious time, and at dawn found themselves on Damekjalek Spur, some two miles from Anzac and a mile short of their chief objectives, Hill Q (900') and Koja Cheman Tepe (971'). The right-hand column climbed the Chailak Dere in good time, but did not attain its goal, Chanuk Bair (850'), the third highest prominence in the Sari Bair complex; one battalion, it seems, had gone astray, missing its rendezvous at the edge of Rhododendron Spur, and the officer in charge decided to await its arrival. He changed his mind too late to enable his exhausted men to cross the spur and entrench themselves on Chanuk Bair, and dawn found them some precious yards short of the height.[22]

Moseley, who had left Murdos on Wednesday, August 4, probably spent Friday night at the base of Chailak Dere, where the remaining half of the 38th had been left in reserve.[23] On Saturday the two advanced columns unsuccessfully renewed the attack, managing only to rectify their lines and to secure a precarious salient on Chanuk Bair. At sunset the spent British force found itself confronting ever increasing numbers of fresh Turkish troops. Had the generals then recognized the situation

---

[21] Aspinall-Oglander, *Gallipoli* II, 127–147.

[22] *Ibid.*, II, 182–203.

[23] Rutherford, *PRS* 93:A (1917), xxii–xxviii, states that Harry fought at Suvla on August 6 and 8, which must mean in the Suvla campaign, i.e., the August offensive, and not in the battles around Suvla Bay. Harry's unit was not landed at the bay where in any case there was no fighting on the 8th (Aspinall-Oglander, *Gallipoli* II, 268–282).

15. The battle of Sari Bair. The map gives the situation at dawn on 10 August 1915. HM was killed near the pennant marked "Baldwin" in the center of the map. From Aspinall-Oglander, *Gallipoli II* (1932).

for what it was—the defeat of the August offensive and of the Gallipoli campaign—Moseley might have avoided combat altogether. They decided to try again. On Saturday night, August 7, the few available reserves assembled in the Chailak Dere under the command of A. H. Baldwin, brigadier of the 38th. In the last desperate attempt, to be made at five o'clock the following morning, Baldwin's force was to attack the northern portion of Chanuk Bair and swing east towards Hill Q, while some New Zealanders, who held the salient above Rhododendron Spur, would advance their line towards the south, and elements of the left attacking column would once again engage Hill Q.[24]

About 300 yards west of Baldwin's primary objective, Chanuk Bair, lies a lower hill which then carried on its western shoulder a piece of open cultivated land known as the "Farm." The ground between the hills was exposed except on the *right*, or south, where the Chailak Dere, through which the 38th intended to reach their attack position, becomes a narrow wooded gully. About half-way up to "Farm Hill" the brigade met a descending ammunition train. In a path one yard wide between precipitous walls rising 600 feet the ascending brigade confronted a hundred explosive mules. The result, as the brigade machine-gunner G. E. Chadwick wrote Amabel, was "frightful confusion." Baldwin could not pass and would not return; he decided that he would have to launch his attack from the exposed *left* flank of Farm Hill, and set off north to reach his position. Again Chadwick: "It was a *cross country* march over high cliffs, deep mullahs, broken river beds and thickly wooded country. At last however we just got to our position on the stroke of time. . . . The attack was carried out by tired and jaded men, who had marched over ghastly country in the pitch dark falling headlong down holes and climbing up steep and slippery inclines. Of course the attack was disjointed and failed." [25] The 38th managed to hold the Farm and part of the hill for the 8th and 9th of August, but it never reached Chanuk Bair.

Early on the morning of the 10th the enemy counterattacked. Machine guns raked Farm Hill from the high ground to the right while 30,000 Turks poured over Chanuk Bair. They annihilated the 6/Loyal

---

[24] *Ibid.*, II, 204–222.
[25] Chadwick to Amabel, 14 and 16 Aug and 27 Sept 15 (LH).

North Lancashire Regiment, a battalion from the 38th which had replaced the exhausted New Zealanders on Rhododendron Hill. They careened down the steep incline to the Farm and smashed into Baldwin's hapless, bone-weary men. They closed hand-to-hand. "So desperate a battle cannot be described. The Turks came on again and again, fighting magnificently, calling upon the name of God. Our men stood to it, and maintained, by many a deed of daring, the old traditions of their race. There was no flinching. They died in the ranks where they stood." [26] Brigadier-General Baldwin and his brigade-major fell in the front line. So did the brigade signal officer, second lieutenant Moseley, the most promising of all the English physicists of his generation.[27]

---

[26] Sir Ian Hamilton, as quoted by Cooper, *The Tenth*, p. 91.

[27] Aspinall-Oglander, *Gallipoli* II, 303–308; information from Army Record Center.

VIII

Epilogue

MOSELEY'S DEATH was widely reported. Belligerents on both sides paused to observe his passing, "ein schwerer Verlust für die Naturwissenschaften," "a matter of great regret," "une mort glorieuse." [1] After recovering themselves the British scientists used his death as a strong stick for bullying (as Harry would have said) the War Office: "The loss of this young man on the battlefield," said Rutherford, "[is] a striking example of the misuse of scientific talent." [2] "To use such a man as a subaltern [is] economically equivalent to using the *Lusitania* to carry a pound of butter from Ramsgate to Margate." [3] It came out that the Royal Society had sought his return; that papers had gone forward, but too late. These facts, together with references to Harry's "immortal discovery" lifted from a lecture by Oliver Lodge, who had himself lost a son in the war, were retailed in the daily press under captions like

---

[1] E. Rutherford, *Nature* 96 (1915), 33–34; K. Fajans, *Naturwissenschaften* 4 (1916), 381–382; Urbain to Rutherford, in Rutherford, *PRS* 93:A (1917), xxvii; Società italiana delle scienze to Amabel, 16 Sept 19 (LH). Obituary notices appeared in *London Times* (1 Sept 15), *Glasgow Herald* (2 Sept 15), *Oxford Times* (4 Sept 15), and *Manchester Guardian* (8 Sept 15).

[2] Rutherford, *Nature* 96 (1915), 33–34; *PRS* 93:A (1916), xxviii, and Memorandum to National Research Council, 8 June 17 (National Archives, Record Group 407); see I. Varcoe, *Minerva* 8 (1970), 192–216.

[3] Reginald Pound, *The Lost Generation* (1964), p. 177, referring to a "conspicuously misplaced volunteer." The same sentiment, with explicit reference to Moseley, may be found in J. D. Bernal, *Social Function of Science* (1967²), p. 171; A. Marwick, *The Deluge* (1965), p. 228; M. Sanderson, *The Universities and British Industries* (1972), p. 218.

"Sacrifice of a Genius" and "Too Valuable To Die."[4] There is little doubt that Harry's death helped Rutherford and his colleagues convince the public that scientific brains, being a national and even a military asset, should be conserved in time of war.

Had the War Office a clear conception of the military value of physicists, it would have asked Harry (as it did Rutherford and Bragg) to develop a weapon against submarines or (as it did Tizard) to improve the performance of bombers. He would have refused both. Well meaning and influential friends did in fact arrange for him to work on aircraft design; he replied that, since the operation was run entirely by civilians, nothing would have pleased him better, had he happened to be physically unfit. As it was, nothing could keep him from the front. He and the 5,000 other Old Etonians who rushed to the colors with him thought it their duty to be under fire. As Harry's old school fellow Charles Lister put it when declining a safe job as an interpreter: "The date of my birth determines that I should take active service." He too pulled strings to enter a combat division and died in the Mediterranean.[5]

Harry received several posthumous honors, most notably a gold medal, the premio Matteucci, from the Società Italiana delle Scienze. Commemorative plaques were put up in Manchester and at Eton, where a verse by Eggar records Harry's first exposure to X radiation.[6] At Summer Fields one of the four competitive "leagues" into which the school is divided proudly took the name Moseley. A certain Professor Hamer, of the University of Pittsburgh, proposed that element 43, of whose imminent discovery he had heard inklings, be called "Moseleyum," "a name," he said, "better and more international in character like true science itself than a latinized name of the discoverer's own kingdom or republic." His suggestion was ignored, except by the editors of *Nature*, who observed that it would be a fitting tribute, despite its want of precedent and euphony.[7] Today, after "Lawrencium," "Men-

---

[4] Lodge, *Nature* 104 (1919/20), 82; Lankester to Margery, 13 Sept 15 (LH): "I was trying to get him called back to use his great scientific skill in some of the work for the war now being done in England"; *Evening News* (23 Oct 19).

[5] Margery's notes (LH); **125**; E. L. Vaughan, *List of Etonians Who Fought in the Great War* (1921); Lord Ribblesdale, *Charles Lister* (1917), pp. 129, 156–157.

[6] Società italiana delle scienze to Amabel, 16 Sept 19 (LH); Eggar to Amabel, 28 April 22 (LH). Eggar's verse: "The rays whose path here first he saw/ Were his to range in order'd law./ A nobler law made straight the way/ That leads him 'neath a nobler ray."

[7] Richard Hamer, *Science* 61 (1925), 208–209; *Nature* 115 (1925), 545. The discovery Hamer anticipated was named "Masurium," after a province in Germany; we may rejoice

delevium," and "Nobelium," there can be no reservation on either count; and we may hope eventually to see "Moseleyum" attached to a deserving element beyond uranium.

Moseley's best monument, besides his work, is the scholarship founded by his will and enriched by the sale of Pick's Hill, which Amabel, in a beautiful and appropriate gesture, bequeathed to the Royal Society. The first Moseley Student was Harry's former colleague H. R. Robinson, whom the grant helped to return to peacetime research under Rutherford. The second tenant, P. M. S. Blackett, became one of England's leading physicists, a Nobel laureate, and the President of the Royal Society.[8]

Oxford had no Moseley Student before the Second World War. This was not the fault of Lindemann, who did his best to bring physics to Oxford, "to minister to the Iroquois" as his friend G. P. Thomson put it.[9] He immediately secured a special university grant, some £1200, to bring electricity, water, and machine tools to the Clarendon. He sent Harry's old tutor, Griffith, now his chief demonstrator, about the country bagging compressors, liquid air machines, and other war surplus apparatus.[10] With such material and his own leadership, informed by his extensive acquaintance with European physicists, Lindemann hoped quickly to establish a research school.

Unfortunately the university declined to provide for much more than the instructional program. Lindemann thereupon turned to private sources like his friends at Metropolitan Vickers. "At present [he wrote] the whole of physics is dominated by the 'quantum' problem"; to resolve it the atom must be attacked; to attack the atom costs money. Could industry not see its way to providing £1000 to £1500 p.a. for, say, five

---

that the nationalistic discoverer, W. Noddack, had no wish to celebrate Moseley, since "Masurium" does not and did not exist. Cf. F. Paneth, *Nature* 159 (1947), 8–10, and *infra*, p. 139.

[8] Will of Amabel Sollas, 25 Feb 27, Somerset House; Robinson, *PRS* 104:A (1923), 479.

[9] Thomson to FAL, c. March 19 (FAL, box 97).

[10] FAL to mother, 12 June 19 (FAL, box 98); Griffith to FAL, e.g., 4 July and 9 Aug 19 (FAL, box 13:I); cf. Birkenhead, *Professor*, pp. 84, 87. The £1200 was not so generous as might appear. During the war Clifton had returned to the university some £420 from the Clarendon's annual statutory grant of £565, and after his resignation in 1915/16 the general university fund benefited from all or part of his salary of £900 p.a. E. S. Craig to FAL, 29 April 19 (FAL, Box 97).

years? "At the end of such time . . . I am confident that the Oxford physics school will have established itself, thanks to this assistance, in such a commanding position, that the university will continue the grant if the private benefactors withdraw." [11]

Lindemann did in fact acquire important apparatus as gifts from industry and he secured extra-mural research funds, although not quite at the level he desired.[12] He also attracted good men. His first recruits—including Griffith—came from air-force scientists who had worked with him at Farnborough during the war. They were supplemented or replaced in the mid-twenties by men trained at the Clarendon, chief among whom was Derek Jackson, F.R.S., who established at Oxford what was perhaps the world's leading laboratory for exact optical spectroscopy. A third wave of recruits, the refugee physicists of the thirties, raised the Clarendon to the standard of the Cavendish. Lindemann, who immediately recognized the opportunity afforded by the exodus from Germany, managed to obtain stipends for several low-temperature men from Breslau who made his laboratory England's center for cryogenic research.[13]

Had Harry lived he would almost certainly have been chosen Professor over Lindemann. Would he have built as flourishing a school? One can scarcely doubt it. He too would have known how to capitalize on the refugees. Jackson's school of spectroscopy would also have developed; it throve not because Lindemann found it funds, but because Jackson was a millionaire able to put £4000 of his own money into his laboratory.[14] No doubt Lindemann was more effective in obtaining the support of industry than Moseley could have been. But Harry certainly would have been more successful in dealing with the colleges over the critical matter of fellowships. Lindemann showed only too clearly that he despised the humanistic dons who controlled the fellowships and continued to deal stingily with physics. (Only six Oxford Fellowships were held by physicists in 1939, and only three of these by Clarendon

---

[11] FAL to Vickers, 8 Nov 19 (FAL, box 13:I); Birkenhead, *Professor*, p. 83.

[12] Birkenhead, *Professor*, p. 88. In the decade 1929–1938 these grants averaged £650 p.a. (Lindemann, "Notes on the History of Physics at Oxford," p. 3 [FAL, box 13:I]).

[13] Birkenhead, *Professor*, pp. 90–91, 97–106; G. P. Thomson, *ORS* 4 (1958), 56; N. Arms, *The Life of F. E. Simon* (1966), pp. 65, 77–78; K. Mendelssohn, *Cryogenics* 6 (1966), 129–135.

[14] Lindemann, "Notes," p. 3 (FAL, box 13:I).

men.) The dons despised him in return as an "intolerably litigious fellow," a semi-alien not "in the least like an ordinary Englishman." [15] Harry, with his public school background and his deep ties to Oxford, would have advocated more persuasively than Lindemann the diversion of fellowships to the support of physics. No doubt his greater scientific distinction, enhanced by a Nobel Prize, would also have strengthened his hand.[16]

As Harry had foreseen, his work, X-ray spectroscopy, contributed importantly to the decisive solution to the problem of atomic structure. Most directly, Moseley's law secured the cardinal result of the English School of atom builders, namely the identification of the rank of an element in the periodic table (Z) with the number of electrons (n) in its constituent atoms. The opposition to this identification, voiced at the British Association meeting in Australia, evaporated as the Bohr-Rutherford atom demonstrated its power in recondite matters, like the Stark Effect and the Franck-Hertz phenomena, for which it had not been designed. *Etiam periere ruinae.* By the war's end most physicists had altogether forgotten the reservations of Hicks, Lindemann and Nicholson; and Moseley's law, recognized (to use the words of de Broglie) as "one of the greatest advances yet made in natural philosophy," was widely taken as proof of the doctrine of atomic number, and as the best available evidence for the equality of n and Z.[17]

Moseley's legacy also contributed to several key improvements in the quantum theory of the atom. In particular, attempts to derive the K_α and L_α formulae forced fruitful alterations in three of Bohr's initial procedures, namely (1) restricting the electrons to a single plane through the nucleus, (2) allowing the populations of the *innermost* rings to increase with Z, and (3) assigning to *every* electron in its ground state,

---

[15] Birkenhead, *Professor*, pp. 114–116, 109; Lindemann, "Notes," p. 6 (FAL, box 13:I); R. Harrod, *The Prof* (1955), pp. 29–30, 39, 55, 101.

[16] According to Harrod, *The Prof*, p. 46, the university probably would have helped Lindemann more had he kept up his professional reputation during the twenties. See C. Hinshelwood and G. P. Thomson in Birkenhead, *Professor*, pp. 110–112 and 365–366, respectively.

[17] De Broglie, *Scientia* 27 (1920), 105. See F. H. Loring, *Atomic Theories* (1921), p. 26; A. Sommerfeld, *Atombau und Spektrallinien* (1921²), p. 65; and the informed discussion in R. Ledoux-Lebard and A. Dauvillier, *La physique des rayons X* (1921), pp. 375–390.

regardless of its distance from the nucleus, an angular momentum of $1 \cdot h/2\pi$. Harry had already guessed that the "one-quantum" atom, as we may call the result of (3), would not suffice, and that the confluence of inner rings with increasing Z, presupposed by (2), would not take place.[18] In the early days of the war Walter Kossel, an associate of Sommerfeld's, provided the basis for further work that would confirm these guesses. Arguing not from the emission spectra Moseley had studied but from absorption data collected by Barkla and by an assistant of Röntgen's, Ernst Wagner, Kossel taught that internal ionization must precede X-ray emission, which accompanies the fall of an electron into the vacancy so created. For K_α, for example, an "L electron," one from the second ring, fills a preexisting hole in the K circle; for K_β and L_α, M is the donor and K and L respectively the recipients. Assuming that the K ring possesses p one-quantum electrons and the L ring q x-quantum electrons, one then wrote equations like

$$\nu_K/\nu_0 = p(Z-s_p)^2 + (q-1) \cdot (Z-p + 1 - s_{q-1})^2/x^2 - \\ (p-1) \cdot (Z-1-s_{p-1})^2 - q(Z-p-s_q)^2/x^2 \tag{6}$$

and hunted for p, q and x to give the best fit. One found that $x = 2$, and that $p + q = 10$ (p being 2 or 3, q 8 or 7) independent of Z.[19] Contrary to Bohr's assumption (2), all atoms beyond neon apparently possessed much the same populations in their K and L regions; and the normal L electrons evidently enjoyed twice the angular momentum allowed by assumption (3). It was thence a small step to the n-quantum atom, in which, in the ground state, each electron of the nth circle possessed angular momentum $n \cdot h/2\pi$.

Sommerfeld's introduction of the azimuthal quantum number k secured the theory of the "n-quantum" atom. According to Sommerfeld, each value of n is to be associated with n values of k ($= 1, 2, \ldots n$); each combination n_k defines an elliptical orbit which is the more eccentric the greater the disparity between n and k. The q electrons of the L "ring," for example, can exist either in a common circular orbit ($n = k = 2$) or in the *Ellipsenverein* of figure 16, in which each electron describes a private

[18] Bohr, *PM* 25 (1913), 477, 482, 493–496; *supra*, p. 108; cf. Heilbron, *Isis* 58 (1967), 462–465, 473–478, and S. Nisio, *Japanese Studies in the History of Science* 8 (1969), 55–75.
[19] Kossel, *VdpG* 16 (1914), 898–909, 953–963; Heilbron, *Isis* 58 (1967), 462–465, 473–478.

2_1 ellipse so phased that, at any instant, all the electrons lie on the same circle about the nucleus. In general each circular orbit or *Ellipsenverein* has a characteristic energy, and can serve either as donor or recipient in Kossel's process; consequently we should expect satellites of K_α and L_α corresponding, respectively, to transitions from the L *Ellipsenverein* to the K circle and from the M levels to the L circle.[20] Harry had caught sight of such satellites, as had W. H. Bragg; and during the war a great number were found and followed through the periodic table by Rydberg's successor, Manne Siegbahn, and his collaborators, who made neutral Sweden the world's center for exact X-ray spectroscopy. Many of these new lines, as Sommerfeld showed, fit nicely into an energy-level scheme based upon the n-quantum ring atom.[21]

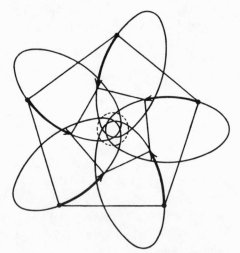

16. Sommerfeld's *Ellipsenverein*, this one incorporating five electrons in phased elliptical orbits with precessing perihelia. From Sommerfeld, *Atombau und Spektrallinien*(1919).

Unfortunately all the lines could not be accommodated and no assignment of ring populations, manipulated in the manner of equation (6), gave formulae of Harry's type which precisely fit the Swedish measurements. It appeared that the trouble lay with the first of Bohr's assumptions, the planar atom, a conclusion confirmed by ancient chemical data and by subtle new calculations regarding the compressibil-

---

[20] Sommerfeld, *Sb* (Munich) (1915), 449–500; *AP* 51 (1916), 125–167; *PZs* 19 (1918), 297–307.
[21] Bragg, *Nature* 93 (1913), 31–32; **IX,** 710; Siegbahn, *JRE* 13 (1916), 296–341; A. Kindh, *Kosmos* 5 (1925/6), 5–63; and Heilbron, *Isis* 58 (1967), 456–459.

ity of crystals.[22] At this point, late in 1920, Bohr renewed his attack on the higher elements. He now not only admitted a spatial atom, but one not quite symmetrical, in which elliptical orbits of outer electrons pierced those of inner groups. This penetration, he said, literally tied the atom together and explained why it adapted so easily to the occasional loss of deep-lying electrons.[23] Here Harry's belief that X-ray spectra would reveal "what the insides of an atom are made of" found its most literal and successful justification. X-ray emission, by betraying the energies released by the removal and readjustment of internal electrons, give a precious clue to the orbital knitting which, according to Bohr's new theory, stabilized the atom. He accordingly took the spectra mapped by Harry and by Siegbahn's group as a principal guide for a new assignment of electronic structures, a characteristic performance which might well be taken as the high point of the old quantum theory.

Bohr's primary object was to determine how many electrons in any given atom possessed orbits of a particular n_k type, and to justify his assignments by appeal to his powerful and mysterious *engine de guerre*, the Correspondence Principle.[24] One detail of the scheme, which was soon enough superseded, deserves our attention. Chemistry and spectroscopy both suggest that each of Mendeleev's periods should be associated with a different value of the principal quantum number n, which is one for hydrogen, two for lithium, three for sodium, and so on. Plainly there must be eight 2-quantum electrons to account for the elements from Li through Ne. How do they divide between 2_1 and 2_2 orbits? Bohr had no principles adequate to answer the question and arbitrarily assigned four electrons to each category. Similarly he divided the eighteen 3-quantum electrons required to complete the fourth period (K through Kr) into three symmetrical groups of three each (3_1, 3_2, 3_3). All this bears on the vexed question of the number of rare earths, or rather, on the nature of the yet undiscovered element at $Z = 72$. The fifth period (Rb through Xe, $Z = 54$), which immediately precedes that containing the earths,

[22] F. Reiche and A. Smekal, *AP* 57 (1918), 124–144; Smekal, *PZs* 22 (1921), 400–402; M. Born and A. Landé, *VdpG* 20 (1918), 202–209, 210–216. Cf. Forman, *HSPS* 2 (1970), 158–165.

[23] Bohr, *Nature* 107 (1921), 104–107; *Zs für Physik* 9 (1922), 10–21.

[24] Bohr, *Zs für Physik* 9 (1922), 21–29; cf. Bohr and Coster, *ibid.*, 12 (1923), 342–374; and Coster, *PM* 43 (1922), 1071–1107, and *PM* 44 (1923), 546–573.

exactly parallels the fourth, and so, according to Bohr, must have eighteen symmetrically distributed 4-quantum electrons $(4_1, 4_2, 4_3)$. The sixth period begins with three 6_1 electrons, which carry it to lanthanum $(Z = 57)$; thereafter the missing 4_4 group is bound deep into the atom, building up the family of rare earths. How many 4-quantum orbits are there? By analogy, they should divide into four groups of eight each, for a total of thirty-two; and since eighteen of them already exist in xenon, there ought to be precisely fourteen rare earths after lanthanum.[25] The space following lutecium therefore could not belong to an undiscovered lanthanide, a point to which we shall return momentarily.

Despite its numerological flavor Bohr's theory contained much truth. With the help of the term schemes worked out primarily in Sweden, and with X-ray absorption data provided particularly by de Broglie's group, others quickly reached a finer discrimination of the atomic sub-shells. Additional quantum numbers appeared which, with the help of n, k and the Pauli principle, fully specified the number and types of electronic species within the atom.[26] With the advent of electron spin a complete correlation of the X-ray term schemes with the energy levels of easily picturable electronic distributions became possible. That, however, marked the closest physicists have come to the solution of Moseley's problem. They were no more able in 1926 than he had been in 1914 to deduce the frequencies of the X-ray spectra from the model; only with quantum mechanics, which explicitly rejected the use of pictures of the kind that Moseley had envisaged, did exact calculation of X-ray frequencies become possible.[27] This is not to say that his program proved fruitless. On the contrary, by enabling physicists to utilize X-ray data in the continuous refinement of Bohr's principles, it contributed significantly to the advent of quantum mechanics.

Moseley's last reckoning left four spaces between aluminum and gold, at numbers 43, 61, 72, and 75. From their positions in the table it appeared that the first and last must be homologues of manganese, and

---

[25] Bohr, *Zs für Physik* 9 (1922), 48, 52–55.

[26] E.g., E. C. Stoner, *PM* 48 (1924), 719–736; A. Dauvillier, *CR* 178 (1924), 476–479; A. Sommerfeld, *PZs* 26 (1925), 70–74; W. Pauli, *Zs für Physik* 31 (1925), 765–783.

[27] The earliest successful computations were L. Pauling's, *Zs für Physik* 40 (1927) 344–350; see Pauling and S. Goudsmit, *Structure of Line Spectra* (New York, 1930), pp. 185–190.

the second a rare earth, intermediate between neodymium and samarium; while the third, which falls between lutecium and tantalum, presented a problem. Everyone agreed that lanthanum (57), the first earth, was trivalent, and that tantalum was pentavalent. Should one consider the remaining known earths, cerium through lutecium, as homologues of lanthanum, and hence reserve space 72 for a quadrivalent element, or should one take the whole group from cerium through 72 as a complex intermediary between lanthanum and tantalum? In the first case 72 would be quadrivalent, in the manner of zirconium and thorium; in the second it would be like a rare earth, closely related to ytterbium and lutecium. The knowledgeable chemists, who recognized that several of the rare earths had quadrivalent oxidation states, inclined toward the latter opinion; and, being ignorant of Moseley's unpublished analysis of Urbain's samples, they tended to label space 72 either celtium or thulium, in accordance with taste or nationality (fig. 17).[28]

In the spring of 1922 Urbain asked de Broglie, who had built an improved machine on Swedish lines, to reexamine a preparation in which Moseley had vainly sought elemental celtium eight years before. The work was entrusted to a junior associate, A. Dauvillier, who greatly gratified the old chemist by reporting the presence on his photographic plates of two exceedingly faint lines which, he said, undoubtedly belonged to the spectrum of element 72. The very faintness of these lines should have warned Urbain that their source could not have been the celtium of 1911, for that "element" possessed an *intense* optical spectrum and measurable magnetic properties. But the desire to confirm his earlier discovery, to secure the glory of finding a new earth, untarnished, as were lutecium and ytterbium, by Teutonic priority claims, overwhelmed his judgment; and in the *Comptes Rendus* for May 22, 1922, he explained that the new techniques of de Broglie had at last accorded celtium, the heaviest and most soluble of the rare earths, its rightful place among the elements.[29] The French scientific press immedi-

---

[28] [Editorial], *Chemistry and Industry* (1923), pp. 787–788; B. Brauner, *ibid.*, pp. 884–885; H. E. Armstrong, *ibid.*, pp. 792–793; L. B. Asprey in E. V. Kleber, ed., *Rare Earth Research* (1961), pp. 58–65.

[29] Urbain, *CR* 174 (1922), 1349–1351. Urbain had hoped that Ct might occupy no. 72 even after Harry's tests; Urbain to HM, 29 June 14 (**102**); to Rutherford, 26 Sept 15 (OHS), quoted by Rutherford, *PRS* 93:A (1917), xxvii, and 28 Sept 15 (OHS). Harry had explicitly ruled it out (**96**); cf. Heimann, *Annals of Science* 23 (1967), 254–255.

a

17. Examples of post-Moseley tables (a) a German version, from Ladenburg, *Zs für Elektrochemie* 26 (1920), which takes number 72 to be Auer's thulium II (b) a French rival, from Ledoux-Lebard and Dauvillier, *La physique des rayons X* (1921), which also takes 72 to be a rare earth, Urbain's celtium.

b

	I.	II.	III.	IV.	V.	VI.	VII.	VIII.
	1 H=1,008							
2 He=3,99	3 Li=6,94	4 Be=9,1	5 B=11,0	6 C=12,00	7 N=14,01	8 O=16,00	9 F=19,0	
10 Ne=20,2	11 Na=23,00	12 Mg=24,32	13 Al=27,1	14 Si=28,3	15 P=31,04	16 S=32,06	17 Cl=35,46	
	19 K=**39,10**	20 Ca=40,07	21 Sc=44,1	22 Ti=48,1	23 V=51,0	24 Cr=52,0	25 Mn=54,93	26 Fe=55,84 27 Co=**58,97** 28 Ni=**58,68**
18 A=**39,88**	29 Cu=63,57	30 Zn=65,37	31 Ga=69,9	32 Ge=72,5	33 As=74,96	34 Se=79,2	35 Br=79,92	
	37 Rb=85,45	38 Sr=87,63	39 Y=88,7	40 Zr=90,6	41 Nb=93,5	42 Mo=96,0	43	44 Ru=101,7 45 Rh=102,9 46 Pd=106,7
36 Kr=82,92	47 Ag=107,88	48 Cd=112,40	49 In=114,8	50 Sn=118,7	51 Sb=120,2	52 Te=**127,5**	53 I=**126,92**	
	55 Cs=132,81	56 Ba=137,37	57 La=139,0	58 Ce=140,25	59 Pr=140,6	60 Nd=144,3	61	62 Sm=150,4 63 Eu=152 64 Gd=157,3 65 Tb=159 66 Ds=162
67 Ho=163,5 68 Er=167,7 69 Tu=168,5 70 Yb=173,5 71 Lu=175,0				72 Ct=?	73 Ta=181,5	74 W=184,0	75	76 Os=190,9 77 Ir=193,1 78 Pt=195,2
54 X=130,2	79 Au=197,2	80 Hg=200,6	81 Tl=204,0	82 Pb=207,20	83 Bi=208,0	84 Po=210,0	85	
86 Em=222,0	87	88 Ra=226,0	89 Ac=227	90 Th=232,15	91 UX₂=234	92 U=238,2		

ately celebrated his triumph. Rutherford, as Moseley's scientific executor, announced the new element to the readers of *Nature*, and the Chemical Society of London, in its influential *Annual Report*, fully endorsed the discovery.[30]

But the physicists refused to follow. According to Bohr's new numerology, element 72 could not resemble the earths, as the last available 4-quantum electron had disappeared in making lutecium. He accordingly doubted the French claim, and applied to Lund for expert opinion. "The business appears clear enough [he wrote to Dirk Coster, the author of the most successful X-ray term scheme] but of course one must always be prepared for complications, which in this case might come from the simultaneous development of two [5_3 and 4_4] inner electron groups." Coster, who had already joined combat with Dauvillier over some obscure lines in heavy metals, replied that the young man's papers were "a mixture of very good and very bad things," and that Siegbahn, who had seen the plates in Paris, reported that "celtium" could not contain more than 0.01 percent of element 72.[31] Of course it could contain less.

Coster had agreed to spend the academic year 1922/3 in Copenhagen. Hevesy, who was already there, proposed that they explore for element 72; but Coster held back, expecting the unknown element to be exceedingly rare. "Finally, however [according to Hevesy], Coster yielded to my argument that the main aim of our work should be to enable me to learn the technique of X-ray spectroscopy and we could just as well at the same time try to find Bohr's element 72." They began with a concentration of Norwegian zircon, which immediately showed the L_α lines of number 72. The new substance was not only not exceedingly rare, it was more common than gold or silver, and turned up in all the samples of "zirconium" on display in Nordic museums. By December there could be no doubt that the elusive element resembled zirconium and thorium. Bohr was then in Stockholm, where he had gone to receive the Nobel Prize. On December 11, 1922, just as he was about to deliver the required address, Coster called with the latest findings. Bohr

---

[30] *La Nature* 51:1 (1923), 182–183, 223; E. Rutherford, *Nature* 109 (1922), 781; *Annual Reports on the Progress of Chemistry* 19 (1922), 52; Urbain, *Chemistry and Industry* (1923), pp. 764–768, gives bibliography.

[31] Bohr to Coster, 3 July 22 (AHQP).

immediately made public the discovery, and announced that the work of Urbain and Dauvillier in no way menaced his new theory of the periodic table.[32]

To celebrate Bohr and the city in which they worked, Hevesy and Coster proposed to call their discovery "hafnium," after the Latin name for Copenhagen. Unfortunately number 72 already had a French name. Urbain and Dauvillier conceded that the celtium of 1911 was not that of 1922, the new element being but a minute impurity in the solution of the old; nonetheless, they said, X-ray detection of number 72 had occurred in Paris eight months before it did in Copenhagen, and the right of names remained with them.[33] Bohr's team found it difficult to dislodge them from this position, especially when old-line chemists, outraged at the "colossal effrontery" of physicists who presumed to deduce from theory, and to know at a distance, the full range of impurities possible in Urbain's complex preparations, supported the French. "[In] my opinion," thundered Bohuslav Brauner of Prague, who had labored over rare earths for forty years, "in my opinion Prof. Urbain is the real discoverer of celtium and there is no hafnium." "We do not know what decision the International Committee on the Elements will announce," editorialized *Chemistry and Industry*, "but we think that Urbain and Dauvillier are quite justified in attaching the name celtium to number 72 until reasons far more disingenuous than any yet adduced are advanced to prove they did not discover the existence of the element." [34]

The French thought hafnium a Teutonic plot. "Ça pue le boche," "it stinks of the Hun." The English too sometimes evaluated the new element in terms of wartime alliances. A past president of the Chemical Society of London wrote Hevesy, who had submitted a paper on the chemistry of hafnium: "we adhere to the original word, celtium, given to it by Urbain, as a representative of the great French nation which was loyal to us throughout the war. We do not accept the word hafnium, given to it by the Danes, who only pocketed the spoils during the war." [35]

---

[32] Hevesy, *Archiv för Kemi* 3 (1951), 543–548; Bohr, *Nature* 112 (7 July 23: supplement), 16; Hevesy, *Chemical Analysis by X Rays* (1932), pp. 278–279.

[33] Coster and Hevesy, *Nature* 111 (1923), 79, 182; Urbain and Dauvillier, *ibid.*, 218.

[34] Brauner, *Chemistry and Industry* (1923), 884–885; *ibid.*, 784–785.

[35] F. Paneth, *Ergebnisse der exakten Naturwissenschaften* 2 (1923), 163–176; Hevesy to Rutherford, 11 Jan 23 (R); cf. Urbain to Rutherford, 17 July 16 (OHS).

Meanwhile Hevesy, who was not a Dane, but something worse, an Austro-Hungarian, or even a cosmopolitan, was busy fueling the fire. He spent the early summer of 1923 in Berlin, where he tried to interest Auer's company in his patents for hafnium extraction. He then went off to the Austrian Alps and the dark castle where his countryman the Baron von Welsbach was still trying to split thulium. He brought a most welcome bit of news. Because experiments at Copenhagen had proved that the old celtium was nothing but lutecium of the purity of Auer's cassiopeium, it followed, according to the "Danes," that Urbain had not carried his separations far enough in 1907 to have isolated element 71 from Marignac's ytterbia. The priority, therefore, belonged to Auer, and with it the prerogative of names; not only "celtium," but "lutecium," must go, and even "ytterbium," had it not been conferred by the sainted Marignac, who was a Swiss. Hevesy had easily convinced the Berlin chemists of the propriety of the new labeling; "without doubt," he wrote Coster triumphantly, "it will win wide approval in Germany." And to be sure, in their next report, which appeared in 1924, the Deutsche Atomgewichtskommission adopted ytterbium, cassiopeium, and hafnium.[36]

Now this German commission was very independent, and necessarily so, because in accordance with the exclusionary policy of the Allies no national of the former central powers could sit on the International Committee on Chemical Elements, the postwar version of the old International Committee on Atomic Weights. In 1923 the committee on the elements consisted of four Anglo-Americans, three Frenchmen including Urbain, and the arch anti-physicist Bohuslav Brauner. Needless to say the committee did not adopt the solution of their German counterpart; their second table, issued in 1925, retained lutecium and omitted number 72 altogether. A compromise was reached in 1930, following a reorganization which reduced its membership to an American chairman, two Germans, Mme Curie and a French replacement for Urbain.[37] Their happy compromise—ytterbium, lutecium, hafnium—was

[36] Hevesy to Coster, 18 April 23 (AHQP); [Deutsche Atomgewichtskommission], *Berichte der deutschen chemischen Gesellschaft* 57:1 (1924), i–xxxvi. For a picture of Auer's castle see Sedlacek, *Auer*, p. 72.

[37] *JACS* 45:1 (1923), 867–874; 46:1 (1924), 529–530; 47:1 (1925), 597–601; 53:2 (1931), 1627–1639.

by no means universally accepted. Moseley's machine brings order to chemistry, not to chemists; and for years one found German texts labeling aldebaranium, cassiopeium and hafnium what the French called ytterbium, lutecium and celtium.

As for the missing Moseley spaces, 75 presented no difficulty—it was found where expected, in manganese ores—while the others, 43 and 61, proved more troublesome than hafnium. Many people claimed to have detected lines of the one in ores of manganese, and of the other in rare earth fractions, a curious case of simultaneous nondiscovery, as neither element exists naturally. When the chemists had vainly looked in all likely corners, the physicists succeeded with one of those powerful mysterious machines that had distressed Professor Armstrong. In 1937 the Berkeley cyclotron filled the penultimate Moseley space (43) with the first of the man-made elements, and a few years later the last of the missing elements (61) turned up in an atomic pile, among the fission products of uranium.[38]

---

[38] Weeks, *Discovery of the Elements* (1956⁶), pp. 862–865; J. C. Hackney, *J. Chemical Education* 28 (1951), 186–1900.

Letters

Besides the abbreviations on pp. xii–xiii, the following are used in the letters: ALS, "autograph letter signed by sender"; and TLS, "typed letter signed by sender." As usual, square brackets indicate material inserted by the editor. Words enclosed in braces { } are guesses; a question mark similarly enclosed indicates an omitted unintelligible word or words. All dashes, parentheses and dots are in the originals. Occasional liberties have been taken with spelling, paragraphing, and punctuation.

A paragraph or a whole letter, which merely repeats other material here printed *in extenso*, has sometimes been omitted. In such cases the nature of the excluded passages is indicated in square brackets. In no case has a letter been suppressed; every item written by or to HM and known to the editor has been given a number in chronological sequence and is either printed or noticed below.

1

Nov 21 [1897] [1]

ALS (LH)

[Summer Fields]

My dear Mother,

I have had a cold and had to stay in bed on Friday. Yesterday I got up. There was another boy in Sick Room besides myself called Bridgeman: and on Saturday we played about a bit (half undressed) which Miss Peirce[2] did not like at all, because she said that 'How would you like it if you were taking great trouble to make you get well soon, the person did the thing to stop you from getting well.' I got in the Black Book once but as I was in Sick Room I could not get punished on Saturday for it, it was for fighting with another boy. The crust that was round was very good. Could you get me another of it! I have still got most of the letters you sent me, I have got about 16 of them. Huge amounts of love from your loving Boy.

---

¹ Date supplied on the assumption that Nov. 21 was Sunday.

² The "forebidding" matron, also said to have been remarkable for "patience and kindness." P. Savage and M. Young in R. Usborne, ed., *A Century of Summer Fields* (1964), pp. 6, 28. Bridgeman is F. R. D. R. Bridgeman (1889–1930), who had a distinguished career in the Royal Navy (*Summer Fields Register* [1929], 75).

2

Monday [c. 1898]
ALS (LH)   [Summer Fields]

Dearest Margery,

I want to know what bird's eggs swaps we have both got together as I want to swap some eggs with Grant¹ and I suppose you would. He has got a gull, a grouse and 2 rooks for swap perhaps 2 gulls. Say which are yours and which mine or if we have both got swaps of the same sort. Write *as soon as you possibly can* back. I will swap your swaps for you of stamps. I am going out in a minute from your loving Boy.

---

¹A. P. F. Grant, born 1887, Minister of Agriculture 1950–52. *Summer Fields Register*, p. 71.

3

Sunday [c. 1898]
ALS (LH)   [Summer Fields]

Dearest Mar,

I am sending you the 2 gulls and 2 rooks which [I] have swapped with Grant ma[jor] with the swallow which Grant does not want after all. I have arranged to swap as follows

        1 gull = long-tailed tit, great tit
        1 gull = linnet, redstart

　　　1 rook = blue tit
　　　1 rook = spotted Fly C[atcher]
　　　1 grouse = Sand M[artin] and Willow Wren
Please send me the redstart, spotted Fly catcher, blue tit.

　　The sticking paper is for Mother she said she wanted some more for my stamps. I am sending you a magnifying glass it does not magnify much I am afraid. The grouse will come soon I have not got it yet.

　　Much love from your loving Boy.

P.S. I thought you might like some black tracing paper as I have been given a lot.

4

ALS (LH)

[Summer Fields]
[c. 1900]

My dear Mar,

　　Parsons[1] found the 4 + 1 (Tree Pipit!) eggs, in a tiny hole in a willow tree, only just big anuff for Parsons' hand, too small for mine. In getting out the eggs he broke one, so off course we took all. I wonder if the one at Marston Ferry had eggs in it. The nest was very difficult to get at, as one had to stand on a pointed stake with one leg nowhere. I found a greenfinch(?)'s nest in a hedge with 4 in, and took one (did not I blow it well with a thorn). Parsons found a Linnet(?)'s nest with 6 in as well today. One boy got a common bunting's egg. It seemed to be nearly　　almost round, and like a yellow Hammer. The eggs have not yet come. Your loving

　　　　　　　　　　　　　　　　H.M.

---

[1] Alan Parsons; *supra*, p. 13.

5

Summerfields Nr Oxford
Saturday [c. 1900]

ALS (LH)

[To Margery]
　　[Itemizes birds' eggs swaps.]

6

ALS (LH)

[Eton College]
[Sept 01]

[P. 1 not found]

sausages and potato mashé. After supper I had a tub and went to bed. In the morning I got up at 6-50 and had roll, butter and tea. Then we did an exam Latin Prose for 1ʰ-30ᵐ. Then we had breakfast. After breakfast I saw Mr: Alington[1] and ordered the books I will want at an Eton shop. Please send me Le Roi de montaines,[2] if it is anywhere where you or Mar can get it. Mr Alington will be in Oxford from Thursday afternoon till Sunday afternoon. After that I did a Latin Trans: Paper for 1 hr and Latin grammar for 1/2 hr. All the exams are very easy. There are 137 new boys this term. The six in Long Chamber seem mostly very nice. The old boys are beginning to come now but I have not seen any in College yet. They will come in the evening. After the grammar paper I went out to get my books and then sat down to write this letter. I must not write you such long letters when you are in France, must I?

They have the absurd fag plan here I find. The boy calls 'Here' and the last arrival is made useful. I am very near the 6th form rooms and have very little way to run, so I am lucky. I like Mr Alington and Mr Goodheart[3] very much and have not come in contact with anyone else. The grammar paper was just a race who could write fastest. I wrote the last word as the bell struck.

We have dinner and supper in the Big Hall with the rest of the 70. I am not a bit shy yet, because no old boy has yet deigned to look at me, except Summerfield boys. My bed is very uncomfortable and my pillow very low, but I shall soon get over that. The chief objection to the Long Chamber is that one can hear snores from one end of it to the other. Your very loving son

H. Moseley K.S.[4]

---

[1] C. A. Alington, HM's tutor; *supra*, p. 18.

[2] E. F. V. About, *Le roi de montagnes* (1857), probably in the school edition of George Collar (1899). It was a standard beginning book. "For French translation we plowed through About's *Roi des montagnes*, and never once did any conception that it was a satire dawn on our minds." W. Peck, *A Little Learning* (1952), p. 87.

[3] A. M. Goodhart, Master in College.

[4] King's scholar.

7

ALS (LH)   [Early Eton]

[To Margery]
  [Designs for a cabinet to store birds' eggs. Miscellaneous news.]
  Today a bishop preached in Chapel, but it did not concern me, for where I sit I cannot hear one word of the sermon. I want the cabinet to hold all my big eggs and some room over. On Sunday I have not much time, as I have 2 prayers (35 m) 2 chapels (2:30) 1 Greek text (:20) 1 Sunday Q[uestions] (2:15) and private (:30) = 6 hrs divinity!

8

ALS (LH)   [Early Eton]

[To Margery]
  [Bird-nesting.]
  I am going to watch on next Sunday early with [Julian] Huxley. He is very good indeed on birds, knowing them all, almost, by song or form. He does not collect eggs.

9

                                                                        Friday evening
ALS (LH)   [Early Eton]

My dear Mar,
  Thank you for your letter. For the last three days I have been suffering from a raging cold, which luckily made my eyes sore, so that I could stay out. I am going into school tomorrow, most probably. There are 3 competitions in Natural History for the end of next half [1] offered this year. (1) original essay on birds of Eton & neighborhood (2) life history of not more than 6 British insects (3) series of photographs of some bird or animal etc. I might go in for the last two, possibly. (I am writing with a pencil, whose lead is just pushed up and into it as I write. I could not imagine how it wore down so extraordinarily quickly.) I got 95 for the last problem paper: The one I have just shown up, I expect to get 90–100 for, but the next one is one of Mr Hunt's, and is absolutely

impossible.—He is evidently trying to show off his knowledge, like last time.

[No ending]

---

¹ Etonese for "term"; there were three "halfs" each year.

10

[Middle Eton]
Moseley. KS
[Marked α+] ¹

(LH)

Europe

Europe was a buxom little maiden,
Sent by her ma to gather for the table.
Primroses, bluebels, buttercups & daisies,
    And to arrange them.

She when strolling through the verdant pastures,
Saw at her side a creamy-coloured creature,
'Billy' was its name, its sire was a famous
    Aldernay First Prize

Picked were the flowers, neatly tied in bunches;
So she approached her pet with easy conscience.
Called it by name and then began to softly
    Stroke it & murmur

Endearing epithets. Gently did the 'Moocow'
Then rub his muzzle over all her great-coat,
To find out whether there was any sugar
    Hidden in the pockets.

Europe thinks it wouldn't be a bad plan
To have a ride on the back of little Billy.
Up she scrambles! Billy thinks its great fun!
    All of a sudden

Billy gives a start and rushes madly forward!
Tears over fields of corn & mangelworzel.
A farmer pursues, uses dreadful language
    Armed with a pitchfork.

Billy rushes seawards: mighty Jove has sent his
Mind into that great creamy-coloured creature.
Such an occasion for a nice elopement
Couldn't be let slip.

---

[1] Mr F. P. Walters, one of HM's particular friends in college, writes (1971) as follows about "Europe": "I had remembered this! & had thought to mention it . . . to illustrate M.'s capacity for unconventional ways of thinking. The $\alpha+$ is a special mark implying that it would in due course be given some kind of prize. A good mark, I think, for the Classics Master who spotted its merits!"

11

ALS (LH)

New Buildings,
Eton College, Windsor

My dear Mar,

Thank you very much for your 3 letters. I have told all the news in Mother's letter. Week before last, there was a lecture 'All about Animals,' by a man who had gone over the world with a full-plate camera. The slides consequently were very good, the patter moderate. He was immensely pleased with himself, as he said that he had proved conclusively that Penguins actually made a nest of 3 and a half bits of seaweed, and that everyone, who said they did not, was wrong. In last week's punch, or the week before, there was a picture called 'A light on Darkest Africa' or 'Mr L-NC-ST-R [E. R. Lankester] on the Okopi.' [1] The drawing was not so very like him, it was not 'light' enough, but he was quite like as to the face.

Aunt Tye is sending me a reading lamp, and adds a postscript that it has a very powerful spring, and is sure to jump out like a jack-in-the-box and murder me.—(Better not tell mother). How are the bulbs in my box getting on? I congratulate you on the prize. How am I to know you have got one, if you never tell me? I am glad the roses are all right. It is so cold now that I think the sproutlets from Miss Hall [2] would like a little charcoal and covering soon. I am astonished to hear that Helium is three or 4 times as heavy as Hydrogen, though it has a lower boiling point. Another {?} of the p.p. [problem paper], which however I have succeeded in doing after much labour is to prove that 16, 1.15.6, 1.1.15.5.6, 1.1.1.1.55.56 etc all sq:s.[3]

Your loving H.M.

---

[1] Not found.

[2] Magdalen Hall, a close friend of HM's mother.

[3] The series is $4^2, 34^2, 334^2, 3334^2, \ldots$; or in general $N(n)^2$, where $N = 3(10^0 + 10^1 + \ldots + 10^{n-1}) + 1$, and the first term $N(1) = 4$. Since $10^0 + 10^1 + \ldots + 10^{n-1} = 1/9(10^n - 1)$,

$$
\begin{aligned}
N(n)^2 &= 1/9(10^{2n} - 2 \cdot 10^n + 1) + 2/3(10^n - 1) + 1 \\
&= 1/9 \cdot 10^n(10^n - 1) + 5/9(10^n - 1) + 1 \\
&= 10^n \underbrace{(1.1.1. \ldots 1)}_{n \text{ places}} + \underbrace{5(1.1. \ldots 1)}_{n \text{ places}} + 1 \\
&= \underbrace{1.1.1. \ldots 1}_{n \text{ places}} . \underbrace{5.5.5. \ldots 5}_{n - 1 \text{ places}}.6
\end{aligned}
$$

12

[Eton College]

ALS (LH)   Sunday 14th [May 05]

My dear Mar,

How lovely to have found a dabchick's nest. I long to have been there. [Some bird-nesting news is here omitted] I will love a dabchick. It will help to fill my white egg drawer.[1] I will be tried for my boats some time next week.[2] Only 7 places alas and I hang, fall forward, etc. etc. etc. College Junior 4's begin in about a fortnight and Bland[3] refuses to begin to take us out 'til after School Pulling. Only 10 days we can't possibly get together in that time. All other 4's have started some time. I expect that I am rowing in A.[4] How College will keep head of the river, I don't see.

Your loving H.M.

---

[1] See 7.

[2] HM did not receive his "Boats," i.e., his aquatic color, until 1906; see 26.

[3] Nevile Bland, Captain of the Boats, later Sir Nevile Bland, Ambassador to the Netherlands, 1942–48.

[4] "College A" was a Junior House Four.

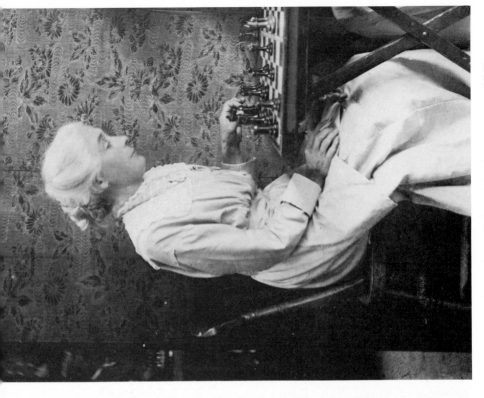

19. Amabel Gwyn Jeffreys Moseley, courtesy of LH.

18. Henry Nottidge Moseley. From H. N. Mosley, *Notes by a Naturalist* (1892[2]).

21. HM about the time he entered Oxford (1906), courtesy of LH.

20. HM as a child, courtesy of LH.

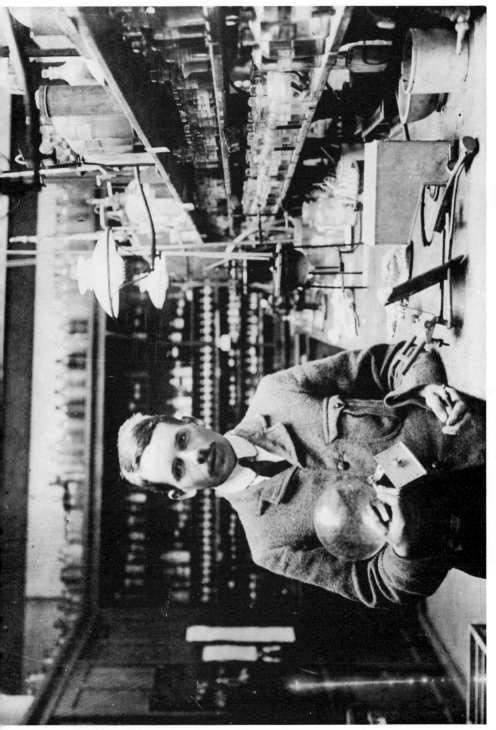

22. HM in the Balliol-Trinity Laboratory (c. 1910), courtesy of OHS.

23. HM in the library, courtesy of LH.

24. HM in his prime (c. 1914), courtesy of LH.

25. HM in uniform (1915), courtesy of LH.

26. 48 Woodstock Road, Oxford, HM's home.

13

ALS (LH)

[Eton College]
[c. May 05]

My dear Mother,

Thank you for the shirts.

My timetable is being considerably changed, so that I will do no physics this half except book-work. Mr de Havilland has arranged for me to do practical Physics etc with Mr Eggar next half.[1] The Physics which I was doing with Mr de H last week is too elementary & gets on too slowly, as the div[ision] which I was doing it with is rather dense. I will be doing lots of Chemistry 13 hrs practical, 1 hr Chemistry private, and 3 hrs prep[aration] in school, besides some out of school. I think that I cannot possibly get you tickets for the Speeches.[2] Do you still want to come? I will try, but I dont think it's any use, and it's a beautiful day for long leave. But I suppose it would disappoint Mar not to come. I have ordered my new tails & trousers. Your letter arrived all right, only on Sunday instead of Saturday evening. How is the Pumpkin. 10 Sunday is to be done.

Your loving son,

H. Moseley

N.B. The time table is altered but we do not go to bed early.
[P.S.] Sending Mar what I suppose are fish scales. Probably nice under micro:

---

[1] Hugh de Havilland, a Fellow of the Linnean Society, was not a specialist in physics; for W. D. Eggar, see *supra*, pp. 21–22.

[2] A celebration, held annually in early June, when the boys dressed in their finery, gave and listened to speeches, etc.

14

[Eton College]
[Nov 05]

ALS (LH)

My dear Mum,

I enclose a letter from Hartley,[1] in answer to one in which I said clearly that any scholarship was better than none, but that I was undecided about the Exhibition question, or whether to try later for other Schol:s. His letter seems to be tantamount to an offer of an exhibition, and to hold out no hopes of the scholarship: which is only natural considering how little I know. My time is chockfull, a game every day. For the rest work, except yesterday, when all my work was put out sadly by two games. A mixture game in the morning, and then asked suddenly to play in a sine match in the afternoon.[2] I was extremely tired after it, but recovered in the evening, and had to speak on 'the practibility of socialism' in College Pop.[3] The light shade has come, and is lovely. I will write to thank Mar for it. It is just what I wanted. My eyes are much better this half on the whole.

Today I breakfasted with Alington; very sleepy indeed, as the debate went on till past 11. last night. I have no chance of playing for College at the Field game, but might quite possibly get my Wall Colour.[4] I am so sorry that I have not time to write during the week, but you know that I have hardly any time. Extras[5] 12–2 on three days 12–1 on one 3:45–5 on two, 6:45–8:45 on five, and then games. I am feeling very well, and by no means overworked.

Your loving son, H.M.

I hope you will come next week Mar too.

---

[1] Harold (later Sir Harold) Hartley, then a very junior fellow and science tutor at Balliol, whose letter must have told HM that he had not won the Balliol science scholarship available for 1906; *supra*, p. 26.

[2] A sine game was one in which no one who already had a football color could play; a mixture game did not discriminate.

[3] Not *the* Pop but a college debating club that met every Saturday evening at 10:00 P.M.; like the Royal Society it did not permit discussions of religion. It consisted of twenty members, usually the senior collegers, and attained a high level in HM's time under the guidance of Knox, Shaw-Stewart *et al.* C. H. Malden, *Recollections* (1905), pp. 102–108.

[4] He won neither. The Field game is Eton football; the Wall game is incomprehensible (*supra*, p. 16).

[5] Studies beyond the required curriculum.

15

ALS (LH)

New Buildings
Eton College
[Nov 05]

My dear Mar,

The shade is exactly what I wanted. Thank you so much. Of course you should not be thanked until after my birthday, but as I am using it, I will count it as given, though never a word to say where it dropped from. I have joined the Essay Society, so that between that and College Pop,[1] I ought to get quite literary. My room is charming, except the wallpaper, which is a hideous faded pink, and covered with patches. I seem however to be never there, except from 10 to 11 at night, when I am so sleepy, that I produce most wonderful Extras Works, Scholarship papers, Essays and Problem Papers. At other times I seem to be always either having Extras or playing games. I get progressively worse at the field game, or rather fail to get better, which is sad; due no doubt to my being too slow for any but a very neat player. On Saturday I subbed for somebody in a Lower College match. The opponents, the 2nd sine[2] of a house, produced the lightest football I have ever played with. Consequently play was almost impossible as there was a high wind, they were lighter, and so had a better time of it with the ball, and I confined myself to stopping dangerous rushes; a matter of great ease, as they were all absurdly slow. On Thursday I was shamefully ill-used, made to play twice, the second time in a mixed game which consisted largely of people who played for the school and Masters. I naturally did not often touch the ball, and was dog tired at the end. I go about now with no hat, and for early school, if I am late, I [wear] a very old pair of pumps. It is a matter of great difficulty running down to the Physics laboratory (1/4 of a mile off) in these, especially on a muddy day. At chamber singing last night I was asked to sing after all the songs I knew had been used up. I had to fall back on the old love-song, which I had unsuccessfully tried four years ago, at my first chamber singing.[3] I had naturally rather forgotten it in that time, but managed to make up where necessary.

    Your loving brother

H. Moseley

---

[1] **14**, n.3.

[2] **14**, n.2.

[3] On the first Saturday after fires were allowed a "Chamber Singing," attended by all of the college, was held in Long Chamber. All new boys and anyone who had not sung before then had to serenade the guffawing assembly with a song of no less than three verses. After the initiation the older boys would sing as requested. Malden, *Recollections*, pp. 68–73.

16

ALS (LH)

New Buildings
Eton College
[20 Nov 05]

My dear Mother,

I saw the Aurora Borealis beautifully on Wednesday evening. I had no idea that it was ever seen so brightly in England, though I am told that it was much better earlier in the evening. Porter[1] says that he has not seen the like for many years. There were two bright pink patches in the sky (no clouds), which alternately faded and darkened. One of them was sometimes in the form of a long pink tongue, or streamer. They were cut across by white bands. A lovely sight.

You are the naughtiest, baddest, wickedest Mum ever seen. You have a bad headache, and then stay up till 12 having a bridge party, which does not end till past 11. In fact you dawdled even after the bridge party had left. How can you be so naughty? I have no wish to see Lewis Balfour,[2] but as you have asked him, I suppose I must bear it. I cant give him Eton news. I dont know the relative merits of the House football teams, etc etc. I have never been asked to their house, so that. . . . [HM's dots]

How ungrateful I am, but never mind as I wont scold my naughty Mum, on Saturday week, and she has put in the stove, and got a parlourmaid. Much more than I hoped for, and very good. A most detestable patronizing letter, but if her own sunbun[3] mayn't call her naughty, who may? My Mum is to have it all her own way next holidays, & she shan't reproach me with being a tyrant.—I never say anything half so nasty to you, and you see it still rankles.

———

I am not a tyrant, only I love being with my Mum, and when I am not doing her things, I like her to be doing mine. As for my loving my own way, it is chiefly in matters of health.[4] I know that my Mum is only too careful about me, and nothing like careful enough herself. And all this came I suppose from a letter which my tutor[5] says he wrote you, but which I had almost forgotten about. It springs from a quarrel which Mr Eggar thinks he had with me, tempered I expect with a feeling that I get my own way more often at Eton than is good for me (see the matters of

Porter instead of De Havilland, repeal of the Head's Early Bed (10.15) edict etc, cessation of problems for the half, etc etc). However in the case of Eggar a molehill has been made into a mountain. I have no respect for the man, because he either cannot or will not explain anything and refers you to books. The consequence is I don't do my work his way, but annoy him by introducing unnecessary complications, simply to prove that they don't matter, instead of taking everything for granted. Evidently the 'quarrel' referred to arose from my drawing a diagram of the apparatus I used myself, instead of learning up the diagram given in the text book, which I told him even if I could conceivably remember it, I had not personally found to work, as mine had. This enfuriated him, but I think my principle is right, as the differences were far from vital.

Tomorrow we have to see the King of Greece off at Windsor station, a nuisance. The Head has abolished 2:45 absence,[6] an excellent thing. I am very much in favour of him at present. I am still debarred from playing in Coll: Wall Games, but make up my exercise somehow. Health excellent.

H.M.

---

[1] T. C. Porter, the Head Science Master; *supra*, pp. 23–25.

[2] The son of Henry Balfour (1863–1939), a student of H. N. Moseley's who became Curator of the Pitt-Rivers Collection of the Oxford Museum.

[3] HM's pet name. The immediate cause of this uncharacteristic explosion appears to have been the reproach that he insisted upon his own way both at Eton and on holidays.

[4] Here HM has interlined almost illegibly: "and perhaps thats when my Mum treats me sometimes not only as her baby boy, but as a {weak} one as well."

[5] Alington.

[6] The reforming Head Master was Edward Lyttelton, who succeeded Warre in 1905; "absence" signifies "roll call."

17

New Buildings
Eton College

ALS (LH)   [c. 26 Nov 05]

My dear Mum,

Wonderful indeed that you are having the pruning done. Virtuous, and wise as it will silence reproaches. I can't remember the day of the dance, is it to be next Thursday?[1] I expect a surplus of men will not turn

up, and if they do, a wall-flower man does not look foolish like a girl. By
the new system I do 3 early schools every week in College, so that
lateness is impossible, but the task of getting up by 7:30 is horribly hard,
when there is no one to know whether you get up or not. I will probably
have a fag next half, as Mozley[2] seems likely to be leaving, to go to
Germany. I would then be Captain of Liberty, an ideal position with a
fag and almost all the authority of VIth form, without any of the
irksome duties, such as 'keeping' the passages at bedtime.[3] The pyjamas
have split in half down the back, and are hardly worth mending, as they
seem quite rotten.

  Your loving son

                H. Moseley

---

 [1] It was Friday, 1 Dec 05, and Harry avoided it (Diary).
 [2] James Frederic Mozley, who went to Oxford and then entered the Church.
 [3] "Liberty" were the six collegers immediately below Sixth Form; their captain
consequently ranked eleventh in college. Since Harry was thirteenth at the end of the
spring half, 1905, when (with one irrelevant exception) the school order was fixed, someone
else must have left to give Harry a chance at the captaincy. Cf. Malden, *Recollections*, pp.
2–6, 29–32, 37–41, and *supra*, p. 14.

             18

                 New Buildings
                 Eton College
ALS (LH)   [15 Dec 05]

My dear Mum,

  It was I who expected a letter from you, who reproach me for not
writing, I got a letter from Mar quick. Still you are forgiven. I was of
course delighted with the news, and very content to go to Trinity.[1] My
Tutor is very pleased, as it is his old college, and he naturally thinks well
of it. Everybody however seems to do that; the Etonians there are at
present few, and I hope Henderson,[2] who is trying for a Scholarship there
now, will come too.

  Porter seems to be very pleased, though rather disappointed at my
not getting the Balliol as he evidently thinks me better than Huxley, in
fact his butter is laid on with an obvious trowel.

Good mum to telegraph so quick, Pelham's[3] letter only reached me in the evening.

Your loving son

H. Moseley

---

[1] The "news" being his election to a Millard Science Scholarship at Trinity College, Oxford; *supra*, p. 26.

[2] George Lockhart Henderson, who after distinguished service in the Royal Flying Corps became a pioneer in commercial aviation; he was killed in a crash during a routine crossing of the channel (*London Times*, 22 July 30, pp. 14a, 16b). He did not win a scholarship to Trinity.

[3] Henry Francis Pelham, President of Trinity 1897–1907.

19

New Buildings
Eton College
ALS (LH)   [16 Dec 05]

Dear Mar,

This is my fourth letter this morning, and I am worn out. Thank you for your nice letter. Butter[1] is in season at times. A most harassing time yesterday evening: the annual scientific society exhibition. It was a great success, someone shewing liquid air, and Professor Miers[2] shewing crystals forming, projected on a screen by polarized light. They were lovely, changing colour as they grew, and such colours.

I shewed phosphine, (put down in the programme as phosphunine— a patent medicine). It worked beautifully. Each bubble as it bubbles up through water explodes on reaching the air with a little flash of light, making a lovely vortex ring of P_2O_5. The smell is of course appalling, but I had a good big draught-cupboard. The chief difficulty was gas, which had to be led through yards and yards of tubing joined together from another part of the room.

Your loving

H. Moseley

---

[1] Cf. **18**.

[2] H. A. Miers, F.R.S., Professor of Mineralogy at Oxford.

20

ALS (LH)

New Buildings
Eton College
[28 Jan 06]

My dear Mum,

I paid 2/6 to the long thin man, but did not pay for the other staining. I know I paid, and my accounts prove it. Lyttelton[1] has changed the whole timetable, cutting off 1/4 of an hour from early school, 1/4 from the time between school and dinner, and so having dinner, and everything after earlier by 1/2 an hour. Thus we get 1/2 an hour more bed, a most excellent arrangement, though of course very unpopular at present.

7:30	early school
8:15	breakfast
9:15– 9:35	chapel
9:35–10:25	2nd school
10:45–11:45	3rd school
1:30	dinner
2:15– 3:15 / 4:30– 5:30	school
5:30	tea
8:30	supper
9:00	prayers
9:10	our supper
9:30	bed for fags
10:00	general bed
10:30	bed for us

As I told you, I am messing with Henderson & Walters.[2] Huxley wanted very much to join us, but we had to refuse, as he and the rest of the mess would never have got on together, though I would quite have liked to have him, had it been consistent with peace. I was so sorry for him, as he was very anxious not to mess alone.[3] Thank Mar for her letter.

I have not enough news to answer it yet. I am so glad the pruning was a success.

Your loving son

H. Moseley

---

[1] **16**, n. 5.

[2] *Supra*, p. 14.

[3] About this incident, which greatly rankled Huxley (*Memories* [London, 1970], pp. 56–57), Walters writes (1971): "our refusal . . . would have been perfectly natural [since Huxley was one year our senior] and would have nothing wounding in it. What might survive of the whole story is the kindness of M's attitude, not so common, I think, in a boy of 17." Presumably Huxley, who returned to Eton for an extra year on the advice of the Balliol staff (*supra*, p. 26), had found no one left among his election with whom to mess.

21

New Buildings
Eton College
ALS (LH)   [7 Feb 06]

My dear Mar,

Now you get your promised reply. Mother has I suppose told you of my great success with Lyttelton. I represented that I could not work at mathematics in a room in which Scoones[1] was teaching. I now therefore work in my own room, or in Reading room, and only write my name, in a special book kept for me at School office, at the end of each school. On Saturday we had a Debate at Coll: Pop[2] on Politics; it lasted for 1 1/2 hours and more, and left off at 11 only because the light threatened to be turned out. It had been preceded by strong private business, but was quite sober itself, several splendid speeches being made, and the general level being much higher than usual. I spoke shortly and hurriedly for Chamberlain, but I was evidently not very explicit in part, as everybody was surprised when I subsequently voted approval that the Liberal government had got in.[3] The speech was cut in two, as I suddenly found in the middle an excellent quotation, on which to sit down.

I have just been dining with my Tutor, a very boring occupation, as Mrs Alington does all the talking, and never talks interestingly. Still she is very amiable, so that . . . [HM's dots]

I have before next Monday to do 4 1/2 Mathematical papers, 3 of this week, 1 1/2 left undone from last. Still there is hardly anything else, so that I have very little work on the whole. I forgot to put a handle to the name of the Limington district clerk, and he has punished me by not answering.

Your loving brother H.M.

---

[1] Paul Scoones; *supra*, p. 23.
[2] **14**, n. 3.
[3] HM's auditors found his matter as surprising as his manner; he was no liberal (*supra*, p. 29).

22

New Buildings
Eton College
[16 Feb 06]

ALS (LH)

My dear Mother,

I am so very sorry to hear of Molly's death. It must be so peculiarly sad for the family that it should follow so quickly on her going to London, which seemed at the time to be so unnecessary a sacrifice.

She has always seemed to me the embodiment of all that an eldest daughter should be, and yet to lack that heavy stupidity, which seems to go with such a nature. She was so good-natured, and so transparent, that she will be missed by all who have met her.

Today I have a cold, which has defied all the superstitions of cinnamon. I stay out, and wait for it to go, thankful that I can do so, without disturbing any work, unlike last half. I am taking a fresh interest in Problems, which are this half just hard enough to be interesting, just not too hard to prevent me from doing them all. Dyer,[1] who had, I fancy, considered that doing science had rendered me hopelessly bad at Mathematics, is mildly astonished, and wonderingly announces that I am far stronger than anyone except Marsden & Carter, that means better than Dalton & Huxley minor,[2] a fact which I have never doubted for a moment. He never forgave me for refusing to do problems last half.

Your loving son

H.M.

---

[1] John Maximillian Dyer, the Head Mathematics Master.

[2] Hugh Marsden, who became a mathematics master at Eton; R. H. A. Carter, later K.C.B. and K.C.I.E., an Oppidan one year HM's senior; Hugh Dalton, *supra*, p. 13; and Julian Huxley's younger brother, Trev.

23

New Buildings
Eton College
ALS (LH)   [17 Feb 06]

My dear Mar,

I am bored to tears by a bad cold in the eyes, and perhaps that is why I am writing. Tomorrow I know whether I get my boats or not for certain. A cold, starting from Parsons,[1] has pervaded the whole election, though of course he has it much the worst, and I am not sure that he is not beginning influenza. The best part is that it is so universal (the cold), that the debate in Coll: Pop is postponed. I had to open, 'That the life of an Eton Master was not desirable,' and would have come off very badly with my cold as bad as it is. You will notice that my style has suffered severely, and is becoming quite Darwinian.

My work with Porter is interesting. This half I made some solution of Potassium Permanganate, found its strength, and thence determined the purity of some oxalic acid crystals. I found finally that 99.6% was pure, a great triumph, as the result was probably very nearly exact, .4% impurity being just what one would expect [?], and the possibilities of accumulated error being great. Now I am to find the molecular weight of something by the lowering of the freezing, and raising of the boiling point, a very long and difficult business. However most of my time is spent in telling Scoones[2] why I have done no Extra Work.

Yr loving H.M.

---

[1] *Supra*, p. 13.
[2] *Supra*, p. 23.

24

New Buildings
Eton College
ALS (LH)   [27 Feb 06]

My dear Mum,

I do hope you were not anxious at not getting a letter. I sent off the postcard before early school on Monday, so that it ought to have arrived fairly early. It is wicked shame that I have not got my boats, though after all I do not lose very much by not getting them till next Half. I get them some time before the 4th, but may not wear the colour till then. The captain of the Boats, Somers-smith,[1] is generally considered to be quite unfit for his post, and I believe that he has made many other such mistakes. Two worse oars than I in College have them given it, which is rather annoying. I believe that leave on Saturday starts directly after early school, and it lasts till 7:15 on Monday. Why shouldn't it last till 10:00? The holidays begin on April the 6th and leave off on the third of May, so that all hopes of late holidays are gone. Still this gives us longer before Term begins, which is nice.

> Your loving son
>
> H. Moseley

---

[1] J. R. Somers-Smith, killed in France in 1915. F. L. Vaughan, *List of Etonians* (1921), p. 231.

25

New Buildings
Eton College
ALS (LH)   [early May 06]

My dearest Mum,

What base ingratitude to eat your birthday cake, and then forget your birthday. I hope however that when one gets to the age of 35,[1] the odd days are less important. And fancy having for birthday present only withered tulips, which should long have been thrown away. You must forgive a penitent sunbun, who will treat you better in future years. The time is soon coming when there will be no need of letters, and with me in Oxford itself, no more anxieties, as a messenger will be dispatched post-haste to bring Mum and cinnamon, when I sneeze. Your fifth birthday hence is to be celebrated in Japan, or perhaps you will not have a birthday at all that year; beware of crossing from Yokahama to 'Frisco in the first week of May, if your birthday is inclined to fall on the Sunday, once gone nothing could bring it back, but then it would be nice to stay 39 for two whole years. If when your 80, they refuse to renew your

license at all, we will emigrate to New Zealand where there will be plenty
of room for the superannuated, and you will find the stupid old age,
which you dread, a most lively and engrossing occupation. But that is so
many years off still, that by that time you will be Lady Croquet
Champion,[2] I married, and I am sure that the importance of games in
English life will by that time be so exaggerated, that you will be allowed
to live, in honourable retirement as long as you care to. I apologize for
the wild letter, but there is really no news.

Your loving H.M.

---

[1] Evidently a family fiction: Amabel, who married in 1881, was nearer 45 in 1906.
[2] Amabel was an enthusiastic and able competitor at both croquet and chess.

26

New Buildings,
Eton College
ALS (LH)   [c. 18 May 06]

[To Margery]
  [Bird-nesting expeditions alone and with Huxley; delays in receiving
aquatic honors.] I have at last been given my Boats, but do not know
which boat I will row in. I care not at all, that makes no difference. On
Tuesday a good many boys were given the colour, and as there are only
10 vacancies in all I thought it was time for them to give it to me.
Fletcher therefore wrote to Bland, the last Captain of the Boats, and he
wrote to Somers-smith,[1] the present Captain, reminding him to give me
it, but before his letter could have arrived here, Somers-smith had woken
up to a sense of his duties.

---

[1] W. G. Fletcher, who returned to Eton as a master and was killed in the war; Nevile
Bland (12, n. 2), and J. R. Somers-Smith, 24, n. 1.

27

Eton College
ALS (LH)   [20 May 06]

[To Amabel]
  [Rowing and bird-nesting.]

28

ALS (LH)

New Buildings
Eton College
[23 May 06]

[To Amabel]
[Long bird-nesting expedition with Huxley.]

29

New Buildings
Eton College
ALS (LH)   [1 June 06]

My dear Mother,

The bumping races are now over, and we have rowed over every night. College is very excited, as College A has kept head of the river, though they were extremely hard pressed yesterday by Vaughan's,[1] and rather badly pressed the other nights. Evans took the cup last year, but Miss Evans' death left College A head of the river, as it has always been.

College B has had a most exciting time of it; as after Monday we were very hard pressed 3 times, and nearly made a bump the other. Tonight Byrne's got right up to us, and almost overlapped, if not quite, at the same place as usual, about 3/4 of the way through the race. They tried to strike, but I watched them carefully, and was sure that they would not touch us, and gave a great spurt as they missed; after that they troubled us no more.

College A, College B, and Heygate's, who were always in front of us, are the only boats on the river, who rowed over the whole course, without bumping or being bumped any night. Tonight all College assembled in Hall to 'ragger' the crews as they processed in, and then the healths of Coll:A, Coll:B, and Fletcher[2] (the Keeper of College Aquatics) were drunk.

Your loving H.M.

---

[1] One of the Oppidan houses, as were Evans, Byrnes and Heygates, mentioned *infra*.
[2] **26**, n. 1.

30

als (lh)

New Buildings
Eton College
[4 June 06]

[To Amabel]

[A bird-nesting expedition undertaken "as a relaxation from rowing." Selection of a parting gift to Alington.] I think that the Mycaenae cup would be an excellent thing for my Tutor, thank you so much for remembering it. The fishes would be right, I think, as anything larger would seem out of keeping with my economical tastes.

31

als (lh)

[Eton College]
[c. 6 June 06]

[To Amabel]

[Rowing (Junior Pulling). Final prizes.] I am going in only for the geology prize [which he won]. I am really eligible for the chemistry again, but am not competing as it would be rather grabbing to take it, while if I am not in there will be quite a good competition for it.

32

als (lh)

New Buildings
Eton College
[22 June 06]

[To Margery]

[Last bird-nesting expedition with Huxley.]

33

als (lh)

New Buildings
Eton College
[24 June 06]

My dear Mum,

My cold has now almost gone, and my eyes are recovered. The next fortnight will for me be cramfull, geology,[1] of which I have as yet done scarcely any, Mathematics, to avoid dissensions with my Masters, sculling for the race directly after Henley. I have done very little sculling yet, as I have out of economy not had a rigger, while rowing. Also I must revisit one or two birdsnests so that altogether till near Lords my time will be very fully occupied. Yesterday I went for a picnic with the Alingtons to Burnham Beeches. I was rather disappointed with their appearance. They are better than anything near Eton, but only in Autumn do they look anything out of the ordinary. [Arrangements for visits here omitted.]

Yr loving H.M.

---

[1] Cf. **31**.

34

Eton College
Windsor
[c. 8 July 06]

ALS (LH)

My dear Mum,

What a villain I feel, to be late two weeks running, or rather with only one virtuous week between; and you so very good over the Billiard room.[1] Have you yet decided when we go to the Tyrol, as though Mrs Alington is not yet trying to peg me to dates, she must be fuming, and wanting to settle her plans. I come directly after chapel on Friday, arriving in the morning some time about 11, and then we will have two lovely days. My sculling is on Tuesday, but I can't scull at all, and am not taking it seriously. It takes such a vast amount of practice to scull, and I am only just learning to feather off the water, a task which requires a horribly even balance, as you can imagine. I enclose two photos of Coll:B, taken by Mrs A[lington], one just before the start, the other while racing. You will see that we are not together, that is not keeping the same time, and that Marsden[2] is not a pretty figure when rowing.

Your loving son,

H. Moseley

---

[1] Which Amabel added to the house at 48 Woodstock Road, Oxford.
[2] For Marsden, **22**, n. 2; for the race, **29**.

35

Gai[n]ay
Orkney Islands, N.B.
ALS (LH)   Thursday Aug.30th.07

My dear Mother,

I arrived yesterday afternoon. Kirkwall Tuesday evening. The hotel there is most comfortable. The passage was rather rough, but not too much, and not much more than usual, as the rollers are always there. I am nearly asleep, so excuse. Today we had a gale of wind, and no dog, and only shot 14 snipe 1 golden plover, no grouse. I naturally missed all my snipe except one half, and shot 1 oyster-catcher, who stayed still for me, and one flying red-shank, also one golden plover in the dusk, which I lost, on the beach.

The island is under 2 miles long, and fairly broad, but there is plenty of room. We[1] have 1 bedroom, 1 sitting-room, accommodations primitive. All kinds of birds. A deserted teal(?) nest. four eggs, 3 of which are not half the right size, evidently first attempt, like chickens. The gun seems excellent. I will write a real letter when I am no more sleepy.

Your loving

H. Moseley

---

[1] HM and his cousin Jack.

36

Hotel du Gold Herens
Ferpécle (Valais suisse)
ALS (LH)   Tuesday, August 3, 1909

My dear Mother,

We[1] arrived here last night. Saturday and Sunday night at Arolla. Friday at Pralong. Thursday.Wednesday at Fionnay. Tuesday. Ollomont. Monday. Gt St Bernard. Sunday, Saturday.Ferret. Friday. Praz du Fort.Val Ferret. We have had great luck with the weather until today. Today it seems to be going to pour continuously, and is cold. Therefore the Col du Torrent must wait until tomorrow. From Pralong we came to

Arolla by the same way as last year, but went up the Pas de Chevres to avoid the zigzags up the Col de Riedmatten. The Pas de Chevres is absurdly easy to get up, but our Alpenstocks were much in the way. Going down it without a rope, one would have to be careful. The pass [Col de Severeux] from Fionnay to Pralong was very delightful. We took a young porter to shew us the way, and he left us near the top to find our own way down to Pralong, and only charged 10 francs! We left Fionnay about 4 in a hot fog, like a Turkish bath. When someway up the hill side the Combin group appeared through the fast vanishing fog as a dim ghost, of which the tips became outlined in orange, until at last we saw the whole group of mountains lit up by the sun, with billowy waves of clouds beneath it. I have never seen a more wonderful transformation scene. Further up we saw a chamois quite close, and a squealing eagle soared above us. For the last half hour or so we went up steps that I cut in the snow with the porter's ice-axe. It was hard work, as the axe was very blunt, and was evidently meant more for show than for use. The Rosa Blanche [Rosablanche] is about 11,000 feet, and the view from the top is amazing. I think that it is about the best I have ever seen. The Savoy mountains, the Graians,[2] the Monte Rosa and Matterhorn group, the Engadine, Oberland, Wildstrubel, Diablerets and Juras made a continuous circle all round, and in the foreground were the Grand Combin, Pleureur, and Mont Blanc de Cheilon with the Val de Dix, and the Fionnay valley below us, and in front the Glacier des Ecoulaies down which we glissaded to the Val de Dix. A lovely day, but no climbing.

[A paragraph on Margery's finances here omitted.] [3]

---

[1] HM and, perhaps, Henry Jervis (*supra*, p. 31).
[2] Alpi graie.
[3] The letter continued to a second page, which has not been found.

37

48 Woodstock Road
Oxford
ALS (LH)   [4/5 Dec 09]

My dear Mar,
    You were a most impertinent little girl to send messages asking for a letter. Do you not know that the home sick young woman newly married

and living in the suburbs habitually finds time hang so heavy on her hands, that she causes the waste paper baskets of all her relatives to burst with repletion; while here in Oxford the heavy eyed student pores unremittingly over dry 'School' books, merely ceasing to snatch an infrequent and unattractive meal, or to dream for a few hours that Schools are over, and he has squared the circle.

And here is the young woman, with no duties or occupations but to see that the pound of sugar is sold by just measure, with but a reasonable modicum of sand, and that the weekly Soda consumption is kept within bounds, sending messages to her studious brother, in which she pretends that she has no time to attend to her 'natural' duties. Now that a letter—and that legible—has really arrived, I thank you for it, merely waiting until term has left off, to emphasize how preposterous is the idea that I have time to spare.

I keep my waist measurement within reasonable bounds by abstaining from lunch,—a source of serious grief to {Mamee}.[1] But of exercise I have had little lately, excepting such as my military duties demand. I am an antimilitarist for myself at any rate, by conviction, a soldier by necessity. I can find no sound argument with which to confute the advocate of universal service, and I am therefore forced either to appear military myself or to argue on what seems to be a losing side.[2] We march about the fields—two men to a skipping rope make a section—imagining ourselves a large army; then the section commanders find themselves behind their 'men,' and advance hastily over the skipping rope to the front—a manoeuvre which would be worth watching if practiced on parade. The skipping rope wheels, and trys to form fours, in which it necessarily fails. Then we skirmish, open into extended order, and fire rapidly wooden cartridges at the trees.

You ask about Hartley.[3] I have not had the pleasure of seeing much of him this term, but one incident was very entertaining. I got the Junior Sci[entific Society] to ask Miss Buchanan[4] to read them a paper on her heart-beats. Apparently Hartley, for reasons known only to himself, objected and tried to induce Balliol men to stir up dissension. They were to pretend that the presence of a Lady in the club was illegal, and as she had agreed to read, before the fuss began, it appeared that things would become very awkward. He was circumvented, because the principal agent on whom he relied told him to come and 'do his own dirty work,' or something to that effect; and as such a thing would be quite contrary to his policy in life, the agitation fizzled out. Lady visitors, who care to sit wrapped in stifling tobacco smoke at the meetings, may now do so: the Balliol objectors, so noisy before, vanished suddenly.

My poor eyes are worn out three days in each week measuring diffraction bands, Newton's rings, etc., which are only just faintly visible in a darkened room. To fix a spider line on the edge of a shadow that is only just visible is trying work. I am delighted to be able to get down to the cottage away from damp, muggy Oxford. Mother is planning Rome with Magdalen Hall in February. I hope she will consent, but she has not yet been asked. It seems stupid for anyone to stay in Oxford in February who is not obliged. Your treasure tells Nelly[5] that she likes the looks of you, which is lucky for you, as it means that she will work well. Would you like me to send you an article on 'The Detection of Adulterants for the House-Wife'. It will tell you how to test for formalin in your milk, salicylic acid in your vegetables, borax in your cream, coca-nut oil in your butter, chalk in your cocoa, and so forth. Surely the duties of a scientific housekeeper include this! Let me know if your money-matters go amiss.

Your loving brother

H. Moseley

---

[1] Evidently the family cook.

[2] Cf. *supra*, p. 30.

[3] **14**, n. 1.

[4] Florence Buchanan, a student of E. R. Lankester's, held a research position at the Oxford Museum for many years. Her studies of the heartbeats of birds and mice (*Proceedings of the Physiological Society of London* 37 (1908), lxxix–lxxx; 38 (1909), lxii–lxvi; and 40 (1910), xlii–xliv) were very highly regarded; cf. *Nature* 127 (1931), 456.

[5] Apparently a maid of Amabel's who knew Margery's new servant ("treasure").

38

48 Woodstock Road
Oxford
ALS (LH)   [early 1910?]

[To Margery]

[Asks to come to visit "next Saturday."] Please excuse a letter, it is late, and I have much Physics to get through.

39

[Oxford]

ALS (LH)   [27 May 10]

My dearest of small Mothers,

I am agitated about the Manchester question, as well as worrying over Schools. It is hot, and my brain is limp as putty, and quite incapable of working hard.

I find divided counsel concerning the Manchester demonstratorship. It has been advertised in *Nature*,[1] and applications have to be sent to the Council before 13 June. This probably means getting large numbers of copies of testimonials printed, but the wretched Registrar refuses to answer the letter I sent on Saturday asking for particulars. Of all people in the world, Registrars have the least excuse for being unbusinesslike. I find my tutor[2] very much in favour of my trying for it: Nagel [3] also, although he does not appear interested one way or the other, advises it, and tells me what testimonials should be sought for. I have approached Clifton,[4] who is very willing to help me, and will either write privately to Rutherford, or send a testimonial, which should have weight, as he was for some time Professor at Manchester himself in quite prehistoric days. It was a surprise to find him so amiable.

Today I spoke to Kirkby,[5] who very strongly urges me to have nothing to do with it, but go to research without teaching. He quite agrees that Rutherford is the best possible man for me to be under, but considers that demonstrating all day for £125 is a gross case of sweating. The question really is, whether teaching would leave enough time for research. All the Manchester demonstrators manage to get some research done, but I do not know how much of it is in the Vac:s, and how much in term. What Kirkby's point of view in fact is, is that I am too good to waste on Manchester demonstrating.

The other side is that I have a strong belief that some teaching would clear my brain,[6] and fix ideas at present uncoordinated more than would any amount of reading. Also teaching is an experience that has to be gone through.

Kirkby's judgment is not very trustworthy for two reasons. Firstly he is by nature rather lazy himself, and therefore his ideal is on a less strenuous plane than my own—he would probably think an Oxford fellowship would be the full stretch of my ambition.

Secondly as an Oxford man he looks down on all things outside, whereas it is a fact that recommendations from Oxford are apt to carry less weight than from places where Science is treated as a more serious profession, and a year or two teaching in a very large well organized Laboratory at Manchester count for more than several years of the easy-going, and less responsible demonstrating at Oxford.

It would thus be, as Rutherford advised, a relief to get through the drudgery early.

At the same time, if there is little opportunity left for research (and I will be less advantageously placed than others, as I will want to devote most of the Vacs to cultivating Pick's Hill [7] and my Mother's society), the advantage of contact with Rutherford is diminished, but the mercenary advantage that he is an excellent stepping stone remains. Again research posts, such as I will want will be easier to get, if I research steadily with undivided attention for a year or two. On the other hand it is notorious how difficult it is for those who let some years elapse between leaving Oxford and taking a job, to get employment. They get past over, and often forgotten. (This would cease to be a strong argument if I happened on successful research, but that would be much a matter of luck.) Two things seem to be equally balanced, either a year's research, then try for a demonstratorship, if I find they have not immensely much to do, and if there appears to be a vacancy.

Or to try to get some teaching over, which would at the same time give me a much better position in the laboratory, and enable me to see more of Rutherford, then after one year drop it, if it left scarcely any time over. Apparently the wage is exceptionally low (Kirkby on leaving Oxford got £180 for only 15 hours work a week at some place in Wales), but that is not very material, is it?

Having thus cleared up my ideas by writing them down as they occur, I send you them, though you will see that they have no pretence of being a letter.

Until Saturday evening

Goodbye
H.G.J.M.

I would like to have your opinion, if this reaches you in time.

What a coup it would be to get the post on the strength of the good testimonials I believe I would get before July 1st and then get a 2nd.

---

1 Not found.
2 Idwal O. Griffith, *supra*, p. 37.
3 D. H. Nagel, *supra*, p. 36.
4 R. B. Clifton, *supra*, p. 34.
5 Reverend Paul J. Kirkby, *supra*, p. 41.
6 Cf. **84**.
7 HM's garden near the New Forest; *supra*, p. 40.

40

Trinity College,
Oxford
ALS (LH)   [17 June 10]

My dear Mother,

Two elementary papers today, not great success.[1] I was fighting inefficiently against time. The heat is overpowering, and an owl squawked all night in the garden, and kept me awake. Tomorrow general Physics, and most appropriately heat.

The testimonials arrived in time, and flattered, and incidentally mentioned that I had very considerable knowledge of chemistry which was a very large fib.

H.G.J.M.

No flowers![2]

---

1 *Supra*, pp. 39–40.
2 I.e., no flowers have arrived from Pick's Hill.

41

48 Woodstock Road
Oxford
ALS (LH)   [21 June 10]

My dear Mother,

The heat here has been insupportable, and Saturday was the worst of all. I have therefore of course spoiled all my chances. It was a chance that could not be guarded against. The two special subjects about which I knew something came on the Friday and Saturday afternoons, on Friday in Heat I did disgracefully, and had no brain at all left for Electricity on the afternoon of Saturday. It was extremely sultry, and the paper on Light in the morning had used up every thought I possessed. By the afternoon I could not even write straight, and I am sure that if the examiners can read what I put down, they are cleverer than I am. It will be no use asking me to assist in deciphering, nor is what I wrote at all worthy of being deciphered. I hear from Nagel that the results in chemistry will be all topsy-turvy; all the worst men at the top of the lists. I suppose that is to be put down to the heat.

My papers have been extremely fair and well arranged, so that it will be no used slanging the examiners, whose only indiscretion lay in putting the two easiest papers first, and the two hardest last.

I gather from what other men have been doing that there will probably be one first and many seconds in Physics this year,[1] but there are one or two who might be pulled through by the practical work.

I am now recovered, but exceedingly glad of a few days rest before beginning the practical work. I did not come to Pick's Hill, because my hay fever is annoying enough here, where I hardly stir from the house, and would probably be bad enough to addle my brain completely at the cottage.

Lady Rhys has asked you to lunch on Thursday, and I have refused for you. Providentially I just remembered in time that she was Mrs no longer. I have heard nothing of Manchester naturally, of course they would not elect me until they heard I had got through Schools, and equally of course I will now have no chance against a man with a double first. Thank you, if I have not done so already, for the lovely Paeonies, they are now reviving, and some are a sumptuous colour. I am glad they are mostly the same colour, they will make a much finer effect presently when massed together, than if they had all been different. I am glad to hear the despised Spanish Irises are flowering. Are the Sparaxis? I hope you do not attempt to work in the garden during the day. It is far too hot. Please don't do it, as I would not like a sunburnt Mum to return to me. We are quite in the dark about the day of your return. Mary[2] says that a chess person[3] is coming to stay in the house on Thursday, and so I suppose that you will be back by then. I do hope the woman will not be here more than one night, as I get so agitated when I am being examined, that I am sure I will be rude to her, and you cannot expect her to be quite as agreeable as Mrs Herring, who I understand to have been the pick of the bunch.

Give my love to Mar and Siesta during the day and sow seeds all the night for your loving

H.G.J.M.

P.S. My health is blooming, so that if you tell people that I am in a decline, and that it is a wonder I lived through my Exams, you will not be believed.

---

[1] There were no firsts and eight seconds, including HM's.
[2] The parlor maid.
[3] An opponent for Amabel.

42

Pick's Hill, Westwellow
Romsey, Herts
July 17 [1910]

ALS (R)

Dear Prof Rutherford,

Thank you for your letter informing me of my appointment. It will be a great pleasure to me to work in your laboratory, and after my failure in 'schools' I consider myself very lucky to have got the opening which I coveted.

I do not know how soon your laboratory starts working in September, but I would like to get some work started as early as there is somebody willing to look after me, as it would be difficult in term-time to spare the large amount of time, which will probably be wanted to start research.

I would like to be guided entirely by you on the subject which I attempt, since until I have had a year or two for reading of a different kind, from that useful for examinations, I cannot profitably choose for myself.

I will spend August in Oxford and will then read up Radioactivity, in the hope that your suggestion may lie in that direction. My present knowledge extends little way beyond your books.

I am

Yrs very truly
H. Moseley

43

ALS (LH)   [Manchester]
                                                       Tuesday [Sept/Oct 10]

My dear little Mother,

Two letters from you, so here a second from me, though I expect at
least two to one to console me for being in the desert.

Firstly the garden, that you may not forget to read: Annuals must be
sown Linum and others. Also I want to hear if my second lot of cuttings
flourishes. Such Penstemons as the mole killed must be replaced. Have
Jap: Iris and Cistus seed been sown, and is the rest of the Cistus seed
stored in safety?

Have you got frame paint and wire from Cooper?

Please occupy yourself in taking many hundreds of rose cuttings.
Long cuttings with a heel burred in the frame with only an inch or two of
nose above ground. Lady Gay, W. A. Richardson, and some of Smith's
roses. Put them quite close together and ram the earth round them.

Has all the Tree Lupin's bed been planted, and have more bulbs
arrived? The Quamashes would like to be planted. I hope the burrowing
progresses and that it is being done with reference to a pretty ground
plan of the garden, when sunk.

I would like to have some seeds collected, if any are available. I had
hoped for flowers, but I dare say there is a scarcity, as there are no
Chrysanth:s. Have cuttings of the geraniums been taken?

I get into Dunwood House[1] on Thursday, which will be excellent as
these lodgings are far from comfortable. Lodgings seem to be cheap and
nasty here in general, the students usually pay a pound or a few shillings
over to include everything except lunch.

I find my teaching work promises to be dull for the most part,
teaching idiots elements. I must hurry through their work before term
begins (Tuesday next), to see what I can make of the experiments myself.

The radioactivity is most interesting. I am being given a preliminary
course of experiments, which a lot of people come to the Laboratory for
a few weeks to go through, so as to learn something of its methods.[2] As to
research, the prospect is quite uncertain. Rutherford wants me to wait til
Christmas before starting, thinking that I will have too much to do at
first, but against that I will kick, when I have found out exactly how
much is expected of me.

He has been extremely kind, in asking me several times to the house, and for a long motor ride one day. I have been grateful, as talking to nobody grows wearisome. I called on the Hicksons on Sunday, and Mrs Hickson evidently wants to invite you for a week-end. I said you would prefer Blackpool if I was in Manchester!

I am told that the weather has been exceptionally kind, and I have really seen the sun several times, though never for more than ten minutes at a time.

Today I am lazy and although it is tea-time, I have not been to the Lab. I worked late there last night, and watching a gold-leaf becomes monotonous after many hours. The Lab is accessible day and night, Sunday included as I have keys, so that I will be there till about 11. this evening, then return to a late-hours-keeping land-lady.

I want my silver and cutlery for Dunwood House, so that if you have any of them at Pick's Hill, perhaps you will send them when you leave. Also I would like two or three napkins.

Your loving son

H. Moseley

---

[1] The boarding house in Withington, Manchester, where HM lived for two years.

[2] Bohr, e.g., took such a course during his first weeks at Manchester; J. L. Heilbron and T. S. Kuhn, *HSPS* 1 (1969), 233–234.

44

Dunwood House,
Withington,
Manchester

ALS (LH) Sunday [Oct 1910]

My dear Mother,

The cupboard arrived late last night, and had to be unpacked at midnight, since it would not get inside the house, and I feared rain.

I think it quite charming: it is so simple and well proportioned, and it will be a great ornament to my study. It arrived in perfect condition, and I have just stuck it up. I have not yet had time to get a carpet, so my study has not yet been used. I fear the blue wall-paper swears at all the pictures, and I may find it unbearable. Furniture here seems dear, {Kalmuc} 4/6–5/- a square yard is surely too much.

I am suffering from an instrument whose tricks drive me wild. I cannot get it to behave rationally, and meanwhile no experiments can start. I am to work with my apparatus on one table, and the measuring electrometer on another table 12 foot away, to avoid as far as possible the disturbance due to the Radium Emanation I will use. The two will be connected by a wire which has to run inside a vacuum to avoid leakage by the way.[1]

On Saturday I was disgusted to find a large proportion of coloured students with the thickest heads among those doing Lab:work. These seemed to include Hindoos, Burmese, Jap, Egyptian and other vile forms of Indian. Their scented dirtiness is not pleasant at close quarters.

Otherwise the work is easy and not troublesome, though naturally not very exciting. The Sir W. daff:s would like to go in herbaceous border. l.h.s. among paeonies. Cytisus will die if moved in the autumn.

Remember this year the myrtles etc who must come into the frame to avoid cold toes. You never mentioned if you took a few thousand rose cuttings, it is still not too late.

My companions here are a well-meaning Psychologist a nice but boring pedagogic Economist and an interesting and probably very nice Literateur.

The house is run by clockwork, and the housekeeper is averse to deviations. The seven day period rotational food supply is good but very stodgy. The most troublesome feature is the distance from the College 1/2 hour walk, 15 to 20 or more minutes tram, as the road has always been up resulting in uncertain delay.

Yr loving

H. Moseley

The letter addressed D. B. Somervell,[2] Magdalen, would like to go.

---

[1] These are setting-up exercises for **III**; cf. *supra*, pp. 49–50.
[2] Donald Bradley Somervell, first in chemistry in 1911, later a fellow of All Souls.

45

ALS (LH)

Dunwood House,
Withington,
Manchester
Sunday Nov 13 [1910]

My dear Margery,

Thank you for your letter. It is indeed unexpected good news that you have your house off your hands. I am glad, as that practically tied you to Sydenham.

The climate here is unusual, but not so bad as it is pictured. The last 10 days have been 2 brown fogs. 1 white. 1 bright frosty day. 1 snow. 5 rain, but never all day long. It is alternately hot and muggy and cold and damp, but except for the brown fogs not one whit worse than Oxford, and not quite so sleepy here.

My work is going through much tribulation. On Thursday I at last induced my apparatus to stay at a pressure of 1/400 mm. that is a three-hundred-thousandth of an atmosphere, after plastering many suspected leaks with a red sticky stuff which resembles butter. Then I started my experiment, but a glass tube of thickness much less than tissue paper filled with Radium Emanation chose to break off its stalk inside, and everything had to come to pieces to get it out. Fishing for a thing which breaks at a touch was too risky to be tried, for to let Emanation loose upon the Laboratory is a capital offence.

The method of getting a vacuum I use is delightfully simple. Heaps of charred cocoanut shell in a bottle are sealed into the apparatus and then cooled by liquid air. The charcoal sucks up almost all the gas in a surprisingly short time, and so long as it is kept cool keeps the pressure down. I am trying to measure the number of electrons shot off by Radium in some of its changes. This is only repeating someone else's work, but is worth doing, as it is possible now to use better methods. I hope later to get on to more interesting work. I want to find how these electrons (β particles) are stopped by matter, a question of importance now much in dispute.[1] My teaching is light 9 hours a week at present, but so distributed that I have only two days quite free, and Saturday and Monday mornings both engaged. This prevents week ends.

The students are docile but mostly stupid, and repeating the same thing to 100 different students becomes at times monotonous. There is however the saving grace of intelligence among a few.

These give more trouble than the rest. They get their experiments finished in one hour, instead of two, and I have to rack my brains to find something to keep them good and quiet for the rest of the time.

My companions in Dunwood House I see not very much of, but find them quite pleasant and easy to get on with. One is not quite to my liking, but the wheels of politeness are well-oiled, which does instead.

I consider my birthday as a time of mourning for vanished youth as you know, but if you really must give me a present, let it be a letter-case, if that is not too dear; that of Mrs Poulton[2] has alas vanished for ever.

Y.l. Brother H.M.

Please thank Alfred [3] for his congratulatory letter of August 1st, which I believe has not yet been answered. On reflection, I called on him instead, which equivilates.

---

[1] Cf. J. L. Heilbron, *AHES* 4 (1968), 265–280.

[2] Mrs E. B. Poulton, wife of the Professor of Zoology at Oxford and a good friend of Amabel's.

[3] Alfred Ludlow-Hewitt, Margery's husband.

46

Dunwood House,
Withington,
Manchester

ALS (LH)   [Wednesday, 30 Nov 10]

My dear little Mother,

Your Monday letter finds itself sadly behindhand, and takes this first opportunity to get written. Today the fog is so thick, that I shall probably get lost on my way to the College; it tastes acrid and tickles the throat. Yesterday the tram in which I came back lost itself badly, and I finally got out somewhere and groped for a side-street on which to find a street name which luckily I recognized. Monday the fog was thinner but more yellow. Sunday it poured all day, but I was enjoying myself in Derbyshire. I walked with a friend over a 2000 ft hill which was deep in snow. I saw many mountain hares and a ptarmigan all in their winter dress. We started in rain, walked through sleet into a foggy snowstorm and down through a blizzard to more rain. The hill-top resembled a snow field. A crust of ice on top, and riddled with holes into which I sank over my knees. The going was hard, especially on the roads, which were glazed, and equilibrium was almost impossible down hill with a blizzard at the back, which seemed a short time before to have stripped the wires from the telegraph poles and festooned them on the road.

The fresh air was none the less very enjoyable, and has left me stiff from about 16 miles, after my sedentary existence here.

Monday was also a strenuous day, 4 hours demonstrating in the noxious atmosphere of 45 Bunsen burners, and a like number of students, then experiments all the evening; which behaved like lambs for once. Yesterday the apparatus was sulky. It complained I think of feeling damp, and refused to become exhausted in consequence, while the evening was taken by a sudden stop-gap demand for bridge until midnight, after which I snooze in my chair, trying to concoct a letter to you. Some gloves and a coat have arrived, sent from Oxford: most shameless of Mums, I have already with me two warm pairs of gloves, but those you send are certainly extra beautiful, and shall be reserved for motoring. The coat is fine and warm, very ostentatious, and more suited for the gold-fob successful business man, than the poor scientific mouse. If I do not return it, please do not accept this as a precedent for further wrong-doing, as even if you do find a coat which can be worn, such luck would not continue. Thank you for taking the trouble to get it for me. If you send the bill, I will pay in order to get the discount.

I believe my duties finish next week except for examining perhaps. We settled the 23rd, did we not, for me to come to Pick's Hill.

Birthday letters must be answered alas. Delicious Choc:s for Aunt Emily. A cushion for Aunt Tye. A letter case for Mar.

I must soon think about preparing lectures for next term, but there is not much time to spare for them at the moment.

Yr loving son

H. Moseley

47

ALS (LH)

Dunwood House,
Withington,
Manchester
[8 Dec 10]

My dear Mar,

Thank you very much for the letter-case, which is just what I wanted and extremely useful. I am at present extremely busy, trying to get some work done on my β rays. It is slow business, but most of the difficulties are behind me, and when my teaching ends next week, I can go at it without interruption. I fear the results are not going to be interesting, and I may shunt onto a side-point which I have discovered incidentally, and which has the advantage of being untrodden ground.

[A description of the "scaling" of the Derbyshire mountain, as in **46**, follows.]

Yr loving H.M.

I will attend to the business affairs.

48

ALS (LH)

Dunwood House,
Withington,
Manchester
[Dec 1910]

My dearest little Mother,

Christmas is coming much too quickly as the days for my experiment slip by and leave nothing behind. I hoped today to have got many of the results I wanted, but alas things went wrong as always when not wanted to, and today and tomorrow are wasted at the least, in remaking much of the apparatus. It passes man's ingenuity to make the apparatus at first just as it will be wanted. Could it be done, it would save much time. Last week the Lab was in horrid confusion an annual soirée which it had ignored for 3 years had to be given attention. I shewed off my steel balls on Mercury, and also proved that the earth was rotating. The latter can be shewn most easily with a long pendulum that keeps swinging always in the same direction. If started north and south, its south end appears to move round to the west, because that end of the floor is nearest the equator and slips by faster then the other. I had never seen this before, and was charmed by the way in which the pendulum payed no attention to the earth.

[Arrangements for Pick's Hill here omitted.]

Yr.l.H.M.

49

Dunwood House,
Withington,
Manchester

ALS (LH) [Dec 1910]

My dear Mother,

[Arrangements for Pick's Hill omitted.]

I most rashly said last Monday that I meant to make a whole series of experiments that day. Since then two air pumps have come to pieces and been made to work again, most of the apparatus has been scrapped and made anew, and at last I am again ready to start. Remaking the apparatus took a long time, as the Laboratory Assistant spent his time mending Rutherford's motorcar, and I had to make everything myself. Turning brass I find a slow business, but I got it done at last, including two bits where a most accurate fit was necessary.

Yr loving H.M.

I will come by the through train, so please let a pony-cart meet me.

50

Dunwood House,
Withington,
Manchester

ALS (LH) [c. 28 Feb 11]

[To Amabel]

[Horticultural instructions. Arrangements to meet at Pick's Hill.] My work does not go forward a bit. Much patience is being worn thread-bare, but still when it does choose to start, I will soon be through with it.

51

ALS (LH)

Dunwood House,
Withington,
Manchester
March 19 [1911]

My dear Mar,

I write to pay my respects to my newphew, but since he lacks a name, he obviously does not want to be bothered by letters. I hope you will lose no time in impressing on him the Erewhonian[1] point of view, that his noisy intrusion into a peaceable household is quite unjustifiable, and that however badly he may think himself treated in the future, he has only his own importunity to thank. Also it is high time to enter his name at all the Public Schools. By the time he has settled which he would prefer, they will all have their lists filled, and a comprehensive policy now only entails the deferred enmity of some dozen school masters, which at twelve years or more is not worth considering.

He is I believe at an age when personalities are resented in silence, but none the less deeply, so be careful that those who cannot resist disparaging his personal beauty should keep out of earshot.

If only he could resemble a young robin instead of a young blackbird.

Wishing him many happy returns of his birthday, I am

Yr loving
H. Moseley

---

[1] A reference to Samuel Butler's *Erewhon* (1872).

52

ALS (LH)

Dunwood House,
Withington,
Manchester
Monday [1 May 11]

My dear Margery,

I will be both honoured and pleased to be godfather to the infant, if you and Alfred mean to bring him up as a Christian. If not, any godfather would be in the position of a trustee, who was both powerless to enforce the fulfillment of his trust, and knew from the first that those who established the trust never intended it to be kept. I think you know that I believe the Christian religion to be of great mental and moral value to those who can believe in it, both in making it easier to behave properly and in taking away the frequent mental worry to which all agnostics are prone.

Thinking then that from the purely personal utilitarian standpoint, Christian religion is a valuable asset to Europeans, I sincerely hope that you do not mean to add to my young nephew's difficulties in life. Personally I do not see how as a schoolboy I could have got on without a definite religion, as Philosophic Ethics seemed even less intelligible to me then, than they do now, and fear of discovery was seldom a sufficiently strong motive for good behavior. Your message seemed to suggest that lack of orthodoxy was a bar to being a godparent. I have gone carefully through the Baptism service and find that that is not so.

Yr loving brother
H. Moseley

Give Henry[1] my kindest regards.

---

[1] The "infant."

53

Physical Laboratories,
The University,
Manchester

ALS (LH)   Thursday [7 Dec 11]

My dear Margery,

I am writing in a Laboratory so steam heated that even with coat off it is hardly bearable, and at the same time I am waiting for an experiment to prepare itself. Teaching for the Term ends tomorrow but I have plenty to keep me busy after that. Examinations next week, with the prospect of more than a hundred men to examine, and other things besides. At present β ray experiments which must be got through while my supply of emanation lasts, and at the same time calculations and curve-drawing for a paper which must be sent off during next week on work I have done with Makower (the senior Demonstrator here).[1] The paper describes a new kind of γ ray which we have found. The work has been at times tedious more arithmetic than experiment, but it has only taken us a very short time, ten days experimenting, followed by arithmetic in our spare moments for a fortnight. Then there is a miserable lecture to Gas Engineers, which I have been bullied into giving early next Term, on a highly technical subject connected with gas lighting. I object to wasting my time looking up a subject of such a kind, of which I know nothing, and holding forth to specialists.

[A paragraph dealing with Alfred's business affairs is omitted.]

The experiment is now clamouring for attention, and I must go to it. I have to do so many things in a minimum of time that it seems more like a conjuring trick than anything else. The experiment begins in the. attic and continues in my room on the ground floor, so that I have to race down three flights of stairs in the middle, to the great astonishment of an occasional student. Your particulars of the farm are meagre indeed.

Yr loving
H. Moseley

Give my kindest regards to the pigs and Henry.

_____

¹ **II**; *supra*, p. 56.

54

Physical Laboratories,
The University,
Manchester
Saturday [9 Dec 11]

ALS (LH)

My dear Mother,

The Term's teaching is now over, and in consequence I am feeling rather tired and lazy, and will be glad when I can get my holiday. There is however much to be done first. I will probably have a hundred men to examine for Rutherford, trying and tedious work, trying because he is responsible for the examination, and will pick haphazard at the papers I correct, and doubtless disagree with my marking. Also I have a few men of my own to examine, and some routine work to get through. Then there is the γ ray paper which Makower is now writing. For it I have many curves to draw, and some calculations to get through. We will send it to the Phil Mag next week.[1] My pockets bulge with unanswered letters and bills: tomorrow I will attack them seriously. My β ray work[2] is now very interesting, but my experiments are complicated, and something goes wrong two times out of every three, so that it is only occasionally that an experiment gives any result. However I will have the point I am now at settled within the next day or two, if I can get over my present laziness. No fear of my overworking until I have had my holiday.

[Alfred's business matters omitted.]

I changed my rooms during the week. From 159 to 81 High St. The new house is larger and more airy than the old. Our sitting room is nearly twice as big, but unfortunately looks out north, onto the road. The removal was carried out marvellously easily considering that there were 4 lodgers who had to be moved and have beds and rooms prepared for them during the day. I kept clear, and escaped all the confusion & fuss. Please remember that I expect to find edging stones waiting for me at Pick's Hill.

Yr loving son

H.M.

---

[1] **II.**
[2] **III.**

55

Dunwood House,
Withington,
Manchester

ALS (LH)   Monday [8 Jan 12]

My dear Mother,

I have got my examination papers satisfactorily off my hands, and my marking has been officially approved. One man, who has been taking this same course for at least four years got but 3 marks out of a hundred. At this rate of progress I fear he will be an old man before he succeeds in passing. I find the experiments I did just before coming to you, and which for lack of tables I could not before now interpret, give a result quite satisfactory and interesting. I am now writing up the paper for the

Royal Society, but I must do a few more experiments as I go. Please tell Babey[1] to mulch the lawn with manure. This is important and we had forgotten it. I stayed only the one night with Margery, and found it rather cold. Here it has snowed much, and everywhere there is deep dirty snow slush. There has here been no fine weather, or cessation of rain through Xmas week, so I was lucky to have escaped. Margery seemed to be thriving, and that wonderfully considering that they exist on porridge and cold bacon, herrings and an egg when one of the 30 or 50 hens lays. There had alas been no egg the day I was there, and the hens all eating their heads off. She is very sensible to economise on the food bill, but how is it that the servants stand it? There seems an unnecessarily big staff about the farm. Apparently there are two cowmen, the small boy, the youth who gets I think 2/6 a day, and does not come on wet days, and the one-eyed handyman on the same terms. The handyman can do everything except milk they say, but does spend his time in Margery's garden. They would be better without him. He cannot dig, and he cannot garden; and he looks lazy. Poor Alfred grumbles at the 157- going week by week into her garden. They are having plenty of trouble from illness, as is natural with such a mixed and nondescript herd. The new horse and one other have parasite mange, some of the cattle have ophthalmia, and some have blinded themselves, probably from that cause. Then there was a litter of pigs which they had to bring up by hand, and which died of cold in the night, and I think a few other casualties. The new petrol engine I should judge to be a necessity. They have a most absurd drainage system, which demands a heavy force pump to send the drainage onto one of the fields.

The one ploughed field, part of which is let in allotments, will be an expense. They have to keep three cart horses to plough it, besides the two light horses and a great quantity of machinery. The horse will of course be of use also for the hay. Alfred is up about 5 or 5.30 I believe to look on at the milking. When they were a man short for a few days he milked himself. There are 50 cows, of which I think 35 are in milk. Those whose record I saw were giving an average of 2 gallons, which is quite good, I believe, but some must be much less, as their total is not anywhere near 70 gallons a day.[2] I went over the land. No chance of flood, as their little stream and the upper Thames have been cleared of weed in the summer drought. The land seemed very good grass. One

field detached the other side of the canal they pay 4 pounds the acre for!
[A short paragraph on Alfred's business omitted.]

H.M.

---

[1] The gardener at Pick's Hill, Herbert Babey.

[2] Alfred became a highly successful breeder and dairyman; cf. A. Ludlow-Hewitt, O.B.E., *Breeding Cows for Milk* (n.d.).

56

24 Rusholme Place,
Rusholme, Manchester
ALS (LH)   Easter day [7 April 12]

My dear Margery,

When I telegraphed to you I was feeling worn out and wanted a country holiday badly, but now a week's comparative laziness has set me on my legs again. It was most convenient that you could not have me, as before your telegram arrived I got a letter from mother to say that she was enjoying a weekend in bed, so of course I went to console her instead, and got her up, and trotted her out for an airing on a hot summer afternoon that I concocted especially for her. Never the less Oxford is but a poor tonic for the jaded.

I enclose two reprints. The one has the diagrams in, which we drew together.[1] They have printed quite well. The other includes my labours with Makower.[2] The table of numbers on the last page represents many grey hairs. I used to keep Makower calculating at them every night until he dropped asleep over his slide rule. I have just finished my β ray paper, and wait till Rutherford comes back from his holiday to publish it. The only difficulty is to find a journal which will take it, as it grows longer every time I look at it, and is much illustrated.[3]

I hope you have got the infantile plants I sent you from Letts. Their cheapness was astonishing, but they grew splendidly with me last year, and so probably will again. The red daisies are for Henry's[4] garden.

I am now trying to get a vacuum. It is a long business, and I have had many accidents and failures, but think that I have succeeded fairly now. I cannot tell, until I get some liquid air, which will not be till Wednesday, since the laboratory servants are keeping holiday. Of all methods the best appears to be to suck up the gas out of the apparatus with charcoal made from cocoanut shell, which is cooled in liquid air, but the charcoal and the whole apparatus has first to be heated for days in electric furnaces, and pumped out with mercury pumps. If only I had some liquid hydrogen, the matter would be simple, as charcoal cooled in it eats up almost every molecule of gas it can get at. Liquid hydrogen is however an extremely expensive luxury. I should like to come to stay with you next Thursday or Friday, I can not yet tell which, if you are free to have me then. I go on Saturday to meet Mother at Pick's Hill. Please let me know if this suits you. I will bring what letters etc. I have got, and talk business then, as it is better than writing. There does not seem to be any cause for alarm about your money matters; as far as I have enquired all is satisfactory. Has Alfred yet seen his grandfather's will? If not I will send him a copy.

    Yr loving brother

                                      H. Moseley

---

[1] A paper written with K. Fajans (**I**); *supra*, p. 55.
[2] **II**.
[3] Rutherford gave it (**III**) to the Royal Society.
[4] HM's nephew.

57

Physical Laboratories,
The University,
Manchester

ALS (LH)   Friday, May 10 [1912]

My dear Mother,

    Thank you for the £5, which comes at the right moment to save me from writing to my Bank. However you shall have your money back; it is not fitting that when you sell your treasures the money should be spent on mutton chops. My paper I got rid of last Monday to my great relief. Now the Royal Society has it, and I have no more bother until they send me the proof. Rutherford was very complimentary both about the work and the paper, and has offered me the University research fellowship in Physics for next year to be held jointly with an American who is coming to work in the laboratory.[1] This is of course a secret, as the fellowship is advertised every year and is nominally open, with appointment by the Senate, and there would be trouble if anything became known. The fellowship is worth £125, so that my share would be half this. I have just sent in my official resignation of my Demonstratorship. I hope I am giving long enough notice; I fancy that I have to give notice by the first of June, but I cannot really remember.

I am now doing rather dull experiments with a very fractious electrometer repeating somebody else's work to please Rutherford. I hope that I will soon be through with it, so that I may go back to my own ploys.

I can't possibly stay at Pick's Hill until the Monday.

Yr loving son
H. Moseley

---

[1] T. S. Taylor; cf. **58**, enclosure.

58

ALS (LH)

[Manchester]
[5 or 6 July 12]

My dearest Mother,

Thank you for the flowers which arrived in quite good condition, erigeron as before beating the rest, but spiraea palmata also very fresh. The raspberries met with the fate common to fruit sent in tin boxes. The dry pulp arrived looking like little red sausages three of them lying in the bottom of the box. The juice did not. The poor P.O. had wrapped it in grease proof paper and then in many thicknesses of newspaper, but even so everything was soaked by the juice. On Saturday I saw Graham White circling above my head in a biplane while I was playing tennis in Fallowfield. The first aeroplane I have seen, and marvellous to behold. The crowds who watched all agreed that they were glad that was not their profession, but it looked and probably was as simple as cycling, as there was no wind. My experiments have again ended in failure, after most exhaustive and exhausting exhaustion of the apparatus. The disease I have not succeeded in diagnosing as yet. It is really too grilling to do much work, more like the damp tropics than genuine summer weather. I must see to it that I get a special exemption from the Insurance Act. I have no wish to be a voluntary contributor all my life, and if I join an approved society or the post office now, I lose any three pences when I come to be insured. I fancy I can get exempted if I have £13 per annum private income. I must have at least that, to have got such a fat money order out of Somerset House.

I am glad to hear of the raspberry abundance, due doubtless to the thinning, which has let in some sun where before there was a thicket. I hope the gardener is keeping the new canes thinned out. He should have left only about 5 young canes to each bush to take the place of the old ones. When he is short of work he may begin covering the path down to the Canada gate with yellow sand. He may quarry for it where he likes close at hand. It is to be found everywhere.

I forget if it is the Nat Union Women Workers the big Trades Union which you joined recently. If it is, please read the speeches at the general meeting yesterday. I object strongly to the way all the speakers are jealous of the Prudential getting part of the new insurance business. Their attitude was Tradesunionism all over. They want to capture the insurance in order to have a hold over the insured, and threaten to diddle them out of their benefits if they are not obedient. I am delighted that the independent societies are getting all the custom.

I shall expect the path to be all yellow and firm the whole quarter of a mile of it, ready for Aunt Emily in August.

Y.l.H.M.

It is *not* a scholarship.[1]

---

[1] Re an enclosed clipping: University Intelligence, Manchester, July 5. The John Harling Fellowship for the encouragement of study and research in physical science has been awarded to Mr. H. G. J. Moseley, B.A., who was until recently an Assistant Lecturer and Demonstrator in the Department of Physics, and to Mr. T. S. Taylor, Ph.D., who is Instructor of Physics in the University of Illinois.

59

Physical Laboratories,
The University,
Manchester
ALS (LH)   July 28 [1912]

My dear Margery,

I enclose the will I promised for Alfred. I am much too busy to look at it myself and it appears to be circumlocutory. I am hard at work trying to get finished and get away from here. It is high time I left as I am breaking all my apparatus, a sure sign that it is time for a holiday. I must this evening write up a short paper on a not very interesting piece of work, and correct the proofs of the paper I read to the Royal Society,[1] and which has lain on my table reproaching me for a month or more. Then I can get away after a last attempt to make my present research work.[2] I am trying to find the potential to which radium hung up in a vacuum charges itself. The radium gives off β rays and positive electricity is left behind which accumulates until a spark passes through the vacuum and discharges it. So far I have managed to get to a hundred and sixty thousand volts, but I have not yet had an experiment which consents to work properly. Usually something breaks or goes wrong at the critical moment, which is a nuisance, when it takes 24 hours continuous labour getting the vacuum alone. If I can get to 300,000 or more I will have a fine new method of getting high potentials, which I can use for a lot of things. At present one has to use a Wimshurst machine, which usually gives 50 or 100,000 volts at the outside.

I hope the horrid little plants I gave you are growing and flowering. Letts afterwards sent me a new supply instead of those you had intercepted and in June they were growing well. None the less he was not the man whom I remembered as giving good plants before; all the other men give better, and do not send rotten lettuces.

I am told by Mother that I would like to stay with you for a few days in the week after next. I was going to propose coming a bit later, but she wants to get away to her chess tournament so that our visit to the Tyrol will be hustled into just under 3 weeks before I return here, and I will not have a day to spare afterwards. So I hope you can have me for a couple of days in that week. It has rained here every day for I cannot remember how long. I hope you have it also to swell the aftermath. I owe you sixpence for a telegram you sent from Cricklade for me.

Y. loving. H.M.

---

[1] **III.**
[2] **IV.**

60

[Manchester]

ALS (LH)   Tuesday [Sept/Oct 1912]

My dear Mother,

Here is a copy of the long-delayed paper,[1] which doubtless you are anxious to read. My virtue has been great and I have distributed about sixty copies with great promptitude. I have been listening to a most interesting paper by Elliot-Smith,[2] who traces back all the Megalithic monuments in the world to the Egyptians who built the pyramids, and produces a great mass of detailed similarity in outline and detail to back it up. The New Zealand platinum you told Percy[3] about is a mistake. It was thorium and notably mesothorium, which the black monazite sand on the beaches contains. A seashore full of platinum would indeed be worth finding. My experiments still go awry.[4] The last attempt was just not successful, but was of some use. Now again for several days I have been stopped through lack of liquid air. Some fitting of the machine has failed to arrive from Germany, and I do not know how long they will keep me waiting.

I am now struggling through a long mathematical German paper,[5] tedious work but very good for me.

I hope you have ordered gunnera manicata etc. etc. including ostrowskia magnifica from Dicksons. Also there is the bed for gunnera $5 \times 5 \times 3 + 3$ barrows of manure.

Fine weather for some time past, cold with sometimes a glimpse of the sun. I hear Tyrol in the latter half of August was intolerable. Everyone fled to warmer climes frostbitten. The Rhone valley at the same time had excellent weather, so there had we known we might have been happy.

Y.l.H.M.

---

[1] **III.**
[2] G. Elliot Smith, Professor of Anatomy at Manchester 1909–1919.
[3] A cousin engaged in some line of chemistry; cf. **68.**
[4] Experiments related to **IV.**
[5] Probably Laue, *Sb* (Munich) 42 (1912), 363–373; *supra*, pp. 63–66.

61

Physical Laboratories,
The University,
Manchester

ALS (LH) Thursday Oct 10th [1912]

My dearest Mother,

From the length of time your Oxford letter took to reach here I fear my postcard may not have caught you at Oxford (Tuesday posted). You deceived me by going to Pick's Hill on the ninth, instead of the 10th as you intended. I am today very busy again the supply of liquid air having been turned on once more this afternoon. I have been hard at work all the evening getting things in order, and am thoroughly tired after struggling til 9 o'clock with the help of the Laboratory steward to fix a huge heavy electromagnet into position on my apparatus. The Professor shewed a marked inclination to keep this particular magnet for his own use, and it is only after much importunity that I have got him to give it up. I am trying at the moment to take a γ ray Radium photograph, to see if radium really gives out waves, like light. Some Germans have recently got wonderful results by passing X rays through crystals and then photographing them, and I want to see if the same results are to be found with γ rays.[1] Tomorrow I start anew the old work[2] which has been now for so many days interrupted, so I have plenty to keep me busy. [Horticultural instructions follow.] I have still much work to do before starting a photograph and then bed.

Y.l.H.M.

---

[1] *Supra*, p. 70.
[2] **IV**.

62

Physical Laboratories,
The University,
Manchester

ALS (LH) Monday [14 Oct 12]

My dear Mother,

I am at present resting from experiments for a bit [of] writing, as I have much to get through. My γ ray photos have not given me what I hoped for, but I have not yet finished with them. The vacuum charging experiment I have now finished with I am glad to say, as it meant sometimes weary watching through the night. I am already devising new methods for my next piece of work, which will be a thorough frontal attack on the γ ray, and will probably keep me good and quiet for the best part of a year.[1] The flowers arrived quite safe, the mignonette smelling sweetly still, for all that their basket had come to pieces. Yesterday I supped with Carpenter (professor of metallurgy, whose parents you know in Oxford I think), and had quite a nice evening. Elliot-Smith was there and kept us amused. Today I was surprised to find a sad blunder in Rutherford's latest paper, in which he gives a new theory of β rays.[2] I fear all his calculations are wrong, but when I demonstrated it to him he philosophically acknowledged his error, and declared that even if the calculations did no longer fit the theory (which was made to suit them) he is sure the theory is right all the same. I saw the Hicksons yesterday, they were properly grieved that you refused to go to stay with them. I must as usual now rush to catch the post.

I have bought a melodious alarm which when required rings intermittently until I choose to get up. It is far less bearable than the old kind, which does give peace after a few minutes.

Y.l.H.M.

---

[1] In fact it was quickly abandoned in favor of X rays (**VI**); *supra*, p. 70.

[2] Rutherford, PM 24 (1912), 453–462, 893–894 (= *Papers* II, 280–287, 292–293); *supra*, p. 52.

63

Manchester
Monday [4 Nov 12]

ALS (LH)

My dear Mother,

I have been lazy for a couple of days recouping after the lecture I gave on Friday on X rays. It was rather anxious work, as Bragg the chief authority on the subject (Physics Professor at Leeds) was present, and so I had to be cautious. However it proved quite successful, and I managed completely to disguise my nervousness.[1] I was talking chiefly about the new German experiments of passing the rays through crystals. The men who did the work entirely failed to understand what it meant, and gave an explanation which was obviously wrong. After much hard work Darwin and I found out the real meaning of the experiments, and of this I gave the first public explanation on Friday. I knew privately however that Bragg and his son had worked out an explanation a few days before us, and their explanation although approached from a different point of view turns out to be really the same as ours. We are therefore leaving the subject to them. The subject is very important, and there will probably be an enormous amount of work done on it in the next few years. I spent yesterday wandering in the Peak, and for a wonder was not caught by a snow storm. It was very slimy underfoot in the valleys, but hard frozen on the hills. This week I make a last attempt on the radium charging problem,[2] by rather a different method, then come to you Sat-Monday, and give a paper on the radium charging on Tuesday to the Manchester Literary and Philosophic Society, a very oldfashioned scientific society founded by Dalton[3] a little over a century ago. I have just had my pass book made up, and am pleased to find that I still have plenty of balance at the bank. I will come on Saturday probably by one of the 10 something trains. I forget which is the fastest. Owing to the incursion of X rays, all my work has been hung up, no writing or experiments for ever so long.

Yr loving H.M.

---

[1] *Supra*, p. 71.

[2] **IV**; nothing came of it.

[3] In fact the society was founded in 1781, thirteen years before Dalton became a member.

64

Physical Laboratories,
The University,
Manchester

ALS (LH) Nov 14 [1912]

My dear Margery,

Thank you for your cheque and letter. I enclose a copy of the paper I read at the Royal Society in the summer.[1] They have taken a very long time publishing it. I am now for the moment fairly free from work. The last thing I have been at, the charging up of radium in a vacuum I have finished with, as there seems no prospect of getting forwarder. Now alas I have to write a paper about it, an odious task. I have also some work done before my summer vac which I should have published long ago and cannot put off any longer.[2] Unfortunately I find I have already forgotten what it was all about. Meanwhile there are many tempting problems to be tackled and I cannot decide which to start on as they all look formidable and as if they would take a long time to work out. On Tuesday I had to read two papers to the grey-haired fogeys who make up the Manchester Literary and Philosophical Society, a very oldfashioned and serious minded little society, founded by Dalton,[3] the chemist, just over a century ago. I had to explain everything in words of one syllable and yet try to appear very technical, lest they should be offended. It is surprising what a lively interest in science is taken by these old merchants and city men. I expect a birthday letter on the 23rd, if you please. Dont bother about a present, as I agree with you that birthdays are best set aside for private mourning, and public rejoicing is discordant. I fear that I will not be able to put up with my excellent landlady much longer. Her temper is disturbing at times: this evening for example, when she took the opportunity of my being in my rooms to serve up my supper at 5.30, and I demanded it at its proper time two hours later. Landladies are all alike in one respect, that if you give in to them in trifles they think you weak kneed, and impose the more. However there is one prime virtue in the evil tempered. They generally preserve an icy silence, which is delightfully restful compared to the plump and garrulous. Are you getting any more roses? if so I believe Bees are good. Mill St Liverspool. The herbaceous plants and little climbers I got from them were cheap and excellent, especially young climatises all kinds 9d each. I have got a big German book to review,[4] and have not yet dared to face it, as it means much weary work with a dictionary. However it is the only way to learn to read German properly.

Yr loving
H. Moseley

[1] **III.**

[2] HM did not write this paper (**X**) until the spring of 1914; *supra*, p. 53.

[3] **63**, n. 3.

[4] T. Svedberg. *Die Existenz der Moleküle* (1912), reviewed by HM in *Nature* 92 (27 Nov 13), 367–368.

65

ALS (LH)

Physical Laboratories,
The University,
Manchester
Monday [18 Nov 12]

My dearest of Mothers,

Here is a very short letter, as I have another more urgent to write after it before the next post goes. I am starting a new piece of work on the new X ray problem which I read a paper about recently. There is no danger of ill effects as for the sake of measurements I keep the bulb inside a lead box, and do not let the rays escape. I have now very much complicated apparatus to arrange and make and have to get crystals cut and buy X ray bulbs. Plenty to keep me busy for the present. Next Sunday I sup with the Akenheads. I have been feeling too stupid to get through the paper-writing, but it must be finished off soon now. I will send you back the authority which is all correct, and a longer letter when time permits.

Y.l.H.G.J.M.

66

ALS (LH)

[Manchester]
Sunday [24 Nov 12]

My dearest Mother,

I spent a properly doleful birthday mourning my vanished youth without a single letter to comfort me. Yours arrived too soon, and Margery though warned by me a few days ago evidently forgot. Today I have been very gregarious, eating lunch and supper, the latter with the Akenheads. Myrtle is still very doleful and subdued; her husband is becoming daily a more crusted tory. They are enjoying servant worries, and a long succession of incompetent nurses. The week has been spent entirely in making apparatus to start work on the X rays. I have not finished yet, and a suitable X ray bulb, the most important point of all, has yet to be obtained. There is nobody here who is an expert on the rays, so I have had to find out details of modern X ray practice from Bragg at Leeds. Tomorrow I must try to squeeze ten guineas out of Rutherford to buy the most up to date kind of mercury interrupter.[1] No crystal sections arrived yet from Germany. They will probably keep me waiting for some time, but I see that I will have enough to keep me busy in getting everything else to work. I will be working with specially purified Helium, and must tomorrow fit up complicated glass apparatus to deal with it. Three week[s] cannot possibly be spared at Xmas I fear, and you know it. Besides I find myself getting so lazy now that I dont really need any holidays at all. Do you know what Margery would like for a Christmas present? If the gardener is idle he might go on a bit with the long path. It is now as always when I write midnight, and therefore post time and bedtime.

Y.l.H.M.

----

[1] *Supra*, pp. 72–73.

67

Physical Laboratories,
The University,
Manchester,

ALS (Bragg Papers, RI)   [c. 20 Jan 13]

Dear Prof Bragg,

The Sanitas Co's mercury break[1] which you recommended works, as far as I can tell, most satisfactorily. Darwin and I have as you know been trying for some time to measure the 'reflected' X rays electrically. We have now succeeded in doing so with the help of your son's device of reflection from a mica surface. All the results which we have got so far point to the reflected radiation being identical in character with the primary. We find the ionisation in air and in Helium very variable in amount, depending of course largely on the reflection angle, but also on other factors which we have not yet unravelled. Sometimes we get 3% of the primary beam,[2] but at times not more than about a third of a %. When the effect is small we multiply it by ionisation by collision in Helium at atmospheric pressure, a method which works splendidly.[3] The reflection is very sharply defined, the scattered radiation on either side of the maximum being quite small. The reflected rays when they hit brass produce a quantity of β rays, which are stopped by a few mm of air. The variation of ionisation with pressure in air also gives the ordinary type of curve.[4] The absorption of the reflected beam by Aluminum is independent of whether the aluminum comes in front or after the mica, which is good evidence that the reflection does not alter the character of the rays. The reflected rays are harder than the main beam: evidently because the harder constituents penetrate further into the mica.

I hear that you also have detected this ionisation, so probably you know already all we have to tell you about it. Anyhow we thought that you would like to know that your technical advice is bearing fruit, and at the same time we are anxious not to overlap your work. The field opened by this reflection is so wide that we can easily keep clear of any special point you are interested in. We are sending a note to Nature about our experiments.

Yrs sincerely
H. Moseley.

---

[1] A critical part of every X-ray installation was a device to make and break the primary circuit of the induction coil. In most interrupters used in 1913 rapidly spinning metal vanes alternately made and lost contact with jets of mercury; the Sanitas' company's "Sanax" break ingeniously avoided the chief difficulty of these devices, viz., the tendency of the mercury to emulsify in the paraffin in which the rotating system swam. Cf. G. W. C. Kaye, *X Rays* (1914), pp. 64–65.

[2] The high reflection, found only for mica, probably arose from a slight curvature of the crystal's surface, which "chanced to focus the very broad incident beam into the narrow opening of the detector [**VI**, 220]"; cf. **V**.

[3] *Supra*, p. 74.

[4] Cf. Barkla and A. J. Philpot, *PM* 25 (1913), 832–856.

68

Physical Laboratories,
The University,
Manchester
ALS (LH)   Tuesday [21 Jan 13]

My dear Mother,

I am sorry that you are being kept so long waiting for your letter. I have been exceedingly busy for the last week. On Thursday we got the result we were searching for with the X rays,[1] and have had a most exciting time since then, working out very hurriedly some of the number of interesting points which arise. Now we have sent off a letter to Nature describing what we have found so far, and so there is a moment in which to rest, and we can do the rest a little more leisurely. However it is necessary to keep on steadily with the work, as many others are on the same track, and we do not want to overlap more than is absolutely unavoidable. It is for this reason that we have written a letter to Nature, fearing that if we kept silence until really ready for publication, all the others who have been writing to Nature on the subject would regard us as interlopers into their preserves. You know that the main discovery was made by a German who found spots when X rays were photographed through a crystal. We worked out the cause of these spots, but left the publication to Bragg, who was a day or two ahead of us.[2] The rays behave as if reflected from planes of atoms in the crystals. W. Bragg the younger shewed that they were also reflected from the surface of a bit of mica. The question of importance was this. Is the reflected stuff what we call X rays, or a kind of wave like light which is mixed up with the rays? The X rays have some properties which seem quite impossible for a wave to possess. The reflected rays have got to be a wave. We have now detected them electrically instead of photographically and find that they are identical in their behaviour with the ordinary X ray. So they are a kind of wave with properties no wave has any business to have. I supped with Myrtle on Sunday. She seemed a little more cheerful.

I will come to you for a week-end I expect if all goes well, but the term is quite short as Easter is so early.

Tonight I am doing my duty nobly writing many letters. One to Percy,[3] a begging letter for materials for my experiments. One may as well make one's relatives useful.

Y.l.H.M.

---

[1] That the reflected rays ionize (**V**).

[2] *Supra*, pp. 74–75.

[3] Cf. **60**, n. 3.

69

The University,
Manchester
Sunday [2 Feb 13]

ALS (LH)

My dear Margery,

I left you to celebrate your birthday in solitary gloom. How terrible to think that you have less than a year of youth left. I will send you some roses when I find some place to get them from. I want some for myself, but Bees have put up their prices enormously and are now as expensive as everybody else. I think souvenir de la jeunesse will be the most suitable kind for you. I am moderately hard at work with X rays but a bit lazy, probably as the reaction from a great spurt a fortnight ago, when interesting results suddenly began to arrive hand over fist. I am working with C. G. Darwin son of Sir George the late tides man. The X ray problem is becoming intensely interesting and lots of people are working at it, so we staked out our claim in the conventional way by sending to Nature a letter which after some delay has now been published. I feel therefore that there is no longer a terrible hurry needed, as we no longer fear someone else claiming a monopoly in the subject. We have now got what seems to be definite proof that an X ray which spreads out in a spherical form from a source as a wave through the aether can when it meets an atom collect up all its energy from all round and concentrate it on the atom. It is as if when a circular wave on water met an obstacle, the wave were all suddenly to travel round the circle and disappear all round and concentrate its energy on attacking the obstacle.[1] Mechanically of course this is absurd, but mechanics have in this direction been for some time a broken reed. There is some most mysterious property of energy involved which the Germans have for some years been groping after, but which we see no immediate hope of comprehending.

On leaving you, when I reached Manchester I found my landlady fled, or rather I discovered her absence when I wanted breakfast the next morning, and so I spent a most uncomfortable weekend. She was not to blame as her mother was suddenly taken ill and died.

Yesterday I went to see a dramatised version of Les Miserables. V. Hugo, at a cinematograph show. The performance lasted 2 1/2 hours without intermission, and is the longest film ever produced. I much enjoyed it, as it was all done by first rate French actors and wonderfully well staged, with real scenery throughout, and quite exciting and easy to follow without knowing the story.

Much love,
H. Moseley

---

[1] This was a favorite argument of W. H. Bragg's, e.g., *PM* 20 (1910), 388.

70

ALS (LH)

[Manchester]
March 10 [1913]

[To Margery]
    [Horticultural.]

71

The University,
Manchester

ALS (LH)

Monday [14 April 13]

My dear Mother,
        [A paragraph of miscellaneous news is omitted.]
    I am now considering the question whether I stay here next year or
not. I will have to decide soon, as if I do my fellowship will no doubt be
reappointed, and if not Rutherford wants to arrange for someone else to
have it. I think probably I will not stay, as it is unwise at the present stage
to be long in one place, but there are cogent reasons on the other side
also. Rutherford to whom I have spoken on the subject wanted me to
stay, but naturally his opinion is not unbiased. The question of working
in Germany involves great difficulties. After consulting several people I
consider that a few months are as much as could profitably be spent
there, simply because there is no laboratory there which comes up to
England in the experimental side of modern physics. They run away
after strange theories and experiment gets neglected. Also their national
bigotry is rather a serious obstacle in the path of any foreigner.[1] In that
respect the French are a hundred times worse, and their suspicion that
their pet ideas will be stolen seems in some cases to be such, that
conditions become intolerable. It is therefore quite possible that I will
go to Leeds for a month or two or perhaps longer, and then return to
Oxford, but my plans are not at all definite yet, and I will have to talk
things over when I take my MA.[2] The weather remains abominable,
snow, rain and cold winds, but perhaps an improvement today.
        Give my love to Aunt Edie.

                                                            Y.l.H.M.

---

[1] Cf. *supra*, p. 79.
[2] No academic achievement beyond the A.B. was required.

72

The University,
Manchester
Tuesday [7 May 13]

ALS (LH)

My dear Mother,

I sent off today an application for the B.N.C.[1] research fellowship, having got permission from Heberden[2] to be late. It is of course not the least use, but it never does any harm to remind people of one's existence. The work is going on the whole very well,[3] but at times it makes us tear our hair. Just now a horrid fellow has polluted the atmosphere with radium emanation, and so work is impossible. There is so much that we want to do, and everything takes so long that the experiments have to lag far behind the imagination. The result will be no doubt that we will have to publish in a half finished state, which will be aggravating.

I expect I can get a few days holiday when this is finished, but I cannot say just when that will be. Then Pick's Hill will be delightful for a change. I do not think that July in Tyrol is practical politics, I am much more likely to be still at it by September, as the work will be ["not" is intended?] bear leaving. There are far too many people at it by now.

Y.l.H.M.

---

[1] Brasenose College, Oxford; *supra*, p. 80.
[2] Charles Buller Heberden, President of Brasenose.
[3] **VI**.

73

The University,
Manchester
11 May [1913]

ALS (LH)

My dear Mother,

I think you are most disloyal going off for a jaunt to a watering place, when your garden has decked itself out with flowers to receive you. Then they are all languishing unadmired and the slug and the centipede roam unchecked and the Romneyas wither unattended. With me it is all work at present, trying hard to wind up the X ray experiments. They show great guile however, and as soon as we settle that one point is really finished with, it discloses fresh complications all of which have to be pursued in turn. I think another fortnight will see the end of it, and then I come to you for a few days fresh air before beginning again. I still have no really definite plans for next year. Rutherford wants me to stay and has offered me the John Harling fellowship to myself as a slight inducement. But I think it is about time for a change, and I will probably end by trying what Townsend's Laboratory is like to work in. I will have a much better chance of a research fellowship if I am on the spot clamorous. I hear there are thirty five applicants for the B.N.C. job.[1] I wonder there are not more. I have rather a feeling against becoming an amateur, if only for a time, so I would like to have some kind of a job.

I find my landlady very doleful, having counted on getting rid of me for Whitweek. She cannot understand anyone staying in Manchester then, but the poor University gets no holiday this year.

Y.l.H.M.

Not more than one game [of croquet] a day please

------

[1] The Brasenose College Research Fellowship; cf. **72**.

74

The University,
Manchester
Sunday [18 May 13]

ALS (LH)

My dear Mother,

Please do not count on my coming to Pick's Hill, for it is very uncertain. So long as I keep fit, I will certainly keep on working, and only take a holiday when I get stale. I have been working at high pressure for some time, and am battening on it. For a few days I got very tired, but now some long nights have quite made me fresh again.[1] There is so much to be done, and it is all so extraordinarily interesting that I live in constant impatience that experimental work is so slow. Darwin and I are now trying to hustle a paper into the Phil Mag of the first of June. Darwin is away for the weekend, and I am making him spend it writing up the paper, putting in all the results which we hope to have ready by the end of this week. Very likely the publishers will refuse,[2] as they usually think three or four months the right time to have for publishing a paper, but we have got Rutherford to coerce them, and may succeed. The whole subject of the X rays is opening out wonderfully. Bragg has of course got in ahead of us, and so the credit all belongs to him, but that does not make it less interesting. We find that an X ray bulb with a platinum target gives out a sharp line spectrum of five wavelengths which the crystal separates out as if it were a diffraction grating. In this way one can get pure monochromatic X rays. Tomorrow we search for the spectra of other elements. There is here a whole new branch of spectroscopy, which is sure to tell one much about the nature of an atom.[3]

Rutherford tells me that he is badgering Heberden and one fellow with reference to the B.N.C. fellowship, but my chances are practically nil, since Townsend [4] is I believe running someone else, and anyhow they do not want a physicist. A few days ago I got the offer of quite a good Government job at the National Physical Lab[oratory] in the aeroplane department. Research work on wind resistance, lifting power and such like. The pay is very reasonable, but I refused it, as I do not wish to get mixed up with technical work.

A pained but polite note from Macmillans reminding me that I have not yet reviewed the German book.[5]

Y.l.H.M.

---

[1] For HM's work habits, *supra*, p. 76.
[2] They did; **VI** appeared in July.
[3] Cf. *supra*, pp. 81–82.
[4] J. S. Townsend, Wykeham Professor of Physics at Oxford and Director of the Electrical Laboratory.
[5] Cf. **64**.

75

The University,
Manchester
ALS (LH)   Tuesday [27 May 13]

My dear Mother,

Thank you very much for the flowers which must have come wonderfully quickly if only sent off this morning. Your letter arrived with them. The Ixias are the finest I have ever seen and as fresh as possible. They and the grass look lovely together. How I wish I was with you, to see all the fresh spring. I cannot tell when I will be free, but will certainly

have a week's holiday as soon as possible. I expect to be quite through
with the present work before June 11, and will keep that day free for you
and the R[oyal] S[ociety] Soirée.[1] I must take my chance of finding you
at Pick's Hill or in Oxford, as dates are impossible with research. The
sudden heat makes me feel most lazy, though there is of course no sun,
and it is not at all hotter than is pleasant. I still am like a gnome after a
long winter of darkness longing for some light, since Easter was not at all
persistently or convincingly sunny. The University is having great fun:
the arts professors have made a secret agreement and are voting
themselves new chairs, much to the disgust of science, which had no
opposition combine ready to defeat them. They have already invented
professorships of Imperial Latin (dog latin), Modern History (the 4th
History Prof.) and we are threatened with Fine Art. The University has
had a rise in its Government grant, and apparent[ly] does not know how
to spend it. The Junior Staff is now peti[ti]oning for a rise of salary all
round, as they want a finger in the pie. Then the Vice Chancellor is
resigning, and no one has a successor ready, though few will seriously
regret him, as he is an oily old wobbler.[2]

Y.l.H.M.

Please have rows and rows and rows of Spart:Junc: [*Spartium junceum*,
Spanish broom] sown. How are Romneyas and roses. Sow all perennials
not sown earlier.

---

[1] Amabel attended as the widow of a Fellow.
[2] Sir Alfred Hopkinson.

76

The University,
Manchester
Tuesday, 29th July [1913]

ALS (LH)

My dearest of Mothers,
    Today has been unbearably hot and stuffy, and even now near
midnight I discard coat and waistcoat and work with windows and door
open to try to get some air. I will come to you as soon as I can get my
apparatus to work before ever I start measurements.[1] It is a wonderfully
slow business. All today spent blowing glass apparatus and then cleaning

it. Working with Nitric acid, then with potash then water, then pure alcohol and all in unwieldly bits of glass all joints which break if allowed to bear their own weight and tubes which spurt acid at you from unexpected angles. I enclose two papers. The X rays is I think quite nice work, the other is thin and unsatisfactory.[2]

[A paragraph of miscellaneous news is here omitted.]

Rutherford left on Sunday and most of the research men followed immediately. There are still 6 of us left in the Laboratory however and will be for some time I expect. A terrible thing has happened to one unfortunate. He was lent a valuable preparation of actinium to purify chemically. After much purification the final solution has just been boiled down and tested radioactively. Alas he has purified the actinium all away, and it is all now down the sink.

Y.l.H.M.

---

[1] Probably preliminary to **VII**; cf. *supra*, pp. 83–84.
[2] The "X rays" is **VI**; the "other," **IV**.

77

The University,
Manchester

Aug 13 [1913]

My dear Margery,

[After a long opening horticultural paragraph:] I am still very busy on the work which I began about Christmas. I enclose a paper describing the work with Darwin, which please read when you have time as you will be interested. I am now struggling with an X ray tube with a truck inside carrying pieces of all the metals I can get hold of.[1] At last it seems willing to work but I dont expect really to get started for another fortnight or so. The truck is pulled back and forwards by silk cords from which hang iron weights. The weights float on mercury, and by altering its level the truck is moved and fresh metals brought into the track of the cathode rays. I want in this way to find the wave-lengths of the X ray spectra of as many elements as possible, as I believe they will prove much more important and fundamental than the ordinary light spectra. The method of finding the wave-lengths is to reflect the X rays which come from a target of the element investigated. I am using as reflector the same big crystal of potassium ferocyanide which Darwin and I used to find the wavelengths of the platinum spectrum. I have then merely to find at which angles the rays are reflected, and that gives the wavelengths. I aim at an accuracy of at least one in a thousand for the relative wave-lengths of the different spectra, but the absolute numbers will be uncertain to about 2%, as the distance between the layers in the crystal cannot be measured accurately.[2] I find the spectra can also be photographed, but horrid diffraction fringes then come round the lines of the spectrum and prevent their positions being measured very accurately.[3] I have a quantity of photographs, and know roughly what causes the fringes, but they must wait until I have more time to give them. Where is my Bible box.

Your loving brother
H. Moseley

Give Henry my love.

---

[1] *supra*, p. 86.
[2] Cf. W. L. Bragg, *PRS* 89:A (1913), 248–277.
[3] Cf. 87.

78

65 High Street,
Oxford Rd,
Manchester
[19 Oct 13]

ALS (LH)

My dear Mother,

There is my address. The rooms are most comfortable as is only fair as I pay £2 instead of £1.5 all told with the last woman. [Some horticultural instructions omitted.]

Rutherford has caught the prevailing X ray reflection fever, and is using my photographic method to find the wave-lengths of some X rays given out by radium.[1] It needs keen eyes to see the resulting spectrum on the photograph, but it is there all right. My own work promises now to go very well. I have arranged a somewhat different and very simple way of finding the wave-lengths of my different elements,[2] and am surprised at the ease with which it is working so far.

Let me know if any fellowships are being advertised.

Y.l.H.M.

---

[1] Cf. Rutherford and E. N. da C. Andrade, *Nature* 92 (1913), 267, and *supra*, p. 78.
[2] Perhaps the substitution of the fishline pull (**IX**, 704) for the mercury wells (**77**).

79

The University,
Manchester

ALS (LH)   Sunday [2 Nov 13]

My dearest of Mothers,

When I last wrote I prophesied that my work was at last going to go well. Since Wednesday it has been astonishingly successful, which you will be glad to hear as it shortens the time that I will have to stay here. I can now get in five minutes a strong sharp photograph of the X rays spectrum, which would mean days work by the ionisation method. In the last four days I have got the spectrum given by Tantalum. Chromium. Manganese. Iron. Nickel. Cobalt and Copper and part of the Silver spectrum. The chief result is that all the elements give the same kind of spectrum, the result for any metal being quite easy to guess from the results for the others. This shews that the insides of all the atoms are very much alike, and from these results it will be possible to find out something of what the insides are made up of.[1]

You are over captious to grumble about the quality of my letter writing. When I break off work in time to write for the midnight post you should feel grateful that I have anything to say at all. Anyhow when you choose to go in for a game (Ladies' Chess) which is run almost exclusively by fussies, it is hypercritical to refuse to accept their standards. I know it does not come natural to you, but it is part of the game as far as I gather from what you tell me, so you ought to see that you are not outmanouvred.

I want to know the result of your two games, as I suppose that £2 hung in the balance, and surely that is not to be despised. The poor

Scotch lady must have [been] heartbroken at throwing away her chances
of the booty. Anyhow I am sorry you missed your two games with her, as
it would have been great joy to you to have beaten her.

I have just corrected the proof of the Nature review,[2] and on second
thoughts am making it a little more venomous, to make up for all the
trouble the horrid fellow has given me.[3] I am emboldened by seeing a
slashing attack on the same book in a French journal, but the reviews in
Nature are usually such pure honey that I feel timid.

I have returned the official postcard of the British Ass[4] on the
question of Australia telling them to put me provisionally on the list of
acceptances, as the time limit expired on Nov 1st, and I thought it a pity
to burn my boats. It is quite easy to cry off later. I fancy that there will
be £100 grant going for anyone who wants it, so that anyone going
second class would be self supporting. The fares are the same by the
Canadian Pacific as by the Red Sea I am surprised to see, though of
course going across Canada takes longer. If our New Zealand scheme
falls through I might like to go.

Y.l.H.M.

---

[1] *Supra*, pp. 115, 129.
[2] Of Svedberg's book; cf. 64.
[3] In fact HM's review is not venomous; his chief complaint is Svedberg's prolixity.
[4] The British Association for the Advancement of Science; *supra*, p. 112.

80

The University,
Manchester

ALS (LH)   Monday [10 Nov 13]

My dear Mother,

I do not like your wallpapers, neither the niggly white which
pretends to be canvas nor the very dirty London smoke colour, and I do
not believe you do either, but choose them as being my taste! Thank you
anyhow for making the attempt. I am sure I do not know when I will be
back. My work has turned out so extremely interesting and important
that I will go on with it for a long time to come, and the only question is
where to break off, publish and start afresh in Oxford. I feel a very selfish

fellow over it, as it is so very easy and so little trouble and gives so rich a
return for a minimum of work that I should like to keep it all to myself.
If I publish, a horde of hungry Germans will be down on it directly, and
if I delay perhaps someone will get in ahead. So for once I feel
thoroughly commercially minded over the whole affair. Anyhow I shall
try to be in Oxford by my birthday.[1] I hear from Rutherford that the
Solvay Institute[2] has given me a thousand francs, which will come in very
useful for getting apparatus in Oxford.

   This evening I must find the spectrum of brass before I get to bed,
so I must hurry up, as it is getting late. It will of course give the two
spectra of copper and zinc.[3] Copper I know already, but not zinc. If I
used the pure metal it would boil in the X ray tube and spoil everything.
Yesterday I saw Myrtle and the twins, both flourishing.

Y.l.H.M.

---

[1] November 23.

[2] Rutherford was one of the committee that dispensed the research funds of the
institute, endowed by the Belgian industrialist Ernst Solvay in 1912. Von Laue had
received a similar grant. Cf. H. A. Lorentz to Rutherford, 17 Sept 12 (R).

[3] Cf. **82**.

81

The University
Manchester
Nov 16 [1913]

ALS (AHQP)

Dear Bohr,

   During the last fortnight or so I have been getting results which will
interest you. After a lot of trials with ionisation methods, I have fallen
back on photography and find the work so easy that I hope to get out the
chief spectrum lines of most of the elements within a reasonably short
time. So far I have dealt with the K series from Calcium to Zinc (leaving
out Scandium). The results are exceedingly simple and largely what you
would expect. Each element gives two main lines, α and β. Of these α is
about 5 times the stronger. β has a frequency about 10% higher than α,
the ratio being nearly but not quite constant.

$$\nu_\alpha = \nu_0 \cdot (1/1^2 - 1/2^2) \cdot K^2,$$

K = N − 1, very exactly, N being the atomic number. ν_0 is the Rydberg spectroscopic frequency in vacuo.[1]

	N presumably is	K =	ν_β/ν_α =
Ca	20	19.00	1.089
Sc	21	—	—
Ti	22	20.99	1.093
V	23	21.96	1.097
Cr	24	22.98	1.100
Mn	25	23.99	1.101
Fe	26	24.99	1.103
Co	27	26.00	1.104
Ni	28	27.04	1.104
Cu	39	28.01	1.105
Zn	30	29.01	1.106

In calculating the grating constant I have taken $e = 4.78$ [$\cdot 10^{-10}$esu]. An error here is not very important as the grating constant depends on $e^{1/3}$.[2]

The reflection was from potassium ferrocyanide in the second and third order. The two orders gave concordant results and they are probably correct to within 1/2%. One or two of the strongest photographs shew a third line which seems to be $\nu_0 \cdot K^2(1/1^2 - 1/3^2)$, but I am not yet certain of it. I have been using exposures of only five minutes in all cases. I will now try long exposures of some hours to see if a series can be brought out. You will notice that the order is the chemical order Fe—Co—Ni, not the order of atomic weights.

The fact that $\nu_{n+1}^{1/2} - \nu_n^{1/2} = $ constant proves your condition of constant angular momentum.[3] For so long as the electron vibrates in the same ring, and the central charge varies, we have both for your radiations and for Nicholson's transverse vibrations $\nu \propto \omega$. (This will not be true in Nicholson's case if the outside rings exert a marked effect, and as they must do so I cannot believe α is of that type.) $\omega_{n+1}^{1/2} - \omega_n^{1/2} = $ constant gives with the equilibrium condition

$$\begin{cases} m\omega_n^2 r_n = \dfrac{ne^2}{r_n^2} - \dfrac{F}{r_n^2} & \begin{array}{l}\text{(force from other}\\ \text{electrons in ring)}\end{array} \\[2mm] \therefore\ \omega_{n+1}^2 r_{n+1}^3 - \omega_n^2 r_n^3 = \text{constant} \end{cases}$$

that $\omega_n^{3/2} r_n^3 = $ constant.

Of course the assumption that $v \propto \omega$ means that the inner ring vibrates as a whole. $K = N-1$ suggests that $s_n = 1$ and that therefore $n = 4$ in the ring. Where is the energy to come from to take 4 electrons from state $h/2\pi$ to state $2 \cdot h/2\pi$? Is it possible that really no inner ring exists and that it is one electron vibrating by itself? Then the principal vibration is obviously $N^2 \cdot v_0(1/1^2 - 1/2^2)$. This would mean that two elements say Argon and Potassium had the same N which is not incredible. Does the vibration β suggest one electron out of a ring going by itself to state 2? I am publishing these preliminary results in the December Phil Mag. The paper is as yet not written, so I must make haste. If you care to send me any suggestions about an explanation of these results I should be delighted to have them. I am puzzled by their apparent simplicity and by the wonderful way in which α fits the simple formula. Of course they shew that it is well worth while to examine every element in this way, and until this is done I do not see the explanation clearly.

I feel however that they lend great weight to the general principles which you use, and I am delighted that this is so, as your theory is having a splendid effect on Physics, and I believe that when we really know what an atom is, as we must within a few years, your theory even if wrong in detail will deserve much of the credit.

Please remember me kindly to Mrs Bohr.

Yrs sincerely,
H. Moseley

---

[1] These results appear without change in **VII**.

[2] Since (*supra*, p. 78) the grating constant d is proportional to $N^{-1/3}$, where N is Avogadro's number, it is known only as accurately as $e^{1/3}$. (N was best determined by measuring the amount of charge E deposited by N electrons, whence $N = Ee^{-1}$ and $d \sim N^{-1/3} \sim e^{1/3}$.) Bohr had used the value $e = 4.78 \cdot 10^{-10}$esu; HM used 4.89 in **VII**, 1027, without giving a source; perhaps it is a misprint. Cf. J. L. Heilbron and T. S. Kuhn, *HSPS* 1 (1969), 251.

[3] Cf. *supra*, pp. 103–104.

82

ALS (LH)

The University,
Manchester
Monday [17 Nov 13]

My dear Mother,

I am exceedingly busy getting ready to publish my results in next month's Phil Mag. I have not begun to write the paper yet, but have nearly finished the experiments, made most of the very long calculations, and measured up nearly all of the fifty odd photographs. Further reproductions of ten of the photos have been made and sent off tonight to the publishers to be engraved. However I must leave the poor publisher a few days to send me proofs and so he must have the manuscript in a day or two. I hope to come to you next Saturday. Whether I stay or not depends on wehther Townsend can supply me with apparatus.[1] If not I have no time to waste and must come back here until apparatus can be got. The results are very satisfactory: the zinc lines from the brass peeped up between the copper lines just where they were expected. Since then I have been working at alloys of iron with vanadium and with titanium but my poor tube is now on its last legs.[2]

No time for more now. Poor Ronald P. to be left 3/4 of a million, what an affliction! I can not imagine a more arduous profession than getting rid of that much money.

Y.l.H.M.

---

[1] In the event HM had to procure most of his apparatus himself (**84**; **IX**, 704).
[2] It died soon after the new year (**85**).

83

Ms copy by Bohr and Mrs Bohr (AHQP)

Øster Søgade 96[iv]
21 [Nov] 13

Dear Moseley,

Thank you very much for your kindness in communicating to me your most interesting and beautiful results.

In the general discussion I quite agree with you in your conclusions as to the constancy of the angular momentum as well as to the total number of electrons in the atoms. As to the latter point the uninterrupted sequency of the values for K for all the elements investigated, including the iron group, is most suggestive; it shall be very interesting to know the values for the other elements especially for those of lower atomic weight.

As to the detailed interpretation I must confess that for the present I cannot offer any valuable suggestion; I hope, however, very much that your further investigations shall be able to throw light on the problem. If the lines should really form a simple series in analogy to the Balmer series such as you think possible, this fact would certainly be very suggestive.

Taking the constancy of the angular momentum it seems not possible that the radiation corresponds to transverse vibrations; for then the frequency of the strong lines should be expected about two times as big as that observed by you.[1]

However, it can hardly be imagined that the lines should correspond to a process by which the angular momentum of every electron in the innermost ring is increased from $h/2\pi$ to $2 \cdot h/2\pi$. As you write: From where should the necessary energy come? How should it be possible to excite the radiation by cathode rays?

Might it not rather be imagined that the radiation corresponds to a passing from a configuration in which the innermost ring contains n to one in which it contains $n - 1$ electrons? Neglecting the outer rings the frequency should be $\nu = \nu_0[n(N-s_n)^2 - (n-1)(N-s_{n-1})^2]$ or approximately $\nu = \nu_0[N - (ns_n - (n-1)s_{n-1})]^2$.

I am sorry that this is all which I can say,* if I think of anything letter [sic], I shall let you know. For the present I have stopped speculating on atoms.[2] I feel that it[s] necessary to wait for experimental result[s]. You will therefore understand that I look forward very much to see your paper in the Phil. Mag. and expect with the greatest interest the results of your further experiments. Once more thanking you for your kind letter and sending best wishes to you and all in the laboratory,

Yours sincerely,
N. Bohr

Mrs Bohr asks me to remember her to you.[3]

* Many processes of the latter kind can readily be imagined, but apparently they do not explain the striking simplicity of your results.

---

[1] With respect to each of the other three electrons in HM's four rings, a given one, displaced transversely by an amount x, would have a potential energy

$$-\frac{e^2}{\sqrt{p^2 + x^2}} \sim -\frac{e^2}{p}\left(1 - \frac{x^2}{2p^2}\right),$$

p being the separation between the interacting particles. The total potential energy of the electron, including the effect of the nucleus, is then

$$\frac{(Z - s)e^2}{r} + \frac{(Z - s')e^2}{2r^3} \cdot x^2$$

where $s' = \Sigma(r/p)^3 \sim 0.83$. This gives for the frequency ν' of the harmonic transverse oscillations

$$(2\pi\nu')^2 = \frac{(Z - s')e^2}{m} \cdot \frac{m^3 e^6 (Z - s)^3}{(h/2\pi)^6},$$

writing for r its value as given by the quantum condition. Taking $s' \sim s \sim 1$, we have for calcium ($Z = 20$)

$$\nu' \sim 2.4 \cdot 10^{18} \ sec^{-1}$$

as compared to ν_{K_α} at about $0.88 \cdot 10^{18} \ sec^{-1}$. This result could have caused little disappointment, as neither Bohr nor Moseley had taken very seriously the possibility that K_α involved a transverse oscillation.

   [2] The following sentences are here cancelled: "(as soon as I get more time I shall, however, finish a paper about the phenomena of magnetism.) Unless somebody get[s] some quite new ideas." The paper on magnetism never appeared; cf. Heilbron and Kuhn, *HSPS* 1 (1969), 131.

   [3] The draft has several verbal improvements which may be of interest as examples of Bohr's great care in composition: line 8, "suggestive" was introduced for "interesting" and "interesting" for "important"; line 13, "light" for "much light"; line 15, "very" for "most"; line 33, "feel" for "think"; line 34, "experimental results" for "the results[s] of work of the kind you are doing."

                                           84

                                                              48 Woodstock Road
                                                              Oxford
ALS (R)   7 Dec [1913]

Dear Prof Rutherford,

   I had written to Cossor's about the X ray tube, and had sent them some pure Nickel sheet, from which to make the anti-cathode, but hearing that you are wanting the tube immediately,[1] I have written again to hurry them up, and have asked them to tell me how soon they can have the one tube ready. Mine can wait, as I am in no hurry for it. I am afraid it will not be ready for some days as I only wrote at the beginning [of] last week, thinking before that that I should be going to London, and so explain matters to them in person.

After seeing Townsend on Saturday I took a week's holiday in Hampshire finding that there was no apparatus with which to begin work forthwith. The last week has been spent in collecting the apparatus, a task requiring patience and tact in one or two cases, but now I think I shall really be able to get started again. It is too early yet to have an opinion on the prospects of working efficiently here, but I find the professor most obliging and ready to make the way smooth. The mechanic however is likely to prove a thorn in the flesh.[2] Things seem to move slowly here compared to Manchester. My wish to get something made in a week is thought to shew unseemly impatience, while liquid air is only made apparently about once a month. However I naturally do not expect such good conditions for doing work as obtain at Manchester; as I am sure that there is no use looking for its like in England.

I want you to know how very much I have enjoyed the three years spent in your department. When I came my brain was full of cobwebs left by reading for examinations, and even if this time has only served as an education it has been very well spent. Especially I want to thank you and Mrs Rutherford for your kindness in interesting yourselves about me, and for the debt I owe you for personally teaching me how research work ought to be done.

Yrs sincerely,
H. Moseley.

---

[1] Rutherford's sudden and acute interest in X rays grew out of his attempt to confirm his theory of β groups (*supra*, p. 52). In collaboration with H. Richardson, he (*PM* 25 [1913], 722–734, and *PM* 26 [1913], 324–332, 937–948, = *Papers* II, 342–360, 410–422) had examined γ rays of several substances by the absorption method, finding many of them approximately homogeneous and of penetrating powers corresponding to K and L radiations appropriate to elements of high atomic weight. When Moseley and Darwin began to prosper, Rutherford adopted the crystal method and, in collaboration with E. N. da C. Andrade, eventually obtained the chief frequencies of the soft γ's of RaB (*PM* 27 [1914], 854–868, = *Papers* II, 432–444). In fact the line fell at L_α of Pb (which the new theory of isotopy made chemically inseparable from RaB), since Rutherford took as "γ rays" characteristic X rays produced by the internal conversion of β rays. Cf. *supra*, p. 53.

HM designed the X-ray bulb with the nickel anti-cathode for comparing the grating constants of the two crystals (rocksalt and barium sulfate) used by Rutherford and Andrade. It apparently was made by A. C. Cossor, Ltd., a firm which still exists as Cossor Instruments Ltd., Harlow, Essex. Nothing ever went to waste in Rutherford's laboratory, and after the bulb had played its part, W. F. Rawlinson used it to study the high-frequency spectrum of nickel (*PM* 28 [1914], 274–277).

A story about HM told by A. B. Wood (Eve, *Rutherford*, pp. 238–239) probably refers to the preliminary stages of the γ-ray reflection experiments. In order to shield their photographic plates from β rays Rutherford and Andrade had placed their source and crystal between the poles of an electromagnet which heated up during the lengthy exposures required, and so tended to burn out the insulation of its winding. To remedy the defect, HM suggested using *bare* aluminum wire which, being oxidized by heating, would become better insulated with time. Rutherford then told of a great electromagnet he had known in Montreal, one "strong enough to draw the iron out of a man's constitution." This was just the kind of tea-table rusticism that HM deplored (*supra*, p. 57).

   [2] The mechanic was probably Townsend's factotum G. A. Bennett; cf. A. von Engel, *ORS* 3 (1957), 257–272.

85

48 Woodstock Road
Oxford

ALS (R)   Jan 5 [1914]

Dear Sir Ernest,

   Please accept my heartiest congratulations on your knighthood.[1] I know well your views on the sorrows entailed by a title in the guise of blackmail levied by servants and so forth, and I am all the more glad therefore that you have sacrificed yourself for the sake of the public reputation of science.

   Things move very slowly with me at present, partly because I have been having a holiday but mostly because I am waiting for apparatus and it is difficult to get anything done just at Christmas time. The old apparatus after holding up gallantly all the time at Manchester was smashed up by a discharge which went astray, just as I was beginning on the Tungsten spectrum. I see in Comp:Rend:Dec 22nd that De Broglie has now photoed this spectrum. He uses a ‖ beam confined by 2 slits and rotates his crystal by clockwork. This arrangement, which I remember you suggested, would be useful for very small < s, as the scattered radiation could be screened off more effectually, but it has the great disadvantage of wanting so much of the X ray beam that much longer exposures are required. De Broglie finds a spectrum very similar to that which I got from Tantalum.[2]

   I find some difficulty in getting the harder spectra such as silver, and am beginning to suspect that for the same voltage the number of X rays obtained from a Nickel target for example is *very much* greater than that obtained from silver.

   I am sorry there was such delay in getting your tube from Cossor's.[3]

I wrote three times and then went to see them, as I happened to be in London. They have recently moved and the firm which succeeded them apparently keeps back their letters.

The nickel is reputed chemically pure, but I know nothing of its history and so cannot vouch for it. The tube ought to be used with a valve as a nickel cathode splatters badly.[4]

You may have noticed that F. A. Lindemann has been going for me in Nature. I propose to reply and enclose a copy of my letter.[5] I have sent it to Nature this evening but as it is long I hardly expect to see it this week.

I need hardly say that I should be very grateful for any criticism or advice, if you could spare time to read it. Here there is no one interested in atom building. I should be glad to do something towards knocking on the head the very prevalent view that Bohr's work is all juggling with numbers until they can be got to fit.

I myself feel convinced that what I have called the h hypothesis is true, that is to say one will be able to build atoms out of e, m and h and nothing else besides. Of the 3 varieties[6] of this hypothesis now going Bohr's has far and away the most to recommend it, but very likely his special mechanism of angular momentum and so forth will be superseded.

Yrs sincerely,

H. Moseley.

---

[1] The New Years Honours list for 1914 included Rutherford, who was knighted at Buckingham Palace on 12 Feb (Eve, *Rutherford*, p. 226). "I shall have to go to a Levie before long to be properly knighted—velvet breeches & coat, cocked hat—a sword & buckles in galore. I am now in the hands of the tailor to fit me up—damn'd expensive but highly humorous." Rutherford to B. B. Boltwood, 27 Jan 1914, in Badash, pp. 290–291.

[2] De Broglie, CR 157 (1913), 1413–1416, found two (spurious) bands and three lines, one a doublet; HM (**IX**, 710) found three lines only. For the method of the rotating crystal, *infra*, **87**, n. 7.

[3] Cf. **84**.

[4] HM and his contemporaries employed several methods to minimize the reverse discharge of the bulb, i.e., the discharge arising from the make of the primary circuit. Often a condenser in the circuit sufficed; but with anti-cathodes which "sputtered," or disintegrated badly when functioning as a cathode, various "valves" or rectifiers were used to suppress the reverse discharge entirely. Cf. Kaye, X Rays (1914), pp. 27–28, 66–67, 76, and *Proceedings of the Physical Society* 25 (1912/3), 198–202.

[5] Lindemann, *Nature* 92 (1 Jan 14), 500–501; **VIII**.

[6] Thomson's, Nicholson's and Bohr's; *supra*, p. 107.

86

48 Woodstock Road
Oxford
ALS (in possession of Prof. K. Fajans)   Jan 6 [1914]

Dear Fajans,

Many thanks for your letter and the suggestions which it contains. A copy of my last paper was already on its way, and by now has no doubt arrived. I am sorry that the M[oseley] and Darwin paper[1] was not sent to you through some oversight. I am sending a copy separately. I am greatly looking forward to attacking the rare-earths by my method. Special apparatus for the purpose is being made, and will arrive I hope next week. In the meanwhile I have been enquiring for specimens of rare-earth compounds. La.Ce.Pr.Nd.Er.Yb. (also Y. and Th.) can be obtained from Schuchardt of Görlitz, and I wrote some time ago for oxides of all of these.[2] I can hear of nobody who sells the rarer elements, samarium.thulium.gadolinium.etc.etc. Do you happen to know of any firm or private person from whom I can get any of these? I do not at all want to have to start fractionating myself.

I think there can be no doubt now about the truth of Broek's theory. It makes all your radioactive chemistry laws seem quite obvious. But what does Antonoff's UrY branch mean, if as Soddy believes X_1 and Y are inseparable? I am very glad that Y is now confirmed. Fleck's denial was I though[t] published in much too great a hurry, seeing the time Antonoff had spent over it.[3]

Please give my kind regards to Mrs Fajans.

If you know anything of the rare rare earths, why remember to let me know.

Yours sincerely,
H. Moseley.

---

[1] **VI**.

[2] The samples arrived by the middle of the month (**87**).

[3] UY (^{231}Th) and UX$_1$ (^{234}Th) are the second members of the actinium and radium series, respectively; no branch in fact exists (pace Eve, *Rutherford*, p. 228), as each descends via α emission from a *different* isotope of uranium. HM apparently had not yet fully digested the concept of isotopy, and even Soddy at first did not make clear the relation between the parents of Y and X_1. The existence of Y had been disputed by (Lord) Alexander Fleck (*PM* 25 [1913], 710–712), and subsequently confirmed by Soddy (*supra*, p. 72).

87

ALS (American Philosophical
Society, Philadelphia)

48 Woodstock Road
Oxford
Jan 17 [1914]

My dear Darwin,

Very many thanks for your three letters, to which I am ashamed to
have sent no reply. The reason of my silence is that I have had very little
news to report. Whether it be the insidious air of Oxford, or merely a
natural and deserved run of ill-luck, the experiments have not yet really
got into their stride again. Partly to blame are all manner of scientific
tradesmen notably those villains Cossor who have been leaving unmade
many X-ray tubes which I have ordered. In the meanwhile I am learning
how to get my own way in Townsend's laboratory, which naturally is a
slow job at first.[1] I am trying to divide the spectrum work into three
parts, and to do all 3 at once. This dangerous arrangement is necessitated
by the impossibility of getting apparatus mended quickly if it slows
down. (1) is the hard K lines, chiefly from the elements in the Rb-I
column. So far I have got the α line only of Zr and Mo, while Bragg gives
α and β for Rh and Pd.[2] Zr_α and Mo_α are given accurately by $3/4 \cdot 2\pi^2 \cdot$
$N^2 \cdot \nu_0$ [where $N = Z =$ atomic number and $\nu_0 = R =$ Rydberg
frequency] as also is Rh_α within I expect Bragg's limit of accuracy (0.1°
out I think).[3] Pd_α seems about to fit $(N+1)^2$. It is quite possible that
about here the relation becomes less simple, because it is no longer quite
safe to ignore electromagnetic possibilities.[4] However, it rather looks as if
the old $(N-1)^2$ relation goes straight through, but with one N missing
from the atomic table somewhere before Zr and another between Rh
and Pd.[5] The reason why these hard rays give trouble is firstly [1] that the
distance [from] cathode to target in my old apparatus is short. This
makes it difficult to get high voltage.—A new appartus which should get
over this is being made—[2] Secondly that for the same voltage the soft
K rays are given out very much more abundantly than the hard. I believe
there must be a big factor in here. Even though the soft rays according to
Barkla[6] do not give as much photographic effect individually, their
numbers seem to be so much the greater that the spectrum lines for the
same exposure are quite a dozen times as strong. This is after all only
what one would expect. The chance of a cathode ray making so intimate

a collision as to lose 1/2 its energy must be very much smaller than the chance of losing 1/4.

[3] A third difficulty is the white radiation which is heaping itself up into most exasperating Barkla fringes. These fringes sometimes look very much like lines, only luckily they are never straight for any great distance. I have got a little information about them. A. they remain quite unaltered when the target is changed. This proves definitely that they are made of white rays. B. as the crystal turns they turn with it at double the rate. They can then be represented by alternate bands on the crystal being supposed to reflect well and badly.[7] I think Barkla's explanation of this is all right. The way to circumvent this is to work at long distances and above all to use a hard tube (I do not know whether this will help when the 'characteristic' is as hard as the average 'white'). After some difficulty I have borrowed a good spectrometer, and mean to measure up the hard K's to 1'.

The second job is the rare earths. Here I mean to use the L's as being much easier. At the present moment I am trying a few L's for lower atomic weights, so as to know what kind of spectrum to expect. Today I tried tin. It has one strong L line just where one would expect $\theta =$ about $40°$ (λ/ρ for Al [8] about 500 I suppose). I have got specimens of several rare earth oxides, the purest obtainable commercially, but probably containing two or three elements apiece. I have not got their spectra yet as I am waiting for an apparatus with which I hope to get the spectra by fluorescence.[9] If this works it will save a lot of bother. It is a big watercooled tube (20 cm diameter) with Iridium target so that it will take a lot of power (I have got hold of a fine modern medical coil to run it). It has a test-tube sealed in with a flat bottom close up against the target. In this way it should be possible to get sufficient fluorescent rays from material placed at the bottom of the test-tube. I have every hope of eventually pigeon-holing all the rare-earths, but this is sure to mean a lot of work. And first I want some preliminary results to justify me in sending round a begging letter to all the owners of the many elements which are unpurchasable.

The third job is the K's of low atomic weight, and L's too if possible. This will be easy and I will start as soon as the vacuum spectrometer which Cook[10] is making for me is ready. If one day you find yourself with nothing better to do, I wish you would have a look at it, and see if Cook is making a sensible job of it. The chief thing is of course the scales, but it is geometrically constructed (Design stolen by me from Pye's)[11] and such is not Cook's strong point.

Bragg's "osmium" [12] is most interesting. I suspect that Müller's really supplied him with Platinum-Iridium-Osmium-Ruthenium. I fancy all that column of elements really has the same kind of spectrum. [For] Ta I found only $\alpha \cdot \beta \cdot \gamma$ but very likely $\delta \cdot \epsilon$ were there too. For W de Broglie found $\alpha \cdot \beta \cdot \gamma \cdot \delta$.[13] Then Bragg's alloy with the three all complete (and also Ru K_α most plain to behold). Thank you for B's[Bragg's] letter which I enclose. Also for the Laue papers. Will you send Laue a copy of our paper?[14] I have v[ery] few left, as a good many people (Germans) have been writing for copies. He never got the copy originally meant for him, as I did not know his address.

In reply to your last letter. I have got Johnson Matthey[15] to deposit osmium on copper and I expect it will be fairly pure. I will try it soon to make sure that B[ragg]'s result was due to a mixture. With regard to the grating model,[16] I no longer have the least paternal tenderness for it, and if it has proved at all useful that is only due payment for listening to my wearisome expatiations on its excellencies. It paid me a scurvy trick by beguiling me into many an unsound conclusion, and I do not want to have anything more to do with it.

I am delighted that you have managed to tame excess scattering.[17] I am sure that the diffraction pattern of an atom is a sound idea. One might learn a lot from the exact shape and amount of excess from a simple atom like carbon, but then it ought not to be an atomic quantity. I imagine for any atom in the solid (not crystalline) the molecular complex would be the true diffraction unit.

I quite agree that X rays must have a refractive index. The mere fact that the scattered stuff lags demands it. But does this mean refraction by a prism? I am not at all clear myself that it does. By the way the accepted idea at present is that atomic scattering q does *not* depend on wave-length.[18] I don't think this has been tested at all precisely, but it seems roughly true.

The nontemperature effect seems to work out very nicely, but where has the infallible Debye[19] gone wrong?

You might ask Marsden when you see him whether the Physical society[20] has blackballed me. What are you going to try experimentally?

Characteristic reflection efficiency badly wants doing. A good hard Ni tube is I believe nearly all characteristic.[21]

Ever yours,
H. Moseley

P.S. You owe me 1/2 of prints   1.8.0
            typing   5.6
                    16/9

---

[1] Cf. **84, 85**.

[2] Bragg, *PRS* 89:A (1913), 246–248.

[3] *Supra*, p. 77.

[4] Using the Bohr conditions and HM's results, the velocity v of an electron in the innermost ring is $v = 2\pi(Z-1)e^2/h \sim 10^{10}$ cm/sec, or about one-third the speed of light, for palladium $(Z=46)$.

[5] No such elements exist.

[6] C. G. Barkla and G. H. Martyn, *PM* 25 (1913), 296–360 (February number).

[7] C. G. Barkla and G. H. Martyn, *Proceedings of the Physical Society* 25 (1913), 206–213. The fringe system would not have moved (with respect to the plate) as the crystal rotated had it been made from characteristic rays. Consider figure 10, where the entrance slit at A and the plate about B lie on a circle centered around C, through which the axis of rotation passes. Initially the crystal face occupies the position EF. Assuming its surface is unflawed, it can reflect toward B only those rays in the divergent pencil admitted through A which strike it at C, i.e., which originally proceeded along AC. Of these rays only those of wavelength λ will be constructively or selectively reflected in accordance with Bragg's law, $d\sin\phi = n\lambda$, where ϕ is < ACE. When the crystal is rotated to GH, there again is only one point on its surface which will reflect rays from A to B in accordance with the law of "reflection." That point, P, lies at the intersection of the crystal face and the circle ABC. Now $\theta =$ < APG $=\phi$, so that in its new position the crystal continues to reflect *selectively* towards B only rays of wavelength λ. (Note that $\phi + \beta = \theta + \alpha$, and since $\alpha = \beta$, $\theta =\phi$.) On the other hand if the "line" in question has been concocted by a particular facet of the crystal surface, it will shift its position with the rotation: if one doubts the credentials of a given line one just turns the crystal slightly and observes the new position of the line. This curious focusing effect also greatly simplifies the reduction of experimental data: one need not worry about the finite divergence of the incident pencil, for from wherever a ray of wavelength λ strikes the crystal at the critical angle, it will be reflected toward the same point on the plate. Cf. W. H. and W. L. Bragg, *PRS* 88:A (1913), 428–438; and J. L. Heilbron, *Isis* 58 (1967), 482–484.

[8] λ here signifies the absorption coefficient, ρ the density of the absorber; "λ/ρ in Al" is the mass absorption coefficient in aluminum, the standard measure of penetrating power.

[9] By exposing targets to X rather than cathode rays.

[10] C. W. Cook, instrument maker at Manchester (*supra*, p. 45).

[11] W. G. Pye, one-time mechanic at the Cavendish (1882–99), ran a scientific instrument business in Cambridge. His design proved very serviceable (**IX**, 705–706). See J. J. Thomson in *History of the Cavendish Laboratory*, p. 82, and *Recollections*, p. 116.

[12] Apparently a private communication.

[13] De Broglie, *CR* 158 (19 Jan 14), 177–190; cf. **85**, n. 2.

[14] **VI**.

[15] A London instrument company.

[16] An analogy between the action of the reflecting crystal and a diffraction grating; Darwin, *PM* 27 (1914), 315–316.

[17] The observed intensity of the scattered radiation exceeds that predicted by the simple theory, which considers each electron to act independently. "Excess scattering," the surplus over the predicted amount, arises i.a. from the electrons in the same atom acting in consort or—in the case of an intimate molecular union—from the electrons in the molecule. Cf. Darwin, *PM* 27 (1914), 327–328, and P. Debye, *AP* 43 (1914), 49–95.

[18] E.g., by J. J. Thomson, *Conduction of Electricity through Gases* (1906²), p. 326; Darwin, *PM* 27 (1914), 327.

[19] In fact Debye was his infallible self. Darwin (*PM* 27 [1914], 328) and HM refer here to Debye's first paper on the temperature effect (*VdpG* 15 [1913], 678–689), which considers a one-dimensional grating, and explicitly ignores certain proportionality factors depending on distance and angle. When Debye introduced them in discussing the three-dimensional case (*VdpG* 15 [1913], 857–875), he obtained the same formula Darwin later published (*PM* 27 [1914], 325).

[20] Ernest Marsden, *supra*, p. 70. The reference to the physical society is unclear.

[21] Cf. **85**.

88

ALS (Hevesy Papers, Niels Bohr
Institut, Copenhagen)

48 Woodstock Road
Oxford
Jan 18 [1914]

My dear von Hevesy,

Very many thanks for writing to me. I am, as you thought, now established in Oxford with no prospect of returning to Manchester. I am continuing the X ray spectra along several lines at once, and see many possibilities of interesting work in front of me. I am therefore especially glad to hear that you mean to come to Oxford in the Summer.[1] We will do great things together. You must of course stay here with my Mother and myself while we find you satisfactory rooms.

I am at the moment trying to fix

(1) the spectra of the atoms of low atomic weight such as aluminum

(2) the K spectra of elements like Silver and tin

(3) the L spectra of the rare earths.

The last of these seems especially interesting, as in this way I do not doubt that it will be possible to put every rare-earth element into its right pigeon-hole, to settle if any of them are really complex and where to look for new ones. The difficulty is of course to obtain salts of the pure

elements. I have got commercially pure ytterbium, erbium, praseo- and
neo-dymium, cerium, lanthanum and can get samarium (all oxides).
They will doubtless have the rarer elements mixed with them, but when I
have preliminary results on these I will be justified in writing begging
letters to those who have separated the really rare elements. You do not
I suppose know where any of the others can be bought? If you do, the
information would be valuable to me. Your tantalum has done valiant
service. I have burnt a hole (or rather boiled it, as it was done by cathode
rays in a good vacuum) in one end of it, and just round the hole the
metal has recrystallized. This gives one an idea of the temperature which
these rays will develop if permitted.

Another thing I want to try is to look for the characteristic line of
the missing Mn homologue between Mo and Ru. It should be possible in
this way to spot a mere trace of it if it exists at all.[2] There are several
other sporting chances along similar lines, so you see that there is plenty
of chemists' work in this business.

I am very interested in your idea of diffusion into a saturated
solution.[3] I have no doubt that it goes on merrily as saturation like most
other things is a kinetic equilibrium. It is a delightful thing to
experiment on as the theoretical conditions are so simple.

Ever yrs,

H. Moseley

---

[1] HM decided to go to the British Association in Australia and the collaboration never
took place (cf. **93, 94**).

[2] It (technetium, $Z=43$) does not; cf. *supra*, p. 139.

[3] In one of the earliest uses of radioactive tracers, Hevesy (*PZs* 16 [1915], 52–54) was
studying the dynamic equilibrium between Pb and a saturated solution of $Pb(NO_3)_2$ by
following the fortunes of a bit of Th B (^{212}Pb) introduced into the system.

89

48 Woodstock Road
Oxford
ALS (American Philosophical
Society, Philadelphia)
Feb 1 [1914]

Dear Darwin,

I decided against the British Ass[ociation Meeting] some time ago,
and on the whole I am glad I did so, as just at the moment I would

rather not spare the time, but naturally I have some regrets. You are to be congratulated on getting your subsidy as you were so very late in applying.[1] I am writing this moderately promptly so that you may continue to look out for a berth-mate, as it is unpleasant being cooped up with a stranger.

My formula

$$\nu = (1/2^2 - 1/3^2)\nu_0(N - s_n)^2$$

for the L rays is turning out triumphant, a great piece of luck as I published it on the slenderest of evidence.[2] So far I have only measured systematically the L_α line from Ru Rh Pd Ag Cd Sn Sb and earlier Ta Pt. They all fit the same formula. An important point is that the Ls_n is much larger than the K for the same element. Evidently L comes from the second ring of somewhere about 18 electrons.[3] I have not worked out the exact number. It is astonishing how the arrangement of the electrons remains the same over such a wide range of atoms. I take it that the formula means that the second ring is a $2h/2\pi$ ring and I believe this is the key to the atom['s] structure.[4] I am going to look for an M series $(1/3^2 - 1/4^2)$.[5]

What the formula means physically I cannot imagine?

It might interest you if you have any spare time to work out the properties of an atom [like the one in the figure] a bit. Obviously the inner ring will have fewer electrons than on Bohr's theory.[6] I will not be ready to publish for a long time so I would rather you kept these results to yourself. In a few days I will be able to tell you how Al behaves, as the spectrometer is on its way. Thank you for looking at it.[7] I wish (and so does my mother) that you would offer yourself for a week end.[8]

Ever yrs,
H.M.

---

[1] HM later changed his mind (**94**) and attended the Australia meeting (*supra*, p. 112); the subsidy, supplied by the Commonwealth government, amounted to about £100, enough for a first-class round trip passage.

[2] **VII**, 1033, based on L_α of only two elements, Ta and Pt.

[3] Assuming four electrons in the innermost ring, and the "vibration" of the second ring as

a whole, $Z - 4 - s_n = Z - 7.4$ (**IX**, 711), whence $s_n = 3.4$, and $n \sim 9$. Evidently HM had not recognized the effect of the screening of the innermost rings; for taking $s_n = 7.4$, $n \sim 16$.

⁴ *Supra*, p. 129.

⁵ It was found by Siegbahn, *VdpG* 18 (1916), 278–282.

⁶ *Supra*, p. 115.

⁷ The spectrometer constructed by Cook (**87**) made possible the measurement of the very soft K rays from aluminum, the lightest element whose spectrum HM published (**IX**, 708).

⁸ Darwin did visit in May (Diary, 30 May 14).

90

48 Woodstock Road
Oxford
March 4 [1914]

ALS (R)

Dear Sir Ernest,

My work on X ray spectra is for the moment going smoothly, and I now feel confident of the main results. The K spectra from Palladium to Aluminium all have their main line α given by $(3/4)\nu_0(N-1)^2$.[1] For the light atoms however other lines become fairly prominent, particularly one ω of slightly *longer* wave-length than α. For Magnesium and Sodium the spectra are extremely complicated and α is lost, being certainly not among the seven strong lines.[2] I think ω is here the strongest, but I have not finished these spectra.

The atomic numbers run as follows: (I only include those measured)

13. Aluminium	30. Zinc
14. Silicon	40. Yttrium[3]
17. Chlorine	41. Zirconium
19. Potassium	43. Molybdenum
20. Calcium	(44. ——————)
22. Titanium (and so on to)	47. Palladium

You will see that there is room for 9 elements between Zinc and Yttrium. Only 8 are known. I feel privately pretty sure that Strontium, which I will try shortly, is $N[=]38$. It seems very probable that N 39 is Keltium,[4] owing to its chemical affinity to Scandium and Yttrium but unless I can get a milligram or two of it from Urbain I cannot tell yet.

The L spectra from Niobium to Gold are all exactly similar. The α line (corresponding to the Platinum α at 13.5°) is alway[s] much the strongest. It is given very approximately by $(1/2^2 - 1/3^2)\nu_0(N - 8.4)^2$. The atomic numbers here are[5]

Niobium	42	Tin	51
(assumed from the K results)		Antimony	52
		Cerium	59
Molybdenum	43	Tantalum	74
(————	44)	(————	76)
Ruthenium	45	Osmium	77
Rhodium	46	Iridium	78
Palladium	47	Platinum	79
Silver	48	Gold	80
Cadmium	49		

The rare earths I am now in the middle of. They give the usual spectra, but the commercial salts which I have been using are fearful mixtures, so that I am not yet sure of the results. I have tried Neodymium. Praseodymium. Samarium. Gadolinium. Erbium.

Now I have got some pure samples from Crookes,[6] and will repeat my results. I find that there are not enough places to accommodate all the elements to which names have been given in this region. It will be a great clearance to put each element in its right place and weed out the superfluous, as the subject is still in terrible confusion. There are some who would split almost every one of these rare earth elements into 3 or 4.

It is surprising that the only numbers not yet occupied are (probably 39) (?Keltium), 44 (?Canadium) and 76 and also possibly one or two between 60 and 73.[7] It says much for the industry of chemists.

Many thanks for your criticism of my letter to Nature. I altered the point to which you objected, and in the published version I believe it to be sound, much as I distrust dimensional arguments in general. I left Lindemann's reply alone. It struck me as dishonest, and as I heard privately that he was of a pugnacious disposition, I thought it better not to let a discussion degenerate into an argument.[8] All the same his point, which you applied to Saturn's rings, is preposterous.

I am exceedingly busy now, trying to get a paper[9] into [the] April [number of the] Phil[osophical] Mag[azine]. There is however a quantity more data which I want first. Yesterday I took 9 successful photographs, a great advance on old times.

As soon as the paper is off my hands I am thinking of coming to Manchester for a day or two, partly to polish off the work with

Robinson,[10] which lies heavy on my conscience and partly to discuss with you the extension of these experiments to the Radio-elements. I shall be very interested to see whether your γ ray results are the same as mine. Is the Radium B L spectrum for example the same as that of lead? [11]

I imagine that I have to thank you for the invitation to discuss atom structure at the Royal Society on the 19th.[12] I shall be glad of the opportunity, as unless something unforseen occurs I shall have my material reasonably complete by then.

No doubt you have heard that Clifton[13] is at last retiring this summer. The election will be about Christmas, but I fear that the electors are not a very satisfactory body. Approximately there are 3 from Christ Church and 2 from the University and no outsiders. An optical man will be chosen almost certainly, but there seems a serious possibility of an Oxford man being chosen. Such a one would be Walker (mathematical optics—I think that there is not much fear of this), Pidduck or I. O. Griffith. The most likely is Pidduck.[14] He is at present senior demonstrator in Townsend's laboratory and has the reputation of being a very clever fellow. He has however done very little research work.

I hope however that with an income of £900 to offer they will have the sense to get a good man from outside.

Yrs very sincerely

H. Moseley.

---

[1] This corrects the error in **87**.

[2] The complexity arises from doubly ionized atoms; at aluminum the K_α lines have become a diffuse band, whose long wavelength edge HM seems to have taken as a new "ω" line. Cf. M. Siegbahn, *Spektroskopie der Röntgenstrahlen* (1931^2), pp. 159–60, 370–378.

[3] HM made yttrium one unit too high by miscalculation (**91**), and so threw all subsequent numbers off by one.

[4] Strontium *is* no. 38, and yttrium 39, leaving no place for celtium.

[5] Since these attributions are based on the atomic numbers obtained from K_α, they are also all one unit too high.

[6] Oxides of Sa, Eu, Gd and Er (**IX**, 706).

[7] The space at 39 was of course an error; those at 44 and 76 (*recte* 43 and 75), correct and standard; between 60 and 73 there were in fact two (61 and 72), but HM, misled by the chemists, tended to accept only one (61). Cf. **IX**, 709.

[8] Lindemann, *Nature* 92 (5 Feb 14), 631; the penultimate paragraph is particularly unfair, as it brings against HM's theory of K emission the supernumerary L lines found by HM and Darwin (**VI**, 222) and de Broglie (CR 157 [1913], 1413–1416, and CR 158 [1914], 177–180). HM's informant was probably Tizard, who knew Lindemann well, and had observed that he "hated anyone of his own age to excel him in anything" (Autobiography, p. 53 [IWM]).

[9] **IX**.
[10] **X**.
[11] Cf. **84**, n. 1.
[12] *Supra*, p. 110.
[13] The superannuated Professor of Experimental Philosophy (*supra*, p. 34).
[14] I. O. Griffith was HM's tutor (*supra*, p. 39); James Walker, a demonstrator under Clifton, worked on physical optics (**101**); F. B. Pidduck (first in mathematics, Exeter, 1906), specialized in applied mathematics, especially kinetic theory and fluid dynamics. Pidduck, a Fellow of Queens, became Ballistic Research Officer at Woolwich in 1918, and returned to Oxford as Reader in Applied Mathematics in 1927. Clifton's chair went to Lindemann in 1919.

91

[Oxford]
ALS (R)   5 March [1914]

[To Rutherford]

On going through my calculations, I find a slip has thrown out all values of N from Yttrium onwards by one unit.

The element between Strontium and Yttrium is therefore a myth, and the N's from Y to Au are all 1 less than given in yesterday's letter.[1] $\nu = \nu_0 \cdot K(N - 7.4)^2$ also is right for the L ray, not $(N - 8.4)^2$. Everything else stands.

H. Moseley.

---

[1] **90**.

92

Electrical Laboratory
Parks Road
Oxford
ALS (R)   March 12 [1914]

Dear Sir Ernest,

I made Pt = 78, Au = 79. Therefore presumably Pb = 82 (α line at 12.0° rocksalt). Perhaps you are reckoning on the values given in my letter,[1] not the corrected numbers on the postcard which followed it,[2] or is there really a discrepancy? I am sorry I have not yet tried Pb itself.[3] I find the K series becomes complicated for high numbers. Hg for example has 4 or 5 lines besides α, though α is still the strongest.[4]

Y[ours] v[ery] sin[cerely],

H. Moseley

---

[1] **90**.

[2] **91**.

[3] The interest in Pb concerns Rutherford's theory of γ rays (**84**, n. 1).

[4] With increasing atomic number further shells come into existence, multiplying the chief lines in the K spectrum, and satellites stand out more clearly from their primaries.

93

Typed transcription, original
not found (R)

48 Woodstock Road
Oxford
[20 Mar 14[1]]

My dear von Hevesy,

I have delayed answering you as I have been too busy. Yesterday there was a great meeting at the Royal Society[2] where Rutherford opened a discussion on the structure of the atom. Unfortunately Thomson was not there, so everyone accepted R's atom without any criticisms, and Thomson did not participate in the funeral of his own. Thanks to Rutherford I got a good place and a clear quarter of an hour for describing my recent experiments. These will appear in the April Phil Mag if only Francis[3] is sufficiently long suffering, but alas the paper is not yet written and the days are few. I have now proof that the atomic numbers increase one unit at a time from Al to Au. There are three unoccupied spaces the first Mo-Ru the next Nd-Sm the third W-Os.[4] All others are occupied. Possibly Keltium may fill the second of these. I am most grateful to you for troubling yourself on my behalf about the rare earths. Will you write to Auer[5] for me, since he is much more likely to oblige a compatriot? Then shall [I] be yet gratefuler. What I want is a few mgs (not more) of the oxides of Pr.Ad.Cp.Tm.Ho.Ds.Tb. Of course I would like best of all a little TmII, but I fear that is asking too much.[6] Even 2 mgs is likely to be too precious. The order of the rare earths is as follows. There can I think be no doubt, though naturally I want these elements to confirm it. The Pr I already know definitely but my specimen contains 90% of La and Ce! so it is not convenient for studying the question.

Atomic number[7]

57	Lanthanum	65	Terbium
58	Cerium	66	Holmium
59	Praseodymium	67	Dysprosium
60	Neodymium	68	Erbium
61	Unknown	69	Thulium I
62	Samarium	70	Thulium II
63	Europium	71	Aldebarium
64	Gadolinium	72	Cassiopeium

I have at present examined and fixed definitely 57, 58, 59, 60, 62, 63, 64, 68, also 66 as an 'impurity' (50%) in commercially pure Erbium, and 69, 70, 66, 67 as impurities in nearly pure Erbium, which Crookes gave me.

Auer's Gd 2.3 and Th 3. must be mythical. When are you coming to Oxford? Term begins on April 26, but there is no special reason to begin then. Only I doubt if I will be back here much before then from my holiday. Also what work do you think you will choose.[8] There are several pleasant things we can do. First there is finishing off the rare earths. Then there are the missing elements to find. Further there are the spectra from Au to Th, the spectra from Al downwards, the M spectra, the N spectra, and many interesting things in other directions to be done, with monochromatic X rays. Shall I tell Townsend you are coming, or shall you?

Now I positively must write my paper.

Yrs.

H. Moseley.

2 copies of my paper[9] under a separate cover.

---

[1] The typed transcript is incorrectly dated "20th May."

[2] *Supra*, p. 110.

[3] William Francis, F.L.S., the editor; **IX** appeared as anticipated, on 1 April, less than ten days after submission.

[4] HM omitted the space between Lu and Ta because he accepted too many thuliums (**IX**, 709).

[5] Carl Auer von Welsbach; *supra*, pp. 93–94.

[6] Indeed, as TmII does not exist (**94**).

[7] For the several errors in this list see *supra*, p. 99.

[8] The collaboration did not occur (**94**) and Hevesy had to postpone his initiation into X-ray spectroscopy until 1922 (*supra*, p. 135).

[9] **VII.**

94

ALS (Hevesy papers, Niels Bohr
Institut, Cophenhagen)

48 Woodstock Road
Oxford
April 23 [1914]

My dear Hevesy,

I am so sorry to hear that electrochemistry will keep you busy until the beginning of June, but I know well myself that research will not always get finished just when one means it to. It sounds from your description most interesting work, and I am sure that your principle of radioactive indicators is a gold mine from the point of view of the physical chemist.[1] Unfortunately my plans also have been changed quite recently. I have accepted one of the grants given by the Australian government to cover travelling expenses to the British Association. Consequently I leave England on June 12th for Quebec, sailing to Australia from Vancouver after a fortnight in the Rocky Mountains. So we will not be able to work together,[2] but if you come over before I leave I can introduce you to all the chemists and other convenient people, and arrange whatever you like before you arrive. You will find Oxford in the summer a very jolly place, but in August it becomes an uninhabited desert and everything shuts up for a month. Many thanks for your offer of rare earths. I have now got Neoytterbium.Lutecium.Terbium. Dysprosium from Urbain,[3] who is a most friendly gentleman. He has also promised me Celtium. There remain only Holmium and Thulium. I have written to demand these of James[4] in America, but have not yet heard from him. If he fails me, I should much like a little of these two so as to complete this bit of the work. The correct order is not as my paper gives it but La-Ce-Pr-Nd-Unknown-Sa-Eu-Gd-Tb-Ds-Ho-Er-Tm-NeoYb-Lu-Ct-Ta.[5]

You see TmII does not exist, and I had got the order Ds-Ho wrong before.

I have been searching unsuccessfully for the unknown element. Either it is very rare or, as is quite likely, only occurs in a few minerals. I hardly think that it does not exist.

Yrs,
H. Moseley

---

[1] **88**, n. 3.

[2] Cf. **88, 89, 93**.

[3] Georges Urbain; *supra*, p. 94, and **96**.

[4] Charles James (1880–1928), an Englishman who became Professor of Inorganic Chemistry at New Hampshire College (now University of New Hampshire), specialized in rare earths from American rocks and had worked particularly on thulium (*JACS* 32:1 [1910], 517–518, and *JACS* 33:2 [1911], 1332–1344). Apparently (**IX**, p. 706) he did not furnish the samples requested.

[5] This order is indeed correct, except for celtium.

95

48 Woodstock Road
Oxford

ALS (R)   May 27 [1914]

Dear Sir Ernest,

I find that I cannot possibly finish the velocity of electrons from X rays experiment before I go, and hope that Rawlinson may have luck with it.[1] I am sending you a box of Wratton & Wainwright high resolution plates, which should I think be useful to him for it. They shew lines .01 mm apart distinctly it appears, and have an exceedingly thin coating. They may well be more sensitive for these very slow electrons, and give small chance for fog. Makower has tried them I think for α rays.

My time has been much taken up lately by extras. Among others a big triennial scientific soirée at which I was shewing some of Strutt's experiments.[2] Next week Prof Urbain comes over from Paris in order to examine with me the X ray spectrum of celtium.[3] Within the last few days he has made the first examination of its atomic weight, and judging from his results the determination of the spectrum is badly needed. I offered to go to Paris with my apparatus, but I fancy Prof Urbain is glad of a Whitsuntide holiday, and I am releiving [sic] at not having to take such breakable things to Paris.

I hear definitely that Clifton retires this summer.[4] The conditions of the new appointment are virtually settled, so that the professor will I think be elected about Christmas or before.

Yrs sincerely
H. Moseley

[1] Cf. W. F. Rawlinson and H. Robinson, *PM* 28 (1914), 277–281.

[2] Perhaps Strutt's low potential discharge *in vacuo* (*PRS* 89:A [1913], 68–74).

[3] *Supra*, p. 100, and **96**.

[4] Cf. **90** and **101**.

96

ALS (R)

Electrical Laboratory
Parks Road, Oxford
June 5 [1914]

Dear Sir Ernest,

We sail next Friday by the Virginian, the boat which has been chartered to take the place of the Empress. It is one of the smaller Allan boats, but big enough. I shall much enjoy going over McGill, and am glad to hear that Eve[1] will be there. I was afraid that it would be vacation time. Thank you for writing to him: I shall write myself also to say when I will be likely to arrive, as soon as I hear from the steamship people.

I am rather exhausted after Urbain's visit. He and his wife stayed with us for two days and proved delightful people, but unfortunately neither spoke a word of English. Ramsay[2] shepherded them from Paris, put them up for a night and very kindly brought them on to Oxford, else they might well have been lost. The attempt to speak dog French all day, and to get definite results in two days at the same time was naturally tiring, but I thoroughly enjoyed it, since Urbain is himself an exceptionally interesting man. I gathered from him that the French point of view is essentially different from the English.[3] Where we try to find models or analogies, they are quite content with laws. He is himself a very unusual type of Chemist, since his idea of Chemistry is the study of the Physical properties of elements and compounds, and of the two he himself prefers to work with elements. Hence his success in isolating these rare elements. He uses every available physical property to identify them.

Celtium has proved most disappointing. I can find no X ray spectrum in it other than those of Lutecium and Neoytterbium, and so Number 72 is still vacant. My own impression is that the very definite spectrum (visible) given by 'Celtium' is a secondary Lutecium spectrum, which is masked in what Urbain calls 'Lutecium' by 50% of Neoytterbium, while 'Celtium' is Lutecium with only a small %age of Ny.[4] These proportions are shewn by the X ray spectra, but it is naturally impossible to say that there is not a third element present which is the true Celtium.[5] The only other probable place for such a one if 72 fails is 61, and there is no sign of the 61 spectrum.

To turn to my personal affairs: I should make arrangements about Birmingham[6] before I leave England, as it is uncertain when I shall be back. My own preference would lean rather towards Oxford or McGill, when it becomes vacant, but at my age I will consider myself extremely lucky if I get any good professorship at all, and I do not wish to let any chance slip now on the doubtful chance of something better being available later. Oxford can wait I think until I return. I will try to find out definitely when the election will take place, but I expect that it will not be for a good many months. For Birmingham if you will give me your support that will of course be the chief thing, but I imagine that it is necessary to provide for the uneducated elector, who counts the number of the testimonials. I fancy such a one is much impressed by the opinion of foreigners. Townsend suggests that I should get a testimonial from Perrin,[7] who knows my work and is a friend of Urbain.—To write to Urbain himself and request a testimonial as a return for hospitality received would be altogether too odious.—Do you think this is a good plan? Then should I try for one in German? I am not acquainted with distinguished Germans, but probably some of them have heard of the recent X ray work?

In England the names of Townsend, Schuster, Bragg[8] suggest themselves, but I have no experience in these matters, and so cannot judge what is advisable.

I will return the ions paper to Robinson in a day or two.[9]

Yrs sincerely,
H. Moseley

I am sorry to hear that the electron photos need such long exposures.[10]

---

[1] A. S. Eve, one of Rutherford's first students at McGill, and his eventual successor there.

[2] Sir William Ramsay, the distinguished chemist, with whom Rutherford was perpetually at war (Badash, *passim*).

[3] *Supra*, p. 100.

[4] HM's diagnosis was quite correct: cf. H. M. Hansen and S. Werner, *Nature* 111 (1923), 461.

[5] This was to be the burden of proof assumed by the discoverers of hafnium (*supra*, p. 137).

[6] I.e., for competing for the professorship of physics made available by the death of J. H. Poynting (*supra*, p. 110).

[7] Jean Perrin, professor at the Sorbonne and France's leading contributor to atomic physics.

[8] All provided (or, in the case of Sir Arthur Schuster, agreed to provide) testimonials (98, 99, 100, 108); HM decided not to solicit from foreigners.

[9] X.

[10] Cf. 95, n. 1.

97

ALS (LH)

48 Woodstock Road
Oxford
7 June [1914]

My dear Margery,

Thank you for your letter. Here are the prints you asked for and also
the promised enlargement. We start for Liverpool on Thursday to sail
on Friday, and so this week I will have to think about getting some
clothes etc, and many other things besides. The French Professor[1] who
stayed here for two days last week proved a charming man, though
naturally somewhat tiring as he spoke no English whatever. Unfortunately the new element for the examination of which he came over,
proves shy and will not disclose itself. I cannot imagine what it can be,
and seriously doubt its existence. This is disappointing and leaves one
more gap in the list of the known elements.

I hope the young chicks are flourishing.

Yr loving brother
H. Moseley

---

[1] Urbain; cf. **96**.

98

ALS (LH)

The University,
Leeds
June 9th [1914]

Mr H. Moseley's experimental work on X ray spectra has attracted
the greatest interest and admiration, on account not only of the value of
the results but the rigour and brilliance of his methods. Before this he
has already carried out researches of much importance. He is a most
enthusiastic and persevering worker: he possesses both insight and
ingenuity to a remarkable degree; and he is sure, I think, to have many
other achievements before him.

W. H. Bragg

99

TLS (LH)

The Physical Laboratories
The University,
Manchester
June 9th, 1914

Mr. H. Moseley was appointed Lecturer and Demonstrator in Physics in the University of Manchester immediately after his graduation in Oxford. He held this position for two years, and then resigned in order to have more time for original research. He was then awarded the John Harling Fellowship and worked in Manchester until his departure for Oxford about six months ago.

Mr Moseley is one of the best research students that I ever had. From the first he showed unusual originality and capacity as an investigator. He has published a number of papers which have contributed materially to our knowledge of the subjects under investigation. His work is all of a high order of merit; I would particularly draw attention to his researches in conjunction with Darwin on the reflexion of X rays from crystals,[1] and the later papers of Moseley himself on the X ray spectra of elements.[2] The results of these difficult investigations are of fundamental importance and have already exercised a strong influence on our ideas of the structure of the atom. His work on the X ray spectra of elements is of great practical as well as theoretical value, and I happen to know that the new methods that he has developed for identifying elements have attracted much attention not only in this country but abroad.

Although Mr Moseley has not had a very wide experience as a teacher, I am confident that he would prove excellent in this respect. I have heard him on numerous occasions give an account of scientific investigations. He has impressed me as a fluent and clear speaker with an unusual capacity for bringing out the essential points under discussion. He has an attractive personality and has always had the pleasantest relations with his fellow workers and colleagues.

I can recommend Mr Moseley as an investigator of unusual promise, and I am confident that as a Professor of Physics he would bring much credit to himself and to the institution with which he is connected.

E. Rutherford
Director of the Physical Laboratories

---

[1] **VI**.
[2] **VII** and **IX**.

100

ALS (LH)

Electrical Laboratory
Oxford
9th June 1914

Mr Moseley informs me that he is a candidate for the Professorship
of Physics at the Birmingham University and asks me to testify to his
qualification for that post.

Mr Moseley studied Physics at the Electrical Laboratory and at the
Clarendon Laboratory, Oxford, where he gained the reputation of being
a very able scholar.

After taking his degree, he was appointed as demonstrator and
lecturer at Manchester where he studied Radioactivity with Professor
Rutherford, and carried out a number of interesting researches.

Last year he returned to Oxford and continued his investigations of
the wave lengths of the characteristic Röntgen rays. These researches are
of great interest and importance and he has carried them out most
successfully by himself without any assistance.

There can be no doubt that Mr Moseley possesses all the qualities
necessary for a Professor who will be expected to assist his pupils by
suggesting subjects for research, in a new and important branch of
Physics.

I have therefore much pleasure in recommending him for the
Professorship at Birmingham.

John S. Townsend
Wykeham Professor of Physics, Oxford

101

ALS (R)

Midland Adelphi Hotel
Liverpool
June 11 [1914]

Dear Sir Ernest,

Very many thanks for your two letters, which both arrived, and also
for the testimonial.[1] I will now send an application to Birmingham as
soon as I hear from Schuster.[2] The successor to Clifton will be appointed
in the autumn, just when cannot be settled until he officially resigns. The
electors are two or three nonscientific Oxford men, Townsend, Schuster,

Rücker, and someone to replace Poynting,[3] who will be chosen by the faculty this week. The two professors are thought likely each to run local candidates, who will not be generally acceptable; Clifton wishes for Walker the physical optics man, Townsend for Pidduck or so at least I am told.[4] Is there any hope that Bragg might be induced to migrate? I fancy that he would be more generally popular than anyone else possibly available, whom I can think of. Such speculations are not my business, but I should be extremely sorry if a really unsuitable man is chosen, since it is one of the few jobs with nearly ideal conditions from the research standpoint, the only serious drawback being lack of elbow room, which could be remedied. We will meet at Melbourne. I gather that I will probably only just pass through Adelaide, as I hope to join the Broken hill party.[5] I hope your search for Darwin's successor is being successful.[6] I have heard of no one.

Yrs sincerely
H. Moseley.

J. J. Thomson's Romanes lecture was very well put together, but contained not much fresh theory.[7] I was amused to hear him accept your α-swerving estimate of the 'amount of positive electricity in the atom,' but say no word about the nuclear charge. I am glad that he is a convert, even if he does still try to disguise the fact. The most interesting point mentioned was that they are trying for the very soft types of X rays at the Cavendish, and that with Schumann (?) plates they can photograph rays which are stopped by celluloid as thin as a soap-bubble.[8] He did not mention how they are to be analysed but there are several possible methods if the truth of $h\nu$ is assumed. I presume they will use the minimum exciting potential or something similar.

---

[1] 99.

[2] Cf. 108.

[3] HM's earlier intelligence about the electors (90) erred considerably, as three of them—Schuster, Rücker and Poynting—were not Oxford men. Poynting (1852–1914) was a Cambridge wrangler (third, 1876) who had held the Chair of Physics at the University of Birmingham since 1880 (J. J. T[homson], *PRS* 32:A [1916], i–ix). Sir Arthur Rücker (1848–1915), an Oxford graduate, had spent most of his career in London, initially as Professor of Physics at the Royal School of Science and lastly as Principal of the University of London (T. E. T[horpe], *PRS* 92:A [1916], xxi–xlv).

[4] Cf. 90.

[5] *Supra*, p. 113.

[6] Bohr succeeded Darwin as Schuster Reader in Mathematics. The war caught Darwin

before he took up another post, and toward the end of 1914 he found himself censoring
letters in France (Badash, p. 301).

[7] J. J. Thomson, *The Atomic Theory* (1914).

[8] *Ibid.*, pp. 32–33; *Proceedings RI* 21 (1914–76), 409.

102

[Paris]

ALS (LH)   29 Juin 1914

Cher Monsieur Moseley,

Je m'excuse tout d'abord auprès de vous d'avoir tant tardé à vous
écrire. J'ai dû à mon retour en France, tant malade, aller dans une
maison de santé où j'ai subi une petite opération chirurgicale d'ailleurs
sans importance. Mais cela m'a immobilisé pendant une quinzaine de
jours.

Maintenant j'ai repris le cours de mes occupations qui sont
nombreuses et je profite du calme de cette belle matinée de Dimanche
pour vous écrire et vous prier de me rapeller au bon souvenir de madame
votre mère dont l'aimable hospitalité et l'accueil souriant resteront
toujours gravé dans ma mémoire et dans celle de Mme Urbain.[1]

Durant mon repos forcé, j'ai beaucoup pensé à mon voyage à
Oxford, à vos belles expériences et surtout à ce qui portera dans la
science le nom de *loi de Moseley*.

Cette loi donne une base à la classification de Mendeleeff qui n'est
d'un point de vue scientifique qu'un joli roman.[2] Je vise non la
périodicité des propriétés, mais les lacunes de la classification.

Entre prévoir d'après une loi rigoureusement scientifique comme la
vôtre et prévoir suivant une conception vague, bien que très suggestive,
comme l'idée de Mendeleeff; il y a une grande différence.

Vive la loi de Moseley! Elle mérite de figurer parmi les lois
fondamentales de la chimie et je puis vous assurer qu'avant peu de temps
elle sera devenue classique en France.[3] Les résultats que vous avez
obtenus pour la série des Terres Rares, du Lanthane au Lutécium,
éclairent définitivement la question. Aux arguments que j'ai péniblement
donnés durant ces 20 dernières années, vous avez apporté très rapide-
ment—ce dont vous avez lieu d'être sûr—la preuve suprême et définitive.
Enfin il reste entre le Lutécium et le Tantale une lacune qui je l'espère
bien sera comblée quelque jour par le Celtium;[4] car il se peut que le

spectre que j'ai observé et au quel j'ai donné ce nom soit très sensible tandis que les spectres des rayons X le soient beaucoup moins.

L'histoire des Terres Rares est très compliquée d'abord parce que les séparations sont très difficiles et rarement complètes et ensuite parce que les spectres ordinaires sont très riches en raies et qu'un spectre ne se comporte jamais comme un bloc, les différentes raies ayant des sensibilités très inégales sans rapport avec leurs intensités relatives. En observant ces spectres on a l'impression d'un fourmillement d'Éléments et c'est pourquoi M. Auer von Welsbach et les spectroscopistes de Vienne[5] ont vu récemment tant de Turbiums, de Dysprosiums et de Thuliums. J'ai eu beacoup de peine à résister à cet entrainement.

Vos résultats me montrent que j'ai eu raison, et dans l'intérêt de la question des Terres Rares, autant que dans l'intérêt de mes propres et pénibles travaux, il y aurait avantage à publier une note spéciale relative aux Terres Rares. Voulez vous rédiger cette note et me l'envoyer?[6] Je la traduirais et la ferais passer aux C.R. de l'Académie des Sciences de Paris.

M. de Broglie est venu me voir et m'a demandé des produits qu'il désire examiner par la nouvelle méthode des rayons secondaires.[7] Je lui ai confié entre autres les produits que vous avez examinés vous-même. Nul doute que ses résultats confirmeront les vôtres. J'ai vu ses spectres et son installation pour les rayons secondaires. C'est très intéressant. Les spectres sont moins beaux que les spectres des rayons X, les raies étant plus diffuses. Les poses sont plus longues et les mesures probablement moins précises; mais la méthode n'a pas dit son dernier mot et il faut espérer que M. de Broglie saura la mettre définitivement au point dans un court delai.

J'espère que vous publierez prochainement les résultats des expériences qui ont justifié mon voyage à Oxford.

Vous pouvez dire que vous avez examiné différents échantillons de mes fractionnements de Terres à Ytterbium, depuis les Terres Thulifères et Erbifères jusque et y compris les terres à Celtium. L'indication des valeurs des coefficients d'aimantation sera un repère trés sûr. Au besoin je ferai de nouvelles déterminations de ces coefficients. Il me serait préférable que vous publiez une telle note à votre seul nom. Je ferais suivre votre publication d'une note personelle qui commenterait la vôtre. Le résultat serait le même que si nous publions ensemble et chacun de nous sera plus libre.

J'espère que vous êtes satisfait de votre voyage ainsi que madame votre mère. Mme Urbain se joint à moi pour lui exprimer ainsi qu'à vous nos sentiments les plus sincèrement cordiaux. Je vous serre amicalement la main.

G. Urbain

---

¹ Cf. **96**.

² Cf. Urbain, *Bulletin des sociétés chimiques belges* 36 (1927), 124–136.

³ Cf. Urbain to Rutherford, 26 Sept 15 (OHS), published by Rutherford, *PRS* 93:A (1916), xxvii: "Le premier, en France, j'ai enseigné la loi de Moseley. Je continuerai à la nommer ainsi, et je m'efforcerai de la rendre classique."

⁴ Cf. Urbain, *CR* 114 (1922), 1349–1351, and *supra*, p. 133.

⁵ F. Exner and E. Haschek, *Sb* (Vienna) 119:2a (1910), 771–778.

⁶ HM never provided the note, nor did Urbain ever write up their joint research, as he once intended (Urbain to Rutherford, 17 July 16 [OHS]).

⁷ *CR* 158 (25 May and 15 June 14), 1493–1495, 1785–1788, and *CR* 159 (27 July 14), 304–305.

103

Transcript supplied to Rutherford
by Urbain (OHS)

R.M.S. Makura
Vancouver
July 8th [1914]

Dear Professor Urbain,

I am now just leaving for Australia after a few delightful days in the Rockies. I enclose a set of prints from the most important of the photos, omitting VII (the purest) which unfortunately the man who made the prints has overlooked.[1] When you want to reproduce the spectra I shall gladly send you the original negatives, and will send a print of VII when I can find someone competent to make it. As a matter of fact, VII differs only very slightly from VIII, the proportion of Ny being slightly *greater* in VIII than in VII; the lines are all the same in the two cases.

The range of the angle of reflection in the photos (all are in 3rd order) [is:]

I to V.	right hand register mark[2]	12 1/2°
	left " " "	19 1/2°
VI to VIII.	right " " "	11°
	left " " "	18°

There is a small constant error, which I must determine by measuring up the photos both in the 2nd and 3rd orders.

27. HM's analyses of Urbain's samples, numbered I to VIII. Column 1 gives coefficients of magnetization (as found by Urbain); Column 2, Urbain's labels; Column 3, HM's results, relative intensities of the L_α lines and percentages of earths in each mixture. Courtesy of OHS.

I will send you detailed measurements of the lines later. You will notice that there is in each case a faint satellite on the left of β, as well as on the left of α. This line I have not noticed in previous cases, but as it is

28. Reduction of data on α_3 (L_α in third order) derived from Urbain's samples (154 = I, 162 = II, etc.). The final column, where the decimal point belongs in the second place (e.g., 1.626), completes HM's survey of the rare earths with values for Tm, Ny (Yb) and Lu; Er, supplied by Crookes, already appears in **IX**, 708. These calculations, probably HM's last, are written on the obverse of stationery of the Hotel Sydney. Courtesy of OHS.

present for each of Er. Tm. Ny. Lu. no doubt I will find it in earlier photos if I examined them carefully.

As you know these photos are only of the left end (long wave-length) of the spectrum in each case. The range includes satellite of α, α strong (reckoning from the left satellite) satellite of β, β strong ϕ and sometimes also γ strong, but not δ, ϵ.

With many thanks for your kindness in giving me this most interesting series of products to examine,

I am,

Yours sincerely,

H. Moseley.

You will I hope have received your specimens back safely long ago.[3]

---

[1] Urbain left eight samples with HM numbered I through VIII; analysis showed all to be mixtures of ytterbium and lutecium (figures 27–28).

[2] For the "register marks," from which HM measured his plates, see **VII**, 1026–1027.

[3] Several small errors in this typescript, made from the original lent by Urbain (Urbain to Rutherford, 28 Sept 15 [OHS]), have been corrected without comment.

104

P.M.S. Makura

Post Office Sydney

July 8 [1914]

ALS (LH)

My dear Aunt Tye,

We are now half way between Vancouver and Victoria in a land-locked sea with mountains all round and Mount Baker appearing magnificent above the clouds. Last night was spent at Vancouver, the night before at Sicamous a railway hotel in British Columbia on the Lake. The only building is the hotel with no roads near but a magnificent lake with a shore line of 600 miles, which winds in many directions through the mountains. In the evening we were taken by travelling acquaintances on the lake in a little motorboat. The hill sides slope down steeply on all sides and are covered with a dense tangle of young fir trees, the original forest having been cut for lumber or burnt wherever there is a railway in sight.[1] Two or three small farmers were trying to make orchards on the hill sides, but the labour of clearing the bush is much too great to make the game profitable, and their chief

desire in that neighborhood is to sell the land at a profit to the green
Britisher. None the less the lake was beautiful and teemed with fish and
the brush with grouse so that there are compensations. Further west
where the patches of level ground are large enough for fair sized farms
the bush was being cleared fast enough and in a few years there will be a
fringe of farmland all along the railway. Still the fruit-farming advertise-
ments of the Government and the C.P Railway were thought a great
joke by the natives, the yield being often a fifth of the promised average.

From Sicamous the train soon enters the dry belt which starting at
Kamloops becomes more and more arid as the Thompson River is
followed, then comes the Thompson gorge where the river has cut deep
through fine windblown sand and nothing lives except sage scrub and
prickly pear. Here there is a most interesting irrigation experiment 3000
acres of this wilderness have been supplied with water by means of long
wooden channels like the swiss Bisse, and the result is promising orchards
and green wheat. The Thompson gorge joins the Fraser a stream flowing
between fine mountains, and together they make the magnificent Frazer
canyon inside which the train crawls for many miles on a wonderfully
engineered track. After the canyon comes Mission from which Mount
Baker appears gorgeous, rather like Mont Blanc but with more snow, and
rising from the plain it appears higher though really quite a low peak of
only 10,700 ft. Vancouver is an ugly uninteresting town, but the
mountains all round are fine. We have been spending Thursday through
Monday at Emerald Lake, a chalet hotel with about 20 rooms in the
Yoho Park, a Rocky mountain reservation where shooting is forbidden.
The wild flowers there were splendid, as plentiful as I have ever seen
them in Switzerland. One day we went on horseback over a pass into the
famous Yoho valley to see the Takakkaw falls and the great Wapta
glacier. On the top of the pass the ground was covered with big yellow
glacier lilies (erythronium gigantium) white anemonies yellow violets.
Lower down comes an abundance of orange red lily (L. Philadelphicum)
like the garden wine-glass lily, white lilac-tipped pansies, gaillardias,
indian paint brush (with splendid red bracts unknown in gardens), white
wild heliotrope, false and real solomon's seal, harebells, Michaelmas
daisies, and many others. On the moraines are mocasin-flower orchids
(cypripedium), large yellow and two kinds of white in great profusion in
the woods various pyrolas, devil's club (Aralia) twin-flower in abundance
(Linnaea) dwarf corne (cornus canadensis) in the bogs the delicious

whitescented Habenaria orchid. Flowering shrubs sweet labrador tea (ledum), a charming dwarf Kalmia, white cross-heather (cassiope), virginian choke cherry on the hill sides. Perhaps most profuse of all are the aquilegias the big yellow and the still finer red with yellow wings (A. formosa). Altogether the flowers were a delight. At Sicamous were wild Syringas, two kinds, one the common tall sweet scented, also the great shrub Spireas, ariaefolia (Spray Bush) Lindleyana and Douglasii (red). Grizzlies were common around Emerald lake also black bear but we saw only marmots, gophers, squirrels, porcupine, chipmunk and mountain rabbit also Jack rabbit all as tame as possible.

    With Love,

H. Moseley

---

[1] This travelogue reads much like H. N. Moseley's description of *Oregon. Its Resources, Climate, People and Productions* (1878).

105

Pango Pango

ALS (LH)   Sept 4 [1914]

My dear Mother,

    This is really Thursday (bis) the lost day regained. It has been delightfully cool so far, but today exceedingly hot and muggy and equatorish. No definite news at all except the capture of Samoa and New Guinea, of which we have heard so often. The Jap fleet is said to [be] hereabouts but we have seen nothing yet of it. The boat is very uncomfortable. Very little deck space, tiny cabins, and various minor discomforts, but quite good food. There are a dozen B. Asses, so we make quite a large enough party to criticize our neighbors in comfort, a large number of prizefighters, four musical geniuses including M. Elman, who is said to be the greatest of violinists, but who has none the less a most swollen head, many Germans, some old others young and either masquerading as Americans or slipped in by telling lies. Three caught before leaving Sydney and turned off. (The military search was so officious that I could not write to you on board before starting.) I am becoming more or less expert in signalling morse and semaphor, and kill time playing bridge with a little chess on calm days, as there are many bad players available, but the boat rolls abominably at the least excuse.

I spent Wednesday evening {?} lecture bad, Thursday Friday on a trip to a village on the South Line some distance from Sydney, country rather like Blue Mountains, then down to the seacoast by motor, a fine drive and back by train. I was with Prof Porter (acting president section A) and Carslaw mathematical Prof at Sydney and enjoyed seeing the country. No rough weather so far, or it would go ill with me in this old tub. I will write again from Honolulu. Alas we may not go ashore at Pangopango, because of the smallpox at Sydney. I hope you enjoy the Barron falls and have cool weather.

Y.l.H.M.

I have written to Sir Philip Sydney Jones.[1]

---

[1] An Australian physician and, like Amabel, a croquet enthusiast, doubtless an acquaintance made on the trip.

106

Cunard R.M.S. Lusitania

ALS (LH)   Sept 28 [1914]

My dear Margery,

I arrive at Liverpool tomorrow morning Sept 29th, having left Sydney Aug 29th. This very quick journey was from Sydney to San Francisco touching at PagoPago (Samoa) and Honolulu. Then straight across America to New York and sailing the same evening. The arrangement when I left Sydney was this. [A paragraph on Amabel's movements is omitted.] I shall start military training immediately so as to be more or less efficient by the Spring. There is no need for the moment to look further ahead than that. I have been reading up a smattering from War Office manuals, and practicing flag wagging Morse and semaphore while crossing the Pacific. The whole journey has been exceedingly interesting and well worth while, even though such a lion's share of the time has been taken up by tedious steamer trips: 10 days to Canada 15 to Fiji. 7 to Sydney. 19 back to San Francisco. 6 to Liverpool. = 57 days. In the train 5 days across Canada. 4 back across America. 7 in Australia = 16 days. In all 73 out of a total of 109. A most unfair proportion.

Mother has been keeping in splendid health and much more lively than usual. She enjoyed Fiji most and then the Pacific side of the

Rockies (Emerald Lake) where the flowers were so beautiful. The Australians were a most pleasant surprise being delightful people when at home and their hospitality was overwhelming. They wanted to feed us ten times a day at least. I did my duty to the B. Ass by talking in an oily general mixed Physics and Chemistry discussion at Melbourne and giving a paper at Sydney.[1] I will give you further details of our adventures later, if I cannot arrange to see you.

Your loving brother
H. Moseley

---

[1] *Supra*, pp. 113–115.

107

48 Woodstock Road
Oxford
TL (LH)   8 October 1914

To the Council of the University of Birmingham.
Gentlemen,
    I beg to apply for the Poynting Professorship of Physics. I enclose particulars of my qualifications, copies of my scientific papers and testimonials from Sir Ernest Rutherford, Prof. J. S. Townsend and Prof. W. H. Bragg.[1] For a further opinion of my abilities, I may refer you to Dr. A. Schuster.[2] I have been nominated for and hope to obtain a temporary commission in the regular army preferably in the Royal Engineers. My services are not therefore likely to be available while the war lasts.[3]
    I am,

Your obedient servant,
[No signature]

---

[1] 98, 99, 100.
[2] Cf. 108.
[3] Cf. 115.

108

48 Woodstock Road
Oxford
ALS (Royal Society of London)   8 Oct [1914]

Dear Dr Schuster,
    Many thanks for your letter which reached me in Australia. When I wrote I intended staying in Australia and New Zealand until November.

Hence my anxiety to arrange matters before leaving England. As it is I left immediately after the Sydney meeting, and am now trying to get a commission. This means that if I succeed the Birmingham chair ceases to concern me so long as the war continues, but as no one can tell how long this will be, I shall still send in an application.[1] I must thank you for allowing me to use your name as a reference.

Yrs truely

H. Moseley

---

[1] **107.**

109

48 Woodstock Road
Oxford
ALS (LH)   Oct 10 [1914]

My dear Margery,

This week has been spent very busily drilling and badgering everyone in turn with a view to finding the weak points in the War Office armour. I have drilled for a few days with the territorials among agricultural labourers and butcher boys, nice fellows for the most part but sluggish and not at all well trained. Then among decrepit dons and scouts and shopkeepers each one guaranteed either over 70 or physically unfit. I have crept in unchallenged, though obviously ineligible, and find them all keen as mustard and very well drilled by an efficient and sharp-tongued serjeant. Also in the afternoons we have a private graduates drill in which a dozen of us represent a whole company with lines of string to represent the absent men, and quarrel violently over the fine points in which the lawyers and philosophers among us find ambiguities in the official drill book. Altogether I am getting a fine and most necessary training as naturally I had forgotten all my drill in four years.[1] At the same time I have got the university to nominate me for a commission, with a strong recommendation for the Royal Engineers. This was last Wednesday, and I shall probably hear nothing further about it for a long time and then get a refusal, since I have not got the qualifications officially required.[2] I shall therefore go up on Monday and bother the War Office,[3] armed with a letter of introduction, and am at the same time trying to pull private strings, but unfortunately find them working rather rustily at present, since nobody seems to know which is the right string to pull. I wrote to Ray Lankester[4] and told him to busy himself, but he replies that he does not know how to, and must first be told whom to attack. He sends you his love and complains that you have never been to see his Putney house, 'which being ruined by the war he must now leave.' I am now going to badger another unfortunate and try to concoct fresh avenues of attack. Meanwhile my paper does not progress as I am tired out daily by my drills.

With love
H.M.

---

[1] **37.**
[2] I.e., being an engineer (**110**).
[3] Cf. **110, 111.**
[4] Prof. E. Ray Lankester.

110

48 Woodstock Road
Oxford
Oct 13 [1914]

ALS (LH)

My dear Margery,

Yesterday I pestered Aldershot armed with an introduction to the officer commanding the R.E. there but quite fruitlessly, in fact I was told that only Civil Engineers were being considered. Today I bothered the War Office and spent the morning standing in a corridor only to be told at lunch time that they were too busy to see me. So I came back in the afternoon and again bothered them, this time with effect, as I got introduced to the man who was really making the appointments. He held out good hopes of there being a job going in December but certainly not earlier as batches of officers for the R.E. are only taken on every two months apparently. However I persuaded him to put me in the batch which is starting work immediately instead, and hope to get started at Aldershot on Saturday. Meanwhile I am getting a uniform made in a mighty hurry.

Mother cabled from Malta on Saturday that she was coming on in the Morea. I think it is 10 days from Malta, so she should be back on the 21st.

Y.l. brother,
H. Moseley

111

48 Woodstock Road
Oxford
16 Oct [1914]

ALS (LH)

My dearest Mother,

I am indeed glad that you have escaped from the perils of the
Emden, the Goeben, and other sharks. It is most tantalising that I have
to join at Aldershot tomorrow morning; but one has to do what one is
told. I did not expect you til about Tuesday next, since your cable from
Malta was dated Oct 10th. I can only imagine that they purposely
delayed sending it and then put the date of despatch instead of the date
when you sent it in, for obviously you can not have got from Malta in 6
days.

I am now a second lieutenant in the Royal Engineers and will no
doubt be attached to one of the RE Companies of the new army. The
term of service is so long as the war lasts, and the general impression is
that we will be trained all through the winter and then sent to the Front
in the spring. I was very lucky to get in so quickly as the R.E.
commissions have been much sought after and there is a long waiting list.
These will probably go into the next batch, which starts training in
December, and no more commissions in the Corps will be given until
then. I should have been very much annoyed to have to wait doing
nothing for two months and then probably only get 3 months training
instead of 5. I got back on the 29th. The first few days were spent in long
walks to get fit varied with pestering of everyone in turn, in order to find
the royal road to a commission. This was by no means easy, since the
War Office is so capricious in its methods that the official channels may
mean waiting for months. On the 7th I got nominated for a commission
by the Oxford University Military Education Committee,[1] a necessary
formality which had to wait until the committee chose to sit. On the
12th I went armed with an introduction to the Chief Engineer
Aldershot,[2] but he flatly refused to be chivied and so I got nothing out of
him. On the 13th I bullied the War Office. I spent the whole morning
waiting in a passage and was told about lunch time that the intended
victim was too busy to see me. So I came back in the afternoon and got
fixed up almost at once. 14th and 15th again in London getting uniform
and kit. Now I stay in Aldershot being trained in R.E. work and taught

soldiering and riding and revolver and sword practice etc. etc. for I know not how long.

Y.l.H.M.

Mrs. Poulton[3] here today. Janet just engaged to young Simmonds, medical student back wounded from despatch riding.

---

[1] Cf. **109.**
[2] Cf. **110.**
[3] *Supra*, p. 178.

112

R.E. Mess, Aldershot
ALS (LH)   18 Oct [14]

[To Amabel]
    [Sleeping accommodations. Request for linens, etc.]

113

R.E. Mess, Aldershot
ALS (LH)   Sunday [31 Oct 14]

My dear Mother,
    Today is very peaceful and lazy after a most strenuous and interesting week. Up every day at 6.45 I am kept fairly busy until 7.15 P.M. signalling: reading Morse by ear and eye and sending and reading semaphore. Riding school: Riding either in the School or out on Laffan's plain; lectures on horsey matters; grooming horses and saddling them. The signalling is easy except the reading of messages sent by lamp. In this case all that is seen is a twinkling light, and I have the greatest difficulty in distinguishing one group of flashes from another. The strained attention needed to pick out the letters is trying to the eyes, which soon get bewildered. The riding is most amusing. We get most unmercifully shaken, as it is only as an occasional treat that we are permitted to rise when trotting, so that fast trotting in the School is not very pleasant. Most of the time we are without stirrups. Cantering is then quite easy, but fast trotting on a big horse which shoots one into the air at every step is a regular acrobatic feat, and I frequently have to grab the pommel, to

regain equilibrium. Jumping we have not yet got very far with and stirrups being allowed we get on easily. Deploying and cantering and crosscountry riding on Laffan's Plain on alternate days is excellent fun and the bumping when trotting not then demanded.

Last night I sat at dinner next to a captain whom I had not come across before. We were mutually surprised to find ourselves drifting into scientific shop, since such academic interests are unknown here. I found that he was a Cambridge don, an astronomer named Stratton,[1] who is normally a light in the O.T.C., and has got a temporary captaincy in charge of a signal company. He was in the Crimea waiting for the eclipse when the War started and had a hard job getting back across Russia to Sweden with no knowledge of the language. He tells me that several of the Cavendish laboratory's best research men are now working in the aircraft factory here. I must look them up when I can spare the time. I understand that I will probably be put to the brigade signal service.[2] This means being attached to the staff of some brigade and looking after communications between the staff and the regiments included in it. I have given up the engineering exam:ship at Oxford.

Y.l.H.M.

---

[1] Frederick Stratton, then Assistant Director, later Director, of the Solar Physics Observatory, Cambridge, and Professor of Astrophysics there.
[2] Cf. **127**.

114

R.E. Mess, Aldershot

ALS (LH)   1 Nov [14]

[To Margery]
[Report on training and riding, as in **113**.]

115

The University,
Birmingham
4 November 1914

TLS (LH)

My dear Sir,

With reference to your application[1] for our vacant Chair of Physics, I have to report to you that the whole subject was discussed at the

University Council meeting today in the light of the special difficulties caused to us by the war. You may be aware that the War Office has commandeered all our New Buildings, including the Physical Laboratory, for use as a Hospital, and that between 500 and 600 wounded are now accommodated there. Under these circumstances the work of the Scientific and Technical Departments has to be carried on in temporary quarters, and the Council feels that it would be unsatisfactory to appoint a new Professor until conditions are more normal. The teaching in Physics will therefore be conducted for the remainder of this Session by the present Staff, namely

G. A. Shakespear, D.Sc., M.A.
Guy Barlow, D.Sc.
H. B. Keene, D.Sc.
J. S. Anderson, M.A., B.Sc., Ph.D.

At some future quieter time I shall hope to be able to write to you again.

Meanwhile I am,

Yours faithfully,
Oliver Lodge

---

[1] **107**.

116

Royal Institution
21 Albemarle Street
[London]
November 7th, 1914

TLS (LH)

[To HM]

[Invites HM to agree "provisionally" to "bring before the Members and the Public in a Friday Evening Discourse what can be included in a Lecture of one hour's duration, which has for its basis 'Spectroscopy of Röntgen Rays' or any equivalent title."]

117

R.E. Mess, Bulford Camp,
Salisbury

ALS (LH)   Dec 1 [1914]

My dear Margery,

Thank you for your long letter. I was naturally uncommonly surprised when I saw Mother immediately after her return home, and gathered what was about to happen.[1] Subsequently before anything was settled I was consulted, and as far as my personal concerns are touched all is satisfactory, since after all this is a case where ones personal convenience and prejudices are so relatively unimportant as not to count. I cannot feel enthusiastic (to put it mildly), largely no doubt because in one direction I am very narrow minded. I go through life perfectly contented so long as I am happy, and do not bother to think whether I could not be happier. In fact a modicum of happiness is as much as I have any use for. This much Mother had already and she seems to be risking it on the excellent chance of getting more;[2] a gamble which would never occur to me. Anyhow it shews very great bravery to be ready to back ones opinion with such high stakes.

Prof Sollas I have known sligh[t]ly for a good many years. He has the merits of being an exceptionally enthusiastic and interesting talker, and the drawback of great deafness in one ear. He is much too unpractical a man to have designs on a rich widow, and I think any such fears you may have had are quite unnecessary. The fact that he is thoroughly a gentleman is also a convenience. I believe the marriage will come off very soon, as there is no possible reason for putting it off. I shall not be there, as I see no chance of being able to get away.

Your birthday present was very much appreciated. It was just what I wanted rather badly, as I felt very ashamed of the nickel thing, and was constantly wanting a cigarette case. You may be sure that it will go to France with me.

This place is incredibly gloomy when it rains, and so far it has done so fairly continuously. I arrived at the station at 10.30 on Sunday night, an hour late, and learned that the camp was about 2 miles off, that no cab was obtainable, and that I should certainly lose my way. Fortunately I was saved by a military policeman, and trudged with him in a regular downpour, arriving only to find the mess asleep and deserted. Eventually

I woke up a servant and camped in the smoking room. Today it cleared up for a bit, and it promises to be quite pleasant if it can stay fine. The Company is made of splendid fellows very keen and well educated, and I shall enjoy having to do with them, if only I can get over the feeling of intense boredom at standing about and doing nothing, while the N.C.O.'s teach them. If only I might take a turn in the ranks.

H.G.J.M.

---

[1] The marriage of Amabel and W. J. Sollas.
[2] Cf. **119**.

118

R.E. Mess, Bulford Camp,
Salisbury

ALS (LH)   Monday [7 Dec 14]

My dear Mother,

[Details, mostly meteorological, about a visit to Margery omitted.] The life here is thoroughly interesting as the men are so keen and quick witted in most cases that it is a pleasure to have to do with them. The C.O. Major Bald is an excellent fellow, Indian army, and quite young. The subalterns: How, rich married and rather heavy, a regular officer of the Royal Irish Rifles and Paige, a temporary commission man. Musson, the fourth subaltern, is still at Aldershot training at the signal school; he is a young Woolwich boy, and a good cheerful fellow. Paige, having been the only junior subaltern for some time has had the whole company to run, and started by resenting the presence of an interloper. This was rather natural and I was prepared for a very cool reception at first. Now the Company has been divided into its proper sections, and so I can look after my own section[1] without fear of being thought an interferer. So relations with Paige, who also shares with me a very small bedroom, have improved.

Y.l.H.M.

Certainly transfer the Union shares.

---

[1] Of about 26 men (**127**).

119

R.E. Mess, Bulford Camp

ALS (LH)   Dec 27 [1914]

My dear Margery,

I got my fly on Christmas Eve, a most perfect winter's day. I rode over to Netheravon, about 7 miles, on a timid mare, who got wild with fright every time we met an aeroplane, but was otherwise amenable. Edgar[1] took me over Tidworth and Bulford Camp to Salisbury, then over old Sarum, which looked most impressive, to Stonehenge, then past the flying sheds and up to Savemake and Marlborough at about 5000 ft, and so back. In all a little over an hour, and a most delightful round. It felt perfectly safe all the time, partly no doubt because it was a thoroughly calm day; and the banking was no more alarming than going round a corner on a bicycle.[2] Coming down was an unexpected experience as the gliding angle was so small that the aeroplane seemed to be hanging stationary in mid air, while gliding against the wind. The machine was the B.E., with lots of room for the observer to stretch himself, but rather a high wall all round, so that in order to see right down below it was necessary to lean out off the side.[3]

Edgar shewed me all over the aeroplanes and tackle, which is altogether a most impressively efficient affair, very different from much army stuff. I am now applying for the job of observer,[4] which would be much more amusing than what I am doing now. This does not involve learning to fly, as they actually prefer observers who know nothing about it, alleging that a little skill in flying merely makes a passenger distrustful and nervous. I went over on Christmas Day on a push-bike to see Mother, about 25 miles through Salisbury, but luckily the roads were hard with frost. She had no objections to raise to my attempt to get transferred, being quite satisfied with my assurance that it was the safer job of the two. She is for the moment very rejuvenescent, eats heartily, and has actually walked to Romsey station and back, which is really a feat at her age. She and Prof S seem thoroughly cheerful.[5] I cycled back in the evening and found the Camp very uproarious. However they seem none the worse for it. Thank you for your Christmas letter and enclosure. With love.

H. Moseley

[1] Edgar Ludlow-Hewitt, a cousin, who saw action in France, helped coordinate the operations of the air force and the artillery, and rose to Brigadier General. R. A. Jones, *War in the Air*, II, 100, 121, 175–176; IV, 214–218; V, 444–446.

[2] Cf. **58**.

[3] The Royal Aircraft Factory's famous "Blériot Experimental," so called because it incorporated the same sort of airscrew that had propelled Louis' Blériot's plane in the first flight across the Channel. Raleigh, *War in the Air*, I, 162–164.

[4] Cf. **120, 121, 122**.

[5] Cf. **117**.

120

R.E. Mess, Bulford Camp,
Salisbury

ALS (LH)   8 Jan [1915]

My dear Mother,

The bunny gloves are most luxurious, and will no doubt be acceptable if I get into the R.F.C. This seems a slow job as is everything connected with the W.O. It has so far taken 10 days for my application to go through the C.O. and C.R.E. to the secretary of the War Office, thence down through the flying hierarchy to the people really concerned, who have written back through the same channel to enquire my weight. No doubt more enquiries will follow through the same chain concerning my eyesight and my moral character etc, each at an interval of 10 days. If only the channel could be short circuited all would be settled quickly enough. I had last week my first motor-bike ride on a company machine, round by Stonehenge and one of the Canadian Camps, Lark Hill, in charge of about 30 men mounted on bicycles. [A lengthy report of the trip and the dismal weather is omitted.]

Your loving
H. Moseley

121

R.E. Mess, Bulford Camp,
Salisbury

ALS (LH)   17 Jan [1915]

My dear Margery,

Many thanks for your letter. I am still trying unsuccessfully to get into the flying corps. I had no idea when I started how difficult it was to get anything done, when in the army. A civilian can go to the man from whom he wants to get a job and insist on being given it. Here I cannot even get my application as far as the flying corps. It is intercepted and sent back by the general commanding the Division, who does not want to lose an officer if he can help it. I have bothered Edgar considerably, keeping him posted in the progress of the affair, and asking him to get me applied for by the flying corps. Whether he has done anything in the matter so far I cannot tell, since I have not heard from him at all. Maybe he has been in France all the time, and so not got my numerous letters. If so send me a postcard, as it would affect my line of attack. My first application was refused as I was over the weight limit. Those over the weight limit 10 st 7 lb could only apply if recommended as especially suitable by the G.O.C., who naturally would never do such a thing. However, I hear that a fresh application, which I have prepared after reducing my weight to the proper figure, will if sent assuredly have the same fate. So now I have written to Edgar asking if he can get me applied for to the General by the Flying Corps. If I get no reply from him, I will go ahead with the new application, and pitch it in strong language and then trust to luck.

With love
H. Moseley

122

R.E. Mess, Bulford Camp,
Salisbury
Sunday [25 Jan 15]

ALS (LH)

My dear Mother,

I am enjoying a quiet day in bed, having been bowled over by a particularly vicious cold. I am now thorough[ly] comfortable having got up after tea to sit by a blazing bedroom fire. The new junior subaltern has had to take my orderly officer duties, church parade etc, and I am not looking forward to starting again at 6.30 tomorrow morning. However the cold will then have had two bad days, and should by rights be on the mend. Yesterday morning I had to go over to Rolleston Camp, a long way off in a most isolated part of the Plain, to pay a lot of R.E. carpenters. It felt quite medieval, jogging on a horse with bulging money bags, with a clerk beside me, and a soldier behind to hold the horses. I cut across from there to Netheravon, and lunched with Edgar L.H., arriving extremely late, having been compelled to make a long detour to avoid the big guns which were firing in that direction. You will no doubt be relieved to hear that I have been barred from the Flying Corps, by an Army Order which appeared yesterday, and which forbids any more transfers to the R.F.C. from Kitchener's first army (officially the Third Army). This looks as if there was some hope of getting out in a reasonable time now. None the less the new Order is most annoying, as I had a fresh application just going in, and had taken a deal of trouble in smoothing the way before it. Also observers are being sent to the front as fast as they can be trained, as there are still not nearly enough, the war having started apparently without any at all. No more flying men are going until the summer, as they want to keep them for use with the new Armies, when they go. The Company has now lost its C.O. Major Bald, who has been transferred to a pioneer battalion to our great sorrow. We are now commanded by How, the rich and fat Lieutenant, who makes a very poor substitute indeed. I fear he will be made a Captain, and left in command.[1] Since the snow the mud has been even worse than usual, though the weather otherwise has been good for the last week.

I now have a 'charger,' quite a nice cob, who galloped beautifully all across the plain yesterday, but is very unamenable to discipline. She seems to pay little attention either to bridle or my legs, so that every time we come to a turning there is a serious difference of opinion which usually ends in my turning her round and round in circles until she loses her direction, and then starting her off with my stick.

Y.l.H.M.

---

[1] He was not (**124**).

123

R.E. Mess, Bulford Camp,
Salisbury
31 Jan [1915]

ALS (LH)

My dear Mother,

The cold abated quickly owing to a day's coddling on Sunday, and has now returned to its normal Bulford condition, ready to flash up again as soon as given a chance. Hence partly my preference for Pick's Hill for the weekend as the interminable delays getting back to Bulford by train are almost sure to bring it out again. This last week I have been particularly busy, company orderly duty until Friday, and regimental orderly duty on Saturday. Besides this there is a great flow of new men into the company, and I have been struggling with them. On Friday evening I had a most successful practice at cable laying from 5 to 8.30, it was a lovely night and we all enjoyed ourselves. This is the first time for weeks that I have been able to get hold of my own section and set them to do what I like. The delightful and obvious plan of each officer training his own unit independently is always baulked here in practice, and I look forward with some uneasiness to running my own little show with men who are I think being taught in the wrong way. We are still with How as C.O., but as he has again been cast as unfit for active service by the medical board, it is possible that this will now be altered. His own wish is to go out, and carry on until he breaks down with neurasthenic dyspepsia, but for the company's sake I hope such a risky plan will be prevented.

Yesterday we arranged a voluntary scheme on a large scale, in which all the best men of the company took part. We had 6 signal officers, 4 under the four junior subalterns and 2 under N.C.O.'s, and we ran them as nearly on active service conditions as possible from 6 pm to 6 am this morning. I, being on regimental duty, was not allowed to leave the Lines, so I established a divisional signal office at our company office.

[Here there is an elaborate sketch.]

As you see from the sketch all the four offices were joined by cable, which was of course laid after dark. The cable cart terminus kept touch with the neighbouring gun station on a hill by cyclist orderlies. The gun station communicated with the infantry at Old Sarum by flash lamp. Besides this cyclists and a large number of motorcyclists were used to carry important despatches. Some of the offices got cover in goods yards, sheds, etc but one was fully exposed, and as it poured twice during the night, got soaked through. Some kind friend probably Canadian went round with a wire nippers cutting our cables, but the line men sent out to do the repairs got the lines mended quite smartly considering the darkness of the night. All the cable offices were worked by telegraphists, who are really essential for this work. How I am to carry on with only 2 in my section as at present I cannot imagine. I should have 10 at least, but the Divisional section absorbs nearly all we get.

Y.l.H.M.

124

R.E. Mess, Bulford Camp,
Salisbury
Sunday [Feb 1915]

ALS (LH)

My dear Mother,

We move to Woking next Tuesday, and are looking forward to the change, and the prospect of getting some kit. All our belongings will be packed up by Saturday, and perhaps already sent off, so the signal scheme is not possible. We are troubled tonight by a man in the company, who is thought to have spotted fever. I hope very much this is untrue, as though it moves by such curious hops that one case does not make it very likely that there will be more in the company, yet it will mean more quarantine. We have an admirable new O.C. by name Capt Crocker, and are very glad to get rid of How. The new man is a very keen signal officer, who knows his job thoroughly, and we are likely to find him invaluable. Too tired for more.

Y.l.H.M.

125

R.E. Mess, Bulford Camp,
Salisbury
Sunday [Feb 1915]

ALS (LH)

My dear Mother,

We spent most of today burying our spotted fever case. [An account of the outing and of other outbreaks omitted.]

Prof Turner's[1] interference was no doubt kindly meant. I have written direct to Lucas,[2] whom I do not know, to tell him that I have never had any wish to go into the Aircraft Factory, and that it is a simple mistake on the part of Prof T.

The aircraft factory is run entirely by civilians, and if I was physically unfit I would like nothing better than to work there.

Yesterday I had a magnificent trot and gallop to pay the Rolleston[3] components. My horse behaved very badly, bolting down every side turning he came to. I will change him as soon as I can for a steady old nag, which can be trusted not to play pranks.

Y.l.H.M.

---

[1] Probably Herbert Hall Turner, Savilian Professor of Astronomy at Oxford, an old friend of the family.

[2] Keith Lucas (1879–1916), F.R.S., Cambridge physicist and biologist, who allowed himself to be enlisted for the aircraft factory at Farnborough just as he was about to enter the infantry as a private. He died in an airplane accident (H. Darwin and W. M. Bayliss, *PRS* 95:A [1918/9], iii–iv). Had Harry gone to Farnborough he would have found himself in the company of Tizard, Whiddington, Griffith and Lindemann.

[3] A neighboring camp.

126

[Woking]

ALS (LH)   [11 Mar 15]

[To Margery]

I hope you can come to Pick's Hill for Saturday-Sunday, I shall be there till Sunday evening, and Mother is to invite you. Too busy for letters now. At work the whole day long, and not long enough. Just got a splendid compass. It has a transparent dial lighted up from below with radium, so that one can take a bearing to within a degree on the darkest night. Tomorrow morning I go out with my 2 chargers. 2 pack mules. 2 mules drawing my limbered cart. and 2 mounted men at the head of my section, to practice getting the whole show under cover—no easy job I expect. Today the King inspected the whole division. I had the luck to be orderly officer, and so stayed at peace in barracks.

H.G.J.M.

127

13th Signal Coy RE
{Cornhill} Common
P—kwood, Surrey

ALS (R)   April 4 [1915]

Dear Sir Ernest,

Many thanks for your letter, which I have not had a chance to answer earlier. I am kept very busy and as we are in tents and out on horseback or foot all day long I am in splendid health. I have quite an interesting little job, as I am responsible for the communications of a Brigade, the 38th, and so I and my 26 men will be quite on our own as soon as we get to the Front. I still occasionally see the Phil Mag, but for the rest I have dropped out entirely, and never so much as hear from anyone in the game. We expect to be in France before the end of the month, and so all my affairs have to be put straight, besides a large number of details of special equipment etc for my section. One thing lies heavy on my conscience, and that is my Sydney B. Ass paper, for I have never published it. I must make time to get ready an abstract for the Phil Mag,[1] before I leave, as to chemists the reality and order of the rare earth elements is of much importance.

    With kind regards to Lady Rutherford [and] you,

Yrs v[ery] sincerely,
H. Moseley.

---

[1] HM did not prepare such an abstract, or the note Urbain had requested (**102**); he sent his notebook on the subject to Amabel just before shipping out (**130**), but it disappeared after Rutherford examined it in 1916.

128

Wednesday
[c. 26 May 15]

ALS (LH)

[To Amabel]

    Our arrangements are being made gradually. I have all my new tropical kit, sun helmet etc, but my men's things have not arrived yet. The wretched War Office is taking away all our new telephones and giving us a most inferior and badly made substitute. Anything is good enough for a division which is not going to Flanders. Rumours continue to be quite uncertain where we are really going. Gallipoli was certainly originally decided, but one never knows from day to day. Anyway it will be somewhere precious hot. Sun protectors arrived today from Oxford (I will send them all back to you with my spare kit). Also a charger arrived from Cogswell and sulpher from you.

    My men having given in their second pair of boots a week ago, now have had them issued again, with this difference that the rest of the Company having had first pick took all my men's boots, and left them with all the down at heels the bad pairs and the insanitary. Tomorrow I have a board of officers convened to condemn them to the rubbish heap, so that I may draw new.

[No salutation or ending]

129

Monday
ALS (LH)   [c. 7 June 15]

My dear Mother,

The 12th[1] was delayed for I know not what reason, so we are kept back also. I expect to go about Friday but have been put off so often that I have almost given up expecting. Now we are complete except for compasses and wire. No wire yet at all. Today respirators and 1300 rounds of ammunition arrived, and all my men's kit bags extra blankets etc etc were sent away, so that we can start at any moment.

Colt automatic .32 rimless ammunition for my pistol (please order at once 50 rounds from Cogswell and Harrison Fleet St who supplied the pistol). Please send me now at once any old tools which may be useful such as screwdrivers if possible one large. a hammer. chisels if sharp. files if sharp. gimlets. bradawls. a small saw. Please send also a pair of canvas shoes size 9 brown.

I hope my 2 packages (1 gladstone 1 valise & sword) and my bicycle sent to you by goods train have arrived. The boots want resoling.

I am taking my aircushion in my pocket so do not worry about the crossing. It will be easy to keep afloat if torpedoed. The HQRS of my Company sent a bomshell on Thursday ordering the immediate return of 3 of my 4 telegraphists, and offering me men either imbecile or of bad character in their place. As the telegraphists are about the best men I have and one is a most valuable N.C.O. you can imagine my dismay, especially when told to take untrained and undesirables in their place. The other brigade sections were treated in the same way, the selection of men to take the place of the telegraphists being left to the office clerk, so little does Crocker[2] care what happens to brigade sections! We naturally all descended on him, and I attacked him hot and strong but within the narrow limits allowed by military discipline, and succeeded in extracting 2 very good men and 1 who is pleasant though incompetent for myself, and some good men for the other sections too. But these cannot make up for the departed and know nothing of brigade section work. The reason is first that the W.O. has suddenly docked us of some telegraphists and these the brigade sections had to produce, and then that Crocker found what his subalterns had known and agreed upon months ago that the cablecarts had not got all the telegraphers they were entitled to by the regulations, so again brigade sections were despoiled.

HQRS 38th Inf Bde.

YI.H.M.

Blackdown[3] (not Brookwood)

---

[1] The twelfth division, which was also shipped to the Mediterranean.
[2] The commanding officer (**124**).
[3] A neighboring camp.

130

HQRS 38th Inf. Bde.
13th Division
British Mediterranean
Force,

ALS (LH)   June 14 [1915]

[To Amabel]

[Last minute instructions for disposing of equipment, paying bills, etc.] I am sending you by registered letter my notebook, X ray spectra of rare earths; it will be posted from Avonmouth and I value it highly.[1]

---

[1] It has not survived (**127**, n. 1).

131

Address HQRS, etc, etc.
Walton Bay

ALS (LH)   15/6/15

My dear Mother,

It is delightful to rest after a very strenuous time indeed. My men's equipment gave very great trouble owing to the incompetence of the

Company's quartermaster I imagine. I finally got them sun helmets a couple of days before starting by going myself to Frimley station demanding a hatchet from the stationmaster and breaking open some cases of helmets belonging to the Worcesters, which were waiting for them in a goods train. I fear their quartermaster will not bless me when the remains reach him, nor will he love the stationmaster, who has no authority for the theft beyond my signature of receipt. The same day I had jogged into field stores Aldershot a very dull 7 miles with my wagon behind me, and drew my wire which had been there for quite a long time, but which the quartermaster being a lazy fellow, and always sending another instead of going himself, swore was unobtainable. I had to go a little short though and that after cleaning out every scrap they had, so the other brigade sections may fail to get any. It is then very lucky for me that our company is so incompetent at drawing stores for us, as had it been successful I should have got only a third of what there was and would have been in a bad hole. I got the brokenarmed man out of hospital and also got a substitute for him from reserve signal depot by writing them just before leaving. This gave me one man over, so I had much pleasure in returning to headquarters of the company the deaf lance corporal whom they had foisted on me. As a precaution I did not let him return until the morning after we had left, so as to prevent the possibility of them ordering me to keep him, and taking away my illegally captured substitute for the broken armed one.

Best love
H.G.J.M.

My air cushion is in my pocket.

132

ALS (LH)

British Med Force
June 20 [1915]

My dear Mother,

Just arriving at Gib after a lazy and uneventful voyage on a glassy sea. Very hot indeed, and sure to become more so. Please send thin socks. You promised me those made by the Belgians, but never sent them. Also my Ingersoll watch, if you can recover it from Driver Harvey. Also a comb lanoline toothpaste (a small tube), and Coleman shaving stick. Our destination no longer in doubt. We have been going a steady 13 knots, much better than I expected. As signal officer I have the run of the bridge, and a signal bridge on top of all; a great boon in this weather. Also so far I have escaped all ship's duties. The chance of posting this is thin, as we do not touch at Gib, but possibly the patrol boat will stop us and take mails. If not I will try to get news from shore by lamp signals from the mast-head.

Y.l.H.M.

133

Malta
June 24th [1915]

ALS (LH)

[To Amabel]

Just arrived in harbour, and do not know how long we stay or if we can go ashore. Have been sleeping on deck, as hot as it can possibly be at sea, but for the last 2 days tolerable at night. No news to give you of course. A very dull trip indeed, nothing to do but eat and sleep which we attempt whenever it is not too warm, but still quite a good holiday before starting real work.

H.G.J.M.

134

Alexandria
June 27 [1915]

ALS (LH)

[To Amabel]

[A note giving financial instructions and listing enclosures, including a power of attorney and the following "will (of course confidential) active service form and quite legal I believe."]

This is the last will and testament of me Henry Gwyn Jeffrey[s] Moseley Second Lieutenant Royal Engineers now on active service with the British Mediterranean Expeditionary Force I give and bequeath all my estate real and personal and my reversionary interests therein[1] to the Royal Society of London to be applied to the furtherance of experimental research in Pathology Physics Physiology Chemistry or other branches of science but not in pure mathematics astronomy or any branch of science which aims merely at describing cataloguing or systematizing. Made on the Twenty seventh day of June 1915 by me

s/ Henry G J Moseley[2]

---

[1] The estate amounted to £2,200 (financial records, RS); Amabel subsequently increased the Moseley Fund by a bequest to the Royal Society of about £10,000.

[2] The text is taken not from the original will, but from the official copy in Somerset House.

135

B. Med. Exp. Force

ALS (LH)   July 2 [1915]

My dear Mother,

Alexandria full of heat flies native troops and Australians. The heat somewhat bested by sleeping on deck all the voyage since about two days before Malta. I hope you got my telegram and registered letter[1] both posted last Tuesday. Keeping very fit. One of my men knocked out already, fever of sorts. He had a very poor constitution, and no doubt I should not have brought him, but alas he was one of my best telegraphists. However I may get him back some day. Much love.

H.G.J.M.

---

[1] **134.**

136

Military form letter (LH)   3 July 1915

I am quite well. I have received no letter from you. H. Moseley

137

ALS (LH)   Sunday July 4 [1915]

My dear Mother,

It is very hot of course and the flies are a sore trial and the cause of a certain amount of illness. The centipedes 8 inches long and very fat look terrifying, but so far no scorpions. I have 1/2 a tent to sleep, a great luxury since almost everyone is bivouaced. We are settling down to a free period of training, where I cannot of course tell you. I have now collected all my men but 3 who are left behind looking after the horses and mules, which have not yet arrived. Please send out another large bottle of chlorodyne and 2 suits khaki with pyjamas 1 for myself one for a friend 5'10" tall. Also another pair stocking puttees, and 2 cells No 12 EverReady price 1/6 and 4 dry cells not more than 4"x2 1/4"x1 1/2" (v. important).

Y.l.H.M.

Also a few handkerchiefs. All my stock[ings?]. also dry milk.

138

ALS, on military form (LH)   7 July [1915]

My dear Mother,

All very quiet and peaceful here. Keeping fit though always rather hot. Have just lost my only serjeant apparently slight appendicitis a dreadful blow. No mail yet.

Y.l.H. Moseley

N.B. address *use no other* HQRS 38th Inf Bde, British Med Exp Force

139

ALS on military form (LH)   July 8 [1915]

My dear Mother,

Much refreshed after a lovely sea bathe. Still abominably hot and many flies but very tolerable also I keep very fairly fit still no mail sorry to have no new[s].

H.G.J.M.

140

ALS on military form (LH)   8th July [1915]

My dear Mother,

It is a great jo[y] to come down to the sea again with bathes twice a day after a few hot days inland. Tiptree[1] jam arrived safe and was very much appreciated. Going inland again soon I fear. A gorgeous blue and red heron lives here. So do horrible centipedes one of which was crawling on my neck this morning. Tomorrow I get innoculated against cholera not that there is any here but as a precaution.

Much love

H. Moseley

---

[1] From Tiptree, Essex.

141

ALS (LH)   July 12 [1915]

My dear Mother,

Your letters up to June 22nd at last arrived. It gets hotter here and again hotter day by day, and only cool nights and sea bathing keep life tolerable. I go about in shirtsleeves and sunhelmet with often a wet handkerchief also over my head and so keep fit. No flowers left here except a few purple cistus and various heath like shrubs which I do not know. I have not yet recovered my invaluable serjeant who had the indiscretion to get appendicitis. We are in the land of famine milk powder. *chlorodyne.* oil of cloves. lemonade crystals. sherbet. bovril. coffee extract or cocoa. A+N vanilla flavour mixed would all be acceptable. Water is uncommonly scarce and of very indifferent quality, but I keep well enough all the same. The one real interest in life is the flies, no mosquitoes, but flies by day and flies by night, flies in the water, flies in the food. The food is very good of its kind bread and ships biscuit, meat fresh and bully, dessicated vegetables, tea and sugar (no milk), a very little lime juice or rum sometimes, bacon, a little cheese, jam (mostly flies). Work is getting on fairly satisfactorily. Anything sent out must be packed in tins hermetically sealed, otherwise contents are sure to be stolen.

Best love

H. Moseley

Unfortunately my general is very much put out if one is late for meals, so I am often in hot water.

142

ALS (LH) July 14 [1915]

[To Amabel]

Another mail just arrived up to June 26, quite reasonable. We moved yesterday to a place where the road is worse than the flies. Sand in boots clothes mouth eyes hair. Sand in the food and the water and the air. All my kit is in danger of being buried. The men are not bearing the heat very well. They are so used to perfect health that some at least give in easily when out of sorts, and naturally diarrhea is extremely prevalent. The heat, the sand in the food, the bad water and the flies are all severally quite enough to account for that. I myself keep reasonably fit by judicious use of chlorodyne, and so far I have cured all dysentery among my men in the same way. But I hope the fresh supplies from you will come quick. Two more chlorodyne {parcels} would be very useful. It is a fresh responsibility being medical officer as well as everything else to my little lot, and the medicine chest (a cigar box) has been quite invaluable. The way they recover from dysentery with nothing but bread bacon biscuit bully tea no milk occasional potatoes onions limejuice {?} is to me a marvel. My serjeant has decided not to have appendicitis. Very glad to see him back again. Large land tortoises live here, but I have not yet had the luck to see one. The birds are very interesting, lots of them, nearly all strange except nightjar and plentiful turtle dove.

Best love
H. Moseley

143

ALS (LH) 26th July [1915]

My dear Mother,

Yesterday I brought in a tortoise and presented it to the mess, but the local tortoise is a very brisk walker and disappeared over the skyline almost as soon as liberated. It must be the climate that makes them so lethargic in England. There are tortoises on the land and tortoises in the streams. Also a land crab I am told, but the one brought for my inspection insisted on departing before my arrival. So did a large hedgehog brought in by one of my linemen. Then there are frogs that sing all night, mantises that v[ery] seldom pray and grasshoppers innumerable. If I was not rather busy I could spend all my time examining the local fauna, particularly the water beasts which are very likely not properly known. The sage and thyme and many other herbs smell delicious, in much variety. No sea bathing now for some days past, but plenty of water from a stream which runs past my abode, so that my servant has washed all my clothes. It is terrible what a genius for getting drowned soldiers have. I think there have been 3 so far in our brigade, though the sea is calm and free from currents and on only a few days has bathing been possible. There was a bad accident to an R.E. officer yesterday. He was challenged after dark by one of our sentries and as he paid no attention the sentry quite properly shot him through the thigh, wounding him badly. Today for breakfast porridge and poached eggs, both luxuries before undreampt of. A wicked soldier has stolen (1) my autostrop razor (2) my soap (3) my shaving brush the three most valuable things I possess. No shops here so cannot replace them possibly. Two men have n[ow] been sent away by me to hospital, one last night the other this morning. I have cured with drugs diet and faith all my other cases of dysentery but these two were getting serious and I did not like the responsibility of keeping them any longer. With love to Margery,

Y.l.H. Moseley

Registered letters and parcels arrive much the sooner.

144

ALS (LH) 3 August [1915]

My dear Mother,

The time here passes pleasantly with nothing to do. In the morning I go into the village and buy eggs lemons grapes watermelons etc. Yesterday afternoon I climbed into the hills with lovely clearcut views and rich colouring. In the evening I may bathe in the sea clear and warm with a jetty from which to jump in and out of my depth. For the last few days the weather has been quite delightful with soft sea breezes to temper the heat of the day and cool at nights. In consequence my inside, which had struck work altogether for a few days, returned to duty and let me once more enjoy the good things which are sent us, foremost among which is your Tiptree jam. It is quite disgraceful how greedy we all are. At present we four others who look on the bright side of life are rather disgusted with the general and brigade major, who grumble at the food and everything else in season and out. Their fussiness and complaints grow tedious and give everyone else a deal of extra work, but I always anticipated this as one of the normal joys of active service and so pay little heed. I have now a small store of arrowroot plenty of condensed milk, a tin of bovril and a little rice so I am forearmed in case my inside again misbehaves as it assuredly will. My section is hard at work mending wire, learning helio, flagwagging and route marching, but I let the NCOs look after the men for the most part. The hilltops are thick with worked flints, all rough but of all ages including an obvious flint from an old flintlock. The flowers are over in this parched land save for {?} grass and thistles. We are still always on the move and you may guess that it is not always as idealic as at present; but after 25 days in the thick of it we were glad enough to have a few days rest. However there is more work ahead and you will probably not hear from me again for some considerable time.

Your parcels to date include silk pyjamas puttee stockings shirts before leaving England, 2 lots Tiptree, 1 'verminous' vest (no use for vest in this country), chocolate 1 parcel, not yet touched, plasticene {?}, watch. sulphur bags (I see no necessity for cultivating vermin) silk pyjamas new very much appreciated. electric torch ditto. malted milk arrived when I was rather moribund and proved invaluable. handkerchiefs. newspapers *no use* too stale. new puttee stockings wrong pattern useless. 1 pair socks thin. 1 pair silk more wanted. The brown canvas shoes I have worn incessantly instead of boots since leaving England size 9, will want a new pair soon. This list will be guide as to what has got lost. Food by post will always be very welcome as bully and army biscuits are trying when the digestion is out of order. The bully I really never touch, though it is very good quality canned beef and in a cold climate would doubtless be excellent. The biscuit crushed to powder and soaked in water overnight makes a fair substitute for porridge—occasionally we get a tin of oatmeal in lieu of cheese or bacon, a real godsend. Really the food question is the only one of any importance here, as given plenty of outside food one can keep fit, and the work is not at all over hard, while the bullets and shells of both of which we get quite our fair share do not trouble me at all, though I duck quite enough when shrapnel comes anywhere near. I am teaching my men prudence by example, and they mostly have now some idea of keeping out of harms way. One of them got shot through the neck while reeling in wire in a place where I had been helping him do the same job the previous day. I had been struck then by his stupidity in standing about in unhealthy spots, and had given him a personal lesson in hurtling over the bad parts and using cover. Whether he was incautious the next day I do not know. Maybe it was just bad luck. Anyhow I think he will get over it. No other casualties except 3 men lost through sickness. I have to harden my heart and be really brutal with the sick, as I think every man in the section has been upset by the heat and unsuitable food at one time or another, and any who have little grit just lie down and collapse, and then they go to hospital and I never see them again. The others made of better stuff carry on and get right again with the simple advice about food and drugs which I can give them. One man I lost to hospital because he breakfasted off bacon while suffering from dysentery, and I have constantly to be on guard against this sort of thing, which arises simply from ignorance. If you send food send a little often, say every week. Milk powder malted or plain in a small tin (square sided if possible and quite full, bulk is all important), rice, arrowroot, custard powder, lemonade powder (genuine not chemical) macaroni, elvas plums, jelly fruit or meat (the blackberry jelly from Tiptree is being consumed with great appreciation), maggi soup squares (not marmalade, can get that as ration sometimes) shrimp or veal and ham {pasta}, grapenuts, dried apricots, guava jelly ventuchel-licum solid. Here is a sufficiently comprehensive list to choose from. The really critical items are lemon or lime essence in solid form, milk powder, arrowroot, meat jelly. Remember to pack everything in as solid a form as possible (e.g. horlicks powder not tablets). We are all getting very dissatisfied with the brigade mess. Chadwick the machine gunner and {?} the staff captain contribute a lot of private extras. I contribute a little, but the General and Brigade Major have nothing sent them, and then grumble at the food. This leads to waste of our precious store. A large tin of turkey is opened for dinner and then one of them demands tongue which has to be opened too. If this continues we will mutiny and tell them to arrange their own messing, then I who have a small appetite will score.

> With love,
> H. Moseley

145

ALS (LH)   4 August [1915]

[To Amabel]

On the move again as usual. Send a little tiny tablet of soap every week. Have bought a razor but want another (mine stolen by a soldier) also a small shaving brush. also 2 flat files smallest size (say 1/8″ stick) also want a dozen pliers wire cutting *fairly small* must cut v[ery] fine steel wire so jaws must fit perfectly [figure]. Pattern sketched is good, about 5″. Price about 1/6 at right place. I badly want a green mosquito net for my head [figure] thus. The flies make sleep impossible between sunrise and sunset impossible without some protection and at present I have only a small scoup of dirty netting. Letters and parcels are much quicker if registered. Very sorry to see death of Bay Balfour[1] in Gallipoli. See Prof Bragg made professor at University College London, a good change from Leeds. I am amazed to see that my batch has been made full Lts but apparently I have been left out by mistake. Please find out for certain Oct 15 Temp Commission RE. It does not interest me enough to make a fuss, but if the case is clear I will have it rectified. I hear we are to have a water ration of a gallon all told. Not much to spare. 1 pint tea breakfast. 1 pint lunch. 1 pint tea. 1 pint supper = 2 quarts. The rest for cooking, washing up and personal washing. Really enough as washing is luckily a luxury which one easily goes without.

[No salutation or closing]

---

[1] Isaac Bayley Balfour, killed 24 June 14, the only son of I. B. Balfour, F.R.S., Professor of Botany at the University of Edinburgh (*London Times*, 10 July 15, 4c).

Inventory of Moseleyana

1. LUDLOW-HEWITT COLLECTION: Mr. A. Ludlow-Hewitt, Whitfield Manor, Apperly, Gloucestershire, possesses a number of documents relating to Canon Moseley and Henry Nottidge Moseley. Most of his material, however, relates to HM: letters from Betty Moseley, Amabel Moseley, Henry Jervis, G. E. Chadwick, E. R. Lankester, and G. Urbain; Amabel's pocket diaries; notes by Margery Ludlow-Hewitt; photographs, most of which are reproduced as figures 19–21, 23–25 in this volume; and HM's letters to Amabel and Margery. These last comprise the bulk of the extant correspondence: **1–41, 43–66, 68–80, 82, 97, 104** (HM to his Aunt Tye), **105, 106, 109–114, 117–126, 128–145**. In addition, the Ludlow-Hewitt Collection contains a few letters to HM, viz., **98–100, 107, 115** (all concerning HM's application for the Poynting Chair, and bound into a book gotten up for the purpose), **102** and **116**. AHQP (Berkeley only) has copies of all HM's letters in LH, and of most of Jervis', Chadwick's, and Urbain's.

2. RUTHERFORD PAPERS, CAMBRIDGE UNIVERSITY LIBRARY: This is the largest collection of HM's scientific correspondence (**42, 84, 85, 90–92, 93** [a typed transcript of a letter to Hevesy], **95, 96, 101, 127**); it also contains material regarding posthumous honors, like the plaque set up at the University of Manchester.

3. OXFORD MUSEUM OF THE HISTORY OF SCIENCE: Several pieces of apparatus HM used at Oxford have ended here, e.g., the spectrometers and discharge tubes in figures 9b and 13b, a few plates showing x-ray lines, and some specimens; a full catalogue will be found in

C. R. Hill, *Chemical Apparatus* (1971), pp. 51–53. The museum also has a few important manuscripts: measurements of Urbain's samples (printed with **103** above); notes made aboard ship, apparently an attempt to reconstruct Planck's quantum theory of 1911 (*VdpG* 13 [1911], 138–148) from memory; notes on the rare earths not in HM's hand; a sheet in Bohr's hand comparing HM's results with Siegbahn's, doubtless preparation for his contribution to HM's obituary notice in *PM* 31 (1916), 174–176; four letters from Urbain, one of which has been printed (*PRS* 93:A [1916], xxvii); and a typescript of a letter from HM to Urbain (**103**). The Minute Books of the Alembic Club, which give valuable information about many aspects of physical science at Oxford, also deserve mention.

4. SCATTERED HOLDINGS: (a) The Royal Institution, London (**67**). (b) Bohr Archive, Copenhagen (**81, 83**), copies in AHQP. (c) Professor Kasimir Fajans (**86**). (d) The American Philosophical Society, Philadelphia (**87, 89**), copies in AHQP. (e) The Hevesy Papers, Niels Bohr Institut, Copenhagen (**88, 94**). (f) The Royal Society, London (**108**).

5. BOOKS: HM's scientific books, which have no annotations of interest, are part of the library of the Physics Department, University of Manchester.

6. PHOTOGRAPHS: Figures 20, 21, 24 and 25, all from the Ludlow-Hewitt Collection, are here published apparently for the first time; figures 22 and 23 have been published often before, e.g., figure 22 by Rutherford in *Nature* 116 (1925), 316, and G. Sarton, *Isis* 9 (1927), 96, and figure 23 by Z. Kopal, *Isis* 58 (1967), 405, L. A. Redman, *The Physics Teacher* 3 (1965), 152, and Birks, p. 22. At least three more photographs have been published (see R. Ferreira, *Isis* 60 [1969], 233): (a) full face, head and shoulders view taken from a group photograph, in R. T. Gunther, *Early Science in Oxford* II (1937), p. 235, (b) HM in a group portrait of the Physics Staff at Manchester, 1913, in E. Rutherford, *Collected Papers* II (1963), p. 304, and (c) HM in a group portrait of the Alembic Club, 1907, in R. W. Clark, *Tizard* (1965), p. 36. Figures 9b, 13b, 27 and 28 are printed through the courtesy of the Oxford Museum of the History of Science, University of Oxford, which owns the copyright.

Bibliography

Some articles cited once and not of general interest are omitted. Unsigned obituary notices are entered under the name of the subject.

Alembic Club. Miscellaneous Papers. G. A. Oxon. 4°. 603 (OB).

Alington, C. A. "Public Schools." In *Facing the Facts. An Englishman's Religion*. Edited by W. K. L. Clarke. London, 1912, pp. 203–222.

———. *A School Master's Apology*. London, 1914.

———. *Eton Faces Old and New*. London, 1933.

———. *Things Ancient and Modern*. London, 1936.

———. *A Dean's Apology. A Semi-Religious Autobiography*. London, 1952.

Anderson, C. A., and M. Schnaper. *School and Society in England: Social Backgrounds of Oxford and Cambridge Students*. Washington, 1952.

Andrade, E. N. da C. "Henry Roper Robinson." *ORS* 3 (1957), 161–172.

———. "Rutherford at Manchester 1913–1914." In Birks, pp. 27–42.

———. "A Physics Research Student at Heidelberg in the Old Days." *Physics Education* 1 (1966), 69–78.

Anonymous. "How to Choose a College at Oxford." *National Review* 48 (1906), 282–288.

———. "The London City Companies' Grants to Science and Education." *Nature* 53 (1897), 425–427.

Antonoff, G. N. "The Disintegration Products of Radium." *PM* 22 (1911), 419–432.

Argles, Michael. *South Kensington to Robins. An Account of English Technical and Scientific Education Since 1851*. London, 1964.

Arms, Nancy. *A Prophet in Two Countries. The Life of F. E. Simon*. Oxford and New York, 1966.

Armstrong, H. E. "The Classification of the Elements." *PRS* 70 (1902), 86–94.

———. "Celtium." *Chemistry and Industry* (1923), 792–793.

[———]. "H. E. Armstrong." *The Central* 35 (1938), 1–94.

Ashmolean Society. Miscellaneous Papers, 1876–1937. G. A. Oxon. 4°. 164 (OB).

Aspinall-Oglander, C. F. *Military Operations: Gallipoli.* 2 vols., London, 1928–1932.

Auer von Welsbach, Carl. "Über die Elemente der Yttergruppe." *Sb* (Vienna) 115:2b (1906), 737–747.

———. "Die Zerlegung des Ytterbiums in seine Elemente." *Sb* (Vienna) 116:2b (1907), 1425–1469.

———. "Zur Zerlegung des Ytterbiums." *Sb* (Vienna) 118:2b (1909), 507–512.

———. "Notiz über die Elemente des Thuliums." *Sb* (Vienna) 120:2b (1911), 193–195.

Badash, Lawrence, ed. *Rutherford and Boltwood. Letters on Radioactivity.* New Haven and London, 1969.

Baeyer, O. von. "Bericht über die magnetischen Spektren der β Strahlen der radioaktiven Elemente." *JRE* 11 (1914), 66–84.

Baeyer, O. von, O. Hahn, and L. Meitner. "Über die β Strahlen des aktiven Niederschlags des Thoriums." *PZs* 12 (1911), 273–279.

———. "Magnetische Spektren der β Strahlen des Radiums." *PZs* 12 (1911), 1099–1101.

Bailey, Cyril. *Francis Fortescue Urquhart, A Memoir.* London, 1936.

Baker, Thomas. *History of the College of St. John the Evangelist, Cambridge.* 2 vols., Cambridge, 1896.

Ball, W. W. Rouse. *A History of the Study of Mathematics at Cambridge.* Cambridge, 1889.

Bardet, J. "Sur le spectre d'arc du celtium." *CR* 176 (1923), 1711–1712.

Barkla, C. G. "Secondary Radiation from Gases Subject to X Rays." *PM* 5 (1903), 685–698.

———. "Polarization in Secondary Röntgen Radiation." *PRS* 77:A (1906), 247–255.

———. "Energy of Secondary Röntgen Radiation." *PM* 11 (1906), 812–828.

———. "The Nature of X Rays." *Nature* 78 (1908), 7.

———. "Der Stand der Forschung über die sekundäre Röntgen Strahlung." *JRE* 5 (1908), 246–324.

———. "The Spectra of the Fluorescent Röntgen Radiations." *PM* 22 (1911), 396–412.

Barkla, C. G., and V. Collier. "The Absorption of X Rays and Fluorescent X-Ray Spectra." *PM* 23 (1912), 987–997.

Barkla, C. G., and G. H. Martyn. "An X-Ray Fringe System." *Nature* 90 (1913), 647.

————. "Interference of Röntgen Radiation (Preliminary Account)." *Proceedings of the Physical Society of London* 25 (1913), 206–213.

————. "The Photographic Effect of X Rays and X-Ray Spectra." *PM* 25 (1913), 296–300.

Barkla, C. G., and A. J. Philpot. "Ionization in Gases and Gaseous Mixtures by Röntgen and Corpuscular (Electronic) Radiations." *PM* 25 (1913), 832–856.

Barkla, C. G., and C. A. Sadler. "Homogeneous Secondary Röntgen Radiations." *PM* 16 (1908), 550–584.

————. "The Absorption of Röntgen Rays." *PM* 17 (1909), 739–760.

Baskerville, Charles. "The Rare Earth Crusade. What it Portends Scientifically and Technically." *Science* 17 (1903), 772–781.

————. "The Elements Verified and Unverified." *Science* 19 (1904), 88–100.

Beerbohm, Max. *Zuleika Dobson or An Oxford Love Story*. London, 1911.

Bellamy, F. A. *A Historical Account of the Ashmolean Natural History Society of Oxfordshire 1880–1905*. Oxford, 1908.

Bernal, J. D. *The Social Function of Science*. Cambridge, Mass., 1967².

Birkenhead, Earl of. *The Professor and the Prime Minister. The Official Life of Professor F. A. Lindemann, Viscount Cherwell*. Boston, 1962.

Birks, J. B., ed. *Rutherford at Manchester*. London, 1962.

Bishop, A. S. *The Rise of a Central Authority for English Education*. London, 1970.

Blakiston, H. E. D. *Trinity College*. London, 1898.

Böhm, C. R. *Das Gasglühlicht. Seine Geschichte, Herstellung und Anwendung*. Leipzig, 1905.

Bohr, N. "On the Constitution of Atoms and Molecules. [Part I]." *PM* 26 (1913), 1–25.

————. ————. II. *PM* 26 (1913), 476–502.

————. ————. III. *PM* 26 (1913), 857–875.

————. "Atomic Models and X-Ray Spectra." *Nature* 92 (1914), 553–554.

————. "On the Quantum Theory of Radiation and the Structure of the Atom." *PM* 30 (1915), 394–415.

————. "Henry Gwyn Jeffreys Moseley." *PM* 31 (1916), 174–176.

————. "Atomic Structure." *Nature* 107 (1921), 104–107.

————. "Der Bau der Atome und die physikalischen und chemischen Eigenschaften der Elemente." *Zs für Physik* 9 (1922), 1–67.

————. "The Structure of the Atom." *Nature* 112 (7 July 1923: supplement), 1–16.

————. "Reminiscences of the Founder of Nuclear Science and of Some Developments Based on his Work." In Birks, pp. 114–167.

Bohr, N., and D. Coster. "Röntgenspektren und periodisches System der Elemente." *Zs für Physik* 12 (1923), 342–374.

Born, M., and A. Landé. "Kristallgitter und Borsches Atommodell." *VdpG* 20 (1918), 202–209.

———. "Uber die Berechnung der Kompressibilität regularer Kristalle aus der Gittertheorie." *VdpG* 20 (1918), 210–216.

Bourne, G. C. "Memoir of Henry Nottidge Moseley." In *Notes by a Naturalist*, by H. N. Moseley. New York, 1892², pp. v–xvi.

Bowen, E. J. "The Balliol-Trinity Laboratories, Oxford, 1853–1940." *Notes and Records RS* 25 (1970), 227–236.

Boys, C. V. "On the Newtonian Constant of Gravitation." *PT* 186:1 (1895), 1–72.

Bragg, W. H. "On the Properties and Natures of Various Electric Radiations." *PM* 14 (1907), 429–449.

———. "The Nature of the γ and X Rays." *Nature* 78 (1908), 293–294.

———. "The Consequences of the Corpuscular Hypothesis of the γ and X Rays." *PM* 20 (1910), 385–416.

———. "X Rays and Crystals." *Nature* 90 (1912), 219, 360–361.

———. "Radiations Old and New." *Nature* 90 (1912), 529–532, 557–560.

———. "X Rays and Crystals." *Nature* 90 (1913), 572.

———. "The Reflection of X Rays by Crystals." *PRS* 89:A (1913), 246–248.

———. "An X-Ray Absorption Band." *Nature* 93 (1913), 31–32.

Bragg, W. H., and W. L. Bragg. "The Reflection of X Rays by Crystals." *PRS* 88:A (1913), 428–438.

———. *X Rays and Crystal Structure*. London, 1915.

Bragg, W. H., and S. E. Peirce. "The Absorption Coefficients of X Rays." *PM* 28 (1914), 626–630.

Bragg, W. L. "The Diffraction of Short Electromagnetic Waves by a Crystal." *Proceedings of the Cambridge Philosophical Society* 17 (1912–1914), 43–57.

———. "On the Spectral Reflection of X Rays." *Nature* 90 (1912), 410.

———. "The Structure of Some Crystals as Indicated by their Diffraction of X Rays." *PRS* 89:A (1913), 248–277.

———. "Die Reflexion der Röntgenstrahlen." *JRE* 11 (1914), 346–391.

Brauner, B. "Hafnium or Celtium?" *Chemistry and Industry* (1923), 884–885.

———. "The New Element of Atomic Number 61: Illinium." *Nature* 118 (1926), 84–85.

Brindley, W. H. *Soul of Manchester*. Manchester, 1929.

Broek, A. van den. "Die Radioelemente, das periodische System, und die Konstitution des Atoms." *PZs* 14 (1913), 32–41.

———. "Ordinals or Atomic Numbers." *PM* 28 (1914), 630–632.

Broglie, M. de. "Reflection of X Rays and X-Ray Fringes." *Nature* 91 (1913), 161–162.

———. "Enregistrement photographique continu des spectres des rayons de

Röntgen. Spectre du tungstène. Influence de l'agitation thermique." *CR* 157 (1913), 1413–1416.

———. "Sur un nouveau procédé permettant d'obtenir la photographie des spectres de raies de Röntgen." *CR* 157 (1913), 924–926, and *CR* 158 (1914), 177–180.

———. "Sur les spectres des rayons de Röntgen, rayons émis par des anti-cathodes de cuivre, de fer, d'or." *CR* 158 (1914), 623–625.

———. "Sur la spectroscopie des rayons secondaires émis hors des tubes à rayons de Röntgen, et les spectres d'absorption." *CR* 158 (1914), 1493–1495.

———. "Sur l'analyse spectrale directe par les rayons secondaires des rayons de Röntgen." *CR* 158 (1914), 1785–1788.

———. "Sur l'analyse spectrale par les rayons secondaires des rayons de Röntgen et son application au cas des substances rares." *CR* 159 (1914), 304–305.

———. "La portée des nouvelles découvertes dans la région des rayons de très haute fréquence." *Scientia* 27 (1920), 102–111.

Broglie, M. de, and J. Cabrera. "Sur le spectre K d'absorption de l'élément 72 (celtium)." *CR* 176 (1923), 433–434.

Byrne, L. S. R., ed. *The Eton Boating Book*. Eton, 1933[3].

Campbell, Lewis. *On the Nationalization of the Old English Universities*. London, 1901.

Carpenter, W. B. "John Gwyn Jeffreys." *PRS* 38 (1884–1885), xiv–xvii.

Chadwick, James. "Intensitätsverteilung im magnetischen Spektrum der β-Strahlen von Radium B + C." *VdpG* 16 (1914), 383–391.

———. "The Charge on the Atomic Nucleus and the Law of Force." *PM* 40 (1920), 734–746.

Challis, James. "Report on the Present State of the Analytical Theory of Hydrostatics and Hydrodynamics." *BA Reports* (1833), 131–151.

Charlton, H. B. *Portrait of a University 1851–1951. To Commemorate the Centenary of Manchester University*. Manchester, 1951.

Clark, R. W. *Tizard*. Cambridge, Mass., 1965.

[Clifton, R. B.] "Robert Bellamy Clifton, 1836–1921." *PRS* 99:A (1921), vi–ix.

Committee on the Position of Natural Science in the Educational System of Great Britain. *National Science in Education*. London, 1918.

Comstock, D. F. "The Relation of Mass to Energy." *PM* 15 (1908), 1–21.

Cooper, Bryan. *The Tenth (Irish) Division in Gallipoli*. London, 1918.

Cordeaux, E. H., and D. H. Merry. *A Bibliography of Printed Works Relating to the University of Oxford*. Oxford, 1968.

Coster, D. "On the Spectra of X Rays and the Theory of Atomic Structure." *PM* 43 (1922), 1071–1107, and *PM* 44 (1923), 546–573.

Coster, D., and G. von Hevesy. "On the Missing Element of Atomic Number 72." *Nature* 111 (1923), 79.

———. "On the New Element Hafnium." *Nature* 111 (1923), 182.

Curie, M. *Traité de radioactivité.* 2 vols. Paris, 1910.

Curzon of Kedleston, Lord. *Principles and Methods of University Reform.* Oxford, 1909.

Dalton, Hugh. *Call Back Yesterday. Memoirs, 1887–1931.* London, 1953.

D'Ans, J. "Carl Freiherr Auer von Welsbach." *Berichte der deutschen chemischen Gesellschaft* 64:1A (1930), 59–92.

Danysz, J. "Sur les rayons β de la famille du radium." *Le radium* 9 (1912), 1–5.

Darwin, Francis, ed. *The Life and Letters of Charles Darwin.* 2 vols. Reprint, New York, 1959.

———. *More Letters of Charles Darwin. A Record of His Work in a Series of Hitherto Unpublished Letters.* 2 vols. New York, 1903.

Darwin, C. G. "The Effects of the Diurnal Rotation on the Upper Atmosphere." *PM* 23 (1912), 664–668.

———. "A Theory of the Absorption and Scattering of the α Rays." *PM* 23 (1912), 901–920.

———. "The Theory of X-Ray Reflection." *PM* 27 (1914), 315–333, 675–690.

———. "Laue Diagrams. Twenty-five Years of Research on X-Ray Diffraction." *Current Science* (1937: special number), 23–25.

———. "The Discovery of Atomic Number." *PRS* 236:A (1956), 285–296, and in *Niels Bohr and the Development of Physics.* Edited by W. Pauli *et al.* London, 1955, pp. 1–11.

———. "Moseley and the Atomic Number of the Elements." In Birks, pp. 17–26, and, as "Moseley's Determination of Atomic Numbers," in *Fifty Years of X Ray Diffraction.* Edited by P. P. Ewald. Utrecht, 1962, pp. 550–563.

Darwin, H., and W. M. Bayliss. "Keith Lucas." *PRS* 95:A (1918–1919), i–xi.

Dauvillier, A. "Sur la distribution des électrons entre les niveaux L des éléments." *CR* 178 (1924), 476–479.

Davis, H. W. C. *A History of Balliol College.* Oxford, 1963^2.

Debye, P. "Über den Einfluss der Wärmebewegung auf die Interferenzerscheinungen bei Röntgenstrahlen." *VdpG* 15 (1913), 678–689.

———. "Spektrale Zerlegung der Röntgenstrahlen mittels Reflexion und Wärmebewegung." *VdpG* 15 (1913), 857–875.

———. "Interferenz von Röntgenstrahlen und Wärmebewegung." *AP* 43 (1914), 49–95.

Dixon, H. B. "D. H. Nagel." *Nature* 106 (1920), 186.

Drage, G. *Eton and The Empire.* Eton, 1890.

Duhem, P. *The Aim and Structure of Physical Science.* Translated by P. P. Wiener. Princeton, 1954.

Eggar, W. D. *Mechanics. A School Course.* London [1905].

Emerson, B. K. "Helix Chemica. A Study of the Periodic Relations of the Chemical Elements and their Graphic Representation." *American Chemical Journal* 45 (1911), 160–210.

Engel, A. von. "John Sealy Edward Townsend." *ORS* 3 (1957), 257–272.

Eton College. *A List of Eton College, Taken at Election*, 1905. Eton, 1905.

Euler, K. J. "Methoden der Energieumwandlung. Radionuklid-Batterien, Galvanische Brennstoffzellen, Magnetohydrodynamische Generatoren." *Physikalische Blätter* 25 (1969), 7–15.

Eve, A. S. *Rutherford*. Cambridge and New York, 1939.

Exner, F., and E. Hascheck. "Zur Spektroscopie der seltenen Erden." *Sb* (Vienna) 119:2a (1910), 771–778.

Fajans, K. "Über die komplexe Natur von Radium C." *PZs* 12 (1911), 369–378.

———. "Über die Verzweigung der Radiumzerfallsreihe." *PZs* 13 (1912), 699–705.

Feather, N. "Richard Whiddington, 1885–1970." *ORS* 17 (1971), 741–756.

Ferreira, R. "Photographs of Moseley." *Isis* 60 (1969), 233.

Fiddes, E. *Chapters in the History of Owens College and of Manchester University, 1851–1914*. Manchester, 1937.

Fitzgerald, G. F. "On Ostwald's Energetics." *Nature* 53 (1896), 441–442.

Fleck, A. "The Existence of Uranium Y." *PM* 25 (1913), 710–712.

Fletcher, C. R. L. *Edmond Warre, D. D., C.B., C. V. O. Sometime Headmaster and Provost of Eton College*. London, 1922.

Föppel, L. "Über die Stabilität des Borschen Atommodells." *PZs* 15 (1914), 707–712.

Forman, P. "The Discovery of the Diffraction of X-rays by Crystals. A Critique of the Myths." *AHES* 6 (1969), 38–71.

———. "Alfred Landé and the Anomalous Zeeman Effect, 1919–1921." *HSPS* 2 (1970), 153–261.

Forman, P., J. L. Heilbron, and S. Weart. "Personnel, Productivity and Funding in Physics *circa* 1900: A Multinational Statistical Study." *HSPS* 4 (1973).

Foster, C. "One Hundred Years of Science Teaching in Great Britain." *Annals of Science* 2 (1937), 335–344.

Friedrich, W. "Röntgenstrahlinterferenzen." *PZs* 14 (1913), 1079–1087.

Friedrich, W., P. Knipping, and M. Laue. "Interferenz-Erscheinungen bei Röntgenstrahlen." *Sb* (Munich) 42 (1912), 303–322.

Galton, F. *English Men of Science. Their Nature and Nurture*. London, 1874.

Gardner, Percy. *Oxford at the Crossroads. A Criticism of the Course of Literae Humaniores in the University*. London, 1903.

Geiger, H. "Strahlungs-, Temperatur- und Potentialmessungen in Entladungsröhren mit starken Strömen." *AP* 22 (1907), 973–1007.

Geiger, H., and E. Marsden. "The Laws of Deflexion of Alpha Particles through Large Angles." *PM* 25 (1913), 604–623.

Glaisher, J. W. L. "The Mathematical Tripos." *Proceedings of the London Mathematical Society* (1886), 4–38.

Goldberg, S. "In Defense of Ether: The British Response to Einstein's Special Theory of Relativity, 1905–1911." *HSPS* 2 (1970), 89–125.

Gouy, G. "Sur le mouvement lumineux." *J de physique* 5 (1886), 354–362.

————. *Notice sur les travaux scientifiques.* Lyon, 1913.

Green, V. H. H. *Religion at Oxford and Cambridge.* London, 1964.

Grenfell, Ethel A. P., Lady Desborough. *Pages from a Family Journal, 1888–1915.* Eton, 1916.

Griffith, I. O. "The Relation between the Intensity of the Ultra Violet Light falling on a Negatively Charged Zinc Plate and the Quantity of Electricity which is Set Free from the Surface." *PM* 14 (1907), 297–306.

Gunther, R. T. *The Daubeny Laboratory Register, 1849–1923.* 3 parts. Oxford, 1904–1924.

————. "Oxford Colleges and Their Men of Science." In Gunther, *Early Science at Oxford.* II. Oxford, 1937.

Gurney, R. W. "The Number of Particles in the Beta Ray Spectra of Radium B and Radium C." *PRS* 109:A (1925), 540–561.

Hackney, J. C. "Technetium—Element 43." *J Chemical Education* 28 (1951), 186–190.

Haddon, A. C. "Henry Balfour, 1863–1939." *ORS* 3:1 (1939–1941), 109–115.

Hahn, O., and Lise Meitner. "Nachweis der komplexen Natur von Radium C." *PZs* 10 (1909), 697–703.

Haines, George. *Essays on German Influence upon English Education and Science, 1850–1919.* New London, Conn., 1969.

Hall, A. R. *The Cambridge Philosophical Society. A History 1819–1869.* Cambridge, 1969.

Hamer, Richard. "Moseleyum." *Science* 61 (1925), 208–209.

Hansen, H. M., and S. Werner. "On Urbain's Celtium Lines." *Nature* 111 (1923), 461.

Harcourt, A. V. "The Oxford Museum and its Founders." *Cornhill Magazine* 28 (1910), 350–363.

Harrison, Frederic. *Autobiographic Memories.* 2 vols. London, 1911.

Harrod, R. F. *The Prof. A Personal Memoir of Lord Cherwell.* London, 1959.

Hartley, H. "The Contribution of the College Laboratories." *Chemistry in Britain* 1 (1965), 521–524.

Hearnshaw, F. J. C. *The Centenary History of Kings College London, 1828–1928.* London, 1929.

Heilbron, J. L. "The Work of H. G. J. Moseley." *Isis* 57 (1966), 336–364.

———. "The Kossel-Sommerfeld Theory and the Ring Atom." *Isis* 58 (1967), 451–485.

———. "The Scattering of α and β Particles and Rutherford's Atom." *AHES* 4 (1968), 247–307.

Heilbron, J. L., and T. S. Kuhn. "The Genesis of the Bohr Atom." *HSPS* 1 (1969), 211–290.

Heimann, P. M. "Moseley and Celtium. The Search for a Missing Element." *Annals of Science* 23 (1967), 249–260.

———. "Moseley's Interpretation of X-Ray Spectra." *Centaurus* 12 (1968), 261–274.

Hevesy, G. von. "The Valency of the Radioelements." *PM* 25 (1913), 390–414.

———. "Über den Austausch der Atome zwischen festen und flüssigen Phasen." *PZs* 16 (1915), 52–54.

———. "Borsche Theorie und Radioaktivität." *Die Naturwissenschaften* 11 (1923), 604–605.

———. *Chemical Analysis by X Rays and its Application.* New York, 1932.

———. "Historical Notes on the Discovery of Hafnium." *Archiv för Kemi* 3 (1951), 543–548.

Hicks, W. M. "High Frequency Spectra and the Periodic Table." *PM* 28 (1914), 139–142.

Hill, B. J. W. *Eton Medly.* London, 1948.

Hill, C. R. *Chemical Apparatus. University of Oxford, Museum of the History of Science. Catalogue I.* Oxford, 1971.

Hill, M. D. "Nature Study." In C. Norwood and A. H. Hope, eds., *The Higher Education of Boys in England.* London, 1909, pp. 395–400.

———. *Eton and Elsewhere.* London, 1928.

Hill, M. D., and W. M. Webb. *Eton Nature Study.* 2 vols. London, 1903–1904.

Hirosige, T. "The van den Broek Hypothesis." *Japanese Studies in the History of Science* 10 (1971), 143–162.

Hollis, Christopher. *Eton. A History.* London, 1960.

Horner, F. J. *Time Remembered.* London, 1933.

Hunter-Blair, D. O. "Oxford as it is." *Catholic University Bulletin* 14 (1908), 627–640.

Hupka, E., and W. Steinhaus. "System of Lines Obtained by Reflection of X Rays." *Nature* 91 (1913), 10.

Huxley, J. S. *Memories.* London, 1970.

Irving, A. "Science in the Public Schools." *Nature* 66 (1902), 459.

Jaffe, Bernard. *Crucibles. The Story of Chemistry.* New York, 1957[2].

———. *Moseley and the Numbering of the Elements.* New York, 1971.

James, Charles. "Thulium. Preliminary Announcement." *JACS* 32:1 (1910), 517–518.

_____. "Thulium I." *JACS* 33:2 (1911), 1332–1344.

Jamin, J. *Cours de physique de l'école polytechnique.* Edited by E. Bouty. 4 vols. in 6. Paris, 1886–1890[4].

[Jeffreys, J. G.] "J. G. Jeffreys." *Nature* 31 (1885), 317–318.

[_____]. "J. G. Jeffreys." *PRS* 38 (1885), xiv–xvii.

Jervis, H. "The Evolution of the Elements." *Transactions of the Oxford University Junior Scientific Club* (1905 +), 241–249.

Jessup, A. C., and A. E. Jessup. "The Evolution and Devolution of the Elements." *PM* 15 (1908), 21–55.

Job, P. "Le jubilé scientifique de M. Georges Urbain." *Annales de chimie* 13 (1938), 509–517.

Jones, L. E. *A Victorian Boyhood.* London, 1955.

_____. *An Edwardian Youth.* London, 1956.

_____. *Georgian Aftermath.* London, 1958.

Jones, R. A. See Raleigh, W.

Kaye, G. W. C. "The Emission and Transmission of Röntgen Rays." *PT* 209:A (1909), 123–151.

_____. "Note on Cathodic Sputtering." *Proceedings of the Physical Society* 25 (1912–1913), 198–202.

_____. *X Rays.* London, 1914.

Keene, H. B. "The Reflection of X Rays." *Nature* 91 (1913), 111.

Knox, R. A. *A Spiritual Aeneid.* London, 1919.

_____. *Patrick Shaw-Stewart.* London, 1920.

_____. "Dr. C. E. Williams." *The Times of London* (15 Mar 41), 7.

_____. *God and the Atom.* London, 1945.

Kohl, Max, [and Co., Chemnitz]. Price List 50. Physical Apparatus. (n.p., n.d. [c. 1912]).

Kopal, Z. "H. G. J. Moseley, 1887–1915." *Isis* 58 (1967), 405–407.

Kossel, W. "Bemerkung zur Absorption homogener Röntgenstrahlen [I]." *VdpG* 16 (1914), 898–909.

_____. _____. [II]. *VdpG* 16 (1914), 953–963.

Laborde, E. D. *Harrow School Yesterday and Today.* London, 1948.

Ladenburg, R. "Atombau und periodisches System der Elemente." *Zs für Elektrochemie* 26 (1920), 262–274.

Langstraff, J. B. *Oxford, 1914.* New York, 1965.

Lankester, E. R. "Henry Nottidge Moseley, F. R. S." *Nature* 45 (1891), 79–80.

_____. "Henry Gwyn Jeffreys Moseley." *PM* 31 (1916), 173–174.

Larmor, Joseph. *Aether and Matter.* Cambridge, 1900.

Laski, M. "Domestic Life." In *Edwardian England.* Edited by S. Nowell-Smith. London and New York, 1964, pp. 139–212.

Laub, J. J. "Über die durch Röntgenstrahlen erzeugten sekundären Kathodenstrahlen." *AP* 26 (1908), 712–726.

Laue, M. von. "Eine quantitative Prüfung der Theorie für die Interferenz-Erscheinungen bei Röntgenstrahlen." *Sb* (Munich) 42 (1912), 363–373.

———. "Zusätze (März 1913)." *AP* 41 (1913), 989–1002.

———. "Les phénomènes d'interférences des rayons de Röntgen produits par le réseau tridimensional des cristaux." In *La structure de la matière. Rapports et discussions du conseil de physique [Solvay] tenu à Bruxelles du 27 au 31 octobre 1913.* Paris, 1921, pp. 75–102.

———. "Die Interferenzerscheinungen an Röntgenstrahlen, hervorgerufen durch das Raumgitter der Kristalle." *JRE* 11 (1914), 308–345.

———. "Nachruf auf Hans Geiger." *Jahrbuch der deutschen Akademie der Wissenschaften* (1946–1949), 150–158.

Ledoux-Lebard, R., and A. Dauvillier. *La physique des rayons X.* Paris, 1921.

Leslie, Shane. *The End of a Chapter.* London, 1916.

———. *The Oppidan.* London, 1922.

———. *The Film of Memory.* London, 1938.

———. *Long Shadows.* London, 1966.

Lindemann, F. A. "Über die Berechnung der Eigenfrequenzen der Elektronen im selektiven Photoeffekt." *VdpG* 13 (1911), 482–488.

———. "Über Beziehungen zwischen chemischen Affinität und Elektronfrequenzen." *VdpG* 13 (1911), 1107–1116.

———. "Atomic Models and X-Ray Spectra." *Nature* 92 (1 Jan 14), 500–501, and *ibid.* (5 Feb 14), 631.

———. "Über die Grundlagen der Atommodelle." *VdpG* 16 (1914), 281–294.

Lindh, A. "En svensk Nobelpristagare [M. Siegbahn]." *Kosmos* 5 (1925–1926), 5–63.

Lockyer, J. N. *Contributions to Solar Physics.* London, 1874.

Lodge, Oliver. "Physics and Chemistry." *Nature* 76 (1907), 414–415.

———. "Aether and Matter: Being Remarks on Inertia, and on Radiation, and on the Possible Structure of Atoms." *Nature* 104 (1919–1920), 15–19, 82–87.

Loring, F. H. *Atomic Theories.* London, 1921.

Lyttelton, Edward. *Memories and Hopes.* London, 1925.

Mack, E. C. *Public Schools and British Opinion Since 1860.* New York, 1941.

Mackenzie, C. "Undergraduates at the Beginning of the Century." *Oxford* 5 (1938), 68–74.

Makower, W. "On the Number and Absorption by Matter of the β Particles Emitted by Radium." *PM* 17 (1909), 171–180.

M[alden], C. H. *Recollections of an Eton Colleger, 1898–1902.* London, 1905.

Mallet, C. F. *A History of the University of Oxford. III. Modern Oxford.* London, 1927.

Marsden, E. "Rutherford at Manchester." In Birks, pp. 1–16.

Marsden, E., and C. G. Darwin. "The Transformations of the Active Deposit of Thorium." *PRS* 87:A (1912), 17–29.

Marsden, E., and R. H. Wilson. "Branch Product in Actinium C." *Nature* 92 (1913), 29.

Marwick, Arthur. *The Deluge: British Society and the First World War.* London, 1965.

McCormmach, R. "The Atomic Theory of J. W. Nicholson." *AHES* 2 (1966), 160–184.

McDonnell, M. F. J. "The Oxford Man, by a Cambridge Man." *Oxford and Cambridge Review* (1908:3), 96–104.

Meadows, A. J. *Science and Controversy. A Biography of Sir Norman Lockyer.* Cambridge, Mass., 1972.

Mendeleev, D. *Principles of Chemistry.* 2 vols. London, 1905³.

Mendelssohn, K. "The World of Cryogenics. IV. The Clarendon Laboratory, Oxford." *Cryogenics* 6 (1966), 129–140.

Meyer, R. J. "Elemente der Cerit- und Ytteriterden (Seltene Erden)." In *Handbuch der anorganischen Chemie* III:1. Edited by R. Abegg. Leipzig, 1906, pp. 129–175.

Moseley, Henry. *A Treatise on Hydrostatics and Hydrodynamics for the Use of Students in the University.* Cambridge, 1830.

———. "Elementary Schools of the Midland District." *Minutes of the Committee of Council on Education, 1845.* London, 1846, I, pp. 224–323.

———. "On the Dynamical Stability and on the Oscillations of Floating Bodies." *PT* 140 (1850), 609–643.

———. "On the Descent of Glaciers." *PRS* 7 (1854–1855), 333–342.

———. *Illustrations of Mechanics.* London, 1859⁶.

[———]. "Memoir of the Late Canon Moseley." *Transactions of the Institution of Naval Architects* 13 (1872), 328–330.

Moseley, H. G. J. [**I**] "Radioactive Products of Short Life." *PM* 22 (1911), 629–638. [with K. Fajans]

———. [**II**] " γ Radiation from Radium B." *PM* 23 (1912), 302–310. [with W. Makower]

———. [**III**] "The Number of β-Particles Emitted in the Transformation of Radium." *PRS* 87:A (1912), 230–255.

———. "Radium as a Means of Obtaining High Potentials." *Memoirs and Proceedings of the Manchester Literary and Philosophical Society* 57 (1912), viii–ix.

———. [**IV**] "The Attainment of High Potentials by the Use of Radium." *PRS* 88:A (1913), 471–476.

———. [V] "The Reflection of the X Rays." *Nature* 90 (30 Jan 13), 594. [with C. G. Darwin]

———. [VI] "The Reflection of the X Rays." *PM* 26 (1913), 210–232. [with C. G. Darwin]

———. [Review of T. Svedberg, *Die Existenz der Moleküle. Experimentelle Studien.* Leipzig, 1912.] *Nature* 92 (1913), 367–368.

———. [VII] "The High-Frequency Spectra of the Elements." *PM* 26 (1913), 1024–1034.

———. [VIII] "Atomic Models and X-Ray Spectra." *Nature* 92 (15 Jan 14), 554.

———. [IX] "The High-Frequency Spectra of the Elements. Part II." *PM* 27 (1914), 703–713.

———. [X] "The Number of Ions Produced by the β and γ Radiations from Radium." *PM* 28 (1914), 327–337. [with H. Robinson]

Moseley, H. N. *Oregon: Its Resources, Climate, People and Productions.* London, 1878.

———. *Notes by a Naturalist. An Account of Observations Made During the Voyage of H. M. S. "Challenger" Round the World in the Years 1872–1876.* London, 1879; New York, 1892^2.

[Nagel, D. H.] "D. H. Nagel." *J Chemical Society* 119:1 (1921), 551–553.

Nagel, D. H., and W. A. Spooner. *The Proposed Statute as to Exemption from Greek in Responsions.* Oxford, 1904.

Nicholson, J. W. "A Structural Theory of the Chemical Elements." *PM* 22 (1911), 864–889.

———. "The Spectrum of Nebulium." *Monthly Notices of the Royal Astronomical Society* 72 (1911–1912), 49–64.

———. "The Constitution of the Ring Nebulae in Lyra (NGC 6720)." *Ibid.*, 176–177.

———. "The Constitution of the Solar Corona. I." *Ibid.*, 139–150.

———. ———. II. *Ibid.*, 677–693.

———. ———. III. *Ibid.*, 729–739.

———. "On the New Nebular Line at λ 4353." *Ibid.*, 693.

———. "Atomic Models and X-Ray Spectra." *Nature* 92 (1914), 583–584.

———. "Atomic Structure and the Spectrum of Helium." *Monthly Notices of the Royal Astronomical Society* 74 (1914), 425–442.

———. "The High-Frequency Spectra of the Elements and the Structure of the Atom." *PM* 27 (1914), 541–564.

Nisio, S. "X-Rays and Atomic Structure in the Early Stage of the Old Quantum Theory." *Japanese Studies in History of Science* 8 (1969), 55–75.

Norwood, C., and A. H. Hope, eds. *The Higher Education of Boys in England.* London, 1909.

Owen, E. A., and G. G. Blake. "X-Ray Spectra." *Nature* 91 (1913), 135.

Oxford University Junior Scientific Club. [Miscellaneous Papers, 1882–1928]. OB.

Paneth, F. "Über das Element 72 (Hafnium)." *Ergebnisse der exakten Naturwissenschaften* 2 (1923), 163–176.

———. "The Making of the Missing Chemical Elements." *Nature* 159 (1947), 8–10.

Pauli, W. "Über den Zusammenhang des Abschlusses der Elektronengruppen im Atom mit der Komplexstruktur der Spektren." *Zs für Physik* 31 (1925), 765–783.

Pauling, L. "Die Abschirmungskonstanten der relativistischen oder magnetischen Röntgenstrahlendubletts." *Zs für Physik* 40 (1927), 344–350.

Pauling, L., and S. Goudsmit. *Structure of Line Spectra*. New York and London, 1930.

Peck, Winifred. *A Little Learning or a Victorian Childhood*. London, [1952].

Pelseneer, P. "John Gwyn Jeffreys. Esquisse biographique." *Bulletin scientifique du département du nord* 16 (1884–1885), 258–262.

The Physical Laboratories of the University of Manchester. Manchester, 1906. [Publications of the University of Manchester. Physical Series. No. 1]

Planck, M. "Die Kaufmannschen Messungen der Ablenkbarkeit der β Strahlen in ihrer Bedeutung für die Dynamik der Elektronen." *PZs* 7 (1906), 753–761.

———. "Eine neue Strahlungshypothese." *VdpG* 13 (1911), 136–148.

Porter, T. C. "Analysis of Röntgen Radiation." *Nature* 54 (1896), 110–111.

———. "Experiments on Röntgen Rays." *Nature* 54 (1896), 149–150.

———. "Contributions to the Study of 'Flicker'." *PRS* 63 (1898), 347–356.

———. ———. [II]. *PRS* 70:A (1902), 313–329.

———. *Impressions of America*. London, 1899.

[———]. "Thomas Cunningham Porter." *J Chemical Society* (1933:2), 1650–1652.

Poulton, E. B. *John Viriamu Jones and Other Oxford Memories*. London, 1911.

———. *Science and the Great War*. Oxford, 1915.

———. *The Life of Ronald Poulton*. London, 1920.

Pound, Reginald. *The Lost Generation*. London, 1964.

The Public Schools from Within. A Collection of Essays on Public School Education, Written Chiefly by Schoolmasters. London, 1906.

Raleigh, W. *The War in the Air. Being the Part Played in the Great War by the Royal Air Force*. Vol. I. Oxford, 1922. Continued by R. A. Jones. 5 vols. Oxford, 1928–1937.

Ramsay, W. "Ancient and Modern Views Regarding the Chemical Elements." *Smithsonian Institution Report* (1911), 183–197.

Rawlinson, W. F. "Note on the X-ray Spectrum of Nickel." *PM* 28 (1914), 274–277.

Rawlinson, W. F., and H. Robinson. "The Magnetic Spectrum of the β Rays Excited in Metals by Soft X Rays." *PM* 28 (1914), 277–281.

Rayleigh, Lord. *The Life of Sir J. J. Thomson, O.M.* Cambridge, 1942.

———. *The Life of John William Strutt, 3rd Baron Rayleigh.* Madison and London, 1968².

Redman, L. A. "H. G. J. Moseley, 1887–1915." *Physics Teacher* 3 (1965), 151–157.

Reiche, F., and A. Smekal. "Zur Theorie der Röntgenspektren." *AP* 57 (1918), 124–144.

Ribblesdale, Lord. *Charles Lister: Letters and Recollections.* London, 1917.

Robinson, H. R. "The Secondary Corpuscular Rays Produced by Homogeneous X Rays." *PRS* 104:A (1923), 455–479.

———. "Rutherford: Life and Work to the Year 1919, with Personal Reminiscences of the Manchester Period." In Birks, pp. 53–86.

Rolleston, George. *Scientific Papers and Addresses.* Edited by W. Turner. 2 vols. Oxford, 1884.

Rosenfeld, L. "Introduction." In Niels Bohr, *The Constitution of Atoms and Molecules.* Edited by L. Rosenfeld. Copenhagen, 1963, pp. xi–liv.

Rothblatt, S. *The Revolution of the Dons. Cambridge and Society in Victorian England.* London, 1968.

Russell, A. S. "Lord Rutherford: Manchester, 1907–1919. A Partial Portrait." In Birks, pp. 87–101.

Rutherford, E. "Charge Carried by the α and β Rays of Radium." *PM* 10 (1905), 193–208; *Papers* I, 816–829.

———. "The Origin of β and γ Rays from Radioactive Substances." *PM* 24 (1912), 453–462; *Papers* II, 280–287.

———. "On the Energy of the Groups of β Rays from Radium." *PM* 24 (1912), 893–894; *Papers* II, 292–293.

———. "The Connection between the β and γ Ray Spectra." *PM* 28 (1914), 305–319; *Papers* II, 473–485.

———. "Henry Gwyn Jeffreys Moseley." *Nature* 96 (1915), 33–34.

———. "H. G. J. Moseley, 1887–1915." *PRS* 93:A (1916), xxii–xxviii.

———. "Identification of a Missing Element." *Nature* 109 (1922), 781; *Papers* III, 64–66.

———. "Moseley's Work on X Rays." *Nature* 116 (1925), 316–317.

———. *The Collected Papers.* Edited by J. Chadwick. 3 vols. London, 1962–1965.

Rutherford, E. *et al. Discussion on the Structure of the Atom.* London, 1914. [A separately published pamphlet, sometimes bound in with *PRS* for 1914.]

Rutherford, E., and E. N. da C. Andrade. "The Reflection of γ Rays from Crystals." *Nature* 92 (1913), 267; *Papers* II, 361.

——. "The Wavelengths of the Soft γ Rays from Radium B." *PM* 27 (1914), 854–868; *Papers* II, 432–444.

Rutherford, E., J. Chadwick, and C. D. Ellis. *Radiations from Radioactive Substances.* Cambridge, 1930.

Rutherford, E., and H. Geiger. "An Electrical Method of Counting the Number of α Particles from Radioactive Substances." *PRS* 81:A (1908), 141–161; *Papers* II, 89–108.

——. "The Charge and Nature of the α Particle." *PRS* 81:A (1908), 162–173; *Papers* II, 109–120.

——. "Photographic Registration of α Particles." *PM* 24 (1912), 618–623; *Papers* II, 288–291.

Rutherford, E., and H. Richardson. "Analysis of the γ Rays from Radium B and Radium C." *PM* 25 (1913), 722–734; *Papers* II, 342–352.

——. "Analysis of the γ Rays from Radium D and Radium E." *PM* 26 (1913), 324–332; *Papers* II, 353–360.

——. "Analysis of the γ Rays from the Thorium and Actinium Products." *PM* 26 (1913), 937–948; *Papers* II, 410–422.

Rutherford, E., and H. Robinson. "Heating Effect of Radium and its Radiation." *PM* 25 (1913), 312–330; *Papers* II, 312–327.

Rutherford, E., H. Robinson, and W. F. Rawlinson. "Spectrum of the β Rays excited by γ Rays." *PM* 28 (1914), 281–286; *Papers* II, 466–470.

Rydberg, J. "Untersuchungen über das System der Grundstoffe." *Årsskrift Lund Universitet* 9:2 (1913), 1–41.

——. "The Ordinals of the Elements and the High-Frequency Spectra." *PM* 28 (1914), 144–149.

St. John Nepomucene, Sister. "Rydberg: The Man and the Constant." *Chymia* 6 (1960), 127–145.

Sanderson, M. *The Universities and British Industry, 1850–1970.* London, 1972.

Sarton, G. "Moseley. The Numbering of the Elements." *Isis* 9 (1927), 96–111.

Schmidt, H. W. "Über den Zerfall von Radium A, B und C." *PZs* 6 (1905), 897–903.

Schott, G. A. *Electromagnetic Radiation.* Cambridge, 1911.

Schuler, P. F. E. *Australia in Arms.* London, 1916.

Schuster, A. "The New Physical Laboratory at the Owens College, Manchester." *Nature* 58 (1898), 621–622.

——. *Biographical Fragments.* London, 1932.

Schuster, E., and E. M. Elderton. "The Inheritance of Ability, being a Statistical Study of the Oxford Class Lists and of the School Lists of Harrow and Charterhouse." *Eugenics Laboratory Memoirs* 1. London, 1907.

Sedlacek, F. *Auer von Welsbach*. Vienna, 1934. [Österreichisches Forschungs-institut für Geschichte der Technik. *Blätter für Geschichte der Technik*, no. 2]

Shaw, G. B. *Sham Education*. London, 1931.

Siegbahn, M. "Über eine weitere Reihe (M-Reihe) in den Hochfrequenzspektren der Elemente." *VdpG* 18 (1916), 278–282.

———. "Bericht über die Röntgenspektren der chemischen Elemente (Experimentelle Methoden und Ergebnisse)." *JRE* 13 (1916), 296–341.

———. *Spektroskopie der Röntgenspektren*. Berlin, 1931².

Simpson, G. C. "Sir Arthur Schuster." *ORS* 1 (1932–1935), 409–423.

Skrabel, A. "Karl Freiherr Auer von Welsbach." *Neue österreichische Biographie* III (1931), 46–56.

Smeaton, W. A. "Moseley and the Numbering of the Elements." *Chemistry in Britain* (1965), 353–355.

Smekal, A. "Über die Erklärung der Röntgenspektren und die Konstitution der Atome." *PZs* 22 (1921), 400–402.

Smith, Frank. *A History of English Elementary Education, 1760–1902*. London, 1931.

Smithells, Arthur. "Presidential Address to Section B." *BA Reports* (1907), 469–479. Reprinted in *Nature* 76 (1907), 352–357.

Soddy, F. "The Existence of Uranium Y." *PM* 27 (1914), 215–221.

Sommerfeld, A. "Theoretisches über die Beugung der Röntgenstrahlen." *PZs* 1 (1899), 105–111.

———. ———. II. *PZs* 2 (1900), 55–60.

———. "Über die Verteilung der Intensität bei der Emission von Röntgen-strahlen." *PZs* 10 (1909), 969–976.

———. ———. II. *PZs* 11 (1910), 99–101.

———. "Über die Struktur der γ Strahlen." *Sb* (Munich) 41 (1911), 1–60.

———. "Die Feinstruktur der Wasserstoff- und Wasserstoffähnlichen Linien." *Sb* (Munich) (1915), 459–500.

———. "Zur Quantentheorie der Spektrallinien. III. Theorie der Röntgenspek-tren." *AP* 51 (1916), 125–167.

———. "Atombau und Röntgenspektren. I." *PZs* 19 (1918), 297–307.

———. *Atombau und Spektrallinien*. Braunschweig, 1921².

———. "Zur Theorie des periodischen Systems." *PZs* 26 (1925), 70–74.

Spronsen, J. W. van. *The Periodic System of Chemical Elements. A History of the First Hundred Years*. Amsterdam, 1969.

Stark, J. "Bemerkung über Zerstreuung und Absorption von β-Strahlen und Röntgenstrahlen in Kristallen." *PZs* 13 (1912), 973–977.

Steele, B. D. "The Place of the Rare Earths Among the Elements." *Chemical News* 84 (1901), 245–247.

Stoner, E. G. "The Distribution of Electrons among Atomic Levels." *PM* 48 (1924), 719–736.

Strutt, R. J. "Peculiar Form of Low Potential Discharge in the Highest Vacua." *PRS* 89:A (1913), 68–74.

Steuwer, R. H. "William Bragg's Corpuscular Theory of X-Rays and γ-Rays." *BJHS* 5 (1971), 258–281.

The Summer Fields Register, 1864–1929. Oxford, 1929.

Svedberg, T. *Die Existenz der Moleküle.* Leipzig, 1912.

Taylor, F. Sherwood. "The Teaching of Science at Oxford in the Nineteenth Century." *Annals of Science* 8 (1952), 82–112.

Thompson, S. P. "Address of the President." *Proceedings of the Physical Society* 17 (1899–1901), 12–25.

Thomson, C. Wyville. *The Voyage of the 'Challenger.' The Atlantic.* 2 vols. London, 1877.

Thomson, G. P. "Friedrich Alexander Lindemann, Viscount Cherwell." *ORS* 4 (1958), 45–71.

———. "Charles Galton Darwin, 1887–1962." *ORS* 9 (1963), 69–85.

Thomson, J. J. *The Conduction of Electricity Through Gases.* Cambridge, 1903.

———. "Survey of the Last Twenty-Five Years." In *A History of the Cavendish Laboratory.* London, 1910, pp. 75–101.

———. "The Structure of the Atom." *PM* 26 (1913), 792–799.

———. *The Atomic Theory.* Oxford, 1914. [The Romanes Lecture]

———. "John Henry Poynting." *PRS* 92:A (1916), i–ix.

———. "James Clerk Maxwell." In *James Clerk Maxwell. A Commemorative Volume.* Cambridge, 1931, pp. 1–44.

———. *Recollections and Reflections.* New York, 1937.

Thorpe, T. E. "Sir Arthur Rücker." *PRS* 92:A (1916), xxi–xlv.

Tillyard, A. J. *A History of University Reform [1800–1913].* Cambridge, 1913.

Townsend, J. S. "The Conductivity Produced in Gases by the Aid of Ultraviolet Light." *PM* 3 (1902), 557–576.

———. "The Genesis of Ions by the Motion of Positive Ions in a Gas, and a Theory of the Sparking Potential." *PM* 6 (1903), 598–618.

Tree, Viola, ed. *Alan Parsons' Book. A Story in Anthology.* London, 1937.

Turner, G. L'. E. "The Discovery of Atomic Number." *Bulletin of the Institute of Physics and the Physical Society* (1965), 54–55.

Urbain, Georges. "Un nouvel élément: le lutécium, résultant du dédoublement de l'ytterbium de Marignac." *CR* 145 (1907), 759–762.

———. "Comment se pose actuellement la question des terres rares." In M. A. Haller, ed., *Les récents progrès de la chimie* III. Paris, 1908, pp. 37–66.

———. "Le rôle de l'atomistique dans l'enseignement et dans la recherche." *Revue du mois* 7 (1909), 417–429.

————. "Sur un nouvel élément qui accompagne le lutécium et le scandium dans les terres rares." *CR* 154 (1911), 141–143.

————. "Les numéros atomiques du neo-ytterbium, du lutécium et du celtium." *CR* 174 (1922), 1349–1351.

————. "Should the Element of the Atomic Number 72 be called Celtium or Hafnium?" *Chemistry and Industry* (1923), 764–768.

————. "Définition de l'élément d'après la commission internationale d'éléments chimiques." *Bulletin des sociétés chimiques belges* 36 (1927), 124–136.

[————]. "Georges Urbain, 1872–1938." *Annales de chimie* 11 (1939), 5–9.

Urbain, G., and A. Dauvillier. "On the Element of Atomic Number 72." *Nature* 111 (1923), 218.

Usborne, Richard, ed. *A Century of Summer Fields. A Collection of Tributes, Reminiscences and Other Items.* London, 1964.

Varcoe, Ian. "Scientists, Government and Organized Research in Great Britain, 1914–1916: The Early History of the Department of Scientific and Industrial Research." *Minerva* 8 (1970), 192–216.

Vaughan, E. L. *List of Etonians who Fought in the Great War, 1914–1919.* London, 1921.

Vernon, H. M., and K. D. Vernon. *A History of the Oxford Museum.* Oxford, 1909.

Vincent, E. W., and P. Hinton. *The University of Birmingham.* Birmingham, 1947.

Vincent, J. H. "On a Numerical Connection between the Atomic Weights." *PM* 4 (1902), 103–115.

Ward, W. R. *Victorian Oxford.* London, 1965.

Waugh, Evelyn. *The Life of the Right Reverend Ronald Knox.* London, 1959.

Webster, D. L., and Leigh Page. "A General Survey of the Present Status of the Atomic Structure Problem." *Bulletin of the National Research Council* 2 (1921), 335–373.

Weeks, M. E. *Discovery of the Elements.* Easton, Pa., 1956[6].

Werner, A. "Beitrag zum Ausbau des periodischen Systems." *Berichte der deutschen chemischen Gesellschaft* 38 (1905), 914–921.

————. *New Ideas in Inorganic Chemistry.* Translated by E. P. Hedley. London, 1911.

Whiddington, R. "The Production of Characteristic Röntgen Radiation." *PRS* 85:A (1911), 323–332.

————. "The Production and Properties of Soft Röntgen Radiation." *PRS* 85:A (1911), 99–118.

Whittaker, E. T. *A History of the Theories of Aether and Electricity. II. The Modern Theories.* London, 1953.

Wien, W. "Über die Selbstelektrisierung des Radiums und die Intensität der von ihn ausgesandten Strahlen." *PZs* 4 (1903), 624–626.

Wimperis, H. E. "The Relationship of Physics to Aeronautical Science." *Physics in Industry* V. Oxford, 1927.

Wingfield-Stratford, E. C. *The Victorian Aftermath.* New York, 1934.

Winstanley, D. A. *Early Victorian Cambridge.* Cambridge, 1940.

Woodward, E. L. *Short Journey.* London, 1942.

Word, H. T. "Harrow in the 50's." *Cornhill Magazine* 50 (1921), 394–412.

Wright-Henderson, P. A. "The Oxford Undergraduate, Past and Present." *Blackwood's Magazine* 185 (1909), 335–343.

Index

103; mentioned, 95, 96, 99, 110, 113, 138, 228, 237, 267n
Urbain, Mrs. Georges: 100, 244

Vacuum: technique for obtaining, 177, 187–188, 191
Vernon, J. H.: 83n
Virginian, S. S.: 236

Wagner, Ernst: 129
Walker, James: 230, 231n, 241
Wall Game: defined, 16
Walters, F. P.: on HM's character, 19, 147n; mentioned, 14, 15n, 29, 30, 156, 157n
Warre, Edmond: promotes athletics, 16; tolerates science, 19n; mentioned, 11, 15, 17, 18, 23, 153n
Welsbach, Carl Auer von: *See* Auer
Welsbach Lighting Company: 94n
Werner, Alfred: 91
Westerham, S.C.: *See* Alington, C.A.
Westminster School: 20
Whewell, William: 3, 34
Whiddington, Richard: 77, 83, 86n, 89, 266n
Whiddington's Law: 77, 102, 104
White, Graham: 189
White Hart Tavern, Windsor: 12, 13
Whitman, Walt: 18
Wien, Willy: 58n
Williams, C. E.: 12, 13n
Wilson, C. T. R.: 38, 44, 74

Wimshurst Machine: 191
Wood, A. B.: 217n
Wood, James: 3
Woodhouse, Robert: 3
Woodward, E. L.: 28
Wratton and Wainright Photographic Plates: 235
Wrangler: defined, 2

X-Ray Spectroscopy: L-Spectra of heavy metals, 75, 205, 223; satellites of K_α and L_α, 130. *See also* Atomic Number; Moseley's Law
———, Apparatus and Techniques: focussing effect, 86; rotating crystal, 86, 222, 224n; apparatus for producing X rays, 73; for surveying K and L spetra, 85, 86, 96–97, 207–208; de Broglie's technique, 218, 243; HM's, 221–222
X Rays: study of at Eton, 24, 25n, 70n; intensity of reflection, 76; effects of temperature, 84. *See also* Characteristic X Rays; Moseley's Law
———, Nature of: corpuscular theory, 60–62, 66 (Bragg's), 66n (Stark's); Laue's, 60, 63–66; pulse, 64; W. L. Bragg's, 67–69; dual nature, 72, 74, 75, 200, 201

ytterbia: 93–94
ytterbium: 99, 100, 133, 138, 139, 236